Marti

PRIESTHOOD OF ALL BELIEVERS

In an Age of Modern Myth

Kristian T. Baudler

Martin Luther's

PRIESTHOOD OF ALL BELIEVERS

In an Age of Modern Myth

Kristian T. Baudler

OXEN PRESS

New York

The time is coming when people will not endure sound teaching, but having itching ears they will accumulate for themselves teachers to suit their own likings, and will turn away from listening to the truth, and wander into myths.

II Timothy 4:3-4

In all the mess of modern thoughtlessness, that still calls itself modern thought, there is perhaps nothing so stupendously stupid as the common saying, "Religion can never depend on minute disputes about doctrine." It is like saying that life can never depend on minute disputes about medicine. The man who is content to say, "We do not want theologians splitting hairs," will doubtless be content to go on and say, "We do not want surgeons splitting filaments more delicate than hairs." It is a fact that many a man would be dead today, if his doctors had not debated fine shades about doctoring. It is also a fact that European civilization would be dead today, if its doctors of divinity had not debated fine shades about doctrine.

G.K. Chesterton

Contents

1. **Ecce Mono**   1

    A Visit to the Queen of Hearts

    In Worms

    At the Wartburg

    The Myth of Article 5

2. **Luther's Bohemian Rhapsody**   39

    The Myth of "Public Ministry"

3. **Ministerium: One *Ampt*, Many *Ämtern***   61

    The Pious Myth of Ordination

    "Ordination is no big deal!"

    Melanchthon's Fly

4. **Luther's "Bibeldeutsch"**   90

    The Wittenberg Triptych

5. **Ad Fontes!**   114

    Luther's "Blessed Examples"

    The Pfarrherr Myth

    Article 28

6. **The Myth of Anglican Succession**   150

   The Myth of CCM

   The German Text

7. **The Myth of Apology 14**   174

   A Diminishing Desire

   The Crisis of 1531

8. **The Jonas Text**   200

   "Rite Vocatus"

   "Coepiscopos"

9. **A Pious Plethora**   222

   "That a Christian Congregation"

   The Unity Myth

   "An Imagined Priestly Dignity"

10. **Beware the Ghost of Speyer**   256

    Ecumenical Enthusiasms

11. **"There's no place like Rome!"**   293

    "It Shall Become Even Worse"

Prologue

In a landmark speech he delivered on the 450th Anniversary of the Evangelische Landeskirche in Württemberg, Germany (1534-1984), world renowned Luther scholar and historian Prof. Dr. Heiko Oberman of the University of Tübingen warned the church against surrendering Luther's concept of the "priesthood of all believers" to encroaching ecumenical attempts to elevate the bishop's office. The *Evangelisches Gemeindeblatt für Württemberg* wrote:

> Commenting on the so-called Lima texts[1] he explained infant baptism as "the sacramental process of justification" which dare not be abandoned in favor of adult baptism. Nor dare one advocate for an upgrading of the episcopal office, given that it was "laicization" that launched the Reformation. He also saw a new danger in today's "theological faith" (*Theologiegläubigkeit*), against which one must pit the priesthood of all believers, in keeping with Luther's statement, "Every Christian must be a theologian."[2]

He reissued his warning four years later in the preface to the English edition of his biography of Martin Luther, *Luther: Man Between God and the Devil,* saying Luther "can only be understood as a late medieval man for whom Satan is as real as God and mammon," whose "relevancy so sought after is not found by purging the record and hence submitting to post-Enlightenment standards of modernity, but rather by

---

[1] *Baptism, Eucharist and Ministry,* Faith and Order Paper No. 11, World Council of Churches, Geneva, Switzerland, 1982.

[2] Walter Rebman, "Priestertum aller Gläubigen nicht preisgeben," *Evangelisches Gemeindeblatt für Württemberg,* (July 26, 1984): 12. Sonntag, 15 Juli, 1984, 11 Uhr, Stuttgart, Brenzkirche Vortrag von Prof. Dr. Heiko Oberman, Universität Tübingen, Thema: *Reformation und Gegenwart - Gegenwärtige Reformation.*

challenging our condescending sense of having outgrown the dark myths of the past."

> [This requires the true historian] to become bilingual, gaining control of the languages of the past *and* of the present — not merely languages frozen in dictionaries, but also those gleaned from the historical record and perceived in contemporary experience . . . The translation enterprise is as hazardous as it is necessary; nuances are easily lost, especially when once vitally important existential expressions are rendered as antiquated parts of an obsolete "belief-system." In the case of Martin Luther this problem is all the more acute, as his interpreters, intent on mining his riches, have been given to present him as "relevant" and hence "modern." Thus they have been inclined to bypass or remove medieval "remnants" — first among these, the Devil Himself.[3]

Oberman's warnings are well founded given Lutheranism's current recidivism to dark myths of the past in a seemingly desperate search for relevancy and modernity. Old ecclesiastical superstitions are being revived and new ones invented in pursuit of an ever elusive "unity of visible church." The ancient fable of episcopal succession has been resurrected, while Luther's hallmark concept of the priesthood of all believers is being buried as a pious Protestant myth of the past. But unlike the Reformation's critics of old, the new purge is being spearheaded not from without, but from within a number of self-described Lutheran institutions that range from the *Dom* to the dorm.

Among the busiest of ecumenical alchemists today is the Evangelical Lutheran Church in America (ELCA). On August 19, 1999 this ecclesiastical body voted to embrace episcopalism by signing an ecumenical pact with the Episcopal Church USA (ECUSA), known as *Called to Common Mission* (CCM). Key to this agreement is the required adoption by the ELCA of a so-called "historical episcopal succession," a belief in an unbroken chain of

---

[3] Heiko A. Oberman, *Luther: Man Between God and the Devil,* (New York: Image Books, 1992), xv.

authority by bishops traceable to St. Peter and the apostles as a visible sign of the unity of the church. The doctrine is central to Anglicanism and is modeled after the Church of Rome. Its predecessor, the *Concordat of Agreement,* was narrowly defeated by a previous ELCA church-wide assembly because of this requirement. It was resurrected with great fanfare and an unprecedented information blitz through the national church offices that included hundreds of lectures, articles, seminars, and presentations by legions of bishops, pastors, seminary faculty, and other individuals.

These officially sanctioned and overwhelmingly pro-Episcopalian presentations were long on opinion and frightfully short on facts. Quoting mostly one another instead of original confessional sources, they presented Lutheran congregations with a Luther who never lived and a Reformation that never occurred. Instead they proffered myths claiming the 16th century Lutheran reformers "deeply desired" the adoption of a historic episcopate, that Luther had a high view of ordination and ecclesial hierarchy, and that the Lutheran Confessions fully support these views. Dissenting opinions, then as now, were dismissed as "pietistic," "democratic," "congregational power grabs" that are contrary to scripture and the Confessions and a formula for total anarchy in the churches.

More than five decades in the making, CCM is the culmination of a widespread distortion of the historical record flowing from the pens of such notable ecumenical enthusiasts as Arthur Carl Piepkorn, William H. Lazareth, Carl E. Braaten, Michael J. Root, Martin E. Marty, and Timothy J. Wengert to name but a few. Their confessional interpretations are accepted as normative for the ELCA today. Piepkorn, a late professor of systematic theology at Concordia Lutheran Seminary, St. Louis, and a high profile member of the "U.S.A. National Committee of the Lutheran World Federation," wrote an essay in 1968 for the LWF entitled "*The Sacred Ministry and Holy Ordination in the Symbolical Books of the Lutheran*

Church,"[4] which has served as a foundation for ecumenical dialogues for nearly half a century.

The purpose of this book is thus twofold. The first is to present the reader with a true sense of how deeply Martin Luther embraced a theology of the priesthood of all believers through the examination of a number of often overlooked primary Reformation sources. The second is to examine some of the claims of the above named in light of these sources, and to show how Luther's theology continues to be deconstructed in the ELCA and elsewhere through misinterpretation, misrepresentation, and mistranslation of the confessional record.

With deep love and gratitude to my father, Pastor Theodor R. Baudler, my brother Pastor Andreas Baudler, and my friend Dr. James M. Kittelson, all Luther scholars par excellence.

---

[4] *Lutherans and Catholics in Dialogue IV:* "Eucharist and Ministry," U.S.A. National Committee of the Lutheran World Federation, (New York, NY, 1970).

Abbreviations

Ap   *Apology of the Augsburg Confession*

BSLK   *Die Bekenntnisschriften der Evangelisch-Lutherischen Kirche,* 8. Auflage, Göttingen: Vandenhoeck & Ruprecht, 1979.

CA   *Augsburg Confession*

CCM   *Called to Common Mission*

C.R.   *Corpus Reformatorum,* edited by C.G. Bretschneider and H.E. Bindseil, Halle/Saale, 1834-1860.

LW   *Luther's Works,* American Edition, Philadelphia: Fortress Press, 1958-86.

MBW   *Melanchthons Briefwechsel,* edited by Heinz Scheible, Bd.1, Stuttgart-Bad Cannstatt: 1977.

RGG   *Die Religion in Geschichte und Gegenwart,* J.C.B. Mohr (Paul Siebeck), Tübingen: 1957.

SA   *Smalcald Articles*

SC   Martin Luther's *Small Catechism*

TPPP   *Treatise on the Power and Primacy of the Pope*

WA   *D. Martin Luthers Werke: kritische Gesamtausgabe,* Weimar: Böhlau, 1912-1921.

Walch   *D. Martin Luthers sämmtliche Schriften,*
edited by Johann Georg Walch, St.
Louis: 1880-1910.

Chapter 1

Ecce mono

In 1930, the Spanish artist Elías García Martínez, painted a portrait of the suffering Christ and donated it to the Catholic Church in Borja. He titled it *Ecce homo,* "Behold the Man," Pontius Pilate's words to the mob concerning Jesus. There the painting remained, gradually deteriorating over the decades as it hung half forgotten in the dank, dark little church. In 2012, Cecilia Giménez, an elderly parishioner and local amateur artist, dismayed by it's flaking condition, decided to give it a makeover. The result was a complete disaster. Attempting to restore the portrait of Christ, she destroyed it, and the image she created was lampooned around the world as a cartoonish figure in Crayola on canvas with a simian semblance. Many sarcastically suggested the title too ought to be changed — to *Ecce mono,* "Behold the Monkey." While suffering initial shame, the town of Borja has since benefitted from the painting's notoriety in the form of tourists who come to see "the monkey." Martinez's family, however, who still live in the village, continue to fume over the loss of their ancestor's original picture.

1

In the 1960s the Lutheran World Federation began formal ecumenical discussions with the Roman Catholic Church, just as it had earlier with the Anglicans. The elephant in the room was the question of a Lutheran subscription to the historical episcopacy, the supposed unbroken succession of bishops dating back to St. Peter. Both Rome and Canterbury regard it as necessary for the definition of church and proper episcopal ordinations, (even though neither recognizes the other's succession). Since they couldn't begin to take the Lutheran church seriously without it, and frustrated with the slow pace of visible church unity in an ecumenical age of, "Why can't we all just get along?," some Lutheran negotiators decided it was time to give Martin Luther — the man of uncompromising *solas* — a complete makeover. They began to alter his time honored portrait as a champion of "the priesthood of all believers" to one of Luther — the life long devout Catholic, a lover of the ordained episcopal office, an advocate for institutional hierarchy and church rule by bishops, who eagerly sought reconciliation and reintegration with the Church of Rome for the sake of Christian unity. In so doing, they managed to turn the medieval man into a modern monkey, a Crayola caricature aping present ecumenical sentiments which like Giménez's "restoration" of *Ecce homo,* has been a total disaster. The Luther being presented in American schools, churches, and seminaries today is for the most part a man who never lived leading a Reformation that never occurred.

Art experts agree that Mrs. Giménez's rendering can never be undone. But the original portrait of Luther and his theology can and must be recovered if Lutheranism is to avoid making a confessional monkey of itself in future ecumenical dialogues. This requires removing decades of pious myth and institutional varnish that have been applied to the reformer over the last half century for achieving ecclesial compromise. As each layer is removed, the portrait of Luther that begins to emerge is one of theological brilliance and confessional clarity in the recovery of the gospel from the distortion of present day myths.

2

A Visit to the Queen of Hearts

(und sonstiger Unfug)[5]

Grammar only teaches the words which are signs for real things, as, for example, "The righteous shall live by faith." Grammar explains the meaning of "faith," "righteous," "live" — but it is the sign of the highest art to defend these words against cavilers; this does not pertain to grammar but to theology.[6]

Martin Luther

In his book *Priesthood, Pastors, Bishops* — "Public Ministry for the Reformation & Today," Timothy J. Wengert, Emeritus Professor of the History of Christianity at the Lutheran Theological Seminary at Philadelphia, excitedly recounts his discovery of the electronic version of the *Weimar Ausgabe* (*WA*) of Luther's works:

> Using the latest technology (the critical Weimar edition of Luther's works in digital form online), I set off to see what Luther had said and immediately ran into the Queen of Hearts. There were no references to this phrase anywhere in Luther's own writings — that is to say, *Das allgemeine Priestertum aller Gläubingen* (the common priesthood of all believers) in all of its Latin and German permutations, was nowhere to be found in Luther's writings.[7]

Thus begins a journey down a rabbit hole in this compilation of five speeches by a leading teacher and apologist of the Evangelical Lutheran Church in America

---

[5] . . . and other nonsense.

[6] *WATR* 2. 506, 2533b.

[7] Timothy J. Wengert, *Priesthood, Pastors, Bishops,* "Public Ministry for the Reformation & Today," (Minneapolis: Fortress Press, 2008), 1.

(ELCA), delivered over time to various gatherings of students, faculty, pastors, laity, bishops, and the "Ecumenical Institute in Strasbourg."[8] Sadly, smoke and mirrors abound throughout his book, beginning with the insinuation that some scholars attribute this exact phrase to Luther (though none do), along with feigned surprise that it cannot be found. "The closest," he writes in his first footnote, "is in *WA* 8.254, 7 (*LW* 39.237), where Luther refers to *das eynige gemeyne priesterthum* (the one common priesthood)."[9] His first error already occurs on his first page. He mistakes the adjective *eynige* for *eine* ("one"), when it is actually a variant form of *einzige* ("only"), which denotes a uniqueness without parallel, that is, *das einzige gemeinsame Priesterthum,* or "the *only* common priesthood," precise wording that makes Luther's point even more forcefully than the phrase he is seeking.

"In fact," he continues beguilingly in his opening chapter, 'The Priesthood of All Believers and Other Pious Myths,' "there is no mention of the priesthood of all believers anywhere in *The Book of Concord* . . . The category of the 'common priesthood of all believers' developed by seventeenth-century pietism and championed by some Luther scholars to this day, has nothing to do with Luther's own thought."[10]

In the 24th Article of the *Apology* of the *Augsburg Confession* (hereafter Ap), Philip Melanchthon, it's chief author and Martin Luther's confessional right hand man wrote, "the priesthood of the New Testament is a ministry of the Spirit,"[11] predicated on righteousness by grace through faith, possessed by all the baptized equally, echoing Luther's rebuttal to the priestly Leipzig antagonist, Hieronymus Emser,

---

8 See Mark Menacher's review of Wengert's book in *Logia: A Journal of Lutheran Theology,* (October 2010), 48-51.

9 Wengert 111 n.1. 1 Peter 2:9.

10 Wengert, *Priesthood, Pastors, Bishops,* 4.

11 *BSLK* 366. 59: *sacerdotium novi testamenti est ministerium spiritus.*

4

a decade earlier in his *Answer to the HyperChristian Book* that there is "no more than one spiritual priesthood." [12] Congregations (*Kirchen*), being the true church (*die rechte Kirche*)[13]have "the right of electing and ordaining ministers," Melanchthon wrote in his *Treatise on the Power and Primacy of the Pope* (TTTP),[14] exercising the office of the keys, administering the sacraments, and proclaiming the word wherever the need exists.

In his *Answer* to the "prattling of the Leipzig goat," Luther thoroughly rejected Emser's Romanizing stance, employing language that would shortly appear in his foundational work of 1523, *Concerning the Ministry* (*De instituendis ministris ecclesiae: ad Clarissimum Senatum Pragensem Bohemiae*). Employing numerous permutations of the *only* common priesthood, he wrote:

> [Peter] names the people and the congregation (*Gemyne*) very clearly . . . the name 'priest' belongs to all of us (*allengemein*), with all of its power, rights, and the respect these robbers and thieves of God would like to tear away from us and claim only for themselves . . . But to exercise such power and to put it to work is not every man's business. Only he who is called by the common assembly, or the man representing the assembly's order and will, does this work in the stead of and as the representative of the

---

12 *WA* 8.254: "*Keyn anderß, denn das eynige gemeyne priesterthum bestehen.*" The Catholic theologian Hieronymus (Jerome) Emser (1478-1527) was secretary to Luther's adversary Duke George of Saxony, and counterpart to Georg Spalatin, secretary to Luther's protector, Elector Frederick the Wise of Albertine Saxony.

13 Luther uses "church" and "churches" interchangeably. Eg., in his 1528 *Ten Sermons on the Catechism*, *WA* 30.1: 92, 528, the communion of saints could be the local *Heuflein* (little gathering), the Wittenberg *Gemeine* (congregation or community), or all of *Christenheit* (Christianity) in a single sentence: *Ubi audis vocem, Ecclesiam intellige den hauffen, ut germanice: der Wittemb(ergische) hauffe, gemeine i.e. ein heiliger Christlicher hauffe, versammlung vel germanice: die heilige gemeine Christenheit.*

14 *BSLK* 491. 21-23: "*wo eine rechte Kirche ist, daß da auch die Macht sey, Kirchendiener zu wählen und zu ordiniren.*"

common assembly and power. It is therefore not true that there is more than only one simple (*eyn eyniges eynfeltiges*) priesthood in the church.[15]

All believers (*die Versammlung aller Glaubigen,* CA 7) for Luther are sacerdotes, priests in common (*allengemein*) by baptism, possessing the same name, power, and rights, choosing one from among their number to represent "the common assembly and power." [16] To be sure, Wengert repeatedly pays lip service to the existence of this one and only spiritual estate, but soon leads the reader through a maze of false claims and obfuscations that are long on opinion, but amazingly short on facts, his apparent purpose quickly becoming evident: If we can be convinced that "the common priesthood of all believers . . . has nothing to do with Luther's own thought," we will need to rethink this signature Lutheran claim and perhaps seek a priestly commonality (*Allgemeinheit*) beyond faith alone through one's baptism. He happily offers us his solution: membership in an ecclesial institution that combines laity and clergy, (or "metaphorical" and "ordained" priesthoods),[17] under a unifying umbrella of *episkope,* (oversight) by bishops in "apostolic succession." We are, after all, we are told, not all bishops in common, but we must all *have* bishops in common, bishops who are "desperately needed . . . for the greater visible unity of Christ's church."[18]

Following this path of "churchy" logic (as Luther put it), the reader curiously finds him or herself seated at the Mad Hatter's Party, sipping tea with Emser's prattling goat. Yes, we are told, it is true that we are all priests in Christ, "However, ordination makes elders *presbyteroi,* not

---

15 *WA* 8. 253, 29-36.
16 *BSLK* 61.1-4.
17 Wengert 11, 115 n. 36. Subscription to a "metaphorical" priesthood requires that Galatians 2:20 be understood as a trope and ignores the reality of baptism, the cross, the proclamation of the gospel, the forgiveness of sins, suffering and death.
18 *Ibid,* 109.

6

sacerdotes."[19] While we are all equally priests by baptism, some of us are more priests than others through ordination. What for the early church was a mere laying on of hands in witness to an existing call from the assembled, is now a semi-sacramental *ritus ecclesiasticus* arising from the apostles' supposed creation of a "historic succession of bishops," which "Luther sought to uphold and revive"[20] and Melanchthon favored as long as it conformed to the gospel for the sake of what is now synonymously "the sacred ministry," "the public office of ministry," the "office of preaching" (*Predigtamt*),[21] and the "office of pastor" (*Pfarramt*).[22] For the sake of good order, therefore, and in keeping with an imagined divine protocol, only bishops should ordain. Present day congregations that seek non-episcopal ordinations do so only for selfish reasons of democracy and misguided piety. Claiming "with one stroke Luther eliminated the laity as a separate category" by affirming that "we are all priests,"[23] (though it was the Levitical clergy class he eliminated, by sending priests without a call back to the pew as laity — Emser's complaint), Wengert sees the *Gemyne* as a metaphorical priestly subset, possessing few rights, with little authority (except in an emergency, though he can scarce imagine one), under the "public office of ministry," entrance into which occurs through ordination alone by a bishop alone. Insisting the priesthood of all believers is a "mythical category," he writes it is "a phrase first associated with Luther's theology in the eighteenth or nineteenth century and much more at home in Pietism's platform of church reform."[24]

It is quite the claim, of course, meant to evoke maximum confessional shock and awe among Lutherans who grew up

---

[19] *Ibid*, 20.

[20] *Ibid*, 24.

[21] *Ibid*, 34.

[22] *Ibid*, 43.

[23] *Ibid*, 9.

[24] *Ibid*, 38.

thinking just the opposite, that Luther actually championed a literal priesthood of all believers predicated simply on one's baptism and a proper call. But if that is not true, what then becomes of this longstanding hallmark of Lutheran identity?

Traditionalists needn't lose any sleep. Of the various myths that have grown up along side Luther's teaching since the Reformation, the priesthood of all believers is not one of them. History proves it was already the hot topic of the day from 1519-1523 and previewed in the summer of 1518 in Luther's exposition of Psalm 110:4, "Thou art a Priest forever after the order of Melchizedek," which he dedicated it to his good friend Hieronymus Ebner, the highly influential Nürnberg layman, pro-Lutheran magistrate and close friend of Albrecht Dürer. Emphasizing Christ's priesthood alone and those who belong to him, he declared, "There are still many clergy (*hochfertiger hailigen*) who go around in their self-righteousness, who alone wish to be known as priests, and do not hear that God is not speaking to them, but to Christ: 'You are a priest.'"[25]

Writing to Wenzel Link that same July in seeming anticipation of the actual blaze he would soon light outside Wittenberg's Elster Gate, he boasted, "I have ignited a new fire."[26] Link was the new leader of the Augustinian church in Nürnberg who, along with Ebner, was a member of the *Sodalista Staupitziana,* a group dedicated to the teaching of Johann Staupitz, Luther's father confessor, and the ushering in of Lutheranism in Nürnberg.

His first articulation of the single priesthood, according to Wilhelm Brunotte, is found in a letter dated December 18, 1519 in response to a query from Georg Spalatin, the personal secretary and court chaplain to Frederick the Wise in Wittenberg.[27] Six months after the Leipzig Debate, Spalatin had asked about the official duties of the office of priest

---

25 *WA* 1: 689-710.

26 Walch II Vol. 15, Col. 2378.5.

27 Wilhelm Brunotte, *Das geistliche Amt bei Luther,* (Berlin: Luth. Verlagshaus, 1959), 134.

(*officia sacerdotis*), to which Luther replied "they do not seem to differ at all from the ministry of the laity," save for a specific office entrusted to them of word and sacrament. "Everything else is the same if you remove the ceremonies and human regulations. And we have to wonder greatly where ordination was ever designated a sacrament. Now isn't that astounding? We'll talk later, along with Phillip, because we've debated this often and sharply."[28]

He would later expound on Psalm 110, hailing it as the most Christian of all psalms, in a series of eight sermons delivered in 1535 and published in 1539. His sixth sermon, delivered on Wednesday, June 9, is a vigorous expansion of his original 1518 exposition of 110:4 and subsequent reply to Spalatin. Attacking both canon law's *Translato sacerdotio*, which asserted Christ transferred his priestly office to St. Peter and the popes, as well as the Sacrament of Ordination, he announced "every baptized Christian is a priest already, not by appointment or ordination from the pope or any other man, but because Christ Himself has begotten him as a priest and has given birth to him in Baptism."[29]

> However, we deal with a different matter when we speak of those who have an office in the Christian Church, such as minister, preacher, pastor, or curate. These are not priests in the sense that scripture commonly speaks of priests. They became priests before they received their office, in fact, when they were baptized. Hence they are not priests because of their calling or office[30]. . . The preaching office is no more than a public service which happens to be conferred upon someone by the entire congregation, all the members of which are priests[31] . . . Even though not everybody has the public office and calling, every Christian has the right and duty to teach, instruct, admonish, comfort, and rebuke his neighbor with the word of God at every

---

[28] *WA* Br 1, 594. *prorsus non differre videatur a laicis nisi ministerio*
[29] *WA* 41:205. 30-32.
[30] *WA* 41:207. 37-208. 21.
[31] *WA* 41:210. 23-25.

opportunity, and whenever necessary.[32]

Wengert's mistranslated "one common priesthood," is from *Dr. Luther's Retraction of the Error Forced Upon Him by the Most Highly Learned Priest of God, Sir Jerome Emser, Vicar in Meissen*. Luther wrote it at the Wartburg in October 1521 at the height of his four year pitched battle with Emser over the true meaning of 1 Peter 2:9, "But you are a chosen race, a royal priesthood, a holy nation, God's own people, that you may declare the wonderful deeds of him who called you out of darkness into his marvelous light." In the same tract he wrote of Emser, "He may interpret 'priests' as he pleases, but all Christians are nevertheless such [physical] priests through this passage."[33] Attacking him four months later in *The Misuse of the Mass* (January 1522), he wrote, "For Peter's words apply to all Christians of whichever priesthood; they make it common to all Christians."[34]

Luther's war of words with Hieronymus Jerome Emser, Spalatin's opposite and bitter rival as personal secretary and court chaplain to Duke George of Saxony, dates back to the Leipzig Debate of 1519. Emser was present at the famous contest between Eck and Luther, though they had become acquainted much earlier when the latter attended Emser's seminar as a student in Erfurt in the summer semester of 1504. Based on a comedic play by Johann Reuchlin about a wicked and injurious monk, it was entitled, *Allotriavorlesung,* or "a lecture on nonsense." Martin Brecht reports the young Luther wasn't impressed.[35] Fifteen years later he would directly confront the nonsense of Reuchlin's mischievous monk incarnate — this time in the person of Emser.

---

[32] *WA* 41:211. 18-20.

[33] *WA* 8:253. 13-15. *Szo sind alle Christen solche priester durch dissent spruch.*

[34] *WA* 8:489. 6-8. *das selbige machen sie allen Christen gemeyn.*

[35] Martin Brecht, *Martin Luther,* (Calwer Verlag, Stuttgart, 1981), Bnd. 1, 51.

Luther "began to smell the roast" (*hat den Braten gerochen*) when his former teacher invited him to a banquet at his home in Dresden on July 25, 1518, while he was a guest preacher at the castle church. At the dinner he engaged the Leipzig Thomist Magister Weissestadt in a vigorous theological debate, during which he was lured into making a few incriminating remarks that would later be used to charge him with heresy. He was quick to recognize a setup and felt his suspicions confirmed the following year when after attending the Leipzig Debate, Emser sent an open letter to the Bohemians telling them that Luther was really not on their side, that he had never sided with Hus during the disputation, but had remained a loyal Catholic throughout, and that it was Eck, not Luther, who was their true friend.[36]

Luther was outraged by the deceit, calling it "a Judas kiss." Emser's fallacious "defense" of him to the Bohemians, in fact, appears little different from Wengert's claim today that "the category of the 'common priesthood of all believers' . . . has nothing to do with Luther's own thought."[37] Emser had insisted in his *Quadruplica* that there are two kinds of priesthood, a "physical" (priestly estate) and a "spiritual" (lay priesthood). Wengert argues similarly, saying that although there is only one priesthood, it nevertheless consists of the "clerical"[38] and the "metaphorical,"[39] with the former being established through ordination.

Luther stood accused of being an admirer of John Wycliffe (1330-1384) and Jan Hus (1371-1415) long before Leipzig, a charge Eck was only too happy to prosecute at the debate. Both of these earlier reformers' teachings contained the genesis of the idea of a priesthood of all believers. Wycliffe was an early champion of the authority of *sola scriptura,* an

---

[36] The letter is dated August 13, 1519 and is addressed in Latin to Johannes Zack, administrator of the archbishopric of Prague and provost of Leitmeritz. See Walch 2:18. 1202-11.

[37] Wengert, *Priesthood, Pastors, Bishops,* 4.

[38] *Ibid,* 3, 37.

[39] *Ibid,* 115 n. 36.

11

opponent of transubstantiation, and a believer in the "invisible" church of the elect over Rome's visible "church militant." Hus, too, advocated the primacy of the canon over the edicts of the Church, was opposed to indulgences, and declared Christ, rather than the pope, to be the only head of the church. He was condemned by the Council of Constance as a Wycliffite heretic and burned at the stake on July 6, 1415. Copies of Wycliffe's Bible and manuscripts were used as kindling for the fire.

At Leipzig Eck had managed to maneuver Luther into endorsing the "heresy" of both men through his rejection of the verdict of the Council of Constance and arguing that popes, councils, and canon law can err, later summarized as "Christ alone is our bishop!" But Hus remained a national hero and the Bohemians felt they'd found in Luther a modern champion to their cause. Emser's letter to them was thus the cleverest of ploys. By ostensibly "defending" Luther as upholding Roman orthodoxy, he cunningly painted him into a corner, leaving him with only one of two choices: To be the good Romanist he'd portrayed him as by retracting his reformist teachings, or admit to being a Wycliffite Hussite heretic. But having already crossed the Rubicon with his favorable comments about Hus, Luther chose the latter and charged Emser instead with deceit, suggesting he at least call him "a Bohemian heretic" as Eck had done, rather than stoop to such treachery.

Their jousting over the only common priesthood exploded into open warfare in 1520 when Emser attacked Luther's powerful *Address To the Christian Nobility of the German Nation,* published on August 18 and dedicated to his nobleman friend Nicolaus von Amsdorf barely a month after Pope Leo X condemned his teaching in *Exsurge, Domine.* Luther made 1 Peter 2:9 his weapon of choice for erasing the medieval class distinction that separated the clergy from the laity, the first of "three walls" of the papacy, (the other two being the pope's exclusive right to interpret scripture and to call a council, both of which depended on the preservation of the first). As is the case with any three legged stool, to lose the first would be the worst in the eyes of the papists.

His appeal to the nobility was at once profoundly personal, startlingly simple and direct, and went beyond church reform in the narrow sense. In arguably even bolder wording than "the priesthood of all believers," he declared, "We are all ordained priests by our baptism."[40] When the clergy fail to address abuses in the church, the laity of the royal priesthood of all believers have a solemn duty to intervene through the calling of a general council. He literally expected the nobility to act as the priests they were by baptism.

> Let us thus begin by attacking the first wall. It is pure invention that pope, bishop, priests, and monks are called the spiritual estate while princes, lords, artisans, and farmers are called the temporal estate. This is indeed a piece of deceit and hypocrisy and there is no difference among them except that of office[41]. . . This is because we all have one baptism, one gospel, one faith, and all are Christians alike: for baptism, gospel, and faith alone make us spiritual and a Christian people.[42]

He debunked ordination as a priestly prerequisite, saying "As far as that goes, we are all consecrated priests through baptism, as St. Peter says in 1 Peter 2, 'You are a royal priesthood and a priestly realm.' Apocalypse says, 'You have made us priests and kings by your blood.'"[43] (He would later announce to the Wittenberg faculty and students that compared to baptism, "ordination is no big deal.")[44] "In cases of necessity anyone can baptize and give absolution. This would be impossible if we were not all priests . . . Because we are all priests of equal standing . . . we all have equal authority,"[45] for "whatever comes crawling out of baptism can

---

40 *WA* 6:407. 22-23.
41 *WA* 6:407. 9-15.
42 *WA* 6:407. 17-19.
43 *WA* 6:407. 22-25.
44 *WATR* 5: Nr. 5428. 142.
45 *WA* 6:408. 1-2; 13-14; 15.

brag that it is already an ordained priest, bishop, and pope, although it is not seemly that just anyone should exercise such an office."[46] What is needed is a call to a community or congregation (*vocatio ad*). He repeated the passage in rejecting Emser's literal versus spiritual priesthood (Wengert's "clerical" versus "metaphorical"). "Christ does not have two different bodies, one temporal, the other spiritual. There is but one Head and one body."[47] Indeed, all of the baptized

> have equal authority . . . A cobbler, a smith, a peasant — each has the work and office of his trade, and yet they are still all alike ordained priests and bishops[48] . . . So, then, I think this first paper wall is overthrown. Inasmuch as the temporal power has become a member of the Christian body it is a spiritual estate, even though its work is physical[49]. . . the keys were not given to Peter alone but to the whole community.[50]

Three days later, on August 21, Luther published *A Treatise on the New Testament, that is, of the Holy Mass* stating that because faith alone is the true priestly office, "It permits no one else to take its place. Therefore all Christian men are priests, all women priestesses, be they young or old, master or servant, mistress or maid, learned or unlearned. Here there is no difference, unless faith be unequal."[51]

On December 10, he directed Melanchthon to post a flyer inviting the students and faculty of Wittenberg to attend a bit of "improvised theater" just outside the town wall. When all were assembled, Luther's student, Johannes Agricola, lit a bonfire containing Emser's works, along with those of Aquinas, Eck, the Italian moralist Chiavasso, and the Code of Canon Law. The fire was his answer to the earlier burnings of his works in Louvain, Cologne, and Mainz. As the blaze grew

---

46 *WA* 6:408. 11-13.
47 *WA* 6:408. 33-35.
48 *WA* 6:409. 5-7.
49 *WA* 6:410. 3-5.
50 *WA* 6:411. 37-412, 1.
51 *WA* 6:370. 25-28.

high Luther stepped forward and cast Leo's *Exsurge, Domine* into the flames with the words, "Because you have violated the truth of God's Word, be destroyed in the eternal fire!"[52] — in effect, burning the pope in effigy before the real thing could be done to him.

In Worms

By the time he arrived for trial in Worms at 4 p.m. on April 17, 1521, Luther's battle with Emser over the only priesthood had reached a fever pitch and become a central focus of the Diet. Of the twenty-two manuscripts placed on the table before him which Johannes von der Ecken,[53] acting on behalf of his majesty Charles V, asked him to simultaneously own and disown, two specifically targeted Emser's rejection of a literal single common priesthood. The first was the German second quarto volume, *To the Goat* (*An den Boch*), written as a personal attack minus any theology on the subject of the priesthood. The second was his highly explosive address to the clergy, *The Babylonian Captivity of the Church,* published on October 6, 1520 barely a month after his address to the Christian nobility, in which he threw out the entire papal sacramental system, using 1 Peter 2:9 to dismantle the sacrament of ordination. "Of this sacrament the church of Christ knows nothing; it is an invention of the church of the pope. Not only is there nowhere any promise of grace attached to it, but there is not a single word said about it in the whole New Testament. Now it is ridiculous (*ridiculum est*) to put

---

[52] Robert Stupperich, *Die Reformation in Deutschland,* (München: DTV-Verlag, 1972), 40.

[53] General secretary to the Archbishop of Trier, sometimes spelled "Eck," not to be confused with Dr. Eck of the Lepizig Debate. Von der Ecken was not a priest and had only limited theological training. See Hermann Ries in *Lexikon für Theologie und Kirche,* (Freiburg: Herder, 1959), Bd. III, 649.

forth as a sacrament of God something that cannot be proved to have been instituted by God."[54]

While not opposed to retaining the rite, he rejected as "human fiction" and "a laughingstock" any notion of sacramental grace or "indelible character" attached to it, demoting it to an *adiaphoron* "on par with many others introduced by the church fathers, such as the consecration of vessels, houses, vestments, water, salt, candles, herbs, wine, and the like. No one calls these a sacrament, nor is there in them any promise."[55] He dismissed the papists' argument that Christ supposedly ordained his disciples at the Last Supper as complete fiction.

> They have sought by this means to set up a seed bed of implacable discord, by which clergy and laymen should be separated from each other farther than heaven from earth, to the incredible injury of the grace of baptism and to the confusion of our fellowship in the gospel. Here, indeed, are the roots of that detestable tyranny of the clergy over the laity[56]. . . For thus it is written in 1 Peter 2: "You are a chosen race, a royal priesthood, and a priestly royalty"[57]. . . Let everyone therefore, who knows himself to be a Christian, be assured of this, that we are all equally priests, that is to say, we have the same power in respect to the word and the sacraments.[58]

Therefore, "Ordination can be nothing else than a certain rite by which the church chooses its preachers."[59]

It was these shocking statements that were the subject of fierce debate at the Diet for the ten weeks prior to Luther's arrival as reported by Spalatin, who came to Worms at the beginning of February to take notes. That the priesthood of all believers was a major issue and hot topic, and not a later pious

---

54 *WA* 6:560. 20-24.
55 *WA* 6:561. 26-33.
56 *WA* 6:563. 27-32.
57 *WA* 6:564. 6-10.
58 *WA* 6:566. 26-28.
59 *WA* 6:564. 16-17.

invention, is clear from the quick action taken by the papists to counter it just days after the January 28 opening bell. In the beginning of February, the Franciscan friar Johannes Glapion, personal confessor of Charles V, presented 32 unacceptable "articles" the papists had gleaned from *The Babylonian Captivity*. Articles 29 to 31 specifically target the priesthood of all believers. Starting at 29:

> "Everyone has to admit that we are all priests, insofar as we're baptized, which we in fact are."[60]

> The Thirtieth Article, where Luther speaks of the priesthood, he says, "What then is left to you that every layman does not have, other than tonsure and vestments? O what a sorry priesthood it is that consists of tonsure and vestments."[61]

Spalatin added in the margin: "This distinction is not found in the Gospel."

> The Thirty First Article, "Let everyone, therefore, who knows himself to be a Christian, be assured of this, that we are all equally priests, that is to say, we have the same power with regard to the word and the sacraments." With regard to this article he said the conscientious wish of His Roman Imperial Majesty is that so learned a man might be returned to the lap of his holy mother, the Christian church, and be received with compassion and grace.[62]

Spalatin's side note: "St. Hieronymus reportedly said of this passage, *Nolite tangere Christos meos* ["Don't touch my Christ"], that all are Christians who have been anointed with the Holy Spirit." He lists in both German and Latin the

---

[60] Carl Eduard Förstemann, *Neues Urkundenbuch zur Geschichte der evangelischen Kirchen-Reformation,* (Hamburg: Friedrich Perthes, 1842), Bd.1, 43.

[61] *Ibid.*

[62] *Ibid,* Bd.1, 44.

following "article, which Dr. Martin Luther must renounce and retract 1.5.2.1."

> "It is most certain and to be recognized, that we who have been baptized, are all equally priests, that is, we all have equal power and authority in word and sacrament."[63]

That Luther's "only common priesthood" was understood by all as the complete rejection of a literal/spiritual (or clerical/metaphorical) distinction via ordination is clear from the papists' appraisal of it: They took him literally — as we see, for example, in the Latin address delivered against him on Ash Wednesday, February 13 in his absence by Girolamo Aleandro, the papal nuncio to Charles V and future cardinal. Chancellor Brück translated it and gave it to Spalatin, (but unfortunately threw away the Latin original). Aleandro declared of Luther:

> He further sins against the clergy of the congregation/community, when he says in the book, *The Babylonian Captivity,* that all lay persons, and all who are baptized, are priests through their baptism, which will lead to a diminishing of the priestly estate (*Stand*) if we don't stop him in a timely manner![64]

Further evidence for it being *the* hot topic at the Diet, (rather than a later development of seventeenth century pietism), is the hastily submitted verdict of the faculty of the University of Paris, Europe's leading university for the defense of scholastic theology, which along with the universities of Cologne and Louvain, officially condemned his only common priesthood on April 15, 1521 just forty-eight hours before his trial. At the very top of their list and the first subject to be addressed are five articles of his which teach the priesthood of all believers, along with their attached verdicts

---

63 *Ibid,* Bd.1, 47.
64 *Ibid,* Bd.1, 33. Aleandro proposed and wrote the edict against Luther in Worms.

devoid of any theology. They appear immediately after Luther's foreword under the title:

Articles from Luther's Book entitled, "The Babylonian Captivity," collected and condemned by the Theologians of Paris

Martinus 1: *The sacrament* [of ordination] *is a new invention.*

Paris: This article that, according to him, the sacrament was recently invented by man and not established by Christ, is frivolous, unchristian, and openly blasphemous.

Martinus 2: *The church of Christ knows nothing about any sacrament of ordination.*

Paris: This article is blasphemous and is an error of the Poor of Lyon, the Albigensians, and Wycliffites.

Martinus 3: *All Christians have equal power in preaching and any sacrament.*

Martinus 4: *The keys of the church are all Christians' equally.*

Martinus 5: *All Christians are priests.*

Paris: Any one of these three articles is damaging to the standing of priests and blasphemous and is the error of the aforementioned blasphemers, as well as the Montanists.[65]

At the Wartburg

Luther didn't receive the Latin text until July 1521 while safely at the Wartburg. He translated it into German and added a short prologue and epilogue, meaning the words "All Christians are priests" are his, a stronger line again than Wengert's word-searched colloquial "priesthood of all

---

[65] *WA* 8:273. 1-18.

19

believers." It would not have escaped his notice that the wording of the Paris verdict is nothing more than a repeat of Aleandro's warning that the teaching "that all lay persons, and all who are baptized, are priests through their baptism will lead to a diminishing of the priestly estate."

If Luther had meant *alle Christen sind Priester* only metaphorically, how does one explain Aleandro's and the papists' alarmed appeal to "stop him in a timely manner;" or the universities' fear the teaching is "damaging to the standing of priests," (which a spiritual or metaphorical priesthood could not do); or the urgent priority assigned the topic at the Diet? If Luther wasn't saying the laity are all literally priests, why were they feeling threatened? Why the great panic?

And Luther did nothing to correct their literal interpretation or diminish their *Angst des Amtes,* even though the Diet provided him the perfect venue for doing so. To the contrary, he boldly upped the ante before the Paris verdict was even announced by issuing yet another tract on March 29, his *Answer to the HyperChristian, Hyperspiritual, and Hyperlearned Book of Goat Emser of Leipzig.* While it wasn't on the table in Worms, it was without question on the minds and tongues of his papal interrogators, having hit the presses three weeks before they could demand a retraction from him in person. Once again his focus is 1 Peter 2:9, making it crystal clear that his opponents have, indeed, understood him correctly — that all Christians are literal physical priests. "The Holy Spirit is the simplest writer and adviser in heaven and on earth. That is why his words could have no more than the simplest meaning which we call the written one, or the literal meaning of the tongue."[66] He sharply attacks Emser's illogic that the "letter" of the passage could somehow refer to ordained clergy as a literal priesthood distinguished from a spiritual role assigned to the laity.

---

[66] *WA* 7:650. 21-24. Luther preferred the phrase "grammatical, historical meaning" to "literal meaning." Cf. *WA* 7:652. 24-26.

St. Peter's words have only one simple meaning which encompasses both letter and spirit . . . [Emser] allows himself to imagine that there are two kinds of priesthood, a spiritual one and a churchy (*kirchische*) one, which he calls "ecclesiastical"[67] . . . Scripture does not tolerate the dividing of letter and spirit, as Emser so outrageously does. It contains only one simple priesthood, and one simple meaning.[68]

Rejecting Emser's accusation that he'd said all Christians are automatically ecclesiasts, the New Testament nevertheless "writes of no more than one spiritual priesthood . . . Scripture makes all of us equal priests . . . but the churchy priesthood . . . we now separate from laymen."[69] To the undoubted shock of the assembled in Worms, he boldly declares, "All of us in the whole mass of people are priests without the consecration of the bishop."[70] Historical episcopal succession is rejected as human teaching (*traditiones hominum*), non-scriptural and without God's command. He accuses Emser of assigning the laity a lesser priestly role than the literal meaning of 1 Peter. Where Emser resorted to prescribing metaphorical "spiritual" meanings for the simple, clear, literal statements that all Christians are priests (*spirituales*), Luther accused him of teaching "more than is written in Scripture."[71]

Now see how well Emser rides along with his twofold Bible. The result is that nothing remains certain. When St. Peter says, "We are all priests" [I Pet. 2.9], he says this is said in the spiritual sense and not in the literal one. But when I ask why it is not the literal sense, he answers, because the literal sense kills.[72]

---

[67] *WA* 7:629. 5-6; 8-9.

[68] *WA* 7:651.22-24.

[69] *WA* 7:630. 2-3; 10-11.

[70] *WA* 7:633. 16.

[71] *WA* 7:629. 7-8: (*Aber Emser macht) was yhm gelüstett auß gottis wortt.*

[72] *WA* 7:651. 9-13.

The gloves truly came off as soon as the Diet ended, after Luther was pronounced an outlaw and had gone into hiding at the Wartburg. From there he issued three powerful tracts in rapid succession against Emser's twofold priesthood. The first, a sermon on *The Ten Lepers* of Luke 17:11-19, published on September 17, 1521 again rejected any notion of an ordained priesthood in the New Testament. "And even less convincing is the flighty argument dreamed up by the Liar of Leipzig [Emser], who writes that two kinds of priesthood are meant to be understood in St. Peter's words: one spiritual (*geistliche*) belonging to all Christians, and one physical (*leypliche*) by which they alone — the tonsured and anointed horde — are the priests. But that myth melts like feet of butter."[73]

The sermon is an expansion of his earlier shocking statement to the Christian nobility that "the keys were not given to Peter alone but to the whole community," a claim that threatened to destroy the clergy's lucrative financial monopoly of confession and absolution. Recalling his earlier 1518 boast to Wenzel Link, he wrote in the prologue, "I, poor brother, have once again lit a new fire, and have bitten a huge hole in the papists' pockets by attacking [the Sacrament of] Penance."[74] It was greeted enthusiastically in Link's free imperial city of Nürnberg, the center of German power and home of the Imperial Diet[75] as a theological manifesto in support of the laity. The city's attempt to rid itself of episcopal authority was being spearheaded by a powerful circle of Luther's friends that included the magistrate Hieronymus Ebner; Anton Tucher, a member of one of the city's wealthiest families; Lazarus Spengler, a leading legislator; and the artist Albrecht Dürer. When Pope Leo X added Spengler's name to the Bull of Excommunication, Nürnberg defied him by sending him to the Diet of Worms to stand at Luther's side.

---

73 *WA* 8:352. 31-353; 1.

74 *Walch* II, 12: 1438, 1.

75 The Diet of 1521 was only moved to Worms temporarily due to the plague and returned to Nürnberg the following year.

Bernhard von Hirschfeld, an advisor to Elector Frederick the Wise, regarded him as such an exceptionally "wise layman" that he sent two expensive copies of the sermonic booklet to Tucher, asking him to keep one and give the other to Spengler with the note, "In reading the aforementioned booklet you will see that the laity also highly esteem the word of God."[76]

Less than a month later Luther published *Dr. Luther's Retraction of the Error Forced Upon Him by the Most Highly Learned Priest of God, Sir Jerome Emser, Vicar in Meissen,* in which he thoroughly debunked Emser's "special uncommon" twofold priesthood. (See Chapter 2 below).

It was quickly followed from the Wartburg in 1522 by *The Misuse of the Mass.* Of its three parts, (against the false definition of the priesthood, the false understanding of the mass as a sacrifice, and the false priesthood of the papacy), the first pressed his attack against Emser's mimic of the pope who "divides the priestly people of Christ into clergy and laity."[77] It is his most thorough exposition of 1 Peter 2:9 as the crux of the argument for "the *only* common priesthood," a hermeneutic from which he would never deviate for the rest of his life. He dismisses the Paris verdict that "this idea is heretical because it casts dishonor upon the priestly estate" by citing 1 Peter 2:9, Revelation 5:10, and Rev. 22 and 20:6. Prayer, access to God, as well as teaching and preaching are common to all. He lambasts Emser, "that worthy priest of God — the god Baal" for interpreting 1 Peter 2:9 as "referring to two kinds of priesthood: first, to the spiritual priesthood common to all Christians; and second, to the 'outward' priesthood, as only the anointed and tonsured — that is, the ordained priests are called."[78] Since "it is irrefutable in the New Testament that there can be no outward priests who are

---

[76] Sina Westphal, *Die Korrespondenz zwischen Kurfürst Friedrich dem Weisen von Sachsen und der Reichsstadt Nürnberg,* (Bern/Frankfurt am Main: Peter Lang, 2011), 563.

[77] *WA* 8:540. 6-10. *Der Papst . . . teylet erstlich das priesterlich volk Christi ynn Clericken und leyhen.*

[78] *WA* 8:488. 27-31.

23

tonsured and set apart from the laity,"[79] it follows that "the holy, pious women and children are also tonsured and anointed priests."[80] Citing St. Paul he challenges those who say the laity have no business preaching, asking

> If all men did not possess the prerogative of preaching and only one had the right to speak, what need would there be to command and keep order [1 Corinthians 14]? It is precisely because they all have the right and power to preach that it becomes necessary to keep order . . .[81] Christ has given to everyone the right and power to weigh and decide, to lecture and preach.[82]

The following year he issued his definitive treatise on the subject in *Concerning the Ministry,* addressed to the citizens of Prague, spelling out precisely the rights and powers all Christians possess through their baptism. Declaring the episcopal "mask of ordination is unnecessary," he once more invoked 1 Peter 2:9 in enumerating the seven offices "common to all Christians" in "the ministry of the word." All have the right to preach, baptize, administer Holy Communion, bind and loose sins, offer praise and thanksgiving, pray, and judge all doctrine. In II Timothy 2:2 "Paul rejects all show of tonsure and anointing and ordaining and only requires that they be able to teach . . ."[83] The community or congregation may choose by right one or more persons to carry out these functions for the sake of good order. As Paul Speratus stated on Luther's instructions in his 1523 German preface[84] to *De instituendis,* Luther flatly rejected the false notion held by some today that his advice to the Bohemians was somehow new, radical, and not meant as a model for all of Christianity (*allen Christen*). It is the model

---

79 *WA* 8: 491. 2-5.
80 *WA* 8:489. 4-6.
81 *WA* 8:495. 31-33.
82 *WA* 8:496. 13-14.
83 *WA* 12:191. 4-5.
84 *Walch* II, 10:1548-1549.

he would personally facilitate and establish in evangelical lands throughout the course of the Reformation in keeping with his incendiary 1518 and 1521 bookend declarations, *"Ich habe ein neues Feuer angezuendet!,"* in between which — he lit a real one.

The Myth of Article 5

Martin Luther (Lucas Cranach the Elder)

Wengert's channeling of Emser for our time is nothing new. In a 1968 seminal essay he submitted to the Lutheran World Federation, noted ecumenist Arthur Carl Piepkorn argued in *The Sacred Ministry and Holy Ordination in the Symbolical Books of the Lutheran Church,* that for the last two centuries churches of the Augsburg Confession have essentially had three views on "sacred ministry" (defined as proclaiming the word and administering the sacraments), two of which he called "extreme," and one reasonable. Said he,

The first extreme view holds that the sacred ministry is only the activity of the universal royal priesthood of believers, the public exercise of which the Christian community has solemnly committed to certain persons merely for the sake of good order and efficiency. At the opposite extreme is the position which sees the sacred ministry as the contemporary form of the primitive apostolate and as the personal representation of Christ. A third view occupies the middle ground between these two positions and incorporates elements of both. It sees the sacred ministry as a divine institution that is essential to the church's existence. It regards the responsible public proclamation and application of the gospel and the administration of the sacraments as the primary content of the sacred ministry. It looks upon ordination as the indispensable act of admission to the sacred ministry.[85]

Further reading of Piepkorn, however, soon makes it apparent that the third view is little more than a pious repackaging of the second, but with the addition of "ordination as the indispensable act of admission to the sacred ministry." Piepkorn's real target is the first view, the "extreme" idea of the priesthood of all believers, which he seeks to constrict by conflating "sacred ministry" with ordination in "the primary sources in the symbolical books."

While hardly original, being essentially Roman, such ecclesiastical posturing over the years nevertheless offers us a convenient looking glass into America's largest Lutheran body's use of pious myth to reconstruct Emser's walls within the *only* priestly estate, a feat that is largely accomplished through the spinning of confessional documents culminating in *Called to Common Mission* (CCM)'s institutionalizing conclusion: *sola fides non satis est* (faith alone is not enough). To read Piepkorn and his successors is to understand a sixty year trajectory of the ELCA's teaching magisterium. In pursuit of the holy grail of episcopalism, (ecumenism's talismanic

---

[85] *Lutherans and Catholics in Dialogue IV:* "Eucharist and Ministry," U.S.A. National Committee of the Lutheran World Federation, (New York, 1970).

26

Wundermittel for the achievement of visible catholic unity), the Roman requisite of an inedible character (*character indelebilis*) is disguised in an ontological institutionalism (*character institutum*) based on custom and practice, where Reformation history is ignored and confessional theology is all but nonexistent. Given such an ecclesial Orwellian scenario, it is not only fair for us to ask whether Luther's common priesthood of all believers is a myth, but also whether the ELCA's ecclesiastical system isn't itself predicated on so much pious myth. The answer is easily found by deconstructing some of that institution's following fables.

Have you ever noticed how many stores and restaurants have begun to refer to their patrons as "guests," even though they're really paying customers? As we wait in line the person behind the counter calls out, "May I help the next guest, please?" At the end of a meal we are handed a "Guest Check," (though if we were truly guests we wouldn't have been handed a check at all, much less been standing in line). It's a bit of slick marketing that creates a slight psychological shift from one of the restaurant having the privilege of serving you, to you being privileged to eat in their fine establishment. Nothing has really changed, you're still paying the bill, yet almost imperceptibly the status of the business has somehow been magically enhanced, while that of the patron has been diminished. The old adage, "The customer is always right," no longer applies.

So it is in the relationship of the ordained to the unordained in contemporary Lutheranism. The old notion of a "priesthood of all believers" we are told, no longer applies, nor is it even Lutheran. (So much for Luther's claim that even "a seven year old child knows what the church is, namely holy believers and sheep who hear the voice of their Shepherd.")[86]

A central focus in recent ecumenical dialogues aimed at diminishing the Lutheran claim to a "priesthood of all believers" is Article 5 of the *Augsburg Confession*. Its title in

---

[86] *BSLK* 459. 20-22.

German is *Vom Predigtamt* ("Concerning the Office of Preaching"); in Latin *De ministerio ecclesiastico* ("Concerning the Ministry of the Church").[87] Translated from the German it reads:

> *V. Concerning the Office of Preaching*

> *In order to obtain such faith, God instituted the office of preaching, giving the gospel and the sacraments, by which as through means, he gives the Holy Spirit who produces faith, where and when he wills, in those who hear the gospel, which teaches that through Christ's merit, not through our merit, we have a gracious God, when we so believe. Condemned are the Anabaptists and others who teach that we obtain the Holy Spirit without the physical word of the gospel through our own preparations, thoughts and works.*

Since at least 1959, when Theodore G. Tappert published his beloved red *Book of Concord*,[88] American Lutherans have taken comfort in the thought that "the office of ministry" includes the laity not only as participants, but also as practitioners. They received this assurance in part through Tappert's paraphrased translation of a footnote found at the bottom of CA 5 in the critical apparatus of *Die Bekenntnis Schriften der Evangelisch Lutherischen Kirche* ("The Confessional Writings of the Evangelical Lutheran Church"), the gold standard for the texts of the Lutheran Confessions. He wrote, "This title would be misleading if it were not observed (as the text of the article makes clear) that the Reformers thought of the 'office of the ministry' in other than clerical terms."[89] Wengert seized upon the footnote while editing his

---

87 The titles of the articles appeared already in 1533, not "in the seventeenth century" as Wengert supposes.

88 Theodore G. Tappert, *The Book of Concord*, (Philadelphia: Fortress Press, 1959).

89 Tappert, 31, n 4.

own version of the *The Book of Concord*,[90] focusing almost exclusively on the German title *Vom Predigtamt* while ignoring the parenthetical sidebar, "as the text of the article makes clear." At the very least, the BSLK footnote requires us to examine not just the title of the article, but what it is in the text that makes this so "clear."

The Diet of Augsburg 1530

When the *Augsburg Confession* was presented to Emperor Charles V on June 25, 1530, the intent of the evangelical party was not to stress their differences with the faith of the Holy Roman Empire, but their faithfulness to the same gospel proclaimed by the early church fathers. Their point was their oneness with, not their difference from the evangelical faith of the *Urkirche,* as the prelude to Article 22 of the *Apology* states: "From the above [first twenty one articles] it is manifest that nothing is taught in our churches concerning articles of faith that is contrary to the Holy Scriptures or what

---

[90] Robert Kolb and Timothy Wengert, *The Book of Concord, The Confessions of the Evangelical Lutheran Church,* (Minneapolis: Fortress Press, 2000; hereafter: *BC 2000*).

is common to the Christian church."[91] To underscore this, the *Augsburg Confession* distinguishes its teaching from the false teachings of others, both past and present, some of which were now being ascribed to the evangelicals. Thus, eleven of the first twenty one "undisputed" articles are defined by what they do not believe, in contrast to what their opponents do believe. CA 5 is a rebuttal, a condemnation of the errors of Sebastian Franck, Casper Schwenkfeld, and the Anabaptists, who taught the old recycled gnostic heresy that the means of grace are not necessary to affect faith in light of the gift of the human intellect. The question on the table in Augsburg was, how does one come to such justifying faith, or as the article begins declaratively, "In order that we may obtain this faith." Thus CA 5 describes the means of faith — not the office holder — about whom it says nothing. It is about the ministry and work of the one who creates this justifying faith, the Holy Spirit, "as the text of the article makes clear."

But Wengert, following in the footsteps of Piepkorn, asserts that "Article 5 refers specifically to clerics,"[92] erroneously believing the Latin title of the article, *De ministerio ecclesiastico* to mean ordained public ministers of word and sacrament — bishops, presbyters, clergy — supposedly implied by the German word *Predigtamt* (the office of preaching).[93] His reasoning is threefold.

---

91 *BSLK* 84. 4-7: *So nun von den Artikeln des Glaubens in unseren Kirchen nicht gelehrt wird zuwider der heiligen Schrift oder gemeiner christlichen Kirchen.*

92 Wengert 37.

93 Cf. Dorothea Wendebourg's review of Wengert's *Priesthood, Pastors, Bishops* in *Lutheran Quarterly,* Vol. XXIII/Number 3, Autumn 2009, 350-351: ". . . Wengert puts forward lengthy theories on the words *ministerium* and *Amt* which show an unfortunate linguistic weakness regarding Latin (see also the completely wrong translation of the title *De instituendis ministris* [18 and 60]) as well as the German of the time (which, by the way, was not *Mittelhochdeutsch* (132), but *Frühneuhochdeutsch*). To begin with the latter, it is an absolutely unfounded contention that '[*d*]*as Predigtamt* can only mean "the office of preaching"' and is to be

First, in what he fantastically calls "one of the most telling distortions of the historical record in North America," he insists Tappert mistranslated the BSLK footnote:

> There, in a footnote to Article 5 of the Augsburg Confession, Tappert insisted that this article was not to be understood clerically, implying that one should read it as a reference to the priesthood of all believers. Not only might he have misconstrued a footnote to the critical edition of the Lutheran confessions — it rejected a clericalistic but not clerical[94] reading of the text — but he also reinforced the completely mistaken notion that the Augsburg Confession says little or nothing about the public office of ministry, despite the fact that Article 5 is expressly about *Das Predigtamt,* the office of preaching.[95]

By restricting "the public office of ministry" to the ordained,

understood as 'clerical' (38). This is true in today's German, but in the sixteenth century the term (*Predigt*)*amt* was used just as well in the functional sense of fulfilling a task (in fact, Wengert himself quotes an example of this usage from Melanchthon on page 132: *Amt der Predigt* paralleling *Handreichung der Sakramente,* 'distribution of the sacraments' — which of course has to be understood functionally). The same applies for *ministerium* which can also mean office as well as service in the sense of διακονία; it is not at all the case that the word 'almost always referred to the . . . public office' (37). We have to ask in every instance where these terms occur whether they are meant in the institutional or in the functional sense. In the case of CA 5 all the indicators point in the latter direction, the article does not speak about the ordained ministry."

[94] Cf. *WA* 30.1:93, 3-4. In a sermon he preached on December 10, 1528 on the Third Article of the Creed, Luther stated, *Clerici sunt extra Ecclesiam, quia per sua volunt salvari* ("The clerics are outside of the church, because they want to be saved through their works"). Cf. *The Papacy at Rome, PE* 1, 354.

[95] Wengert 3. Cf. Wendebourg, 349-350: "Equally unsatisfying as Wengert's treatment of Luther's writings is his interpretation of the Lutheran Confessions . . . He contends this article is on ordained ministry. Yet he not only fails to put forward convincing arguments, he also dispenses with invalidating the data that speak against his assumptions."

Wengert fixes a notion of synonymity in the mind of the reader, a device he uses early on and often in his work, ascribing it to Luther.

But it isn't Tappert who has misconstrued the footnote, which Wengert and his translator Eric Gritsch dropped from their Wengert/Kolb version of the *Book of Concord*, "and changed the translation to reflect the actual meaning of the text." It is Wengert who has, who appears to have no idea who wrote it, first blaming Tappert for insisting this article "was not to be understood clerically," calling it "Tappert's position," "what Tappert and others imagined;" [96] then Ferdinand Kattenbusch whose work on the subject the footnote references. In fact it was Luther who so insisted — the footnote being from Heinrich Bornkamm who wrote, *Luther verstand das Predigtamt nicht clerical,*[97] "Luther did not understand the office of preaching as clerical,"

Attempting to circumvent Luther's core conviction (before making it disappear altogether in his own version of the BoC, Wengert, who exhibits limited ability in the German language, invents a word for the footnote that it never uses — "clericalistic" — saying "it rejected a clericalistic but not clerical reading of the text." But if Bornkamm and the highly esteemed theological editorial board of the BSLK had actually meant "clericalistic," they would have said *klerikalistisch,*[98] not *klerikal,* as Tappert rightly has it. Nor would they have included the same footnote in all twelve editions of the BSLK had there been any doubt whatsoever regarding Luther's position.

Wengert also contradicts himself from one chapter to the next in *Priesthood, Pastors, Bishops,* arguing in Chapter 1 that Tappert was wrong to say CA 5 "was not to be understood

---

[96] Cf. www.valpo.edu/ils/assets/pdfs/05_wengert.pdf

[97] *BSLK* 58.

[98] Cf. Bertelsmann, *Wörterbuch der deutschen Sprache,* [Gütersloh: Rheda-Wiedenbrück, 2004], *Adj., o. Steig.; [abwertend] die klerikale Haltung in extremer Weise vertretend.* "[disparaging], to represent the clerical position in an extreme manner."

clerically,"[99] while saying in Chapter 3, "To be sure, this office is not to be understood clerically,"[100] (one of the pitfall of turning speeches into books.)

Second, he asserts the footnote, which cites Luther's 1520 *Sermon on Good Works*[101] putting "the preaching office on par with marriage and governing authorities," and his *Confession of 1528,*[102] is without merit because "Kattenbusch [though it's Bornkamm] gives no proof that the word *Predigtamt* is not 'clerical'"[103] — (so therefore, it presumably is).

This is known in rhetoric as an *argumentum ad ignorantiam,* a proposition that is presumed to be true because it has not been proven false. It's like saying, "You have no evidence there is no teapot on the moon, so there is one." (Or conversely, "Because Luther never used the words 'a common priesthood of all believers,' there isn't one.") While the evidence for the BSLK footnote showing that CA 5's office of preaching was not understood by Luther as clerical is overwhelming, Wengert ignores the theology altogether. Luther's obvious point is that if marriage and the governing authorities have parity with the preaching office, it is because they are already part of the office of proclamation in the single Christian *Stand,* ("standing"), which itself has many *Stände.*

Both of the footnote's cited works of Luther are lead-ins to CA 5. In his *Confession of 1528,* he identifies the "holy orders and true religious institutions established by God." There are only three in number, equally commanded by God and equally holy: the office of priest, the estate of marriage, and the civil government.[104] Melanchthon refers to them in CA 16 as the

---

99 Wengert 3.

100 *Ibid,* 37.

101 *WA* 6.250.

102 *WA* 26.504-505.

103 Wengert 37.

104 *WA* 26.504, 30-31: *"Aber die heiligen orden und rechte stiffte von Gott eingesetzt sind diese drey. Das priester ampt. Der Ehestand. Die weltliche Oberkeit."*

"true divine order,"[105] and Luther expounds upon them in the Fourth Commandment of his *Large Catechism.* There he even elevates the teaching and preaching role of parents to a priestly one, to the "highest *Stand"* of them all. "God has put this *Stand* at the very top, indeed, in his stead on earth" (*Denn Gott hat diesen Stand obenan gesetzt, ja an seine Statt auf Erden gestellet*). [106] Hence Luther's repeated references to parents and overseers of households as "bishops" *episcopoi* (overseers), a *Stand* he meant no more metaphorically than he did the priesthood of all believers.

Wengert's third argument, that "Article 5 refers specifically to clerics" because the German title *Das Predigtamt* means "the public office of ministry," is a nonsequitor, as is clear for instance from Luther's 1528 sermons on the Large and Small Catechisms preached just prior to their publication. In November he proclaimed, "Every father of a family is a bishop (*Bischoffe*) in his house and the wife a bishopess (*Bischoffyn*). Therefore remember that you in your homes are to help us conduct the office of preaching (*helfft das predigampt treiben*),"[107] switching from Latin to German to emphasize the role of the laity in the *predigampt*. Doberstein translates the phrase in *Luther's Works, American Edition* rather tepidly as "help us carry on the ministry." And a few lines later, "In these sermons there will be five parts. These we call the catechism,"[108] though Luther again switched to the German, twice substituting *kinder predigt*[109] or "children's sermons," for "catechism" to show that the preaching in the parlor is the same as in the pulpit.

---

105 *BSLK* 70.12f.

106 *Ibid,* 592.39-41.

107 *WA* 30 I.58: *Quisque pater familias in sua domo est Episcopus, ipsa Episcopa, ideo cogitate/das yhr uns in domibus helfft das predigampt treiben ut nos in Ecclesia.*

108 *Luther's Works,* General Editor Helmut T. Lehman, (Philadelphia: Fortress Press, 1967), 51, 137-138. (Hereafter *LW.*)

109 *WA* 30 I.58: *Habetis in ista praedicatione 5 particulas. Die heissen wir die kinder predigt, quae doceri debent pro simplicibus.*

34

As if suddenly having an epiphany that all ministry of the Spirit is inherently public, Wengert offers a curious logic that would have positively delighted the Queen of Hearts:

> In the writings of Philip Melanchthon, the word *Predigtamt* always referred to the public office of the ministry. The same can be said for the vast majority of Luther's use of the term. To be sure, this office is not to be understood clerically (as if it were referring to a separate estate or walk of life [*Stand*], and in an emergency, any Christian can fulfill this office), but, in fact, Article 5 refers specifically to clerics, that is, to those publicly called to teach and preach the gospel. Moreover, in an official document of this kind, to use the term *Predigtamt* meant the public office that included pastors, preachers, and bishops.[110]

That it includes them is without dispute, as Luther demonstrated to Emser, but not to the exclusion of all other Christians. To restrict public ministry to the clergy, as Luther asserted, is to seek to restrict the "where and when" of the Holy Spirit. The title of the article, after all, is *Vom Predigtamt* — not *Vom Pfarramt,* or *Pastoramt.* Just as *Gottes Wort* for Luther at times referred specifically to scripture, and at other times not, but could be any word of law or gospel emanating from it,[111] (*was Christum treibt*),[112] so *Predigtamt* could be understood specifically as the office of the preacher or pastor, or in the general Pauline sense of anyone called to "proclaim" the kerygma of God (*kerykeuo = verkündigen, bekanntmachen,* "to make known").[113] Luther's concern wasn't whether the preacher was a cleric or not, but whether

---

[110] Wengert 37.

[111] Cf. *Luther the Expositor,* "Introduction to the Reformer's Exegetical Writings," Jaroslav Pelikan, *LW* Companion Volume.

[112] See Luther's famous compass in his preface to the books of James and Jude in his 1522 *Septembertestament* (Neudruck: Stuttgart: Deutsche Bibelgesellschaft, 1994): *der rechte prufesteyn alle bucher (ist), . . . ob Sie Christum treyben* ("the proper test of all books is whether they drive Christ home").

[113] *Griechisch-Deutsches Schul-u. Hand-Wörterbuch,* 9. Auflage, Tempsky, (Wien: Freytag, Leipzig 1908).

they were learned or unlearned (*Gelehrte oder Verkehrte*) in the gospel,[114] as his two catechisms make clear: "In a word, a priest was a man who could say mass, even though he could not preach a word and was an unlearned ass. Such in fact is the spiritual estate even to the present day." [115]

Wengert also misconstrues the use of the term "cleric." Contrary to his claim that "the Reformation often avoided using the late-medieval terms like 'priest, cleric, or spirituals' in favor of the simple word 'minister,'"[116] Luther used them often and to great effect against the papists and enthusiasts, claiming the title "priest" and *spirituales* for "all Christians," as demonstrated against Emser. Not only are we all sacerdotes by birth, said Luther three years after the penning and presentation of CA 5 in Augsburg, we are also all born clerics. He writes in 1533 in *The Private Mass and the Consecration of Priests* (*Von der Winckelmesse und Pfaffen Weyhe*):

> In opposition to this [priestly chrism and consecration] you should again exalt and praise your baptism, and, on the other hand, as much as you are able, weaken and abolish the disgraceful abomination. For within Christendom producing and consecrating clerics is not important. I say that the chrism and the bishop will not make clerics out of us. We do not want them to make us clerics nor do we want to receive this from them. I repeat, if we are not true clerics beforehand without a bishop and chrism, then the bishop and his chrism can never make clerics of us . . . [117] For this reason also the Holy Spirit in the New Testament diligently prevented the name *sacerdos,* priest, or cleric, from being given to any apostle, preacher, teacher, pastor through baptism, but we are all born simply as priests and clerics. Afterward, some are taken from the ranks of such born clerics and called or elected to these offices which they are to discharge on behalf of all of us.[118]

---

114 *WA* 56.417-418.

115 *WA* 30 II.529b, 32f..

116 Wengert 38.

117 *WA* 38.229, 10-16.

118 *WA* 38.230, 13-20. Luther's many post-1530 statements and actions concerning the priesthood of all believers prove Arthur Carl

In *A Treatise on the New Testament, that is, the Holy Mass* (*Eyn Sermon von dem newen Testament. das ist von der heylige Messe*), from his prolific year of 1520,[119] the writings of which serve as the basis for the *Augsburg Confession* and all of Luther's later theology, he writes that the true priestly function is the sacrificing of oneself by faith, the yielding of oneself to the will of God in response to "Thy will be done," through prayer and praise. It is not something we do, but something Christ does to us as our one and only true high priest and bishop:

> Thus it becomes clear that it is not the priest alone who offers the sacrifice of the mass; it is this faith which each one has for himself. This is the true priestly office, through which Christ is offered as a sacrifice to God, an office which the priest, with the outward ceremonies of the mass, simply represents. Each and all are, therefore, equally spiritual priests before God. From this you can see for yourself that there are many who observe the mass and make this sacrifice properly, yet themselves know nothing about it. Indeed, they do not realize that they are priests and can hold mass.[120] . . . All such, then, wherever they may be, are true priests. They truly observe the mass aright and also obtain by it what they desire. For faith must do everything. Faith alone is the true priestly office. It permits no one else to take its place. Therefore all Christian men are priests, all women priestesses, be they young or old, master or servant, mistress or maid, learned or unlearned. Here there is no difference, unless faith be unequal. [121]

Piepkorn's assertions to the contrary to be patently false. Piepkorn claimed, "The doctrine of the universal priesthood of all believers had receded into minor importance — even for Luther himself — by the time the symbolical books were being framed." (*Lutherans and Catholics in Dialogue IV,* "Eucharist and Ministry," 1970, 107). Instead, it increased dramatically.

[119] Published on August 21, 1520 between *An Open Letter to the Christian Nobility* in June and *The Babylonian Captivity of the Church* in September.

[120] *WA* 6.370, 7-14.

[121] *Ibid,* 370. 22-28.

What is truly remarkable here, is that in a treatise about the sacrifice of the mass, a function understood to be the exclusive domain of the ordained, Luther points to the only true priestly office there is, given to all Christians in common (*allengemein*): faith. To that end he states, "I quite fail to see why a man, who has once become a priest, cannot again become a layman, since he only differs from the laity by his ministry" (*Babylonian Captivity of the Church,* 1520).[122] For Luther, one is ordained through (*durch*) one's baptism, and certified by one's election and calling. "It follows that, if needs be, anyone may baptize or pronounce absolution, an impossible situation if we were not all priests" (*An Appeal to the Ruling Class,* 1520).[123]

---

[122] *Ibid,* 567.18-20. The ELCA retains its retired bishops as "bishops emeriti" to lay hands on new bishops to complete the chain for historical succession in imitation of the episcopal character conferred through Catholic orders, i.e., once ordained a priest, always a priest. Luther rejected episcopal succession as "fictitious," emphasizing the finite "call" of the congregation instead.

[123] *Ibid,* 408.1-2.

Chapter 2

Luther's Bohemian Rhapsody

Bornkamm, Kattenbusch, and the BSLK could just as easily have pointed to any number of Luther's correlative writings, beginning with the elephant in the room, the very namesake and basis for CA 5: *De instituendis ministris ecclesiae: ad Clarissimum Senatum Pragensem Bohemiae,* ("Concerning the Ministry"). [124] Luther addressed this extraordinary treatise of 1523 to the Senate and people of Prague in Bohemia, who a century after Jan Hus, found themselves in schism with Rome due in large part to their insistence on receiving the sacrament in both kinds. Having been refused an archbishop by Rome, they were at a loss as to how to properly call and ordain pastors, and appealed to Luther for help. His reply is a summary of the seven "functions," or "offices" (*officium*) common to all Christians: preaching, baptizing, administering holy communion, keys, praise and thanksgiving, prayer, and judging doctrine.

Much cautionary ink has been spilled in our day emphasizing the uniqueness of the Bohemian situation, all of it similar to Conrad Bergendoff's warning in *Luther's Works,* "But it should be remembered that the situation in Bohemia was highly abnormal and that Luther's suggestion is confined to an emergency. He advocated no such solutions for Germany."[125]

Neither of Bergendoff's statements is true. The Latin text of *De instituendis,* which first appeared on Friday, November

---

[124] *WA* 12, 169-195.

[125] *LW,* 40.x. At least Bergendoff added, "The statement does clearly prove that apostolic succession in the Roman sense . . . meant nothing to Luther."

13th, 1523,[126] was quickly followed by an official German translation on Luther's direct orders to Paul Speratus in Wittenberg in January 1524.[127] In the preface, which Speratus signed, he states Luther's clear intent is for the treatise to be thoroughly studied and applied not just in Bohemia, but throughout all Christendom.

> Not without cause have I been moved, dearest brethren [in Würzburg and Salzburg] to specifically commend to you the Germanization of this little book of the Christian ecclesiast (preacher) Martin Luther, whose book, as one might judge from the title, is addressed only to the Christians in the Kingdom of Bohemia. But to whoever thinks a bit further, it is obvious, just as his heart stood and still stands for the same, so it is always minded to advise all Christians (*allen Christen*) . . . that he ordered me to render this book in German *with the expressed intent that it be read and understood not only in Bohemia*, but by all the families comprising the German Nation for their betterment and understanding.[128]

Speratus would himself become the very embodiment of the Prague prescription in Germany six years later, when the Bishop of Pomerania, Erhard of Queiss, suddenly fell ill and

---

126 Cf. Georg Buchwald, *Luther-Kalendarium*, (Leipzig: Heinsius Nachfolger, 1929), 32.

127 Walch X.1549-1603. Speratus signed the preface: *"Am Tage St. Pauli Bekehrung, Wittenberg im 24. Jahr."*

128 *Ibid*, 1549f: *"Nicht ohne Ursache bin ich bewegt worden, allerliebste Brüder, euch zumal zuzuschreiben die Verdeutschung dieses Büchleins des christlichen Ecclesiasten (Predigers) Martin Luther's; welches Büchlein, wer nach dem Titel urtheilen will, er allein an die Christen im Königreich Böhmen geschrieben haben geachtet wird. Wer aber weiter gedenkt, leichtlich erkennen mag, gleichwie sein Herz hierin gestanden ist und noch steht gegen dieselben, also ist es auch allewege gesinnt, allen Christen zu rathen . . . daß er [Luther] dieses sein Büchlein mir in desutsche Sprache zu bringen befohlen hat, nämlich damit gewollt, daß es nicht allein von Böhmen, sondern von allen Geschlechtern deutscher Nation zu Besserung gelesen und verstanden würde."*

died. At Luther's urging, Duke Albrecht of Brandenburg simply "appointed" Speratus, the castle preacher at Königsberg, to be the new Bishop of Pomerania. "Speratus was introduced for the first time as the Bishop of Pomerania on January 7, 1530, and recounted himself how he was 'installed' (*eingewiesen*) to his office in the presence of notaries and witnesses before the assembled congregation in the Marienwerder Cathedral."[129] In other words, there was no episcopal ordination or historical succession.

What Luther saw in the Bohemian dilemma was not an "emergency" — a latter day term he never applied to a situation that was already more than a hundred years old before he ever addressed it — but an opportunity to spread the evangelical cause further east. Not only did he advocate such solutions for all of Germany, he personally implemented them throughout Saxony and beyond, Speratus being "Exhibit A," with many more examples to follow.

He also thoroughly rejected the claim, popular today, that his counsel to the Bohemians was somehow "highly abnormal," or "novel" or "unprecedented."[130] "It is the most ancient custom" (*es ist eine ganz alte Meinung*), he argued, citing the example of Hus a hundred years before, as well as those of the apostles and the patriarchs long before him. And even if his instruction were a novelty, he asks, so what? "Was it not a new thing for the children of Israel to pass through the sea? Will it not be a new thing for me to go through death to life? In all these things it is the word of God, not the novelty that we regard. If we should stop at the novelty of a thing, we would never be able to believe anything in the word of

---

[129] "Speratus," *Realencyklopädie für protestantische Theologie und Kirche*, (Leipzig: Johann Hinrichs, 1906), 628.

[130] A much touted modern myth in the promotion of CCM. Cf. Carl E. Braaten, *Principles of Lutheran Theology*, [Minneapolis: Augsburg Fortress, 2007], 55: "Luther and his followers did not expect to see the emergency situation develop into a state of normalcy."

God."[131]

One can argue, of course, that all the world was in a state of eschatological crisis for Luther, in which man found himself torn between God and the devil. Wherever the word is not being proclaimed, there an immediate and obvious emergency exists, since the church and her bishops are certainly no guarantors of the gospel. It is therefore both right and necessary for Christians to choose servants in the word "by common vote," to lay hands on them, and so elect one or more as pastors, bishops, and ministers for the community. All of this is "accomplished through no other right than that inherent in baptism and faith, especially in places lacking any other ministers," all having "no other priesthood than that which the laity possesses."[132]

Luther sees an emergency only where there is no such community of faith to exercise its God given baptismal right for proclamation, where the word does not go forth. In that case it is up to the individual Christian to take a stand in the gospel. For it is one thing to exercise a right publicly; another to use it in time of emergency. Publicly one may not exercise a right without the consent of the community or of the congregation. In time of emergency each may use it as he deems fit.

But for Luther no such emergency existed in Bohemia. They already had a community of faith, which is the very point of his treatise:

> It is of the common rights of Christians that we have been
> speaking. For since we have proved all of these things to
> be the common property of all Christians, no one
> individual can arise by his own authority and arrogate to

---

131 WA 12. 192-193. Cf. Joseph A. Burgess, *Lutheran Forum,* "Evangelical Episcopate, Yes — Sacramental Requirement, No," 1992, Vol. 26, No. 4, 32: "The term 'emergency situation' should, to be sure, always be used *cum grano salis:* To the victor belongs the definition of 'emergency situation.'"
132 *Ibid,* 189-192.

himself alone what belongs to all. Lay hold then of this right and exercise it, where there is no one else who has the same rights. But the community rights demand that one, or as many as the community chooses, shall be chosen or approved who, in the name of all these rights, shall perform these functions publicly.[133]

The "individual" who may not "arise by his own authority and arrogate to himself alone what belongs to all," is often misconstrued by today's hierarchists as referring to "rogue" lay members of a congregation preaching the word. Luther, however, is speaking about the pope. [134]

Were there an actual emergency in Bohemia, individual Christians would need to act unilaterally by right and command. But as this community of faith already exists, as it did in Hus's day, there is no need for individuals to arrogate these powers and rights for themselves (whether bishop or pope), rather they should act as the *communio sanctorum* and collectively call whomever they wish, for "A PRIEST IS NOT THE SAME AS A PRESBYTER or minister, the former is born, the latter is made," (*SACERDOTEM NON ESSE QVOD PRESBYTERVM VEL ministrum, illum nasci, hunc fieri*).[135] In other words: Priests are born (by baptism), ministers are made (by electing and calling); so being the born priests you already are, make your own ministers!

Wengert's cynical response that one wouldn't want the janitor of an operating room performing open heart surgery, (the unordained proclaiming the gospel) has no legitimacy in light of the word in baptism. Luther liked to emphasize that not one of the apostles was ordained. Jesus chose lepers, fishermen, tax cheats, and escort ladies to proclaim the good news of justification — Luke being the only "surgeon" among them. While Luther himself compared the skills needed to

---

133 *Ibid.*

134 Clement VII was elected pope on November 18, 1523.

135 *WA* 12, 178. Luther wrote this sentence in the upper case for emphasis.

43

properly distinguish law and gospel to those of a fine surgeon, he also made clear that it is not we who proclaim law and gospel, but the word itself — *Scriptura est suipsius interpres* ("Scripture interprets itself") — separating soul from spirit, joints from marrow (Heb.4:12), the same word being either law or gospel, however the Spirit gives one ears to hear it.

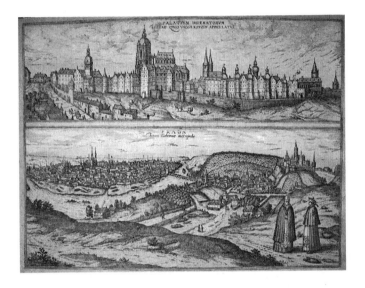

Prague ca. 1600

Not so fast, Wengert says. In an apparent bid to put the lay toothpaste back into the clerical tube of such a wildly democratic suggestion, he writes in a brief commentary on the Bohemian situation:

A final tract sometimes used to "proof text" Luther's doctrine of the priesthood of all believers is his *De instituendis ministris Ecclesiae* (*On the Instituted Ministries of the Church*). This tract was written in 1523 for the Utraquist bishops of Bohemia, who, despite their relative independence from Rome, still sought from the pope confirmation of their appointments as bishop. However, in his (to be sure, somewhat mistaken) account of early church life, Luther traced the development of bishops *not* from the

44

priesthood of all believers but from the paterfamilias of Christian households. The crucial thing here is that Luther was thinking *not* about a democratization of Christianity but rather that, in the absence of the preaching of the gospel in the assembly, the head of the household was to take action to read the gospel and even to baptize.[136]

Setting aside his nonsequitor that *patresfamilias* are somehow not the priesthood of all believers, and his short-changing of the laity from Luther's prescribed seven functions of ministry to only two, Wengert's assertions are simply not factual, beginning with his own, to be sure, somewhat mistaken account of the tract's recipients. As the full title, *De instituendis ministries Ecclesiae, ad clarissimum senatum Pragensem Bohemiae (Den Fürchtigen und Weisen Herren Bürgermeistern und Rath auch ganzer Gemeinde der Stadt Prag in Böhmen)* proves, it was sent not to "the Utraquist bishops," but "To the Illustrious and Wise Mayor, and Senate (*Rath*) as well as the entire Citizenry (*ganzer Gemeinde*) of the City of Prague."[137] This mixed package of recipients included the Utraquists of the bourgeoisie and lesser nobility, Neo-Utraquists,[138] Roman Catholics, Bohemian Brethren,[139] lay preachers (*Laienprediger*), and many others,[140] as is evidenced

---

[136] Wengert 18. In a witty but nonsensical statement he writes on p. 8: "As Paul Rorem of Princeton Theological Seminary once said, the democratic, American misconstrual of the priesthood of all believers means, in actuality, the priesthood of no believers."

[137] Walch 10.1548-1603. The authoritative German translation was made by Paul Speratus already in 1524.

[138] *sub utraque specie* = "in both kinds."

[139] Also known as "Waldenses" or "Picards." Luther had a generally benevolent correspondence with them, and they are the focus of his tract, *The Adoration of the Sacrament* (*WA* 11.431-456) written for them the same year.

Cf. Karl Heussi, *Kompendium der Kirchengeschichte,* Siebente, Durchgesehene Auflage, Verlag von J.C.B. Mohr, (Paul Siebeck, Tübingen, 1930), § 69.

[140] Thomas Müntzer, who lived in Prague for five months, addressed his *Prager Manifest* of 1521 in similar fashion: " . . . *und die*

45

by his opening sentence, "Often, many times, and through many correspondences I have been asked to write to you" (*Oft und vielmals, auch durch vieler Schrift, bin ich gebeten worden, euch zu schreiben.*).

While those who requested the tract are not necessarily identical to those to whom Luther sent it, it is nevertheless clear he was responding to many entreaties *durch viele Schriften* ("through many correspondences") sent to him on many occasions by many citizens.

Rome denied the see of Prague an archbishopric from 1421 to 1561.[141] After the last archbishop, Johann von Rokyczana died in 1471, the Utraquists had elected a consistory (*Konsistorium*) of burghers, aristocrats, and clergy (*die Stände*), 1/3 of whom were lay members (*4 Laien, 8 Geistliche*), with the administrator doing the ordinations, a very bold move indeed in complete defiance of the Catholic rules, and a consistory that was already fully functioning when Luther finally addressed it in 1523.[142] The question being put to Luther now was: How does one choose and put in place church servants? His answer is implicit in the German title of the treatise, *Wie man Kirchendiener wählen und einsetzen soll,* ("How One Should Choose and Put in Place Church Servants"). They, the Bohemian senate and people, by virtue of their baptism, were to exercise the public office of ministry and pick and install their own pastors. Contrary to Wengert's claim that Luther was not thinking "about a democratization of Christianity," he tells the Bohemian citizenry,

---

Hussiten, einmal an das einfache Volk, an die dortigen Humanisten, an die ganze Kirche der Auserwählten und an die ganze Welt."

141 Anton Brus of Möglitz in Moravia was installed into the office in 1561. His predecessor had been Johann von Rokyczana, who died in 1471, fifty years before Luther wrote his letter.

142 At the Diet of Prague the Utraquists demanded the introduction of the Augsburg Confession, and in 1575 the *Confessio Bohemica* was adopted. It was Lutheran in doctrine, but Calvinistic in its interpretation of the Lord's Supper.

Then let those [citizens] who are the most prominent among you (*die Vornehmsten unter euch*) lay hands on them, and certify (*bestätigen sie*) and commend (*befehlen sie*) them to the people, the church, or the community. In this way alone shall they become your bishops and shepherds (*und durch das allein sollen sie eure Bischöfe und Hirten sein*). It is not necessary, I think, to put this form of election immediately into practice in the Diet of Bohemia as a whole. But if individual cities adopt it for themselves the example of one will soon be followed by another. The Diet might well consider whether this form should be adopted by all of Bohemia, or if one part might accept, and another part postpone decision or even reject it altogether. For none should be forced to believe. [143]

No mention is made here of ordinations, episcopal or otherwise. There is no need to rush. No "emergency" is being spoken of. The Bohemians can decide these things for themselves peacefully and calmly over time. It is therefore very misleading to say, "Luther advised the Bohemian bishops to begin to consecrate their own bishops," or that Luther's purpose was "to empower the Bohemian bishops and clergy to act on behalf of the public ministry of the word,"[144] as if he were advising the bishops to decide and act on behalf of the people. That is episcopal *Amstliebe* run amok, and it completely ignores the fact that Luther's Easter treatise of 1523, *That a Christian Assembly or Congregation Has the Right . . . to Call and . . . Dismiss Teachers . . .* (without a bishop's authority), fully anticipates his November counsel to the Bohemians in *De instituendis*. All modern day attempts to turn the Bohemian situation into a cautionary tale against breaking the episcopal hierarchical glass, except "In the Case of an Emergency," completely fails the historical and confessional litmus test.

Yet it doesn't keep some from trying. In his brief treatment of this document, Wengert performs a clever slight of hand

---

143 Walch 10.1598.85.
144 Wengert 24.

that thoroughly misconstrues Luther's famous line, "A PRIEST IS NOT THE SAME AS A PRESBYTER or minister, the former is born, the latter is made," by shifting Luther's emphasis from PRIEST to PRESBYTER, or more precisely, from baptism to ordination. He writes, "This single line, capitalized in the original, makes it clear that, when Luther used the word 'priest' (Latin: *sacerdos*), he did not mean the public office of ministry," adding "ordination makes elders *presbyteroi*, not *sacerdotes*." Yet neither the Latin nor the German make any mention of ordination, and Luther's focus becomes even clearer in Speratus's German: *Es ist nicht Ein Ding, Priester und Diener: zum Priester wird einer geboren; zu einem Diener wird man durch Wahl oder Berufung* (THEY ARE NOT THE SAME THING, PRIEST AND SERVANT; ONE IS BORN A PRIEST; ONE BECOMES A SERVANT BY ELECTION OR CALL).[145] The Bohemian priestly pool, in other words, from which servants for ministry may be drawn, already exists in the baptized. They may therefore call or elect whomever they wish. Nevertheless, Wengert adds:

> Ordination was the means of "instituting" servants of the word. The Latin verb *instituo* means, literally, "to put in place" and, more broadly, "to establish, institute or appoint to an office." Here we see most clearly that Luther, far from eliminating the ordained ministry or making it subservient to the laity or the congregation, understood that the "public ministry of the word" is the means by which "the mysteries of God are dispensed." There is nothing higher or greater in the church than that word.[146]

His inference is clear: The "public office of ministry" refers exclusively to the ordained, to the clergy, who dispense the highest mysteries of God, and not to the sacerdotes, the priesthood of all believers. Yet Luther's whole point in *De instituendis* is that in baptism we are all *born* to public

---

145 Walch 10.1569.29.
146 Wengert 19.

ministry, baptism superseding ordination as high as the gospel supersedes the law. Indeed, one could hardly find a work of Luther's which more closely identifies the sacerdotes with the priesthood of all believers for the "public office of ministry," than this treatise. The very purpose of the upper case statement is to show the Bohemians that they have no excuse for sneaking across the Italian border to be ordained (mostly by Venetians) for the sake of maintaining a subterfugal semblance of historical episcopal succession, a modern day veil of Moses. Why do so when they've already been ordained as priests in their baptism? As members of the *only* (*einzige*) royal priesthood, they already have all that is needful for church, possessing every right, power, and authority to exercise the fullness of public ministry — with or without an archbishop—including preaching, teaching, calling, administering, and ordaining. He contrasts bishops' ordinations *iure humano* ("those whom the bishops have shorn and anointed"), with our baptismal promise *iure divino* immediately after his upper case statement, adding:

> You will not triumph over this scandalous condition unless with closed eyes you disregard usage, tradition, and great numbers, and with open ears heed only the word of God. . . For a priest, especially in the New Testament, was not made, but born. He was created, *not ordained*. He was born not indeed of flesh, but through a birth of the Spirit, by water and Spirit in the washing of regeneration [John 3.6f.; Titus 3.5f.]. Indeed, all Christians are priests, and all priests are Christians.[147]

He says to the Bohemians:

> It is obvious that these pseudo-ordainers, the bishops, blaspheme and err in holding that their anointing and ordinations are so necessary that without them no one can be a priest, however holy he may be, be he Christ himself . . . So it follows naturally that Christ has been made the first priest of the New Testament without shaving, without anointing, and so without any of their

---

[147] *WA* 12.178.

"character" or all the masquerade of episcopal ordination. He made all his apostles and his disciples priests, but through no such masks. So this mask of ordination is unnecessary. And if you have it, it is not enough in order to be a priest.[148]

He also gently chides them for their timidity, for were they to implement his counsel,

> Then Bohemia would return again to its rightful and evangelical archbishopric, which would be rich, not in large income and much authority, but in many ministers and visitations of the churches. But if you are altogether too weak to dare to attempt this free and apostolic way of establishing a ministry, we will endure your weakness awhile longer and permit you to go on accepting those ordained by papal bishops, such as your Gallus... Let it be thus until you grow up and fully know what is the power of the word of God. Clearly we cannot advise you in any other way at this time. For it is not possible for you to accept papal ordination and those ordained by it without sin and disobedience, and therefore without the risk of the destruction of souls.[149]

In what appears to be a rather desperate bid to confine Luther's radicalism to a strictly Bohemian "emergency," Wengert ties himself into a bit of a pretzel, on the one hand decrying what he calls today's "pious construal of a democratized priesthood of all believers and congregational autonomy," while conceding the public office of ministry "is given to all in general and requires that everyone be in agreement."[150] Yet what greater exercise of a democratized priesthood is there, than all the people of God agreeing to call their next pastor, who cannot be imposed upon them without their will?

---

148 *Ibid,* 179.
149 *Ibid,* 194; Walch 10.1598.87.
150 Wengert 82.

The Myth of "Public Ministry"

"Take some more tea," the March Hare said to Alice, very earnestly. "I've had nothing yet," Alice replied in an offended tone, "so I can't take more." "You mean you can't take less," said the Hatter, "it's very easy to take more than nothing."

Lewis Carroll, *Alice in Wonderland*

In a speech he delivered at Valparaiso University in which he declared the priesthood of all believers to be "a mythical category" having nothing to do with Luther's thought, Wengert channeled Goat Emser, stating "it is important to realize that Luther does insist that, by virtue of our baptism, we are all priests, bishops and popes, that is to say, we are all Christians," but cautioning, "In this sense, we are all priests, but only in the sense that the word 'priest,' is used here, namely, as 'a Christian or spiritual human being.'"[151] But as we have already seen, Luther argued the opposite, that all Christians are truly priests, and all (baptized) priests are truly Christians. One's baptism doesn't come with restrictions.

In a chapter he acerbically labeled, "Other 'Proofs' for the Existence of the Priesthood of All Believers," Wengert slyly mixes two of Luther's tracts in a way that would have positively tickled the March Hare. Referencing *Concerning the Ministry*, he writes:

> Later in the tract, Luther went so far as to approve a distinction made by his opponent Jerome Emser, who had insisted, in an earlier refutation of Luther, that there were two groups described in the 1 Peter text, all Christians spiritually and communally and some specially and externally.[152]

Luther, in fact, approved nothing of the kind. To make it

---

[151] Cf. Cf. www.valpo.edu/ils/assets/pdfs/05_wengert.pdf
[152] Wengert 22.

appear as if he'd given his assent to Emser's two priesthoods, Wengert attached a footnote directing the reader to *Dr. Luther's Retraction of the Error Forced Upon Him by the Most Highly Learned Priest of God, Sir Jerome Emser, Vicar in Meissen,* in which Luther acknowledges that Emser's "physical priests" are, along with all other Christians, also "spiritual priests." By mistakenly assuming Luther's concession is genuine — as if Emser had somehow caught him out and his "error" were real — he falls down the same rabbit hole as the Leipzig monk, who completely missed the sarcasm of what Brecht calls "the ironic fiction of Luther's writing,"[153] who stated facetiously:

> I, Martin Luther, confess that in complete agreement with the highly educated man and priest of God, Mr. Jerome Emser, I hold and insist that the saying of St. Peter is to be understood not only concerning the spiritual but also concerning the bodily priesthood. Or, that I may say it most clearly, it applies to every priesthood that there is in Christendom. This I say in all seriousness, for I did not in truth rightly perceive the thing before this. Now I hope that Luther is no longer a heretic and that I am in complete agreement with Emser. [154]

Luther, who obviously regarded Emser as neither "highly educated" nor "a priest of God" (but "of Baal"), "concedes" Emser's marvelous grasp of the obvious — that ordained or "physical priests" are along with all other Christians "spiritual priests" — but then turns the tables on him by taking it to its logical conclusion: If all ordained physical priests (clerics) are also spiritual priests, then all spiritual priests (all Christians) are also physical priests ordained in their baptism, merely needing a call, something Emser couldn't possibly accept because it eliminates his "twofold" priesthood, (and Wengert's "two groups . . . all Christians spiritually and communally and

---

153 Martin Brecht, *Martin Luther,* (Stuttgart: Calwer Verlag, 1981), Bnd. 1, 361.
154 *WA* 8.250.

some specially and externally").[155] Wengert, who appears either unable or unwilling to recognize Luther's clever use of "ironic fiction" for the setting up and knocking down of the Vicar of Meissen, then simply walks away from the text without bothering to quote the remainder of Luther's *coup de grâce* for the reader in which he completely destroys Emser's (and Wengert's) fanciful notion of a metaphorical priesthood:

> In case anyone thinks I am being facetious, I shall earnestly prove that this interpretation of Emser is indisputable. Is it not indeed true and sufficiently evident that Emser says St. Peter also speaks of the physical priesthood? That is why he has lied so abominably and slandered me until I was forced to grant it to him. Thus it is even more indeed true and evident that no man can deny that St. Peter's saying is addressed to all Christians, be they young or old, men or women. Clearly, therefore, everything that is comprehended in [the physical priesthood] must be understood as given to all these Christians. For since all Christians are called priests when he says, "You are a royal priesthood" [I Peter 2:9], and since it is also to be understood in the sense of the physical priesthood, which is consecrated and tonsured, as swordsman Emser teaches and constructs, we have to confess that all Christians are undoubtedly such physical priests. Otherwise, we are heretics and the devil's property, as Emser threatens. Perhaps

---

155 Cf. Dorothea Wendebourg, *Lutheran Quarterly,* Vol. XXIII/Number 3, Autumn 2009, 349: "Where [Luther] writes about all of us being priests the stress is on what follows from our common baptism for our spiritual *potestas* (power): 'that we all have the same *potestas* in the word and in whichever sacrament' (*WA* 6:566.27f). It is this statement which everyone — and rightly so — associates with Luther's discovery that all Christians are priests. For it means that baptism, the celebration of the Lord's Supper, absolution, and so forth, are acts 'any Christian' can perform (*WA* 12:189.41 ff). Luther really says 'any Christian,' and when shortly before he writes 'all Christians in common,' this is meant in the same sense — not in the sense of something which is 'given to all Christians communally,' as Wengert translates thereby shifting the sense (21). Only because Luther is serious about every Christian having this same *potestas* does his argument make sense that order forbids every Christian to make use of it in public on his own initiative."

this is why women wear veils and young maidens wear braids —
so that no one can see that they are consecrated and tonsured.
Well then, this is finished. But it still has one major fault. I shall
be glad to humble myself and hear women and children preach.
But how do we convince Emser, the cuirassier-eater, to do the
same? He will not want to be in the common priesthood (*gemeyne
priesterschafft*). Besides, he will not permit women to teach
him[156] — even if they were only pretty, smooth young maids —
because he is too chaste. But I wish he could be persuaded to
make his confession to such a confessor at a secret place and to
wait most humbly for his absolution! So that he does not get
angry and complain that his cause is tomfoolery and a joke —
which is true, however — we ourselves shall have to reflect what
should be done in this matter.

I shall give my advice. Since they boast and brag about a
special,[157] uncommon priesthood, and since all priesthood —
spiritual, physical, or whatever it may be or may be called — is
ascribed to all Christians in Peter's words as the passage
demands, it follows that the Emserian *priesterey* is a strange un-
Christian thing. Therefore I think it best if from now on we no
longer call this special and strange priesthood "priests" but rather
"tonsure-bearers," and drive this useless crowd from the land.
What good does such a tonsured crowd do us? They are neither
spiritual nor physical priests. And why do we need them if we
ourselves are all physical, spiritual, and all other kinds of
priests?[158]

With Emser's false claim of a twofold priesthood clearly in
his crosshairs, Luther proceeds to outline the seven-fold office
of public ministry which belongs to all Christians in
Concerning the Ministry, starting with his introductory words:

But let us go on and show from the priestly offices (as they call

---

156 Two American Lutheran groups that still bar women from
becoming pastors are the Lutheran Church-Missouri Synod and the
Lutheran Church-Wisconsin Synod.
157 E.g. Wengert 22: ". . . some specially and externally."
158 *WA* 8, 251-252. Luther would no longer reply to Emser, who
continued to harass him for another two years before dying suddenly
in 1523.

54

them) that all Christians are priests in equal degree . . . Mostly the functions of a priest are these: to teach, to preach and proclaim the word of God, to baptize, to consecrate or administer the eucharist, to bind and loose sins, to pray for others, to sacrifice, and to judge all doctrine and spirits . . . Therefore when we grant the word to anyone, we cannot deny anything to him pertaining to the exercise of his priesthood.[159]

Thus, the very first office he points to is the *Predigtamt,* (the preaching office):

The first office, that of the ministry of the word, therefore, is common to all Christians. This is clear, from what I have already said, and from I Pet. 2 [.9], "You are a royal priesthood that you may declare the wonderful deeds of him who called you out of darkness into his marvelous light." I ask, who are these who are called out of darkness into marvelous light? Is it only the shorn and anointed masks? Is it not all Christians? And Peter not only gives them the right, but the command, to declare the wonderful deeds of God, which certainly is nothing else than *to preach the word of God.*[160]

For Luther, "there is no other proclamation in the ministry of the word than that which is common to all, that of the wonderful deed of God, so there is no other priesthood than that which is spiritual and universal, as Peter here defines it."[161] This is the *public ministry* of the word for the salvation of those who hear. "Paul confirms this in 1 Cor. 14 as he speaks not to the shorn or to a few, but to the whole church and *each individual Christian:* 'Each one of you has a hymn, a lesson, a revelation, a tongue, or an interpretation.'" This ministry of the word is the highest office in the church, and "is unique and belongs to all who are Christians, not only by right, but by command. Indeed it is not a priesthood if it is not unique and common to all. Nothing can prevail against these divine thunderings, be it numberless fathers, innumerable

---

[159] *WA* 12,179-180.
[160] *Ibid,* 180.
[161] *Ibid.*

councils, the custom of ages, or a majority of all the world."

That Luther was thinking here not only of the laity receiving the sacrament, but even administering it, given a call, is clear from *The Babylonian Captivity of the Church* written three years earlier. There he states that

> . . . to offer the mass is only to receive the sacrament. What function, then, is left for you as a priest which is not equally appropriate for a layman? Tonsure and vestments? It is a poor sort of priest that is made up of tonsure and vestments! Or is it the oil that anointed your fingers? But every Christian whatsoever has been anointed with the oil of the Holy Spirit, and sanctified in body and soul. Formerly laymen used to administer the sacraments as often as priests do now . . . Therefore everyone who knows that he is a Christian should be fully assured that all of us alike are priests, and that we all have the same authority in regard to the word and sacraments, although no one has the right to administer them without the consent of the members of his church, or by the call of the majority, because when something is common to all, no single person is empowered to arrogate it to himself, but should await the call of the church.[162]

In other words, agreement by the members for the sake of good order through a call is the only thing that prevents more than one or two from preaching and administering the sacraments in the assembly.

In *Concerning the Ministry* he even wonders in his discussion of the second office how it is that the laity are allowed to baptize, but not administer the Lord's Supper. Using a tongue-in-cheek example of Rome's attitude toward women, he writes,

> The second function, to baptize, they themselves have by usage allowed in cases of necessity even to ordinary women, so that it is hardly regarded any more as a sacramental function. Whether they wish or not we deduce from their own logic that all Christians, and they alone, even women, are priests, without tonsure and episcopal "character." For in baptizing we proffer the

---

[162] *WA* 6.566.

life-giving word of God, which renews souls and redeems from death and sins. To baptize is incomparably greater than to consecrate bread and wine, for it is the greatest office in the church — the proclamation of the word of God. So when women baptize, they exercise the function of priesthood legitimately, and do it not as a private act, but as a part of the *public ministry* of the church which belongs only to the priesthood . . . They themselves have established it as the first sacrament and have permitted no one but priests to administer sacraments. But one sacrament cannot be of greater rank than another, since all are founded on the same word of God.[163]

Hence,

"There is something ridiculous about this conferring of orders. For the episcopal dignity is not a sacrament nor has it a 'character.' Yet it gives a priestly dignity and power supposedly above all others."[164]

This imagined priestly dignity and power is what the Bohemians sought to gain through their Italian ordinations in order to qualify for the third function or office common to all Christians, "to consecrate or to administer the sacred bread and wine." In what was no doubt shocking to many in Prague, Luther boldly asserts, "we hold that this function, too, like the priesthood, belongs to all, and this we assert, not on our own authority, but that of Christ who at the Last Supper said, 'Do this in remembrance of me,' . . . So it follows that what is given here is given to all." That the power and right to consecrate or administer the bread and wine is given to the whole *Gemeinde* is clear, he says, from St. Paul's words in 1 Cor. 11.23, "'For I received from the Lord what I also delivered to you,' etc.'"[165]

Yet here again Wengert blows smoke in asserting that Luther instead counseled the Bohemians to "live without the

---

163 *WA* 12. 181.
164 *WA* 12, 182.
165 *Ibid.*

supper," because it "could not occur in the house church."[166] But once again, Luther did nothing of the kind.[167] The Lord's Supper, he says, "is nothing else than a preaching of the word." Mindful of delicate consciences, though, he advised heads of households who "neither would dare nor could receive" the sacrament, to forego this nonessential, but "this condition is grievous and inevitable *only in the case of the weak and over-scrupulous (nisi forte infirmis et scrupulosis).* The others who have faith and know the truth, possess full freedom and means to drive away unworthy ministers and to call and appoint only such worthy and devout men as they choose."[168] Thus, "Christ here enjoined the same ministry of the word on them all equally. All of them are given the right and command to hold the Lord in remembrance, so that God may be praised and glorified in his marvelous deeds."[169] "Here Paul addresses all the Corinthians, making each of them, as he himself was: consecrators (*consecratores*)."[170] To cling to a hierarchical episcopacy, as Emser, the papists, and the Bohemians were doing, was to reject "the marvelous light into which we have been called. If then that which is greatest, namely, word and baptism, is conferred on all, then it can rightly be maintained that the lesser, the power to consecrate

---

[166] Wengert 19.

[167] In *On the Councils and the Churches,* Luther writes, "Christians can become and remain holy without these things, if the preaching is done on the street, without a pulpit, if sins are forgiven, if the sacrament is administered without an altar, baptism without a font, and indeed it is of a daily occurrence that, because of peculiar circumstances, sermons are preached and baptism and the sacraments administered in homes. But for the sake of the children and the simple folk, it is a fine thing and promotes good order to have a definite time, place, and hour for these things, so that people can adapt themselves and meet together, as St. Paul says, in I Corinthians 14, 'Let all be done in fine order' . . . Nevertheless, these things ought to remain free." *WA* 50.649.

[168] *WA* 12.172.

[169] *Ibid,* 181.

[170] *Ibid,* 182.

(*consecrare*), is also so conferred, even if there be no direct authority of scripture."[171] In his summation he boldly states,

> Here we take our stand. There is no other word of God than that which is given all Christians to proclaim. There is no other baptism than the one which any Christian can bestow. There is no other remembrance of the Lord's Supper than that which any Christian can celebrate (*begehen mag*) and which Christ has instituted.[172]

---

[171] *Ibid,* 183. Wengert here shares Piepkorn's erroneous conclusion that, " . . . the opinion of the Church of the Augsburg Confession of this period holds that a layman may not celebrate the eucharist even in an emergency (*WA* Br 7.338-39, 365-66; *WATR* 5.621, no. 6361)," (Piepkorn 117). Of the three examples Piepkorn cites, however, the first contradicts him, Luther asserting: "since there is *no emergency* nor call there" (*nun hie kein Note noch Beruf ist*); the second is a rejection of Matthes Lotther, a *Schwärmer,* for teaching a mix of evangelical and Catholic theology; and the third states the community already has a pastor, so the Corinthian principal of good order applies. While the need for a call is common to all three, ordination is never mentioned.

It was simply for good order, not reasons of theology, that Luther stated in his 1535 Sermon on Psalm 110: "This office cannot be attended to by all the members of a congregation. Neither is it fitting that each household do its own baptizing and celebrating of the sacrament [since the congregation would grow too slowly and one wouldn't know who was baptized]. Hence it is necessary to select and put in place (*ordenen*) those who can preach and teach, who study the scriptures, and who are able to defend them." *WA* 41.214. (*Ordenen* is mistranslated as "ordain" in *Luther's Works* 13.334. For the meaning of *ordenen* see Ch. 4 below.)

Lutheran lay administration was also widely exercised during the Roman Catholic suppression of the *Emigrationspatent,* issued on October 31, 1731, and enforced by Archbishop Leopold Firmian of Salzburg against all churches of the Augsburg Confession. Lay heads of households regularly instructed, baptized, and communed their families throughout Austria and the Alsace, which was known as *Geheimprotestantismus,* or "secret Protestantism." Cf. *RGG*, IV. Band, 1592.

[172] *Walch* 10, 1590.71.

Seeking to bolster their Bohemian backbone, he applies the same logic to the remaining offices belonging to all Christians. Of the fourth, the office of the binding and loosing of sins, he says, "this office of the keys belongs to all of us who are Christians, as I have so often proved and shown in my books against the pope," and "as we have declared already, the ministry of the word belongs to all." The fifth and sixth, the offices of praise, thanksgiving, and prayer, clearly belong to all Christians, as does the seventh, the right "to judge and pass on doctrine." Of the latter he writes, "Clearly it is not without good reason that the mask priests and counterfeit Christians have claimed this office for themselves. For they could foresee that if they allowed all to have this function they could not monopolize any of the aforementioned privileges."[173]

The Bohemians, in the end, sadly lost their nerve and no major gains for the Reformation could be achieved there, but the point had nevertheless been made loudly and clearly to pope and emperor alike: In the absence of the proclamation of the word, the royal priesthood of all believers has the command, power, and authority of Christ to act in accord for the sake of the ministry of proclamation. In order to do this, however, they would first need to know what they're talking about.

---

[173] *Ibid,* 1585.64. A modern parallel is found in the Lutheran-Episcopal agreement *Called to Common Mission,* which states that the role of the bishops as overseers, "is to safeguard the Gospel." One can well imagine Luther wondering when the Holy Spirit had abrogated that role, and if so, asking *Quis custodiet ipsos custodes,* ("Who will guard the guardians themselves?"). His answer is clear: All the sacerdotes do, the baptized, exercising the office of public ministry in common *allengemein.*

Chapter 3

Ministerium: One *Ampt,* Many *Ämptern*

Luther was appalled by the level of biblical illiteracy in both the parish and the parlor, of pastors and their flocks, which he discovered during the 1528-1529 Saxon Visitations. To remedy this emergency situation, he quickly and simultaneously produced both a *Large Catechism*[174] (*Deutsch Katechismus* April 1529) for the education of pastors, and a *Small Catechism* (SC) (May 1529)[175] for their flocks. The smaller was truly formatted as a teaching textbook, free of the admonitions and polemics of the larger, and was to be employed by the *Hausvater,* or head of the household to instruct the children and all present in the home. Wengert wisely includes "teachers" (like himself) in the *Predigtamt,* since the SC is nothing short of an instruction manual for teachers and preachers in the kitchen and the classroom. If Luther had been a stickler for hierarchical office (*Amtsliebe*), or had only thought of the priesthood of all believers metaphorically, he would never have literally entrusted the "uneducated" (*gemeine*)[176] parents and teachers with this all important task in the one office of proclamation. The catechisms' publication was both bold and unheard of in an age of "show thyself to the priest" for all instruction, and ran the risk of emboldening *das gemeine Volk* once again in the immediate aftermath of the Peasant Wars. Yet here at last, in

---

[174] Luther did not give it this title.

[175] Some of today's English versions that purport to be correct translations of Luther's catechism are in fact not, most notably the Lutheran Church Missouri Synod's widely purchased *Luther's Small Catechism with Explanation,* [Saint Louis: Concordia Publishing House, 1991], which is not Luther's, nor his explanations, but Missouri's.

[176] *ungelehrten, BSLK* 501 n.1.

Saxony, was the exercise of the true order of the priesthood of Melchizedek, a priesthood *iure divino* by baptism, a *ministerium verbi divini* of a single *Ampt* with many *Ämptern,* or offices/functions (*officia*) *de iure humano.*

That Luther did not think of this *ministerium* in clerical terms, reserved for the ordained, but as the domain of all the baptized for the proclamation of God's word in all times and all places, is clear from his explanation to the 4th Commandment in the *Large Catechism.* Parents should "consider that they owe obedience to God, and should earnestly and faithfully discharge the duties of their office (*Ampts, officium*), not only to provide for the material support of their children, servants, subjects, etc., but especially to bring them up to the praise and honor of God. Therefore do not imagine that the parental office is a matter of your pleasure and whim. It is a strict commandment and injunction of God, who holds you accountable for it." [177]

The parental *Ampt* is first and foremost the conveyance of the gospel, the preaching and teaching of parents to their children for the praise and honor of God. On November 29, 1528, the First Sunday in Advent, he admonished parents from the pulpit to see to the Christian education of their charges. "You have been appointed their bishop and pastor; take heed that you do not neglect your office over them."[178] In fact, he added, if parents actually took their *Ampt* in the gospel seriously, no teachers would ever need to be hired to re-teach what is preached from the pulpit. "The fault lies with us householders. Necessity has forced us to engage teachers because the parents have not assumed this responsibility. But every master and mistress should remember that they are all bishops and bishopesses for Gretel and Hans," a line he repeats twice for emphasis.[179]

In the *Small Catechism* we see what constitutes for Luther the "new normal" for the evangelical faith. The *Predigtamt*

---

[177] *BSLK* 603.
[178] *WA* 27. 444.
[179] *WA* 30 I.61.

has literally come home. Parents are literally bishops who possess an office by God's command, docents of the domicile, who share the same catechetical handbook with schoolmasters and pastors, who together proclaim his word of law and gospel within the single priestly *Stand* — not just "spiritually" (Emser), or "metaphorically" (Wengert), but "literally" (Luther). The catechism addresses the pervasive emergency which continues in our time, wherever the good news is not being proclaimed.

Luther's new normal hit the streets a full year before the 1530 Diet of Augsburg and provided the context for the *ministerio ecclesia* of CA 5. He made sure of it by expanding on the revolutionary theme of the priesthood of all believers offered in his explanation to the 4th Commandment, firing off a new tract, *A Sermon on Keeping Children in School* from the Coburg Castle, even as the Diet was in session. He completed it by mid-July and hurriedly gave it to Nickel Schirlentz in Wittenberg for publication. When it failed to appear immediately, he wrote to his wife Katie with great agitation, telling her to "take the manuscript from Schirlentz and give it to Georg Rau" to be published "as soon as possible!"[180]

This marvelous work sought to address both the unfortunate abandonment of the old educational system for reasons of misguided Christian liberty, and the claims of pious fanatics (*Schwärmer, himmlischen Propheten*) that being filled with the Holy Spirit was education enough.[181] The remedy for both problems lay in a thorough grounding of young people in a liberal arts education[182] for the spiritual estate. But as things

---

[180] *WA* Br 5.545-546.

[181] Luther wrote in *Against the Heavenly Prophets,* 1525, that they appeared to have "devoured the Holy Spirit feathers and all" "*. . . der den heyligen geyst mit feddern und mit all gefressen habe.*" *WA* 18.66.

[182] *LW* 46. 252, n.73: "The liberal arts were traditionally seven in number. Grammar, rhetoric, and dialectic comprised the trivium of the medieval elementary schools; music, arithmetic, geometry, and astronomy comprised the quadrivium of the secondary schools."

stood, a simple soldier in Caesar's army was better educated "than all the bishops, priests and monks of Germany rolled into one."

But its intent was even more far reaching. It "paints a picture of a future territorial and bureaucratic state in which Rome and the bishops no longer have a role," says Wilhelm Maurer. "Theologians and jurists rule, both exercising spiritual and temporal authority. The work is arranged under this double heading; in lively colors it describes the picture of the two authorities that Melanchthon had only sketched in the *Augustana*. In the process it provides a graphic commentary on CA 28."[183]

Luther compares and contrasts the two "spiritual estates" — the true one of believers purchased with the precious blood and bitter death of Christ, with the false one of monastic houses and foundations, "which give no heed to God's word and the office of preaching." The one true "spiritual estate" (*der geistliche Stand*) is "the office of preaching and the service of the word and sacraments and which imparts the Spirit and salvation, blessings that cannot be attained by any pomp and pageantry. It includes the work of pastors, teachers, preachers, lectors, priests, (whom men call chaplains), sacristans, schoolmasters, and whatever other work belongs to these offices and persons," including any "helpers and assistants."[184] Theirs is a "preaching office" as well, and Luther calls them *Lehrer zur Gerechtigkeit* ("teachers unto righteousness"),[185] *paidagogoi* of the one spiritual estate. Such

---

183 Wilhelm Maurer, *Historical Commentary on the Augsburg Confession*, (Philadelphia: Fortress Press, 1986), 73.

184 E.g., Joachim Camerarius and Eobanus Hess, who taught Greek and poetry respectively at Nürnberg's new school which was dedicated by Melanchthon in 1526. Luther was positively elated, boasting that not even the university of Paris had such fine teachers, nor distinguished city council. "For this they have shown generous Christian consideration on their subjects, contributing faithfully to their eternal salvation as well as to their temporal well being and honor." Cf. *WA* 30II.518, n. 1 & 2.

185 *WA*, DB 11 II. 221.

pedagogues, as he had already made clear six years earlier in *To the Councilmen of All Cities in Germany That They Establish and Maintain Christian Schools,* must be understood in the custodial sense of Galatians 3:24, which he consistently translated as *Zuchtmeyster,* literally, "one who educates, trains, or disciplines in home, court, or school."[186]

Ordination does not make one a *presbyteros,* or bishop, as far as Luther was concerned — Latin does, and even more specifically, Greek and Hebrew do! At a minimum he required the simple or unlearned (*gemeine*) pastors and preachers to be well versed in Latin, and the more learned (*gelehrten*) to be proficient in Greek and Hebrew.[187] These are the languages that are utterly essential in the schools for making *Gottes rede,* "God's speech" (Rom. 3:1-2; Ps. 147:19-20) comprehensible and known, the *Zuchtmeyster* being absolutely indispensable for the proper communicating of the means of justifying faith in the spiritual estate. Nor is the custodial role only one of producing future priests, monks, and nuns, but one by which all young men and women are "taught in a Christian manner," for the temporal world and "for their souls as well." Trained this way, "Even though a boy who has studied Latin should afterward learn a trade and become a craftsman, he still stands as a ready reserve in case he should be needed as a pastor, or in some other service of the word."[188] "For although the

---

[186] *WA,* DB 7.182-183; Grimm, *Deutsches Wörterbuch,* VII. 275; Cf. *LW* 45. n.16. This is in keeping with Luther's translation of *matheteusante* in Mt. 28:19. Mark Menacher notes: "Luther translated this phrase *lehret alle Völker* (instruct all peoples), as did the Vulgate and other common sources. The Swiss Reformers tended to translate this as 'make disciples,' as well as the English. Lutherans have never understood this so, and only in the later 20th century did this poor rendering sneak into German translations, strangely without critical assessment or sound rationale."

[187] *WA* 30 II.547: "Ordinary pastors (*gemeinen pfarher*), however, must be able to use Latin. They cannot do without it any more than scholars can do without Greek and Hebrew, as St. Augustine says, and canon law even prescribes." Cf. *BSLK* 501, n.1.

[188] *Ibid,* 546.

gospel came and still comes to us through the Holy Spirit alone, we cannot deny that it came through the medium of languages, was spread abroad by that means, and must be preserved by the same means. For just when God wanted to spread the gospel throughout the world by means of apostles, he gave the tongues for that purpose."[189]

Peter Waldo (also Pierre Vaudès, (1140-1218)[190]

Thus, it is one thing to be a simple preacher (*gemeine Pfarrherr*) of faith, but quite another to be a person who

[189] *WA* 15.37.

[190] The Luther Memorial, Worms, Germany, by Ernst Rietschel. Waldo was a merchant and preacher, a founder of the Waldensian lay preachers whom Luther praised for their honorable living and reform-minded doctrine (WATR, No. 2864b) even though they didn't fully grasp the doctrine of justification by faith. His chief criticism of them was their lack of education in the biblical languages. Waldo was excommunicated by Pope Lucius III in 1184, and the Waldensians eventually joined the Reformed movement.

actually knows the *Gottes rede,* who can teach and expound upon the languages, "which are absolutely and altogether necessary in the Christian church." Such teachers Luther calls "prophets," and the church must never be without them, "although it is not necessary that every Christian or every preacher be such a prophet, as St. Paul points out in I Cor. 12 and Eph. 4."[191]

These teachers, whom God equips with the Holy Spirit for the communication of his word, are praised by the word itself in Luther's view of their pedagogical role in the spiritual estate:

> This estate the scriptures highly exalt and praise. St. Paul calls them God's stewards and servants [I Cor. 4:1]; bishops [Acts 20:28]; doctors, prophets [I Cor. 12:28]; also God's ambassadors to reconcile the world to God, II Cor. 6 [5:20]. Joel calls them saviors . . .[192] In Psalm 68 David calls them kings and princes...[193] Haggai [1:13] calls them angels, and Malachi [2:7] says, "The lips of the priest keep the law, for he is an angel of the Lord of hosts"[194]. . . Christ himself gives the same name, not only in Matthew 11 [:10], but where he calls John the Baptist an angel, but also throughout the entire book of the Revelation to John.[195]

---

[191] *WA* 15.40.

[192] *WA* 30 II.528b; (*LW* 46.221): *Heilande,* which may have reference to Joel 2:23, where Luther followed the Vulgate (*doctorem iustitae*) in his 1545 German Bible by rendering the ambiguous Hebrew *hammoreh litsedaqah* ("early rain for your vindication" in the RSV) as *Lehrer zur gerechtigkeit* ("teachers unto righteousness"). *WA,* DB 12 II.221.

[193] *Ibid:* Luther consistently understood the "kings" of Ps. 68:12 as "the host of those who bore the tidings" in the preceding verse. In his German Psalter he translated the verse, "The kings of the armies are friends with one another," and in marginal gloss he noted that "[kings] are the apostles whose teaching is in harmony." *WA,* DB 10 I.321-313.

[194] *Ibid:* Etymologically the term "angel" means "messenger." The Hebrew *malak* is translated both ways in German and in English.

[195] *Ibid.*

A Zuchtmeyster in the classroom.

Luther assigns the same titles and attributes to servants in both the spiritual and temporal realms, even as he distinguishes these *Ämtern* from the preacher's or pastor's *Amt.*[196] He wrote in *To the Christian Nobility,* "A cobbler, a smith, a peasant — each has the work and office of his trade, and yet they are all alike consecrated priests and bishops."[197] Indeed, far from eliminating the laity "as a separate category of Christian existence,"[198] he points to the pious among them as the Christian ideal, eliminating instead the clergy (*klerus*)

---

[196] For Luther the terms "pastor" and "preacher" are completely synonymous in this treatise. Cf. E. Harris Harbison, *The Christian Scholar in the Age of Reformation,* (Grand Rapids, Michigan: Wm. B. Eerdman's Publishing Company, 1983), 125: "Luther's conception of his professorship was not that of the nineteenth century. To him the duties of the doctorate included both preaching and teaching, and he never separated the two. His sermons tended to be lectures, and his lectures, sermons. He was always both teacher and preacher, whether in the pulpit or the classroom."

[197] *WA* 6.409.

[198] Wengert 9.

class as a monopoly in the word.[199] He cites Imperial Law, for example, as a gift from God, not so much for its fist and force, but for the wisdom and reason it provides to government, even though Christians who can instinctively exercise it, such as Duke Frederick the Wise and Fabian von Freilitzsch[200] are "pretty rare birds" indeed. In Luther's new normal, these Christian laymen (in this case a ruler and a jurist), are also *"the new generation of clergy," "true bishops before God,"* and should be given the same names given to *"preachers."* "And just as in the kingdom of Christ, a pious theologian and sincere preacher is called an angel of God, a savior, prophet, priest, servant, and teacher, so a pious jurist and true scholar can be called, in the worldly kingdom of the emperor, a prophet, priest, angel, and savior."[201] Theirs is a "divine work," a God-given calling to provide for the greatest blessing of all: peace. To that end, Luther was quite prepared to turn the pulpit over to the laity, to Lutheran jurists who would obey and enforce the kingdom against the false claims of the Catholics. "I wish to offer our jurists the pulpit (*predigtstul*)," he announced on February 23, 1539. "The papists in Augsburg themselves pleaded with the pope to call laypersons to the office of preaching (*Predigtamt*) and church service. In the same way St. Ambrose was also called to be the bishop of Milan, even though he was a layman and man of the world. Honest preachers will surely soon be scarce."[202]

---

[199] Cf. *WA* 12.187-188. Bornkamm notes that Luther initiated and consummated the theses "in and after the Leipzig Debate: No ecclesiastical vocation enjoys any religious advantage. There is no clergy (*Klerus*). The pope possesses no power of the keys over the souls of the believers. The councils are subject to error. The individual believer has the prerogative to interpret the Scriptures; and this means that he is a priest." Heinrich Bornkamm, *Luthers geistige Welt,* (Gütersloh: Carl Bertelsmann Verlag, 1959), 3. Auflage, 143-144.

[200] *LW* 46.239 n. 47.

[201] *WA* 30 II.528b ff.

[202] *WATR* 4.4743. *"Ich wiel unsern juristen den predigtstul anbitten illisque oboediam, modo non urgeant contra conscientiam papae*

In summary, the *ministerio ecclesiastico* for Luther is the office and work of the Holy Spirit in a single spiritual *Amt*, with many *Ämtern*, for the preaching and communicating of the *Gottes rede* of law and gospel to whomever, whenever, wherever, by pastor, teacher preacher, lector, priest, sacristan, schoolmaster, ruler, and parent; messengers of the word in the one and *eynzig* office of proclamation. These are truly the "new clergy!"[203]

---

regnum . . . Die Papisten haben zu Augsburg selbs vom Papst gebeten, daß man Laien zum Predigtamt und Kirchendienste möchte berufen. Gleichwie S. Ambrosius auch zum Bischof zu Mailand berufen ward, ob er wol ein Laie und Weltman war. Rechtschaffene Prediger werden wahrlich balde dünne werden."

[203] See Hans-Martin Barth, *Rechtfertigung und Amt, MD* 2/2002: "Sodann kennt Luther, wie bereits angesprochen, das institutionalisierte Amt das aber keineswegs allein *Prediger* oder *Bischofe* ausfüllen: Zu ihm gehören *"alle die, so im Pfarramt oder dienst des Wortes finden werden... als die da predigen, Sakrament reichen, dem gemeinsamen Kasten vorstehen (also die diakonische Arbeit betreuen), Küster und Boten oder Knechte so solche Personen dienen"* (*WA* 26, 504, 30ff). In gewisser Weise gehört auch das Schulmeisteramt in diesen Zusammenhang (vgl. *WA* 30/2, 580, 19f). Kaum bekannt ist, daß Luther auch das Diakonenamt in seiner ursprünglichen, von der Apostlegeschichte vorgezeichneten Form wiederbelebt sehen wollte. Das institutionalisierte Amt der Verkündigung differenziert sich in eine Fülle von unterschiedlichen Aufgaben aus." ("So then Luther recognizes, as mentioned, the institutional office which in no way consists only of preachers and bishops. It includes 'all who are in the office of pastor or the service of the word . . . such as those who preach, hand out the sacrament, are in charge of the common treasury (in the work of the diaconate), sextons, lectors or those who assist them.' To a certain extent the office of schoolmaster is included as well. Less well known is that Luther wished to revive the diakonate in its original form according to the example of the apostles. The office of proclamation is characterized by a multitude of occupations.")

The Pious Myth of Ordination

"We see in what high regard Luther held both ordination and the public ministry, and we discover how he connected the two things." [204]

Timothy J. Wengert

It is a long standing myth in American Lutheranism that Luther had an exalted view of ordination. Picking up an old copy of the *Concordia Triglotta* at a recent church rummage sale, I happened to turn to Article 28 of the *Apology's* discussion of the power of bishops. In the margin were notes and arrows written by a pastor in 1937, pointing to Melanchthon's statement, "We are pleased with the ancient division of power into power of the order and power of jurisdiction (*potestate ordinis* und *potestate jurisdictionis*)." The pastor had boldly underlined "Power of the Order" and written next to it "to sanctify thru ordination."[205] Four score later the confusion and illusion of the ordained continues.

A *Lieblingstext* of those for whom ordination is a big deal is Melanchthon's famous remark in Article 13 of the *Apology*: "If ordination is interpreted in relation to the ministry of the word, we have no objection to calling ordination a sacrament." Assuming incorrectly that Article 14 is about ordination, Wengert writes, "So Article 14 stands on the border, so to speak, between the sacraments and the church. No wonder that in *Apology* (13.11), Melanchthon suggested that one could understand ordination, interpreted now as referring to the public ministry of the word (audible and visible), as a

---

[204] Wengert 19.

[205] Present-day Lutheran flirtations with episcopal orders and ordination as a sacrament are a throwback to the papal bull *Exultate Deo* (1439) of the Council of Florence, and reaffirmed at the Council of Trent (1563): "Among these sacraments there are three — baptism, confirmation, and orders — which indelibly impress upon the soul a character, i.e., a certain spiritual mark which distinguishes them from the rest."

sacrament!"[206]

Wengert, like Piepkorn,[207] however, doesn't bother to cite the remainder of the statement, which clearly shows Melanchthon's tongue-in-cheek. What he says is that if ordination is strictly "the office of proclamation and the gospel" (*dem Predigtamt und Evangelio*), one can call it a sacrament insofar as these contain the command and promises of God. But he continues, expanding on Luther's sarcastic question to the papists a decade earlier in *The Babylonian Captivity:* "But if everything the apostles did is a sacrament, why have they not rather made preaching a sacrament?" One could then also call the laying on of hands a sacrament, Melanchthon reasoned, for "the church has the command to appoint ministers." Or one could add marriage, because "it has the commandment of God and also certain promises." Indeed, "If matrimony should be called a sacrament because it has God's command, then many other states or offices might also be called sacraments because they have God's command, as for example, government . . . And ultimately, if one wants to give such a glorious title as sacrament to everything that has God's word and command, one should call prayer for others a sacrament . . . Alms could be listed here, as well as afflictions, which in themselves are signs to which God has added promises." Seeing where this would all lead, his very next words are, "But let us pass over all this. No intelligent person will quibble about the number of the sacraments or the terminology, so long as those things are kept which have God's command and promises. It is much more necessary to know how to use the sacraments."[208]

Here he is in complete harmony with Luther, who could find no good reason to call ordination (much less alms or afflictions) a sacrament, and who recalled their earlier

---

206 Wengert 41.

207 Compare Piepkorn, 112: "The term 'sacrament' is applicable both to the sacred ministry and to ordination by the laying on of hands (Ap 13.9-13)."

208 *WA* 6.549.

disagreement in his famous ("we are all priests") letter to Spalatin of December 18, 1519: "We have to wonder greatly where ordination may have gotten this designation as a sacrament. Isn't this amazing to you? More [later] verbally, together with Philip, because we have argued often and sharply about this."[209] A few months later he destroyed the myth of ordination as a sacrament entirely in his sharp attack on sacramentalism and clericalism in *The Babylonian Captivity*:

> Of this sacrament the church of Christ knows nothing; it is an invention of the church of the pope. Not only is there nowhere any promise of grace attached to it, but there is not a single word about it in the whole New Testament. Now it is ridiculous (*ridiculum est*) to put forth as a sacrament of God something that cannot be proved to have been instituted by God. I do not hold that this rite, which has been observed for so many centuries, should be condemned; but in sacred things I am opposed to the invention of human fictions. And it is not right to give out as divinely instituted what was not divinely instituted, lest we become a laughingstock to our opponents. We ought to see that every article of faith of which we boast is certain, pure, and based on clear passages of scripture. But we are utterly unable to do that in the case of the sacrament under consideration.[210]

Luther never appealed to his ordination — only to his academic credentials, to his *Doktorhut*. He didn't mince words in his disdain for canonical ordination by bishops which supposedly creates a *character indelebilis*: "If they offer us proof of their priesthood by pointing to their bald pates and grease, including their long skirts, we'll give them their boasting in these filthy things, because we know one can just as easily shave and grease a sow or a block of wood and dress them up in a long skirt."[211] After demolishing the notion of

---

[209] Walch 21, 1. 246.

[210] *WA* 6.560.

[211] Walch 10,1590.70.

ordination as a sacrament in *De Captivo*, he concludes, "Baptism, however, which we have applied to the whole of life, will truly be a sufficient substitute for all the sacraments which we might need as long as we live."

"Ordination is no big deal."

"A Christian thus is born to the office of the word (*zu dem Amt des Worts*) in baptism," says Luther in *Concerning the Ministry*.[212] Baptism is everything. It is literally the birthplace of public ministry, the beginning and end all by which the gospel is made known (*öffentlich, allgemein bekannt*) by all sacerdotes in common. That he did not have the "high regard" for ordination that Wengert and others claim, is well documented. Nevertheless, in a book he coauthored with Gordon Lathrop, *Christian Assembly: Marks of the Church in a Pluralistic Age,* Wengert writes,

> This high regard for the public office of ministry in general matches Luther's high regard for the specific, episcopal office of oversight. He counseled the Bohemians in 1523 to establish bishops by gathering the clergy, praying, and electing bishops, and laying hands on them to receive the office of bishop, minister, or pastor. The bishops themselves may then come together and elect one of their number to be archbishop, "who would serve them and hold visitations among them, as Peter visited the churches according to the account in the book of Acts."[213]

This fuzzy paraphrase makes it sound like Luther was advocating a return to the old Catholic hierarchical system of clergy picking bishops to pick an archbishop. What Luther

---

212 Walch 10, 1593.76.

213 Timothy J. Wengert/Gordon Lathrop, *Christian Assembly: Marks of the Church in a Pluralistic Age,* (Minneapolis: Augsburg Fortress Press, 2004), 95.

actually says is that the people, "individual cities" (and later, if they wished, the Diet of Bohemia), by right and command of their baptism should "cast their ballots" and elect pastors (whom Luther also called "bishops"), who in turn may choose one or several from among their number to be their leaders through service and visitation.

> As the venture succeeds, with the help of the Lord, and many cities adopt this method of electing their bishops, then these bishops may wish to come together and elect one or more from their number to be their superiors, who would serve them and hold visitations among them, as Peter visited the churches, according to the account in the Book of Acts. Then Bohemia would return again to its rightful and evangelical archbishopric,[214] which would be rich, not in large income and much authority, but in many ministers and visitations of the churches.[215]

It is a thoroughly democratic process belonging to the community, which has "both right and command to commit by common vote such an office to one or more."[216] Tübingen historian, Volker Leppin, notes:

> In Protestant Reformation endeavors, especially in Pietism, the concept of the priesthood of all believers was always relevant. In substance it remains an important element for every modern evangelical understanding of the church, and is — though it wasn't originally thought of as a democratic theory — an important point of contact for the adoption of democratic elements in church structuring.[217]

---

[214] A metaphorical archbishopric, as it were.

[215] *WA* 12.194.

[216] *Ibid,* 190-191. That such democratic elections broke with clerical orthodoxy is clear from Luther's anticipation of the Bohemians' hesitation: "They object and say, 'A new thing and unprecedented, so to elect and create bishops.'"

[217] Volker Leppin, Gury Schneider-Ludorff, *Das Luther-Lexikon,* "Allgemeines Priestertum" [Regensburg: Verlag Bückle & Böhm, 2014], 49: *In protestantischen Reformationsbestrebungen, insbesondere im Pietismus, wurde die Vorstellung vom allgemeinen*

An excellent example of Luther's true view of ordination is found in an event that took place in the home of Dr. Caspar Cruciger in Wittenberg on Tuesday, April 11, 1542. On that day, he and Philip Melanchthon attended a farewell party for Johannes Mathesius, a student whom Luther had ordained on March 29 to the *Predigtamt* at St. Joachimstahl. [218] The celebration was attended by the entire theological faculty of the University of Wittenberg, including the authors of the *Augsburg Confession* and *Apology*, along with other professors and guests. The dialogue is recorded twice in the *WATR* (Nr. 5428, 133-142) and so needs to be read synoptically. Melanchthon reports to the esteemed gathering that a Bohemian (*einer aus Ungern*) has arrived in Wittenberg from Breslau seeking ordination.

Afterwards Philip said, "There is one who has come here out of Hungary from Ferdinand's side, who was to be ordained to Breslaw; so the Breslawers sent him over here."

Luther: "Why don't the Breslawers ordain him?"

Philip: "Ferdinand has forbidden it."

Luther: "Do they think in Hungary that ordination is a big deal?"

Philip: "Yes, Herr Doctor, they think it is a big, marvelous thing, even bigger than when one is baptized."

Luther: "It is true. In the papacy no one is allowed to touch the sacrament, unless he has been ordained. But ordination is no big

---

Priestertum immer wieder relevant. Der Sache nach bleibt es ein wichtiges Element für jedes moderne evangelische Kirchenverständnis und ist, obwohl es im Ursprung nicht demokratie-theoretisch gedacht war, ein wichtiger Anknüpfungspunkt für die Aufnahme demokratischer Elemente in die Kirchenstrukturen. Cf. *BSLK* 491,36-492,1.

218 Three years later Mathesius would be called to the *Pfarramt* in the same town, but not re-ordained.

deal (Aber Ordination ist nicht so ein groß Ding); baptism is much bigger than ordination. Baptism makes one holy and forgives sins; ordination doesn't justify, it doesn't forgive sins. I have baptized, administered the sacraments, preached the remission of sins, these are the highest works and offices (officia ecclesiae) of the church. O, baptism is one big splendid thing!"

From this remarkable exchange, a number of important conclusions may be drawn:

1) Luther clearly rejects the Bohemian fixation that ordination makes elders p*resbyteroi*; only baptism does, (coupled with a call), a point still being lost on them nearly two decades after he first addressed their situation in Prague.

2) He speaks of the *Predigtamt* outside of the context of ordination, consistent with its proper use in CA 5 in reference to the means of grace being the *officia ecclesiae (Amt des Worts)*,[219] not ordination.

3) By contrasting the preaching and distribution of the word with ordination, Luther makes clear that not only is the former greater than the latter, but the latter is unnecessary for the former to be in accord with CA 5.

4) Luther not only downplays the canonical ordination of the papists, but ordination per se, including the evangelical one he himself just performed for Mathesius, since it is by baptism that we preach, teach, and administer the word.

---

[219] Walch 10.1593.76.

Johannes Mathesius (1504 - 1565)

Ordination is no big deal, not even that of Mathesius, (poor fellow), even though he is presently being feted![220] Indeed, in Luther's estimation, this Bohemian's journey to Wittenberg to receive ordination was entirely unnecessary. Even if the Breslawers weren't prepared to ordain him, his baptism certainly entitled him to preach and administer the word without it, as long as he has a call. If Luther had desired in any way to "uphold" "apostolic, historic succession among bishops" (as Wengert and the ELCA claim), why did he not insist that the Breslawer be sent back to Breslaw for ordination? If the Wittenberg faculty and authors of the *Augsburg Confession* and *Apology,* all of whom were present and accounted for, had really desired to return to a Catholic style *Kirchenregiment*, why didn't they refer the ordinand to Balthasar von Promnitz, Bishop of Breslaw (Breslau), who not only stood in "apostolic succession," but looked favorably on the Reformation and was not opposed to Lutheran ordinations? While Ferdinand was clearly in violation of

---

[220] Mathesius announced that such ordinations without bishops should be continued, since it is Christ himself who is doing them. *"Solche Ordination und Handauflegung will Gott kräftig halten und der Sohn Gottes ist selber bei solcher Weihe und gießt die Gnade des Heiligen Geistes aus über christliche Ordinanden."*

mixing the two kingdoms, had Luther had such a "deep desire," he would nevertheless have insisted that Balthasar step up to the plate and assume his episcopal responsibility.

But in this case Luther treats ordination as an *adiaphoron*, a non-essential, an ecclesiastical rite that is neither necessary nor divine in contrast to baptism.[221] And he never changed his mind on the subject. In his original letter to the Senate in Prague, Luther had written:

> Even before such elections [of pastors by the community] we have been born and called into such a ministry through baptism. If we ask for an example, there is one in Acts 18, where we read of Apollos who came to Ephesus without call or ordination,[222] and taught fervently, powerfully confuting the Jews. By what right, I ask, did he exercise the ministry of the word except by the general right common to all Christians? . . . This man was afterward even made an apostle without any consecration or ordination (*ohne alle andere Weihe oder Ordination*), and not only functioned in the ministry of the word, but also proved himself useful in many ways to those who had already come to faith. In the same way any Christian should feel obligated to act if he saw the need and was competent to fill it, even without a call from the community. How much more then should he do so if he is asked and called by the brethren who are his equals, or by the whole community?[223]

After declaring "the perpetuity of the office is shown to be

---

[221] Compare Piepkorn's claim that ordination is divine *ipso facto*: "The term 'sacrament' is applicable to the sacred ministry itself and to ordination by the laying on of hands (Ap 13, 9-13). Ordination is effective (*rata*) by divine right (TPPP 65). Obviously this implies as a lesser included principal that ordination itself is by divine right. Ordination can be called an adiaphoron only in the most narrow and technical sense" Piepkorn, 112.

[222] On this basis Luther installed an unordained Georg Röhrer in 1525 as a deacon in the church in Wittenberg. Cf. Martin Brecht, *Martin Luther*, Band 3, (Calwer Verlag Stuttgart, 1987), 128.

[223] Walch 10, 1592.77-1594.78.

fictitious,"[224] he cites II Timothy 2, "Here Paul rejects all the show of tonsure and anointing and ordaining and only requires that they be able to teach, and to them alone he wants to entrust the word."[225] Such statements are a continuation of his formulation of the priesthood of all believers in his 1520 *Address to the Christian Nobility*. "All Christians are truly of the spiritual estate, and there is no difference among them except that of office . . . This is because we all have one baptism, one gospel, one faith, and are all Christians alike; for baptism, gospel, and faith alone make us spiritual and a Christian people." Contrasting the true spiritual estate with ordinations and consecrations, he writes:

> As far as that goes, we are all consecrated priests through baptism, as St. Peter says in I Peter 2, "You are a royal priesthood and a priestly realm" . . . That is why in cases of necessity anyone can baptize and give absolution. This would be impossible if we were not all priests. Through canon law[226] the Romanists have almost destroyed and made unknown the wondrous grace and authority of baptism and justification. In times gone by Christians used to choose their bishops and priests in this way from among their own number, and they were confirmed in their office by other bishops [pastors] without all the fuss that goes on nowadays. St. Augustine, Ambrose, and Cyprian each became [a bishop in this way].[227]

How authoritative baptism was for Luther is seen in his use of not "who" — but "*what(ever)*" — has crawled out of the baptismal font, may rest assured, that *it* is already ordained (*gewehet*) a priest, bishop, and pope, though it is not seemly for each to exercise such an office," (*Dan was ausz der Tauff krochen ist, das mag sich rumen, das es schon priester,*

---

224 *Ibid*, 1591.73.

225 *Ibid*, 1592.75.

226 *Corpus Iuris Canonici*

227 *WA* 6.407-408. Ambrose was not even baptized when the people elected him Bishop of Milan.

Bischoff und Bapst gewehet sey).[228] Here we have his powerful anti-synergistic Pauline theology of the bondage of the will that excludes any cooperation on the part of the baptized; passive recipients of grace who are dragged kicking and screaming against their will to the waters for drowning, God's work alone, receiving the authority given to all the baptized to proclaim word and sacrament, to bind and loose sins, and to call and install shepherds over his flock (Matt. 28). While every Christian is a priest, and baptism is the true sacrament of ordination, public ministry among God's people still requires a call.

Piepkorn tried to prove otherwise, claiming that ordination in the Reformation superseded the call and was a prerequisite for administering the sacrament — a myth still popular among today's American Lutheran ecclesiasts. Making the case for the Lutheran World Federation he wrote:

> The case (1531) of John Sutel in Göttingen makes it clear that in the mind of the early Lutheran community the mere possession of a call without a public ordination through the laying on of hands did not authorize the recipient to preside over the eucharistic assembly and pronounce the formula of consecration. Luther counsels Sutel to refrain from celebrating the sacrament of the altar until he "publicly before the altar with prayer and the laying on of hands receives from the other clergymen the evidence (of the legitimacy of his status) and authority to celebrate the sacrament of the altar" (*tum publice coram altari a reliquis ministris cum oratione et impositione manuum testimonium accipies et autoritatem coenae tractandae* [WA Br 6, 43-44].[229]

Had anyone from the LWF actually bothered to fact-check Piepkorn, they would have found that he mischaracterized Luther and cherry picked the citation without context to suit his ends. Sutel had been the rector of the Latin school in Melsungen before being a pastor in Göttingen. The cited letter

---

[228] *WA* 6. 408, lines 11-15.
[229] Piepkorn, 105-106, n 5.

81

is dated March 1, 1531.[230] But its proper context was established two months earlier in two previous letters Luther had written concerning the matter dated January 11, 1531. The first, addressed to the City Council of Göttingen, informs the mayor and council that the preacher Johannes Birnstiel, and licentiate Bastlius Schumann, are on their way to assume their pastoral duties.[231] The second, addressed to Sutel and dated the same day, counsels him to be patient with regard to church ceremonies; Birnstiel is coming, though Schumann is delayed due to the harvest he must still sell to make ends meet.[232]

Birnstiel would end up leaving Göttingen already in July, (probably because the people were displeased with his High Frankonian accent), and Schumann never arrived at all.[233] Sutel asked Luther if he should go ahead and administer the sacrament even though he doesn't have the tonsure and chrism of ordination. The situation was a prickly one. The Göttingen *Gemeinde* was both difficult and extremely miserly toward its pastors. Luther complained bitterly about them, and Sutel later wrote a tract against them. Luther replies on March 1, "Thus with regard to the question you ask, whether you should administer the sacrament without tonsure and chrism, I cannot answer" (*Daher kann ich über das, was du fragst: ob du ungeschoren und ungesalbt das Abendmahl des Herrn handeln sollest, nichts antworten*). He advises:

> If there is no serious [situation] there (*wenn es dort kein Ernst sein sollte*), I wish for you to continue to conduct yourself as heretofore (*so möchte ich, daß du, wie bisher, dich dessen enthieltest*). But if the situation becomes truly serious, you could have the other ministers publicly lay hands on you at the altar with a word of affirmation and authority to administer the sacrament (*wenn es aber ein Ernst sein sollte, alsdann kannst du öffentlich vor dem Altar von den übrigen Kirchendienern mit einer Rede und Auflegung der Hände Zeugnis empfangen und die*

---

230 Walch 21, Nr. 1767.
231 *Ibid*, Nr. 1747.
232 *Ibid*, Nr. 1748.
233 *Ibid*, n. 1.

Macht, das Abendmahl zu verwalten).

Luther's "ministers" (*ministris*), as we've already seen, were not necessarily ordained "clergy" as Piepkorn translated it, but "church servants" (*Kirchendienern*). A church council could just as easily have lain hands. The "serious situation" to which he refers is not the absence of the sacrament — he believed its reception once in a lifetime was sufficient — but the congregation's possible objections to Sutel's administration of it. As Reinhard Schwarz observed:

> Johann Sutel was called to be a pastor and administer the sacraments by the city council of Göttingen in what was his first pastorate. He was installed without ordination, a frequent occurrence in the Reformation. Luther did not consider ordination to be absolutely necessary for him; only in case of doubt on the part of the congregation as to his legitimacy. He should then let himself be ordained before the congregation by recognized office holders, in witness to his right to teach/administer with prayer and laying on of hands.[234]

In other words, as far as Luther was concerned, Sutel's pastorate was totally legitimate, including administering the sacraments. The issue was only one of perception. Here again, as in the case of the fellow from Bohemia, ordination was no big deal. Sutel's baptism, along with his call, was quite sufficient. As he put it in the spring of 1533, "When somebody has the authority to preach he also has the authority to administer the sacraments, for we hold that the sacrament is

---

[234] Reinhard Schwarz, *Luther*, (Göttingen: Vandenhoeck und Ruprecht, 1986), 193: "Sutel war in Göttingen vom Rat in ein Pfarramt mit Sakramentsverwaltung — es war Sutels erste Pfarrstelle — berufen, aber nicht mit einer Ordinationshandlung eingeführt worden,was im Zuge der Reformation mehrfach vorgekommen ist. Luther hielt bei ihm eine Ordinationshandlung nicht für unbedingt nötig; nur im Fall eines Zweifels der Gemeinde an seiner Rechtgläubigkeit sollte er sich zum Zeugnis für seine rechte Lehrüberzeugung vor der Gemeinde von anerkannten Amtsträgern mit Gebet und Handauflegung ordinieren lassen."

less important than preaching."[235]

But if troubled, (or in this case trouble-making) Christian consciences remained unsettled, an ordination could be performed in witness to his existing authority. Also critical here is the fact that the Imperial Verdict, issued in Augsburg on November 19, 1530, only offered the Lutherans a grace period until April 15, 1531 to rethink their position and return to the *status quo ante*; meaning that at the time of these letters, all things were still in flux, and the reformers needed to tread very carefully. Their "sharper" response in the German *Apology* was still forthcoming, appearing as soon as the grace period ended. Luther would reiterate that call and ordination are the same thing in his 1533 *Von der Winkelmesse und Pfaffenweihe*: "Our consecration shall be called being ordained or called to the office" (*Unser Weyhe sol heissen ordinirn odder beruffen zum ampt.*).[236] He further maintains that "ordination . . . is solely the command (*befelh*) to teach God's word. Whoever has it, him St. Paul regards as a pastor, bishop, and pope, for everything depends on the word of God as the highest office, which Christ himself regarded as his own and as the highest office."[237] As Maurer put it, "[Ordination] really means nothing more than the choice of a preacher."[238]

Finally, the lack of ordination as a non-issue for the fellow from Bohemia, which included Luther's declaration "Ordination is no big deal," occurred more than a decade after the Sutel letters, when extreme caution in deference to Roman rites was no longer necessary. Sutel would eventually go on to become the Lutheran Superintendent of Göttingen, whose writings would include *An Article Against the Papists in Göttingen*, and *The Gospel of the Gruesome and Dreadful Destruction of Jerusalem* for which Luther wrote the preface.

---

[235] *WA, TR* 1.Nr.512.

[236] *WA* 38.256.

[237] *Ibid*, 253.

[238] Maurer 82.

Melanchthon's Fly

Philipp Melanchthon

A fly in the ointment for the ordination-obsessed remains Melanchthon's 1537 *The Power and Primacy of the Pope* (TPPP). He writes, "But, since the distinction between bishop and pastor is not by divine right, it is manifest that ordination administered by a pastor in his own church is valid by divine right." [239] Similarly, Maurer notes in Luther's *Sermon on Keeping Children in School*:

> Luther deals with the church's power to make ordinances, which was the main question at stake in the Augsburg negotiations. He treats it from his anti-hierarchical understanding of the church, placing the word of God above the church and not the church over the word (theses 1-8, 15). The church, that is, the local congregation rather than the entire church, can make its own liturgical rules as long as they are valid only for itself, do not

---

[239] BSLK 490.65.

conflict with the articles of faith, do not harm consciences, do not claim unchangeable validity, and are not impractical (theses 9-13, 18).[240]

In a scramble to limit the damage such episcopal *Ersatz* could cause the ecclesiastical institutions of our day, Wengert qualifies Melanchthon's otherwise straightforward statement because it "has often confused people."

> First, it is important to note that Melanchthon did not say "any ordained person," but rather "pastor" (German: *Pfarrherr*). Preachers, who were also ordained to their office, and teachers, who were called to their offices, were not mentioned here. In fact, the idea that someone who did *not* preside in a church (which for Melanchthon meant, for example, *the* church of Wittenberg) — that is, who was not at least head pastor of a major town or zip code (as one might call it today) — had the right to ordain was the furthest thing from Melanchthon's mind — or those of his readers or the signers of this document.[241]

But what Melanchthon actually says is, because there is no distinction by divine right between "bishops, pastors, and parish pastors" (*Bischofen, Pastoren, Pfarrherren*), any of them can ordain in their own congregations. And where none of these are to be had, or have become enemies of the gospel, a layman can ordain, (even preachers, teachers, or parents, if need be). The call of the *Gemeinde* is key, not ordination *per se* as the examples of Ambrose, Speratus, Sutel, the Bohemians, and others, clearly show. As Wengert says, "The mail must get through!" Indeed, if it was really the furthest thing from Melanchthon's mind that someone other than the resident *Pfarrherr* could ordain, by Wengert's definition Luther could not have ordained Mathesius (or anyone else for that matter), since Johannes Bugenhagen was the resident *Pfarrherr* of Wittenberg, the head pastor of the zip code, not Luther — and Bugenhagen signed the *TPPP* twice, (once for

---

240 Maurer 74-75.
241 Wengert 96.

himself, and once for Johannes Brenz). Fortunately for Mathesius, and all the others though, Luther thought of himself as being all four of these: a pastor, preacher, parent, and teacher.

"Moreover," Wengert persists, "for Melanchthon, the 'right' to ordain did not devolve to individuals (pastors) or to groups (the ordained clergy or the laity or the individual congregation)" — though that is precisely what Melanchthon is saying: "*Where the true church is*, therefore, the right of electing and ordaining ministers must of necessity also be." He had already literally handed the definition of "true church" directly to the emperor in Augsburg, and through a legate to the pope in CA 7, as had Luther in SA 12, the Catechisms, and his sermons and writings, namely simple believers (*Glaubigen*) among whom the gospel is purely preached and the sacraments rightly received, who though they are never the full church, are nevertheless fully the church and "able to do all things" (*Babylonian Captivity*).

In order for this not to be true, Wengert would need to change the confessional definition of the church — which he obligingly does. The church, we are told, cannot simply be "an isolated congregation," because "church for the reformers was always more event than organization and always encompassed all times and all places as the assembly of believers gathered around the events of word and sacrament."

By shifting CA 7's emphasis from the concrete (believers) to the abstract (event), and confusing the means of grace with its recipients, his inference and agenda now become clear: For the church to be truly church it needs a greater representation than Christ's "two or three," or Luther's *kleine Heuflein* ("tiny gathering"); it needs a "wider expression" (or "church in three expressions" in ELCA-speak) governed by the *episcopoi*. Indeed, he adds, "At this point Melanchthon used 1 Peter 2:9 ('You are a royal priesthood') not as a reference to the laity but as a reference to the entire church, which by virtue of this priesthood could not lose the authority to ordain folks to public ministry."[242]

Melanchthon's invocation of 1 Peter, however, is without question his direct defense of the shocking example he has just given, not only of a single pastor (*ein Pfarrherr/a pastore*) ordaining in his local church (*in seiner Kirchen/in sua ecclesia*), but of "any" (*igliche*) congregation to ordain where the bishops/pastors are not preaching the gospel: "Finally, this is confirmed by the declaration of Peter, 'You are a royal priesthood' (1 Peter 2.9). These words apply to the true church which, since it alone posses the priesthood, certainly has the right of electing and ordaining ministers." As is the case in the *Smalcald Articles*, the reference here is not to the church universal, but to "a pastor in his own congregation," to the *ecclesia particularis,* possessing all things in the fullness of baptism,[243] holy believers, be it only "two or three gathered in his name" around word and sacrament (Matt. 18.20). He'd made the same case five years earlier in his *Commentary on Romans* (based in part on Luther's notes), "It is necessary that this true church always remain, because the kingdom of Christ is everlasting and it is written [Mt. 28:20]: 'I shall remain with you until the end of the world.' Nevertheless, we must know that this true church is not always flourishing equally, but often is only small, and is to be divinely restored later when true teachers are sent, as in Noah's time the church was oppressed and an assembly of only a few persons;" "small seed" he called them.[244]

Luther had no use for six degrees of separation by ordination.[245] Given that we are all equally baptized as priests, "ordination, *if it is anything at all*, is nothing else than a certain rite whereby one is called to the ministry of the

---

242 *Ibid,* 97.

243 Cf. *WA* 11.408-416.

244 Philip Melanchthon's *Commentary on Romans,* trans. by Fred Kramer, (St. Louis: Concordia, 1992), 239-284.

245 E.g., Dyonysius's (c. 500 AD) enumeration of six sacraments in his *Ecclesiastical Hierarchy,* ordination being one of them.

church."[246] He writes with a note of sarcasm in the same treatise:

> I therefore admit that ordination is a certain churchly rite, on a par with many others introduced by the church fathers, such as the consecration of vessels, houses, vestments, water, salt, candles, herbs, wine, and the like. No one calls any of these a sacrament, nor is there in them any promise. In the same manner, to anoint a man's hands with oil, or to shave his head and the like is not to administer a sacrament, since no promise is attached to them; they are simply being prepared for a certain office, like a vessel or an instrument.[247]

In his rebuttal to the cleric Emser in *The Misuse of the Mass* he states, "It is enough now that we know that a Christian people is undivided, without any distinctions of sects or persons, a people among whom there is to be no layman, no cleric, no monk, no nun — no differences at all."[248] As Maurer notes:

> The famous distinction between the general priesthood of all believers and the special ecclesiastical office (found in *To the Christian Nobility*) rests on the assumption that in this serving office there can be no hierarchical degrees; where each one serves, no one else can rule the others. There is no special consecration; the only sacramental prerequisite for priestly service is baptism, which consecrates everyone. Episcopal ordination is dropped. Ordination is selection and designation for a specific service; no bishop can carry it out without the cooperation of the congregation. In emergencies the latter can act alone.[249]

---

[246] *WA* 6.564, 16-17.
[247] *Ibid,* 561.
[248] *Ibid,* 503.
[249] Maurer 81.

Chapter 4

Luther's "Bibeldeutsch"

Title page of Luther's Bible, 1534

In *Rechtfertigung und Amt,* Hans Martin Barth rightly castigates the "conservative, right wing interpretation" of the "Joint Commission on Roman Catholic/Evangelical Lutheran Dialogue: Church & Justification," for claiming the Lutherans endorsed a historic episcopate both during and immediately following the Reformation, calling it "an audaciously one sided interpretation of *Apology 14.*" The reason is "because it is clear from Luther's German translation of the Bible that the word *Amt* does not refer to an ordained office (*ordiniertes Amt*), but to the power and mission that is every Christian's in the gospel, namely to spread the news about justification, as seen in Luther's, *A Sermon on Keeping Children in School.*" This *Amt* is specifically arranged (*geordnet*) and under the auspices of the congregation for the proclamation of justification, and represents the one public office common to all of Christianity:

> This office for Luther is the "ordered" (*geordnete*), not the "ordained office" (*ordinierte Amt*) of the pre-Reformation sense, or the sense in which one encounters it in today's Catholic-Lutheran consensus papers. The term "ordained office" is without question a linguistic misnomer, since the office isn't ordained, but the one who is in office, regardless of the fact that we don't know what scripture meant by the term. Lutherans who have an affection for the office tend to translate *ordinate* as "ordain," whenever it appears in Reformation texts, which at a minimum is problematic, and at times is flat out false.[250]

He offers the example of Avery Dulles and George Lindbeck's mistranslation of *ordinate* as "ordination" in CA 8.2 [What is the Church?]: "The sacraments and the word are effective by reason of the ordination and commandment of Christ," the Latin phrase being *propter ordinationem et mandatum Christi.* Tappert translates *ordinationem* as "institution," Kolb/Wengert as "ordinance," while the German text skips it altogether: "The sacraments are efficacious even if the priests who distribute them are impious" (*so sind die Sakrament gleichwohl kräftig, obschon die Priester, dadurch sie gereicht*

---

[250] Hans Martin Barth, *Rechtfertigung und Amt*, *MD* 2/2002. Cf. *WA* 44.695. Luther saw *Handauflegung*, "the laying on of hands," as a good and "very ancient" custom that predates Christianity and was later imported into the New Testament. As a secular practice it was applied to emperors, kings, counts, and knights, none of whom were, of course, considered "ordained" as clergy (*als Geistliche*).

werden, nicht fromm sind . . .).[251]

Martin Brecht points out that latest from 1530 on Luther called it quits with the Catholic Church's established ordination rites. To him, *"ordinieren"* simply meant to call someone to an office (*Sendung*), and this did not require a bishop. "Every pastor was the bishop of his congregation and could also ordain into a church office for other congregations, if necessary, as occurred in Wittenberg."[252]

Today, when American ecclesiasts use the word "ordain," it is often in the Anglican canonical sense, which is not surprising given the Lutheran-Epicopal dialogues and America's long history with *The King James Bible* and it's affinity for the term. It employs the word forty three times, though rarely in reference to a church rite (e.g., "the stars which thou hast ordained" Psalm 8:3; "I have ordained a lamp for my anointed" Psalm 132:17, etc.).

Any discussion of its use in the Lutheran Confessions, however, must take into account not the English, but Luther's *Bibeldeutsch,* especially those texts that refer to the choosing of elders, bishops, or pastors. After all, "there is not a single word said about [ordination] in the whole New Testament,"[253] he concluded in 1520. So where, for instance, the KJB uses the same generic word "ordain" for at least three different expressions in the Greek, Luther translates the Greek three different ways consistent with the Koine of the Septuagint and New Testament. In Mark 3:14 the KJB reads, "he ordained twelve;" but in Luther "he ordered (*epoiesen*: "to place an order for") the twelve" (*vnd er ordnete die zwelffe*).[254] In John 15:16, "I have chosen you and ordained you," versus Luther "I have chosen you and placed (*etheka*) you" (*ich habe euch erwelet vnnd gesetzt*). And in the text most often misapplied in support of canonical ordination, Titus 1:5, "thou shouldest set

---

251 *BSLK* 62.

252 Martin Brecht, *Martin Luther,* Band 3, 84; 128.

253 *WA* 6.560.

254 Cf. *New College German Dictionary,* [Langenscheidt KG, Berlin & Munich, 1995], *ordnen*: to put in order, to sort out, arrange .

in order the things that are wanting, and ordain elders in every city," Luther translated "that you should . . . set(tle) (*katasteses*) into towns here and there the oldest ones," (*das du soltist . . . besetzen die stedte hyn vnnd her mit Elltisten*).[255] The *Elltisten,* or "elderly," were just that: older, more mature, and therefore presumably wiser and more experienced members of the congregation.[256]

One can add to this last much lauded canonical "proof" text the fact that Ananias, who "put his hands on Paul," was neither an apostle nor a bishop, Acts. 9:17. And those who performed the ceremony of the laying on of hands in the case of Timothy were simple presbyters, pastors, elders, 1 Timothy 4:14. (Ironically, the first person who was ever accorded the title "bishop" *episcopos* in the New Testament, was none other than Judas Iscariot, overseer and thief of the disciples' common purse, Acts 1:20.)

From these passages we see that for Luther, ordination was simply an orderly call (*rite vocatus*) of the church, the appointing and putting in place of a servant of the word. "Our consecration shall be called ordination, or a call to the office," he wrote in *The Private Mass and the Consecration of Priests* (1533).[257] Melanchthon affirms the same in *The Power and Primacy of the Pope* where he translates the Latin *ordinatio* with the German *"ordnet, ordnete,"* and not with *ordinieren.*[258]

A classic example of an attempt to anglicize Lutheran

---

[255] Cf. *WA* 7.631.

[256] Cf. Theodore Engleder in *Popular Symbolics,* St. Louis, Concordia, 1934, p. 109 ff. Not ordination, but the call of the congregation makes the minister (p. 150), as attested to by CA XIV, AP VII and VIII, XXVIII, SA III.X, TPPP 24f., 68 f. The doctrine of the Catholic and Episcopalian churches that episcopal ordination by virtue of an "apostolic succession" confers "holy orders" deals with two additional myths: The "holy order" of sacerdotalism does not exist (p. 155), and there are no bishops *iure divino* (p. 154).

[257] *WA* 38.256.

[258] *BSLK* 490.

ordination is found in Wengert's misreading[259] of a letter sent by Melanchthon to the court of Henry VIII, dated October 4, 1535.[260] It is addressed to the English ambassador, Christopher Mont, as part of Melanchthon's negotiations with the English crown. It reads in part:

> Paulus commanded Titus to ordre priests, and to Timothe he sayth: "Putt thy hands upon no man hastely," and therefore he willyd as well the examination as power to ordre to be in the bisshoppes. He willid nott prists to bee ordryd withowte examination, and this examination he hath committyd to the bisshoppes to whom it apperteynth to holde stedfastly the doctrine of Christe. And therfor this hath byn observyd ever sens the begynnyng in the churche, that the bisshoppes shulde both: judge of them that shuld be ordred and also ordre them . . .

Wengert claims, "The verb *ordre* is the sixteenth-century English word for 'ordain,'"[261] and concludes,

> This means that the English church received encouragement from the Saxon church, specifically from Philip Melanchthon, author of the Augsburg Confession and its Apology, to give bishops (understood: who preach the gospel) the power to ordain. That some Lutherans object to fellowship with Anglicans or Episcopalians simply because their bishops do all the ordaining means, ironically, that they are rejecting a principle Melanchthon insisted upon in negotiations with the English crown.

He repeated his hypothesis in an article for the Episcopal Diocese of Pennsylvania,[262] saying, "Indeed, in the agreement between the Evangelical Lutheran Church in America and the Episcopal Church, USA (*Called to Common Mission*), the Episcopalians were simply re-gifting to today's Lutherans

---

[259] Wengert 45.

[260] *MBW* Vol. 6, Nr. 1640, (Stuttgart: Frommann-Holzboog, 2006), 470.11-18.

[261] Wengert 126, n.35.

[262] "Ordaining Bishops: An Episcopalian Re-Gifting for Lutherans," July 5, 2009.

what in an earlier age Lutherans themselves had defended before the English king, namely, that bishops ordain candidates for the public ministry!" — (implying Melanchthon was advocating for historical episcopal succession à la CCM).

His theory, however, falls flat on numerous fronts. To begin with, the requirement of ordination by a bishop was still an open question in the Church of England until 1662.[263] Also, Melanchthon's letter was obviously strictly written within the context of his newly minted *Augsburg Confession* and *Apology*, specifically Ap 14, which pits evangelical ordering (*rite vocatus*) against canonical ordination (*ordinatione canonica*). Even though Henry's court would officially break with the papacy in the *Act of Supremacy* the following month, (stating all power flows from the throne, not Rome), his church was still thoroughly Catholic and canonical, believing in both a *successio apostolica* and a *character indelebilis* through sacramental ordination, neither of which Melanchthon and the Lutherans subscribed to. Henry always intended for Catholicism to remain the faith of the realm, but without the Pope. The holy orders of English sacerdotalism were still those of Rome, and stood in sharp contrast to the holy "orders" of Luther's *Small Catechism,* which consisted of a common priesthood of all bishops, pastors, preachers, teachers, governmental officials, citizens, employers, laborers, husbands, wives, children and widows. What appealed to the king, for obvious reasons of political expediency, was the Lutheran principal of *cujus regio ejus religio* ("whose region,

---

[263] The necessity of ordination by a bishop was unsettled in the realm at this time. Tyndale, a Catholic priest, (martyred 1536), who rejected episcopal succession, taught in *The Obedience of a Christian Man* (1528) that ordination itself is unnecessary. "They simply told the appointed ministers their duty and gave them a charge and warned them to be faithful in the Lord's business, just as temporal officers are chosen and their duty read to them and they are admitted to their office on their promise to faithfully discharge their duties." R.J. Cooke, *The Historic Episcopate - A Study of Anglican Claims and Methodist Orders,* (New York: Eaton & Mains, Cincinnati: Curtis & Jennings, 1896), V.91f.

his religion"), that is, the religion of the ruler is the religion of the ruled. Or as the former Archbishop of London, J. W. C. Wand, put it in our time, "Perhaps the best description of the king's position would be to say that he was Lutheran in politics and Catholic in theology."[264]

A so-called historical episcopal succession through ordination, (as imagined in the mythology of *Called to Common Mission*, for example), is the last thing Melanchthon had in mind. His concern was simply to get the gospel out, even to the point of a local pastor (also being a bishop) ordaining by divine right in his own congregation, a practice dating back to the early church, and one he points to in Paul's command in Titus 1:5, (a passage he also put in Georg von Anhalt's ordination certificate).

Examining Melanchthon's English, (though the original might have been in German or Latin),[265] the question is: Was he saying Paul directed Titus to "ordain" elders? Or was he simply saying Paul directed Titus to order (*ordnen, bestellen,* "select, procure, place an order for") elders? To make his case for Episcopalian ordination, Wengert insists that "the verb *ordre* is the sixteenth-century word for 'ordain.'" But in fact, the sixteenth-century English word for "ordain" at the time was *ordeyne,* as is evidenced by Tyndale's 1526/27 translation of the very same verse: "For this cause I left ye in Creta that thou shuldest performe that which was lackynge and shuldest *ordeyne* elders in every citie as I apoynted the." Melanchthon's use of the word *ordre,* instead of *ordeyne,* is consistent with Luther's "Bibeldeutsch" *ordnen/bestellen,* meaning "to procure" — who may have *ordryd* a beer while at Hampton Court — but not in the English canonical sense. Mont (whose name was originally "Mundt," then "Mount," or "Montaborinus") was after all, not an Englishman (as Wengert

---

264 J.W.C. Wand, *Anglicanism in History and Today,* (London: Shenval Press, 1961), 17.
265 Melanchthon was in Jena on October 4; Mont may well have been in Wittenberg.

seems to suppose) — but a German — a lawyer and native of Cologne, who was made a denizen of England on Oct. 4, 1531. A friend and *Landsman* of Melanchthon, he actually spent very little time outside of German lands between the time Henry dispatched him there in 1534, and his death in 1572. Originally in Cromwell's employ (who was certainly no friend of bishops), during which he translated German documents into Latin, he served as one of Henry VIII's emissaries in negotiations with the Saxons. And to top it all off — he was himself a Lutheran! In fact, the English court considered him "an advanced Lutheran." [266] Thus, given both his German and confessional background, it is perfectly reasonable to assume that Mont/Mundt would have easily understood Melanchthon's wording in the Lutheran confessional sense, if not the actual German letter of their mother tongue. [267]

---

[266] Cf. *Dictionary of National Biography,* Edited by Sidney Lee, Vol. XXXVIII, (New York: Macmillan and Co., London: Smith Elder & Co., 1894), 204-205.

[267] Were one to translate Melanchthon's English back into German it would approximate the following: *Wenn ich von kirchlicher Macht rede, meine ich nicht grundsätzlich den Primat des Bischofs von Rome. Vielmehr spreche ich im allgemein von der Vollmacht von Bischöfen und meine damit das Verfahren wonach gewisse Bischöfe, die zur **ordnen** von Priestern verpflichtet sind, kirchliche Urteil umsetzen und die Lehre beurteilen sollen. Diese gebräuchliche Form hätte ich gerne in jeder Nation fortgezetzt, denn es ist wahrhaftig notwendig, dass gewisse Superintenden vorhanden sind, durch die die Priester **bestellt/geordnet** werden. Paulus befahl Titus, Priester zu **bestellen/ordnen**, und Timotheus sagte 'Lege keinem deine Hände auf.' Damit wollte er auch, dass Prüfung als Teil der Ordinationsvollmacht der Bischöfen angesehen wird. Er wollte nicht, dass Priester ohne Prüfung **bestellt/geordnet** werden. Und diese Prüfung hat er den Bischöfen anvertraut, zu denen er gehört, dass sie an der Lehre Christi unentwegt festzuhalten. Deshalb ist von Anfang an in den Kirchen daran festgehalten worden, dass Bischöfe beides zu tun schuldig sind, die ordiniert werden sollen, zu beurteilen und sie zu **bestellen/ordnen** . . . Einen Grund diesen Brauch der Kirche zu ändern, erkenne ich nicht, so lange die Bischöfe gute Lehrer*

Melanchthon isn't issuing a rogue letter here, but is submitting it in the context of Ap 14, of evangelical "ordering." He writes in the same letter:

When I name the ecclesiasticall power, I mean nott principally the primacye of the bishop of Rome, butt I spek generally of the authorite of bisshopps and chiefly I mean this discipline, by cause there bee certain bisshoppes the which oweth to ordre prists, the which shulde exercise the ecclesiasticall jugements and consider the doctrine. This accustomyd forme I wolde gladly have contynuyd in every nation, for of truthe it is necessarye that ther shuld bee certain as superintendents of whom the prists may be ordryd.

Again, he is not saying anything new outside of the *Augsburg Confession,* making clear that by "eclesiasticall power" he does *nott* mean "the primacye of the bishop of Rome," (which includes canonical ordination via a *successio apostolica),* but is speaking of the evangelical ordering exemplified in the Visitations, of "superintendents" who should procure (*ordre*) pastors, exercise ecclesial judgment and consider doctrine. In short, he contrasts the Lutheran confessional position with "the ecclesiasticall power . . . and primacye of the bishop of Rome," a primacy and power to which Henry's church still clung at the time of the writing of this letter. He was of the same mind four years later when he wrote against those who

imagine the church to be a state of bishops and bind it to the orderly succession of bishops, as the empires consist of the orderly succession of princes. But the church maintains itself differently. Actually, it is a union not bound to the orderly

---

bestellen/ordnen. *Das heist: Sofern diese Bischöfe nicht Feinde des Evangeliums sind, gute Lehre nicht umbringen und das regieren der Kirche nicht verdorbenen Lehrern überlassen.*

succession but to the word of God.[268]

And again two years after that he fired off a letter to the emperor at the 1541 Regensburg Conference in which he condemned historical episcopal succession (*episcopos successisse*) as an "error" that carried with it "many errors."[269] His stance was entirely consistent with Luther, who stated that year,

> Also in the church the succession of bishops does not make a bishop, but the Lord alone is our bishop raising up bishops wherever, from whomever, and whenever he wills — as we see to be the case with Jerome, Augustine, Ambrose, Huss and ourselves — neglecting succession (*neglecta successione*) which the papists keep insisting on.[270]

It is thus simply not credible to suggest that Melanchthon, after rejecting canonical ordination in 1530, embraced it in 1535, only to reject it again in 1539. But no matter how Mont may have read it, the negotiations sadly came to naught with Henry's 1538 rejection of the *Augsburg Confession* and *Apology,* ending any prospects for the Anglican Church to be considered a church of the Reformation. Nor did Luther ever consider it one — not even for a moment — knowing full well that Henry was only playing games with the Lutherans, having no interest whatsoever in theology, but only in politics, hoping to be named not only the "Defender" of the Protestant League, but its head. Believing Melanchthon's negotiations with the crown (which dragged on fruitlessly until 1540),[271] to be a

---

[268] *Melanchthons Werke in Auswahl,* ed. Robert Stupperich, [Gütersloh: Gerd Mohn, 1951], 1:330, 16-23.

[269] *C.R.* 4.415.

[270] *WA* 53.74.

[271] In a letter to Elector Johann Friedrich dated Oct. 23, 1539, Luther dismissed the negotiations as theologically pointless, discussions that might as well have been "sealed with a Bratwurst": *War es alles mit einer Bratwurst versiegelt,* adding, *Und zü mehr malen Sagt D. Antonius* [Robert Barnes], *Unser konig achtet der Religion und*

huge waste of time and money, he reacted negatively to his colleague's attempts to ingratiate himself with the royal court, including his dedication of a copy of his *Loci* to Henry that same year (1535).[272] "I regret that Master Philip wrote his nicest prefaces for the loosest knaves," Lauterbach recorded him saying on July 10, 1539; Mathesius adding a year later, "The doctor [Luther] said [of Melanchthon], 'The little fellow is a godly man, and even if he should do wrong, his intention's not bad, but it's because he's taken captive by others. He hasn't accomplished much by his method, and he used bad judgment in dedicating his books."[273] Finally, it should be noted that for Wengert's pastor/bishop distinction to be true, Melanchthon's understanding of Titus 1:5 would have to be radically out of sync with Luther's, and more in line with Jerome Emser's. Luther had written:

> Thus Emser too certainly knows from St. Jerome that priest and bishop are one and the same thing in scripture. For St. Paul says in Titus 1 [:5], "You should appoint[274] a priest in every town" (that is, an elder over them); and soon afterward he says about the same priest, "But this same bishop must be a blameless man" [Titus 1:7]. He clearly calls the same man priest, bishop, elder, and watchman. But no one should be surprised that bishop, pastor, priest, chaplain, cathedral dean, monk, and many similar names have different meanings now, since no word of scripture has retained its true meaning.[275]

He reiterated the point of I Timothy 3 in his ordination

---

evangelii nichts uberal. ("And many times Dr. Antonius said, 'Our king couldn't care less about religion and the gospel.'") *WA* 8, Br. 3397.578.

272 Henry VIII personally thanked Melanchthon on Oct. 1, 1535 and paid him the generous sum of 200 gülden for his exposition on the book of Romans. Cf. *MBW* Vol. 6, Nr.1637.

273 *WATR,* No.4699 & 5089. Melanchthon's dedications included Archbishop Albrecht of Mainz who, along with Henry VIII, was regarded as an enemy of the Reformation.

274 *setzenn*

275 *WA* 7.631.

liturgy: "Herein you hear that we bishops — i.e., presbyters and pastors — are called not to watch over geese or cows, but over the congregation God purchased with his own blood."[276]

On those occasions when Luther did think of ordination as an ecclesiastical rite, (e.g. in the case of Mathesius), he saw it simply as an affirmation or witness to a preexisting agreement between the one called and those doing the calling. He compared it to the role of a notary public, or to a pastor at a wedding whose presence, while perhaps desirable for the occasion, is technically not necessary to consummate what has already been agreed to by the bride and groom. Just as baptism is greater than the Lord's Supper, so *vocatio* is far greater than *ordinatio*. In keeping with Ap 14, he saw the call itself as "the true consecration." Thus a priest directed to a (private) bishop to be further invested or inducted "was a confirmation of such a call and was not necessary. For the called pastor would also have been able to perform the office of his ministry without such a confirmation . . ." Why? Because the election and call already are an ordination, hence Luther and the evangelical party would "get pastors and preachers on the basis of baptism and God's word without their chrism, ordained (*geordinirt*) and confirmed by our election and call."[277]

[276] *Ibid* 38.427.
[277] *Ibid*, 236.

The Wittenberg Triptych

The Cranach altar in the Stadtkirche of Wittenberg

For a Christian "all things are lawful; though not all things may be helpful" (1 Cor. 6.12), and so he or she does not act unilaterally in the *Gemeyne,* but by its call. There is no greater call than to preach the word and administer the sacraments, a point the great official portraitist of the Reformation, Lucas Cranach the Elder, made on canvas in many and various ways. The artist had been a witness at Luther and Katherina von Bora's wedding, was the godfather to their first child, Johannes "Hänchen" Luther (b. 1526), twice Bürgermeister of Wittenberg, and the publisher of Luther's *De instituendis ministris ecclesiae: ad Clarissimum Senatum Pragensem Bohemiae.*

A most wonderful example of his confessional witness is found in his famous triptych on the altar of the Stadtkirche in Wittenberg, installed a year after Luther's death. At the height of the American Lutheran debate over the claims to historical episcopacy espoused in CCM, *Lutheran Forum* magazine reproduced the left panel of the triptych on its Fall 1998 cover which depicts Melanchthon baptizing an infant, and offered the rather lame explanation, "This panel from the altarpiece of the parish church of St. Mary in Wittenberg shows Philipp Melanchthon baptizing a child; thus demonstrating that infants should be baptized because Baptism is 'necessary for salvation' (*Augsburg Confession IX*)." While that is an obvious, generic, ecumenically safe, and indeed timid interpretation, to stop there is to completely miss the confessional forest for the trees, making the painting no different from thousands of other renderings of infant baptism at the time.

If that had been Cranach's only point he could just as easily have depicted Luther administering baptism, or any other member of the clergy for that matter. But at least as important for Cranach's purposes as the focus on baptism, is the one who is doing the baptizing: Philip Melanchthon, an unordained layman, who by virtue of his own baptism, possesses the right and command to do so. The hugely oversized font, with its central lay figure, proclaims from ground zero of the Reformation that the power and authority of baptism bestowed in the "Great Commission" (Mt. 28.19) belongs to all Christians *allengemein*.[278]

And in the center panel we see Jesus administering the sacrament of the Last Supper to his disciples, specifically to Judas Iscariot (the communing of the unworthy!), while Luther as Junker Jörg receives the cup from Cranach who is wearing a white serving apron and holding the flagon in his right hand (an unordained layman administering the sacrament, and to the clergy no less!).[279] There is nothing at all

---

[278] Cf. Joachim Rogge, *Martin Luther: Sein Leben, seine Zeit, seine Wirkung,* (Gütersloh: Gütersloher Verlag, Grd Mohn, 1983), 186 & 367.

[279] The younger Cranach would repeat the scene in a 1565 epitaph for Joachim von Anhalt, with all of its illegal acts, only this time

safe, legal, or generic about this picture. All three panels, in fact, depict highly *illegal* acts under canon law. Bugenhagen, who is featured in the righthand panel, was not canonically installed in Wittenberg, yet performed ordinations without the permission of bishops and freely dispensed bishops' titles (a rejection of canon law!).[280]

Cranach created the altarpiece with his son Lucas the Younger in the 1530s, but it wasn't installed and dedicated (by Bugenhagen) until a decade later as an act of supreme defiance against Roman "ecclesiastical and canonical polity," not just for its bold theological depiction of the priesthood of all believers, but because of the date chosen for its installation: April 24, 1547. On that day the Lutheran armies of the Smalcald League were decisively defeated by Charles V at the Battle of Mühlberg. The Lutheran Elector Johann Friedrich was captured and deposed, Wittenberg ceased to be his residence and the protection of the Ernestine rulers had vanished. Only three weeks later, on May 19, the emperor himself would stride into the church to find himself confronted by this magnificent protest sign which proclaims at its head, "No other foundation can man lay than that which is laid, which is Jesus Christ" (I Corinthians 3:11). With all material support for the evangelicals seemingly lost, the altar (which was completed in close consultation with the Wittenberg theological faculty), clearly proclaims the words of CA 7, "It is taught among us that one holy Christian church will be and remain forever. This is the assembly of all believers among whom the Gospel is preached in its purity and the holy

---

substituting himself for his father in *Das Abendmahl.*
280 Cf. Michael A. Mullett, *Martin Luther,* [Routledge: London and New York, 2004], 110: "[Luther's 1520 *Address to the Christian Nobility*] is about so much more than Church reform narrowly understood. Proposals also involved reform of the universities, the elimination of canon law and most of the works of the 'blind pagan' Aristotle from their curricula and the primacy in the syllabus of Scripture rather than Scholasticism."

sacraments are administered according to the gospel!"[281]

In an amusing aside in *Priesthood, Pastors, Bishops,* Wengert tells of an incident that greatly upset him when a couple of unordained parishioners assumed the role of the ordained:

> A graduate student recently told me the story of his vacation in Montana, where he and his family visited a congregation when the pastor was away for a synod function. Without any explanation, some lay persons climbed into the pulpit and spoke and then led the congregation in the celebration of the Lord's Supper. Where was the emergency? Where was the pastor? Now, to be sure, even when we do stupid things, God still manages to use our broken words and bad form. But what bothered my student — and me — was not that, from time to time, in certain circumstances (whether quite at what I would define as the level of emergency or not), someone other than the one called to public ministry may be called upon to do these things in a particular place. Rather, what bothered us was the complete lack of explanation.[282]

(He makes no mention of whether his student thought he had actually heard the gospel that day, or how an explanation to either of them would have made what the laypersons said and did any more kosher.)

One could, of course, ask the same questions of Cranach's panel that Luther had asked the Bohemians in Prague, or the fellow from Breslaw: Where is the emergency? Cranach's baptismal scene is perfectly peaceful, the congregation appears completely unperturbed, and the priesthood of all believers, including Melanchthon, is even smiling. But where is the pastor? Actually, he's just to the left of the font, not

---

[281] The emperor's party considered disinterring Luther's body from the Schloßkirche (Castle Church), but after being assured the Reformer was already in hell, one or more of them reportedly urinated on the grave for good measure.

[282] Wengert 30.

attending a "synod function," but far worse — simply standing by as a layman performs the sacrament in his stead! Why isn't he doing it? Why not *Pfarrherr* Bugenhagen, who occupies the second half of this "sacred" space and is exercising the office of the keys? After all, these are not "Christians trapped in a desert and unable, by virtue of this emergency, to avail themselves of the normal order of the church," as Wengert claims Luther demanded.[283]

Joining Luther in this panel are his family, his wife "Katie," and son, "Hänchen," as well as Frau Cranach (the lady in the front, her back to the viewer), all of which raises some interesting questions: Is this the recording of an actual scene? Did Melanchthon (who preached in the Castle Church) ever baptize a child there, or anywhere else, even though he wasn't ordained? Is this a child or grandchild of the Cranachs? Is it his own? The panel certainly suggests the potential for all of these. It also thoroughly refutes Piepkorn's absurd unsubstantiated claim: "The doctrine of the universal priesthood of believers had receded into minor importance — even for Luther himself — by the time the symbolical books were being framed."[284]

The Wittenberg triptych finds its complement in the same church in a marvelous painting by Lucas Cranach The Younger, "The Lord's Vineyard" (*Der Weinberg des Herrn*). Painted in 1569, this masterpiece shows a large vineyard divided into two halves. The left half (kingdom of the left or civil kingdom) is occupied by the followers of Rome. The parched, barren, stoney, and weed choked soil is being worked on in futility by monks, priests, bishops, and cardinals. The right half (kingdom of the right or spiritual kingdom) is tremendously lush with vines hanging heavy with grapes. The soil is being tilled by Luther in the center who is clearing the

---

283 *Ibid*, 10.

284 Piepkorn 107. If the doctrine of the priesthood of all believers was invented in the 17th century as Wengert purports, it couldn't possibly have receded in the 16th century as Piepkorn claimed.

"Roman weeds" to reveal the true apostolic tradition, along with Bugenhagen and the evangelical reformers, many of whom are instantly recognizable. In the lower left hand corner we find the pope and his minions emerging from the vineyard at the end of the day to demand more money from Christ who refuses them (Mt. 20). In a desperate effort to water the barren soil on the left, workers are throwing large stones down a well to raise the water level (by their works). By contrast, in the vineyard on the right, Melanchthon is once again easily drawing abundant (baptismal) water from a well (again with his Mona Lisa smile), while Johannes Forster, the Wittenberg Hebrew scholar who helped Luther with his bible translation and was a preacher at the Castle Church, is pouring it out. At the top of the vineyard we see Spalatin crossing from the vineyard of the left to the vineyard of the right, (the two kingdoms), transporting a hefty load of Roman manure to be used for the evangelical side. Clearly this "in your face" evangelical message that the priesthood of all believers can do all things in the word through the power of baptism remained undiminished in Wittenberg more than two decades after Luther's death.

In *De instituendis ministris,* Luther noted with clear tongue-in-cheek that the Catholics allowed even ordinary women "in cases of emergency (*Noth*)" to baptize, "so that one can hardly still regard it as belonging to the office of the priest (*Priesteramt*)." Indeed, Luther continues,

> To baptize is incomparably greater than to consecrate bread and wine, for it is the greatest office in the church — the proclamation of the word of God. So when women baptize, they exercise the priestly office (*Priesteramt*) legitimately, and do it not as a private act, but as part of the common and *public office* of the church, which alone belongs to a priest.[285]

---

[285] *WA* 12.181. *sondern mit einem gemeinen und öffentlichen Amt der Kirche, welches denn allein einem Priester zugehört*

"The Lord's Vineyard," Lucas Cranach the Younger

As Wilhem Brunotte notes, "That every Christian, not only one who is consecrated/ordained, may certainly perform the office of baptism, is shown by the fact that according to Romanist teaching even a woman may baptize in an emergency, who otherwise could not have such a priestly function under canon law. If baptism belongs to the office of priest, then every Christian is a priest."[286] Thus the modern mantra that the laity may baptize "only in case of an emergency" because said function belongs to the clerics is, according to Luther, nothing more than a spurious appeal to canon law.

The baptismal panel in the Wittenberg triptych pointedly rejects that appeal, for we see clearly there is no panic, the

---

[286] Wilhelm Brunotte, *Das geistliche Amt bei Luther,* (Berlin: Lutherisches Verlagshaus, 1959), 84.

baby is not dying, and the pastors are just standing by. This marvelous instructional altarpiece of Lutheran theology was installed just a year after Luther's death, and though the Lutheran church obviously became much more conservative after his and Melanchthon's deaths, one can easily imagine a smile on the lips of Melanchthon as he continued to walk past it for the next thirteen years of his life.

Luther's answer to Wengert's Montana question, "By what authority do you do these things?" is the same one Jesus gave to the Pharisees in Matthew 21: Baptism! If the laypersons who preached and administered the word in the church in Montana did so with the assent of the pastor and congregation, they had a confessionally unimpeachable divine call, having been ordained in their baptism for proclamation in word and sacrament. With all of the baptized being equally priests, the only remaining issue is a call.

That Melanchthon, for instance, was not ordained was simply no big deal. What mattered was whether he had a call. And in fact he did. Luther already saw to it while hiding out at the Wartburg Castle in 1521. In a letter dated the 9th of September, he wrote to Spalatin (who sat with Lucas Cranach on the Wittenberg city council):

> I really wish Philip would also preach to the people somewhere in the city on festival days after dinner to provide a substitute for the drinking and gambling. This could become a custom which would introduce freedom and restore the form and manners of the early church.[287] For if we have broken all laws of men and cast off their yokes, what difference would it make to us that Philip is not anointed or tonsured but married? Nevertheless he is truly a priest (*sacerdos*) and actually does the work of a priest, unless it is not the office of a priest to teach the word of God. In that case Christ himself would not be a priest, for he taught now in synagogues,

---

[287] Cf. *LW* 48.308, n.27: "I.e., freedom for the laity to preach and freedom from the domination of the clergy; this is a reference to the priesthood of all believers."

then in ships, now at the shoreline, then in the mountains.[288] In a word, [Christ] was always and everywhere all things to all people at all times. Since therefore, Philip is called by God and performs the ministry of the word, as no one can deny, what difference does it make that he is not called by those tyrants — who are bishops not of churches but of horses and courtiers.[289]

He goes on to say that if Melanchthon were to do this, he would be a "German bishop" in addition to being the "Latin bishop" he already is.[290] He urges Spalatin to "consult with friends who will help you push this." Spalatin did and the city council followed suit through Justus Jonas, to appoint Melanchthon to be a preacher, not just "somewhere in the city," but in the *Stadtkirche*, the city church.[291]

---

[288] In contrast to bishops of fixed "zip codes."

[289] *WA* Br 2.387-389.

[290] Piepkorn wrote: "The assertion has repeatedly been made . . . that Melanchthon . . . presumed to celebrate the eucharist in Wittenberg in 1521. This assertion is based on a misunderstanding of a Latin account of Melanchthon's attendance with his students at a celebration of the eucharist in which both kinds were distributed to the communicants. Melanchthon says explicitly of himself: 'I do not possess the authority to administer the sacraments (*Non habeo administrationem sacramentorum*)' (CR 24, 313)," (Piepkorn 117-118, n. 28).

Nevertheless, Melanchthon also added: *Doctores sunt infra ordinem Pastorum, nisi simul aliqui sint et Pastores et doctores* ("Doctors are below the order of pastors, unless they are simultaneously pastors and teachers."), and as Luther's letter to Spalatin shows, he not only considered Melanchthon to be both of these, but also a bishop twice over.

[291] *WA* Br 2.390.

Georg Spalatin   *Lucas Cranach the Elder*

From this we again see clearly that for Luther, the call —
not ordination, makes elders *presbyteroi*. [292] The public
ministry of the priesthood of all believers has a far wider
context than a simplistic *adiaphora* of hierarchy, succession,
or ordination, so that faith may be taught far beyond the
campus and proclaimed well beyond the ecclesiastical
institution.

In what appears to be a rather desperate attempt to rescue
Melanchthon from the "anachronistic" and "mythical view of
him as a 'lay theologian,'"[293] Wengert lists Melanchthon's
credentials in order to bring him (and perhaps himself?) under
a limited umbrella of those called to the public ministry of CA
5 and Ap 14 (pastors, teachers, preachers). Yet Luther himself
called Melanchthon "a layman." Writing that same day
(September 9) to Nicholas von Amsdorf, he says, "I have
written to Spalatin that he should push the idea of our Philip
lecturing to the people in German on the gospels; Philip
should do it on festival days and in some place like a lecture
hall. Thus it would gradually come about that the gospel
would be preached in the old manner," a phrase he used twice

---

[292] It is clear from Luther's 1539 *Ordination of Ministers of the Word*
that the call of the church (*Gemeinde*) is the ordination of the Holy
Spirit. Bishops ordaining is simply an affirmation of that call.
[293] Wengert 42.

in one day to express a deep desire, not for the episcopal hierarchical status quo, but for a far simpler church governance. He would use it again four years later in urging the Bohemians to "recover an earlier kind of health."[294] "You have a fitting answer," he continued, "if someone wants to object that a layman (*laico*) should not preach (*dicendum*) the gospel in a corner; answer that he is doing it under the auspices of the university, and ex officio."[295]

We find here no interest expressed by Luther in establishing a hierarchical, successive form of church government through ordination (*successio episcoporum/successio apostolorum*); his only interest is in the continued preaching of continuous faith (*successio fidelium*). While Melanchthon was a professional teacher, indeed a "preacher" of the gospel, he was also a layman with a bona fide call, in this case, from the university, which Luther happily touted as a feather in the Reformation's hat. As we shall see later in the examination of Apology 14, all who are "rightly called" may in fact teach, preach, and administer in the church, "whatever has crawled out of the baptismal font" — even "stupid" folks from Montana.

Luther's deep desire to recover the health, freedom, form, and old manners of the early church without all of the hierarchical fuss and bother of his day is expressed throughout his works. In Article 10 of the *Smalcald Articles*, for example, he writes "St. Jerome, too, wrote concerning the church in Alexandria that it was originally governed without bishops by priests and preachers in common;" and again in *The Babylonian Captivity*, "This is an interpretation of the apostolic injunction which cannot be denied, for the church was formerly governed by the older members (*Eltesten*) *without any being ordained and consecrated;* and they were

---

[294] *LW* 48.311, n.9: "I.e., as was customary in the apostolic church, when the exposition of God's word was not restricted to the actual worship service, and the right to preach was not restricted to 'ordained' clergy, an institution of the second century."
[295] *WA* Br 2.390.

elected for this purpose on account of their years and long experience of affairs."[296]

These are hardly sentiments that reflect a "high regard" for ordination `a la Wengert. They show instead a reformer going out of his way to downplay ordination's importance. Heinrich Bornkamm accurately describes Luther's anti-hierarchical sentiment, noting:

> [Luther's] view is that the holiness of the church consists in "the word of God and true faith." This is a return to early Christianity. Luther was quick to adopt the New Testament expression "body of Christ" for the church. It does not mean what the Catholic Church is wont to designate as the *corpus Christi mysticum*, which is based on the mysterious presence of Christ in the sacrament and on the unity in the hierarchy; Luther means the body in which the Spirit of Christ lives, the body permeated with his Spirit, namely, the believers in all the world. To this concept of the church Luther adhered to the end of his life.[297]

---

[296] *WA* 6.569.

[297] Heinrich Bornkamm, *Luther's World of Thought*, (St. Louis: Concordia Publishing House, 1958), 142-143

Chapter 5

"Ad Fontes!"

In his drive to redefine "public ministry" as the exclusive domain of the ordained in Luther's thought, Wengert resorts to a bit of creative editing in his 2000 Kolb/Wengert version of *The Book of Concord,* (hereafter *BC 2000*). Article 14 in the *BSLK* reads:

> *XIV. Vom Kirchenregiment*

> *Vom Kirchenregiment wird gelehrt, daß niemand in der Kirchen offentlich lehren oder predigen oder Sakrament reichen soll ohn ordentlichen Beruf.*[298]

But in *BC 2000* it reads:

> *XIV. Concerning Church Government*

> *Concerning church government it is taught that no one should publicly teach, preach, or administer the sacraments without a proper [public] call.*

He adds footnote 78: "On *ordentlichen Beruf. Beruf* means both 'call' and 'vocation.' The 1531 *editio princeps* and the 1580 Book of Concord add the word [*public*] in brackets."[299] Also footnote 81: "*Rite vocatus* means called in a regular manner by a proper public authority. This is not a matter of 'ritual.'"[300]

---

[298] *BSLK* 69.
[299] *BC 2000*, 46.
[300] *Ibid*, 47.

Both his translation and his footnotes are incorrect. Not only does *Beruf* (from *berufen* "to call") here not mean "vocation," but rather one's "call" to a vocation or calling (*die Berufung zur Berufung*), as shown in Ap 14 (*gebührlich berufen sein*) — the bracketed word *public* does not exist in either of the cited works — not in the German nor in the Latin, which even a cursory glance at the BSLK makes clear.[301] When I notified Wengert of his error, he advised me to read his footnotes more carefully. When I assured him I had, and suggested his word appeared to be conveniently biased for tilting the Episcopal-Lutheran CCM debate in favor of equating public ministry with ordination by bishops, he replied after a time that upon closer examination he had indeed made a mistake.

I requested he publicly retract his claims to the ELCA bishops, as well as in any future printings of his *BC 2000*, but received no reply. When the second printing appeared in 2001, the bracketed word "public" and its accompanying footnote had mysteriously disappeared without explanation. Yet he went on to repeat and embellish his claim in a teaching paper he delivered in 2004 to the ELCA's "Bishops' Academy," (as they briefly referred to themselves) entitled, "The End of the Public Office of Ministry in the Lutheran Confessions":

Third, the important word in CA XIV is "public." This is the eschatological purpose of church government and order: to see to it that what has been whispered in secret is shouted from the rooftops (Matthew 10:27). In fact, the point is so important that both the official German printing of the CA in 1531 and the

---

301 Maurer warned against putting "a one-sided emphasis on this juridical understanding of *publice docere* in the exegesis of CA 14. No matter how self-evident the Roman law's concept of public office was to people like Melanchthon, it was never dominant in the tradition of the church . . . The ecclesiastical 'public' context was in worship, and *publice docere* meant to preach in conformity with the apostolic tradition and in service of the spiritual unity of Christendom." Luther, Maurer says, derived the public character of the preaching office from his call. 198 ff.

version printed in 1580 in The Book of Concord repeated the word "public" in the final phrase (shown in brackets above). This emphasis is contrasted directly to self-appointed, so-called radical preachers who based their authority solely on themselves and their personal or private, "congregational calls."[302]

The false scenario he's created has the authors of the Augsburg Confession "officially" adding the word [public] to "call" to "contrast" and "emphasize" the need for episcopal ordinations over "congregational calls" — despite Melanchthon's insistence in his *Treatise on the Power and Primacy of the Pope* "that ordination administered by a pastor in his own church is valid by divine right."

Another eight years would pass before he would acknowledge his misinformation in *Priesthood, Pastors, Bishops* — during which time it was sold as an "official" confessional text for aiding the passage of *Called to Common Mission*. In a footnote he wrote, "I am grateful to Pastor Kris Baudler for pointing out an error in CA 14, in *BC 2000*, 46, which has been rectified in subsequent printings. This citation reflects the textual history more accurately [Ch. III, n. 27]."[303] Incredibly, he repeated the same fiction in the same book, insisting "one very important word in Article 14 is *public*,"[304] again quoting the above paragraph. Dr. Meg Madson, systematics professor at Luther Seminary in Minneapolis, recently observed:

---

[302] Luther emphasized the validity and authority of "congregational calls," e.g., *That a Christian Congregation . . . has the Right and the Power to . . . Call* (1523). Wengert erroneously adds, "Although the Roman authorities often accused Luther and the evangelicals of such usurpation of authority, in fact all the leaders of the evangelical movement were duly called pastors and preachers of the existing church." In fact, most of the evangelical leaders were not pastors and preachers, and not all were called by the church, but by the nobility, town councils, and faculties, — not to mention the senate and people of Prague, further evidence for the priesthood of all believers.

[303] Wengert 125 n. 27.

[304] *Ibid*, 42.

The first printing of *BC 2000* was large enough that most libraries own only the first printing. For example, Luther Seminary has four copies of *BC 2000* — all from the first printing! Who would even know there is a second printing? Most non-Lutheran libraries would have only one copy, the first printing of *BC 2000* and would have no idea of errors in it. Moreover, the second printing of *BC 2000* contains no notice — nothing in the Preface, Forward, or text of Article 14 — that a serious error was made in the first printing. This error is not a typo.[305]

Sadly, such deception is par for the course in the current debate, where false information repeated often enough is presumed to be fact. In this case, by not identifying the "error," readers of the first edition of *BC 2000* are left with false information, while readers of the second edition — assuming there are any — are left clueless as to what the error might have been, and why a point that "is so important" in such a key article, has now simply vanished.

It is worth pointing out here that the world's confessional gold standard, the *BSLK*, which first appeared in 1930 to mark the 400th anniversary of the *Augsburg Confession*, remained essentially unchanged through 10 ensuing editions. In 2014 it underwent a thorough updating and was reissued in three heavy tomes. It makes no mention of Kolb/Wengert's BoC.

It is certainly fair to say of the current debate that a good deal of what is passed off as American Lutheran confessional "research" is half-baked, where Melanchthon's personal dictum, *ad Fontes!* ("to the sources") is completely ignored. In the year in which he installed me in my present parish, then Metropolitan New York Bishop William H. Lazareth, produced a book called, *Two Forms of Ordained Ministry —* "A Proposal for Mission in Light of the Augsburg

---

[305] Meg Madson, "Wengert errs 'publicly' in the Book of Concord," CrossAlone Lutherans, February 1, 2016, http://thesurfboard.net/crossalone/?page_id=2257

Confession."[306] Already in the first chapter, which had grown out of an essay he had published in the *Lutheran Forum* a few years earlier, the author repeated his routine defense of the notion of an "evangelical episcopate" in light of the *Augsburg Confession*. Lazareth claimed that the "confessional documentation" he presented underscored the need for a "churchwide debate within the ELCA" based on (unidentified) "ecumenical research" on several of the CA's twenty eight articles. Yet, his study on the episcopate is backed up by no more than three footnotes, the first of which refers to his own "abbreviated" article on the same topic published in 1988. In a broadside at Wilhelm Maurer, undisputedly one of the world's leading experts on the *Augsburg Confession* and Melanchthon, Lazareth described the work of the late German church historian from Erlangen University as mere "personal conjectures" in need of some correction. (Wengert parrots Lazareth's shot at Maurer, calling it "questionable work," though neither of them produces any evidence to back their claims other than Lazareth's footnote to a now discredited 1989 Michael Root article in *Dialog*.)[307]

Most revealing is Lazareth's third footnote: his reference not to any original documentation but only to "the Augsburg Confession's most recent edition in English," Theodore G. Tappert's translation of *The Book of Concord*. In a number of places he misidentifies the English translation as being from the German, when it is the Latin and vice versa, and cites the Latin text of Ap 14.1 and 14.5 as evidence for the Lutherans' "official endorsement of the church's traditional polity in the historic episcopate,"[308] recommending Piepkorn who also

---

306 William H. Lazareth, *Two Forms of Ordained Ministry* — "A Proposal for Mission in Light of the Augsburg Confession" [Minneapolis, Augsburg Fortress, 1991].

307 Cf. Michael Root, "The Augsburg Confession as Ecumenical Proposal: *Episcopacy, Luther, and Wilhelm Maurer,*" *Dialog*, Vol. 28. No. 3 (Summer 1989), 223-232.

308 Lazareth, 19-38. He appears to have copied material from Piepkorn, to wit: "Although the hierarchical structuring of the church is of human right only, the symbolical books affirm their preference

provided no evidence. His footnotes show no use of original confessional material, yet his book was episcopally foisted upon pastors of the Metro New York Synod "for study and teaching" prior to the adoption of *CCM*. Assuming any of them ever read it, they would have remained completely clueless as to what the original texts of the *BoC* actually say.

Wengert engages in similar antics. For his invention of "public" in CA 14 in "The End of the Public Office of Ministry in the Lutheran Confessions," he quotes his own faulty footnote, not the German original, referring the reader instead back to Kolb/Wengert's fictitious "CA XIV, in *BC 2000*, 47." In *Priesthood, Pastors, Bishops,* he lines up and then mows down dead church historians by offering personal conjecture in place of hard evidence, relying on secondary sources. In one ironic bid he writes:

> Bernhard Lohse, in "The Development of the Offices of Leadership in the German Lutheran Churches: 1517-1918," in *Episcopacy in the Lutheran Church?*, makes a mistake in his first sentence: "Luther did not outline any definite program for the implementation of the implications of the Reformation nor did he make any specific proposals for a new evangelical Church organization." This contradicts Luther's work on the German Mass (*Deutsche Messe*), and the "Instruction by [*sic*] the Visitors" (*Der Unterricht der Visitatoren*) in the 1520s and any of the countless memoranda of the 1530s and 1540s.[309]

But once again it is Wengert, not Lohse, who has made the mistake by again relying not on the original German, but on a poor English translation by Victor R. Gold who adds words that Lohse never said.[310] Lohse wrote, *Luther hat für die*

---

for episcopal polity (Ap 14, 1.5)." Piepkorn, 110.

[309] Wengert 58.

[310] Wengert's reliance here on secondary literature appears to violate his own rule expressed in Chapter 4 of *Priesthood, Pastors, Bishops,* ("What Scholars Are Saying about Bishops in Early Lutheranism"): "Material written in English is often dependent on German scholarship and does not always provide helpful approaches to the

Durchführung der Reformation sowie für den Aufbau des neuen evangelischen Kirchenwesens kein festes Programm entworfen. ("Luther did not design a *fixed* program for the execution of the Reformation nor for the construction of the new form of the evangelical church.")

Luther had already made it clear in his preface to the *Instructions* that what he is offering are suggestions and blessed examples (*ein selig Exempel*), "without any compulsion."[311] He writes:

> While we cannot issue any strict commands as if we were publishing a new form of papal decrees, but are rather giving an account or report which may serve as a witness and confession of our faith, we yet hope that all devout and peaceable pastors who find their sincere joy in the gospel and delight to be of one mind with us will act as St. Paul teaches in Phil.2 [:2]. and will heed our prince and gracious lord.[312]

In the *German Mass* he repeatedly uses the word *Exemplum,* and in the very first paragraph of the *Preface* he says, "Do not make it a rigid law to bind or entangle anyone's conscience, but use it in Christian liberty as long, when, where, and how you find it to be practical and useful."[313] Indeed, when his good friend, Nicholas Hausmann, called for the establishment of an evangelical council to enforce liturgical uniformity, Luther opposed it in the name of Christian freedom. Law is law, he replied, so even the Latin mass should not be banned for those who desire it.[314] In the

---

historical material. For example, Merlyn E. Satrom, in 'Bishops and Ordination in the Lutheran Reformation of Sixteenth Century Germany,' is almost exclusively dependent on secondary literature." 56.

311 Cf. Maurer, 285. Even when it came to Luther's development of doctrine, "[Luther] was not equally enthusiastic about making balanced formulas binding on his church."

312 *WA* 26.200.

313 *WA* 19.72-113.

314 *WA,* Br 3, No. 793, 373-374.

same year that he wrote the *German Mass* (1525), he wrote in *Against the Heavenly Prophets*, "I am happy the mass is now held among the Germans in German. But to make a necessity of this, as if it had to be so, is again too much. This spirit cannot do anything else than continually create laws, necessity, problems of conscience, and sin."[315] Thus, far from being fixed programs, they are simply examples offered according to the law of love in hope, the formula which Luther reverted to again and again. Or as Melanchthon put it in the *Instructions: The Human Order of the Church,* "Let each one peacefully keep to his custom."[316] Besides, fixed programs for the Reformation were the purview of the princes to whom Luther deferred, not the theologians, the *Augsburg Confession* itself being a political document from its inception.

Nevertheless, claiming Lohse and Maurer are refuted by Luther's *German Mass* and the *Instructions*, Wengert opines: "Lohse's assumption that Luther rejected episcopal claims of the right to rule in the church is incorrect, as proven by Luther's attempts to establish an episcopal leadership of the church." And where Lohse states that there is "really no fundamental difference between the bishop and pastor," he says, "It is too general a statement to be of much help . . . Equating bishop and pastor (*Pfarrherr*) is not the same as equating bishop and preacher (*Prediger*) or teacher (*Lehrer*). For these reasons (and others), his exposition of Article 28 (pp. 57-58) underestimates the positive assessment of bishops

---

[315] *WA* 18.123.

[316] *WA* 26.222. Luther showed no interest in establishing a *Rituale Lutheranum,* but only suggested models to congregations or individuals who specifically requested them. While these included marriage, confession, and baptism, his formulary for ordination was simply hand written and never published during his lifetime. He composed no order for burial, and none for confirmation, a special service for which he disapproved of, along with blessings, dedications, special ceremonies, etc. Cf. Georg Rietschel, *Lehrbuch der Liturgik* (Göttingen: Vandenhoeck und Ruprecht), II (1952), 630-631, 872-873.

by the reformers."[317]

But what Lohse really said is that Luther saw superintendents as important, not according to the Catholic hierarchical model, but in an evangelical sense in which "bishop" and "pastor" are completely synonymous, *Superintendent* simply being the Latin translation of the Greek *episcopos.* "The office of *Superintendent* is in fact that of bishop . . . the office of bishop belonging not to the *esse,* but to the *bene esse* of the church."

Luther's "Blessed Examples"

Wilhelm Maurer famously stated in his *Historischer Kommentar zur Confessio Augustana,* that the focus of "original Reformation theology" needs to be the theological statements of the 1520s, specifically Luther's three key treatises of 1520 which serve as the basis for the 1530 *Augustana.*[318] Key also are writings and letters actually written during the Diet as well as the examination of "classical testimonies" that immediately follow 1530. But instead of examining the theology of the core elements that comprise the CA, (e.g., Luther's credo in his *Confession Concerning Christ's Supper,* or the *Schwabach* or *Torgau Articles*), Wengert looks to Melanchthon's 1540 *Confessio Augustana Variata,* which was rejected by the Lutherans in Naumburg in 1561 for its various concessions to the papists, (especially Article X: Holy Communion), and writes, "It should be noted that the preface to *The Book of Concord* does not forbid the proper use of the *Variata,* as Melanchthon's revisions came to be known. See the preface, par. 17, in *BC* 2000:11 (*BSLK* 751,

---

317 Wengert, 59.

318 I.e., *To the Christian Nobility of the German Nation respecting the Reformation of the Christian Estate, The Babylonian Captivity of the Church, Concerning Christian Liberty.*

37 - 752, 24)."[319]

His assertion, again, appears to be a rather desperate attempt to prop up a weak argument, given that the preface actually does the opposite by affirming the 1561 decision making the 1530 confession the official Lutheran gold standard, "the first Augsburg Confession as it was submitted." That decision was made because in the *Variata*

> some have attempted to hide their error concerning the Holy Supper as well as other adulterated teaching under the words of this same second edition and in their open writings and in public print have tried to palm them off on simple folk in spite of the fact that this erroneous doctrine is expressly rejected in the confessions submitted at Augsburg . . .[320]

The preface's point is to say the only reason the *Variata* was even used in the Naumburg negotiations is because (using Wengert's own translation of par. 17), "it was never our will or intention to gloss over, cover up, or confirm as consonant with Evangelical teaching any false or impure teaching that might be concealed therein," because at the time they didn't perceive it as having the errors they've just acknowledged it has, errors now "apparent to us" and "to everyone." Finally, the *Formula of Concord, Rule and Norm,* also reaffirms "as the unanimous consensus and exposition of our Christian faith . . . the first and unaltered *Augsburg Confession,* which was delivered to Emperor Charles V at Augsburg during the great Diet in the year 1530 together with the Apology thereof and the articles drafted at Smalcald in the year 1537."[321]

Wengert's *Variata* argument is also frivolous for other reasons. He writes:

> In Article 14 (*Variata*), Melanchthon added a single sentence to show that he assumed bishops would regulate the public office of ministry. To the phrase *rite vocatus,* Melanchthon added: "As

---

[319] Wengert 126, n. 34.
[320] *BSLK* 9.
[321] *Ibid,* 768.

also Paul commanded Titus [1:5] that he should set up elders [presbyters] in the towns." As we have seen, he then used this very instruction of Paul to Titus in the ordination certificate for one of the first evangelical bishops in order to indicate that the bishop alone was to perform all ordinations within his diocese.[322]

That this was simply not the case is shown by Luther's ordinations in Merseburg in 1545, including that of Georg von Anhalt, the bishop in question. As Wengert acknowledges in his own footnotes, "The document was signed by Luther, who presided at the consecration, *and others,*" (even though Luther and the others were not diocesan bishops). He had employed the same pattern for ministry at Nicolaus von Amsdorf's installation three years earlier in 1542. Both installations occurred at the behest of the Elector, not Luther, meaning Luther was going through the motions to satisfy the Elector, who was a student of Melanchthon, rather than for any spiritual or theological reasons. In the case of Amsdorf, the Elector even ordered Luther to do it (though he wasn't opposed), and had him physically carted off to the shackled cathedral in Naumburg in what was little more than political gamesmanship to prevent the Catholic Julius von Plug from assuming the position. There too, Luther *and others* presided and installed the candidate.

In early March of that year, in response to the Elector's request for a written defense of what they had now done, (which disproves Wengert's *Variata* theory), Luther recounted Amsdorf's installation in accordance with the spirit of Titus 1:5 in *An Example of the Way to Consecrate a True Christian Bishop* (1542). In one of his strongest arguments that non-diocesan bishops (namely pastors) may ordain, he compares his actions and others' to Augustine's taking over the bishop's highest office (preaching) from St. Valerius, Bishop of Hippo, because he was a poor preacher. (Augustine ceased his episcopal activities only after the Greek bishops objected to his action.) Clearly distinguishing himself and others from the

---

[322] Wengert 47.

124

existing diocesan bishops, Luther asks, "How would it harm our bishops if they were to follow the example of St. Valerius, and have *others* carry out those tasks which they cannot perform themselves?" [323] These include administering the sacraments and "other auxiliary functions," of which ordination is one, thereby freeing up bishops/pastors to preach the word.[324] Rejecting hierarchical episcopacy, he writes:

> Let the papists say whatever they wish, our consciences are safe and free before God, that we did the good and right thing.[325] For I was not the only one who participated in this ordination (*bei solcher Weihe*) and who laid on hands, but also the following bishops (*Bischöfe*), or as one calls them, *'Pfarrherren'*: Doctor Nicolaus Medler, Pfarrherr and Superintendent in Naumburg; Master George Spalatin, Pfarrherr and Superintendent in Altenburg; Master Wolfgang Stein, Pfarherr and Superintendent in Weissenfels; as was practiced in the church tradition of old and taught in the ancient canons, that one should consecrate (*weihe*) a bishop with the participation of the bishops of neighboring towns, as was done here, which included the church and the people, as well as the lords and knights who were all present.[326]

Their actions were thoroughly consistent with the views Luther had expressed nine years earlier in *The Private Mass*, namely that Christ had begun to destroy the Roman chrism,

> to commit and concede to the churches once again the call or true consecration and ordination to the office of the ministry as it

---

[323] *WA* 53.254.

[324] *Walch* 10, 1548: "To whomever the office of preaching is committed, to him the highest office in Christendom is committed: he may then also baptize, celebrate Mass, and perform all the cure of souls [*Seelsorge*]; or if he prefers not to, he may tend only to the preaching and leave the baptizing and other auxiliary functions to others, as Christ did, and Paul and all apostles, Acts 6."

[325] A similar justification is in the German text of Ap 14: " . . . our obedience to the bishops is withdrawn, and we are excused before God and all people of faith." *BSLK* 297.

[326] *WA* 53.257.

possessed it from the beginning, but which the great bishops arrogated to themselves alone and took away from the small bishops or pastors.[327]

The local pastors, at last, were once again ordaining.[328] In answer to the question, "Who ordained von Amsdorf (and von Anhalt)?" Luther is saying, "We all did! Because we're all priests, bishops, and popes by baptism!"[329] His opening words

---

[327] *WA* **38.252**. *ordinirn zum Pfarrampt widderumb der kirchen zusprechen und einreumen wie sie von anfang gehabt hat.* It is clear from this that the reformers' failure "to perpetuate the historic episcopate with apostolic succession" was not the result of a "practical impossibility," as Piepkorn and others have maintained (Piepkorn, 111), but a theological rejection of the doctrine itself. Had they had a succession obsession, they could have acquired it from Bohemia, or Sweden, or even Venice. Or they could simply have gone the route of Henry VIII and reinvented the practice altogether.

Indeed, Rome itself hadn't maintained the practice, as the Jesuit scholar Hans Jorissen makes clear. Cf. Hans Jorissen, *Concilium*, "Erwägungen zur Struktur des geistlichen Amtes und zur apostolischen Sukzession in ökumenischer Perspektive," (Matthias-Grunewald-Verlag, Oktober 1996), 442-448. He declares it "a dogmatical fact of the first order that there were non-bishop ordinations in the pre-Reformation church up to the 15th Century," (*factum dogmaticum ersten Rangens daß es in der vorreformatorischen Kirche noch im 15. Jahrhundert nichtßbischöfliche Ordinationen gegeben habe*).

[328] Luther, though not a *Superattendent* or bishop, performed the ordination with the others. It was not the case that there were no traditional bishops to do von Amsdorf's and von Anhalt's installations, as Michael Root and others have argued. There were four. They were Bishop Johannes VII of Meissen, Bishop Vinzenz von Schleinitz of Merseburg (who died in 1535 and was succeeded the same year by Bishop Sigismund von Lindenau), and Bishop Philipp Pfalzgraf of Naumburg-Zeitz. The Lutherans, however, felt they weren't needed.

[329] Bugenhagen especially advocated for ordinations by local pastors, which Luther also favored, assuming the procedure was fairly standardized and the ordinands were properly educated. Cf. Walch 21b.2028: *"Bugenhagen hält dafür, es solle ein jeglicher in seiner*

are a defiant tongue in cheek boast, "We poor heretics have once again committed a huge sin against the hellishly unChristian Church of the most hellish Father the Pope, in that we have ordered and ordained a bishop in the cathedral in Naumburg without [the oil of] chrism, also without butter, lard, bacon, tar, fat, incense, charcoal, against their will, but not against their knowledge."[330]

All such sarcasm aside, Luther's defense is vital for understanding the pattern of ministry he envisioned for Saxony, and indeed for all of Germany, a pattern he already laid out in his 1528 preface to Melanchthon's *Instructions*. Here we truly see what Luther had in mind as a role model for all of Germany, in which the canonical bishops' system of the day isn't reconstituted, but is replaced with "visitors" (*Visitatoren*), who are pastors and laity alike. Ordination, being both the education and call to an office, rather than a sacramental consecration, is overseen by *Pfarrer, Pfarrherr,* and *schössene Lehn Herren,* that is, *Privatpersonnen* (tax paying members of the aristocracy).[331]

Gemeinde von seinen Ältesten ordiniert werden." Cf. Martin Brecht, *Martin Luther,* Bnd. 3, 127-137.

[330] *"Wir armen ketzer haben abermal eine grosse sünde auffs new begangen wider die hellische unchristliche Kirche des aller hellischten Vaters des Papsts, das wir einen Bischoff im Stifft Neumburg ordinirt un Eingeweihet haben on allen Cresem, auch on butter, schmaltz, speck, ther, schmer, weirauch, kolen, und was der selben grossen heiligkeit mehr ist, dazu wider jren willen, doch nicht on jr wissen."*

[331] For the similar practice in Brandenburg, see Beate Fröhner, *Die evangelische Pfarrstand in der Mark Brandenburg 1540-1560.* Sonderdruck aus dem Wichman Jahrbuch 19 und 20 Jahrgang 1965-66.

Nikolaus von Amsdorf   *Georg III. von Anhalt-Dessau*

These are not only Luther's priesthood of all believers —
they are his bishopric of all believers, his *coepiscopoi.* Indeed,
it was Luther's hope that this clever model, this "blessed
example," would be copied by "all German princes," from the
North Sea to Italy. "And God grant that it is and becomes a
blessed example for all other German princes to fruitfully
emulate, which Christ will also richly reward at the last
[day]."[332]

Yet turning to Melanchthon's 1537 *Treatise on the Power
and Primacy of the Pope* (hereafter *TPPP*), Wengert arrives at
an oddly different conclusion. Where Melanchthon says in
paragraph 11 that all pastors are equal because the church is
above its ministers, he offers:

> What is worth noting here is that Melanchthon wished to prove
> two things: first, that the bishop of Rome was the equal of other
> bishops during the early history of the church, and second, that
> the consecration of bishops took place with the consent of local

---

[332] *"Gott gebe das es ein selig Exempel sey und werde allen anderen
deutschen Fürsten fruchtbarlich nach zuthun."* *Der Unterricht der
Visitatoren 1528,* Hrsg. Hans Lietzmann, (Bonn: Marcus und
Weber's Verlag, 1912), 5. Bergendoff's translation in *Luther's Works*
is a bit weak: "May God grant that it may be and become a happy
example which all other German princes may fruitfully imitate, and
which Christ, on the last day, will richly reward." *LW* 40.272.

bishops — the very practice that the evangelicals tried (unsuccessfully, in the end) to follow at the installation of the first evangelical bishops in Naumburg (Nicholas von Amsdorff [*sic*]) and Merseburg (George von Anhalt).[333]

Yet here again, Melanchthon is emphasizing just the opposite: Not that the pope is equally a pastor, but that all pastors are actually popes, possessing the very same right and authority as the Bishop of Rome, an audacious point that had already been daringly made in the *Torgau Articles*: "Since the keys are nothing other than the preaching of the gospel and the distribution of the sacrament, the pope has no more power through the keys than any other pastor."[334] As far as the Lutherans were concerned, the Naumburg and Merseburg ordinations were therefore perfectly "successful" and completely consistent with this position. The participating pastors had been recognized as local bishops, the pope's equals, and the result was proper (*recht gebührlich berufen*) ordinations à la Ap 14 in both cases.

The *Pfarrherr* Myth

Conceding in *Priesthood, Pastor, Bishops* that Luther "spoke of something akin to the priesthood of all believers" in *A Treatise on the New Testament, that is, on the Holy Mass* (1520), Wengert, who never quotes it, tries to push the lay toothpaste back into a clerical tube, saying, "There, however, he uses the word *Pfaffen* (cleric)."[335] But here again, Luther's statement is not just "somewhat akin" to a priesthood of all believers, but he states it emphatically, at once incredibly bold, completely radical, and the basis for the *Augsburg*

---

[333] Wengert 89.
[334] *BSLK* 124. *Item dieweil die Schlussel nicht anders sind, denn Evangelium predigen und Sakrament reichen, hat der Babst nicht mehr Gewalt durch die Schlussel dann ein jeder Pfarrner.*
[335] Wengert 4.

Confession:

> Faith alone is the true priestly (*priesterlich*) office. It permits no one else to take its place. Therefore all Christian men are priests (*pfaffen*), all women priestesses (*pfeffyn*), be they young or old, master or servant, mistress or maid, educated or lay. Here there is no difference, unless faith be unequal.[336]

Pfaffe, from the Greek *papas* "father," was in common usage as a priestly designation by the 4th century and is related to "pope."[337] In Luther's theology, not only are all pastors popes — so are all moms and dads! In this essay he also uses *priester* and *pfaffe* interchangeably, making all modern attempts to arrange them hierarchically a false distinction.

Wengert adds, "[Luther's] interest in the language problem dated back at least to 1519, when, in a letter to Georg Spalatin (dated December 18, 1519), Luther stated his uncertainty about the Latin term *sacerdotes* (sacerdotal priests)." But in the letter, already discussed as Luther's first mention of a priesthood of all believers, he isn't stating his uncertainty about the term, but his unfamiliarity with any duties belonging to it beyond word and sacrament. Having already said in the letter that he has no interest at all in writing a tract about any so-called "sacraments" outside of baptism, the Lord's Supper, or confession, he answers Spalatin's query as to what the differences are between the duties of a priest, and those of a layman:

> I don't know of any priestly duties about which you ask, and the more I think about it, I can't find anything to write about ceremonial things, so then the Apostle Peter moves me very deeply in saying in 1 Peter 2: 5, 9 that we are all priests; so too John in Revelation [5:10], so that we who are in this priesthood,

---

336 *WA* 6.370. CA 28 also rejects ranks or "orders of ministers" (*von unterschiedlichen Orden der Kirchendiener/ gradibus ministrorum seu ordinibus*).

337 Gerhard Wahrig, *Deutsches Wörterbuch,* (Gütersloh: Bertelsmann Lexikon-Verlag, 1978), 2788.

appear to be in no way different in ministry from the laity, except for the office (*Amt*) (*prorsus non differre videatur a laicis nisi ministerio*) by which the word and sacrament are administered. Everything else is equal when you get rid of all of the ceremonial and human regulations.[338]

In the end it wasn't the term *sacerdotes* the Wittenberg reformers were uncertain about — it was the word "bishop." Indeed, Luther was for using a different word altogether to better convey the Greek's pastoral meaning:

On the 10th of April [1538] the name "bishop" was greatly and thoroughly disputed, as to what a huge office it is, to be placed upon a shepherd of Christ. And [Luther] said he cannot express this title *episcopos* clearly enough in the German, upon reflecting the word *episcopein* meaning to be watchful, to bear burdens. "For this reason it would be best to call pastors superintendents [*Curatoren*] and care givers. And several [of us] think it is not inappropriate that bishop means 'by-sheep,' one who should be with the sheep, who constantly and diligently watches over them. . . In the time of Hieronymus there were neither cardinals, nor primates, nor patriarchs, nor metropolitans, nor an archbishop, but just a bishop, that is, an elder, a pastor, and a deacon."[339]

---

[338] Walch, *Briefe aus dem Jahre 1519*, No. 246: *Die Pflichten eines Priesters, nach denen du mich fragst, kenne ich nicht, da ich, je mehr ich darüber nachdenke, nichts finde, was ich schreiben könnte, als ceremonielle Dinge; sodann bewegt mich sehr der Apostel Petrus, welcher 1 Petr. 2: 5, 9. sagt, das wir Alle Priester seien . . .* Cf. Wilhem Brunotte, *Das geistliche Amt bei Luther*, 134f.

[339] Walch, Bnd. 22, Cap. 31, *Von Cardinälen und Bischöfen*, 980-981, 3-5: *"Am 10. April wurde viel und sorgfältig disputiert über den Namen Bischof, was für ein großes Amt es ware, dem eine Herde Christi befallen ware. Und er sage, er kenne diesen Namen episcopos nicht klar genug in deutscher Sprache wiedergeben und das Wort episcopein, worauf denken, Achtgeben, Sorge tragen. Darum wurden die Pastoren am besten Curatoren und Versorger genannt. Und etliche leiten es nicht ungeschickt ab Bischof bei Schaf, der bei den Schafen sein soll, stets und fleißig auf sie merken . . . Zu der Zeit des Hieronzmus was weder Cardinal, noch Primus, noch Patriarch, noch*

As we have seen in Luther's September 9, 1521 letters to Spalatin and Amsdorf, Lohse and Maurer were correct: Luther was completely comfortable mixing up ecclesiastical titles and even applying all of them simultaneously to the same person, for instance, to someone like Melanchthon the layman, who was a preacher, teacher, bishop, and public minister of the word, (all latter day appeals to "metaphorical" interpretations notwithstanding). Indeed, for all of the palaver that Piepkorn, Lazareth, Wengert, and others raise insisting *Pfarrherren* were exclusively "head pastors in a city or town,"[340] Luther used the titles *Pfarrherren, Pfarrer, Pfaffen, Pffeffyn, Bischoffe,* and *Bischoffyn* interchangeably in his catechetical sermons,[341] letters, table talks, and writings.

Pfarrherr and *Pfarrer* are etymologically the same thing. *Pfarrherr* is simply another word for *Pfarrer,* in Mittelhochdeutsch: *Pfarraere;* in Althochdeutsch: *Pfarrar,* equally applicable to Catholic and evangelical. The *Pfarrherr/Pfarrer* in Luther's day was the one who was called to the *Pfarrstelle,* and who possessed (*ad possessionem*) the rights to the altar and pulpit ministry. In southern Germany they were called *Pfarrer,* in Switzerland *Leutpriester* (Latin *plebanus*),[342] while in northern Germany they were (and still

---

Metropolit, noch ein Erzbischof, sondern ein Bischof, d.i. ein Ältester, und ein Pfarrer un ein Diaconus."

[340] Based on the erroneous conclusions of Markus Wriedt in *Luthers Gebrauch der Bischofstitulator in seinen Briefen,* in Martin Brecht, ed., *Martin Luther und das Bischofsamt* (Berlin: Calver Verlag, 1990). Wengert paraphrases Piepkorn: " . . . in an attempt to return to the definition of bishops used in the early church, [Melanchthon] recognized that head pastors in a city or town (*Pfarrherren*) exercise the same level of spiritual authority as any bishop" (Wengert 65, also 100, 127 n. 52). Compare Piepkorn's wording in his 1968 LWF essay: "[The symbolical books] use the term 'bishop' both for the head of a medieval diocese and — on the analogy of the episcopal 'parish-sees' (*paroikiai*) of the first three centuries — for the chief pastor of a town." Piepkorn, 109.

[341] E.g., *WA* 30.

[342] E.g., Zwingli served as Leutpriester in Einsiedeln.

are) called *Pastor,* from the Latin word for "shepherd." One need look no further than Luther's catechisms to prove the point. The official title for his *Small Catechism* is: *Der kleine Katechismus fur die gemeine Pfarrherrn und Prediger.* That *Pfarrherrn* also refers to simple pastors or *Pfarrer,* is made clear from the word *gemeine,* which both Tappert and Kolb/Wengert rather tepidly translate as, "The Small Catechism for Ordinary Pastors and Preachers." But the word "ordinary" fails to properly convey the meaning of *gemeine,* which actually refers to the less educated clergy, (*ungelehrten*), many of whom were not even schooled in Latin. For example, if one consults the Wittenberg *Ordiniertenbuch,* one finds that for the educational background of the 1979 persons ordained between the years 1537-1560, 1025 are listed as simple *Handwerker* (common laborers), and 44 as *Bürger* (regular citizens).[343] Though these are hardly likely to be "head pastors in a city," Luther nevertheless addresses all of them as *Pfarrherr,* the very same title he gives to the more educated ("big city" clergy, if you will) in the *Large Catechism.*

In a chapter he calls "The Central Arguments of Article 28," Wengert correctly observes that "Melanchthon did not distinguish pastors and bishops," but then adds:

> In fact, on several occasions in this article, he lumps the two together [CA 28.30]. However, rather than leading to a denigration of the episcopal office, it resulted in the raising of the pastoral office to its proper, ancient level. In this regard, it is important to note that the word used in paragraph 53 is not *ministri* (which included preachers and teachers), but *pastores* in the Latin text or *Pfarrer* in the German. The reason Melanchthon on occasion associated the two terms was precisely because the evangelical authority of bishops is nothing other than pastoral: to comfort the terrified conscience with the gospel. Thus, the initial definition of the evangelical bishop in paragraph 5 exactly

---

[343] Cf. *BSLK* 501, n.1.

133

parallels the language of Article 5.[344]

But Melanchthon doesn't so much "lump together" as simply identify what is already one and the same thing: *episcopi sue pastores*, rendering them as a single word: *Bischofe*. In CA 28 § 53 the Latin *pastores* is *Pfarrer* in German, and in §30 it is *Bischofe*, making the titles identical and completely interchangeable in the evangelical sense. But with reasoning as disjointed as the notion that Titus 1:5 was added to von Anhalt's certificate to connote ordination by diocesan bishops only, Wengert again emphasizes episcopal authority by claiming Melanchthon lumped the titles together to indicate "the authority of the bishop is nothing other than pastoral" — though *pastores* is a noun — not an adjective.

Far more likely is that he rendered both *pastores* and *Pfarrer* as *Bischofe* to underscore the completely unorthodox claim of the reformers in Augsburg that every evangelical (non-canonically ordained) pastor is, in fact, an *episcopos;* not metaphorically, but in reality! This is the scandal of Ap 14, the dispute over what is meant by *recht gebührlich berufen,* which caused the article to be tabled, and then rejected in the *Confutatio.* This is the point Melanchthon repeated in no uncertain terms in *TPPP* that "ordination administered by a pastor (*pastores*) in his own church is valid by divine right," that Luther emphasized in *That A Christian Congregation Has the Right . . .*, that was put into actual practice in Merseburg and Naumburg, and was proclaimed to the Bohemians in Prague: You already ARE BISHOPS in your baptism, in every sense of the word! This, in fact, is the "equality" (*aequi!*) Melanchthon is demanding in Ap 14 — an evangelical status Rome refused to grant the Lutherans then, and has not to the present day.

CA 28.5 is not "the initial definition of the evangelical bishop," in "the language of Article 5," as Wengert has it, but of the office (*Amt*) itself, the "office of the keys" (*Von Vermöge der Schlussel/De potestate clavium*), the preaching

---

344 Wengert 74.

of the gospel, the binding and loosing of sins, and the administering of the sacraments, as is clear from Melanchthon's use of the direct object in his *Vorarbeit* of said article in March 1530: "This alone is the bishop's or priest's office" (*Dies allein soll der Bischof oder Priester Ampt sein*), [345] affirming in *TPPP*, " . . . it is necessary to acknowledge that the keys do not belong to the person of one particular individual but to the whole church . . ."[346]

The office of *Prediger*, or "preacher," on the other hand, while part of the job description of the *Pfarrer*, was also a separate office and calling. "The preacher is confined to the function of preaching, whereas the pastor performs additional functions, providing for the full care of souls."[347]

So, on the one hand, the *Predigtamt* of CA 5 cannot be referring solely to the *Prediger*, whose role is limited to preaching without the distribution of the sacraments. Nor, on the other hand, can it be referring solely to the *Pfarrer/Pfarrherren* (pastor), as it would then be called *Vom Pfarramt* or *Pastoramt*. Clearly CA 5 is about one thing only: the means of grace, the work of the Holy Spirit, who alone creates justifying faith through word and sacrament, "as a part of the *public ministry* of the church which belongs to the priesthood" of all believers.[348]

Crypto-Catholics make much ado of Melanchthon's wording in CA 28.21 of divine right being accorded to "bishops as bishops" (*episcopis ut episcopis*). Piepkorn, for example, wrote, "The ministry of the divine word and sacraments is committed to *bishops as bishops* (AC 28.21)."[349] Paraphrased thusly, the statement is somewhat misleading,

---

[345] *BSLK* 120. See also n.3.

[346] *Ibid*, 478.

[347] *Ibid*, 545, n. 2. *Der Prediger ist nur auf den Predigtdienst beschränkt, während der Pfarrer daneben noch die Kasualien ausübt, also der Träger der gesamten Seelsorge ist.*

[348] *WA* 12.181.

[349] Piepkorn, 103. Cf. Maurer 190: "Luther recognizes no apostolic succession in the sense of divine right."

given Melanchthon's rejection of bishops possessing divine right *ipso facto,* as is clear from the article's negative formulation:

> Hence according to the gospel (or, as they say, by divine right) no jurisdiction belongs to bishops as bishops (*episcopis ut episcopis*), (that is, to those to whom has been committed the ministry of word and sacraments) except to forgive sins, to reject doctrine which is contrary to the Gospel, and to exclude from the fellowship of the church ungodly persons whose wickedness is known, doing all this without human power, simply by the word. Churches are therefore bound by divine law to be obedient to the bishops according to the text, "He who hears you hears me." However, when bishops teach or establish anything contrary to the gospel, churches have a command of God that forbids obedience: "Beware of false prophets" (Matt. 7:15) . . . [350]

In 1537 many of the Reformation's leading Lutheran theologians signed the *Smalcald Articles*, the summation of the Lutheran stance, including Luther, Jonas, Bugenhagen, Creutziger, Amsdorf, Spalatin, Agricola, Brenz, Dietrich, and Osiander. Melanchthon signed it with reservation, concerned about its polemics, stating, "I, Philip Melanchthon, regard the above articles as right and Christian. However, concerning the pope I hold that, if he would allow the gospel, we, too, may concede to him that superiority over the bishops which he possesses by human right, making this concession for the sake of peace and general unity among the Christians who are now under him and who may be in the future."[351] He hoped to avoid short-circuiting future negotiations. But within days he had changed his tune in his *Treatise On the Power and Primacy of the Pope.* There he called the popes and the papacy "antichrists!" And unlike the *Smalcald Articles,* the *Treatise* was officially adopted in Schmalkalden as a confession of

---

350 *BSLK* 123-124.

351 This line is often pointed to by ecumenists as "evidence" of Melanchthon's desire for a papal office. But as is clear from his TPPP, within a week he harbored no such illusions and reservations.

faith.[352]

In fact, Melanchthon saw a return by the evangelicals to the Catholic system as a retreat. At the 1541 Regensburg Conference, he rejected the Catholic-Protestant compromises that had been negotiated in the "Regensburg Book." Stung by criticism that he was now little more than Luther's mouthpiece, merely mimicking the latter's rejection of the compromises, he wrote to the emperor that he had no instructions from Luther at all:

> I know that the doctrines of our [Lutheran] churches are the doctrines of the church catholic. This, I think, is confessed by many wise men, though they think that in removing abuses we are harsher than necessary. They wish to retain a kind of saint worship, private masses, and the like. Hence they want us to take a backward step, and to approve the beginning of abuses. Since I cannot do this, I ask again to be dismissed.[353]

Addressing so-called historical succession, he wrote:

> And there were these errors in the article that state that bishops stand in succession (*episcopos successisse*) in the place of the apostles. From this saying many errors immediately follow — that the church is tied to the orderly succession (*successionem ordinariam*), as if it were impossible for the bishops to err because they hold the place of the apostles, or as if these were bishops, so they are called, and it were necessary to listen to them as heads of the church.[354]

In a classic example of hierarchical overreach, Piepkorn conflated the role of *bishops as bishops* (CA 28.21) with that of *rulers* (TPPP 60-61) by mistranslating Melanchthon in the latter to read: "The gospel gives *those who rule over the churches* the command to teach the gospel, to remit sins, and

---

[352] It was adopted as a supplement to the *Augsburg Confession,* and not as an appendix to the *Smalcald Articles,* as some have supposed. Luther was only prevented from signing it because of ill health.

[353] *C.R.* 4.318.

[354] *Ibid* 4.415.

to administer the sacraments . . . This authority by divine right is common to *all who rule over churches,* whether they are called pastors, presbyters, or bishops," [emphasis his.][355]

Of course, the last thing the reformers ever saw true bishops as was *rulers,* spiritual or otherwise (rejected in e.g., Ap 28.6), the church being "ruled and seized only by the eternal word; for it is very disgraceful to rule consciences before God with human law and old custom," as Luther reminded the citizens of Leisnig.[356] Both the German and Latin (*furstehen / praesunt*) are translated "preside" in all English BoC versions. A *Fursteher* is an overseer, a *Betreuer* or *Wächter* (caretaker, watchman), one who watches over his flock as a shepherd (*pastor*) does his sheep. Thus Luther corrected Emser:

> "Bishop" too stems from the Greek language. For he whom they call *episcopus* is called *speculator* in Latin and "a guardian or watchman on the tower" (*warttman odder wechter auff der Wart*) in German. This is exactly what one calls someone who lives in a tower and is supposed to watch and to look out over the town so that fire or foe do not harm it.[357]

In other words, bishops may serve as Smokey the Bear, but they do not rule the forest. The *potestas ecclesiastica* is nothing more or less than the *ministerium verbi,* the authority being not the bishop's, but the word's. Says Lohse: "In so far as the ministry of the bishops was truly the ministry of the word the congregations were obligated to be obedient to them *iure divino.* If the bishops should teach or resolve something against the gospel the congregations should not obey them. This shows clearly that the office of the bishop was without

---

355 Piepkorn, 103-104. Others have repeated Piepkorn's mistranslation, e.g., Wengert 59: "Lohse's assumption that Luther rejected episcopal claims of the right to rule in the church is incorrect, as proven by Luther's attempts to establish an episcopal leadership of the church."
356 *WA* 11.409.
357 *Ibid,* 7.630.

exception subordinate to the word of God."[358]

Melanchthon added to his signature in the *Smalcald Articles* that even the pope, as the bishop of bishops (*summus pontifex*), is only such by human authority.[359] The ministerial office of word and sacrament, as the means of grace, is alone divine; while the ordering of persons to the office is by human arrangement.

Article 28

One of the most frequently mischaracterized confessional articles in present ecumenical dialogues is CA 28, "The Power of Bishops." This last article of the *Augsburg Confession*[360] is popularly described today as a "proposal for reconciliation" offered by the Lutherans to the Catholics in Augsburg, an ecumenical euphemism promoted by the likes of Michael J. Root, the chief author of *Called to Common Mission*. The central issue in Augsburg, Root and others maintain, was the question surrounding the authority and status of the bishops,[361] an assertion that, if true, would make CA 28 the premier article of concern in the Confessions. Wengert devotes most of his *Priesthood, Pastors, Bishops* to that assumption, the result being that it reduces the central sticking point in Augsburg to a question of church polity, of canonical order rather than

---

[358] Lohse, *Episcopacy in the Lutheran Church?*, 58.

[359] *BSLK* 464: ". . . sein Superiorität uber die Bischofe, die er hat *jure humano* . . ."

[360] It is sometimes assumed that because CA 28 is the longest article in the *Augsburg Confession*, it is also preeminent, (e.g., fourteen pages in Tappert to CA 4's three paragraphs on justification). In the *Apology*, however, it occupies a mere four and a half pages to CA 4's sixty.

[361] Michael Root, *Inhabiting Unity, Bishops, the Concordat, and the Augburg Confession*, (Grand Rapids: Eerdmans, 1995), p. 50: "The issue was more narrowly the status and authority of the Catholic bishops."

confessional fidelity — which is also how it was sold in CCM. If this canonical polity of the authority of the bishops could somehow be reframed as "evangelical," the ecumenists reason, historical episcopal succession could be perfectly adaptable to confessional Lutheranism. The obvious and inherent contradiction, though, was never lost on Luther. As Scott Hendrix notes:

> Attempts to separate the issue of authority from the doctrine of justification in Luther's break with Rome impose a distinction on Luther's thinking which would have been foreign to him. For example, Kolde argued that the question of authority and not the doctrine of justification was the "cardinal question between Protestantism and Catholicism": Th. Kolde, *Luther's Stellung zu Concil und Kirche bis zum Wormser Reichstag, 1521* (Gütersloh, 1876), p. 112. In fact, the issue of authority was the most important concrete application of the doctrine of justification.[362]

Luther left no doubt of this when he and the reformers demanded Melanchthon break off all polity negotiations on authority with the papists in the summer of 1530.[363] Since the *Augsburg Confession* had already been delivered, canonical negotiations were little more than the devil's distraction from the real issue of justification.

Nevertheless, claiming support from the work of Wilhelm Maurer, Root maintains that CA 28 is a Lutheran attempt at reconciling the two parties' disparate positions. He quotes Maurer out of context[364] and deftly sidesteps all evidence to the contrary, starting with Maurer himself, who insisted instead that the article was an attempt at *Kompromiß* (a tradeoff)[365] — that is, a matter of political accommodation, not

---

362 Scott H. Hendrix, *Luther and the Papacy,* Stages in a Reformation Conflict, (Philadelphia: Fortress Press, 1981), 194 n.. 15.
363 See Ch. 9 below, "The Unity Myth."
364 Cf. James M. Kittelson, *Enough is Enough! "Confusion over the Augsburg Confession and its Satis est."* http://www.ccmverax.org/kittel.html
365 *Langenscheidt's New College German Dictionary, German-*

doctrinal harmonization. CA 28, after all, belongs to the chief "practices or 'abuses' over which there was disagreement or 'dispute,' as [Melanchthon] put it."[366] While not in theological harmony with the prince-bishops, the reformers were nevertheless willing to accommodate *some* of their juridical demands at the time, provided they accept the specific conditions set down by the evangelicals.

Luther summarized those conditions in his *Exhortation to All Clergy Assembled at Augsburg,*[367] which he published at the time of the diet as an invitation to the bishops to take seriously the gravamina previously presented at the Diet of Worms. Says Maurer:

A pact between [the] Lutheran Reformation and the bishops is still

---

English, (Berlin and Munich: Langenscheidt KG, 1995), 364. Cf. Wilhem Maurer, *Historischer Kommentar zur Confessio Augustana,* Bnd 1, (Gütersloh: Gütersloher Verlagshaus Gerd Mohn, 1976), 86 n. 128. Cf. Maurer, 72 n. 128: "Luther's letter of July 6 [1530] to the cardinal archbishop of Mainz (*WA* 30.2: [391], 397-412) shows that by that time he no longer held to the compromise. He considers it no longer possible to produce unity in doctrine, and he asks the cardinal, like Gamaliel, to work toward toleration and peace; at the same time he is quite ready to use Psalm 2 in an attack against the princes of the old religion. Luther's other writings from the Coburg — with the exceptions mentioned in the text—belong to this period, when the results of the diet had taught him that the compromise was unworkable. They therefore offer, at best, supplementary commentaries to CA 28."

That Luther wasn't in a particularly compromising mood is also clear from his letter to Melanchthon from the Feste Coburg, dated July 15, 1530: *"Ich schisse dem Legaten und seinem Herrn in seine Disputation, wir wollen Disputationes genug finden."* Walch 21a. 1517-1519, Brief Nr. 1627.

[366] James M. Kittelson, "Enough Is Enough! Confusion Over the Augsburg Confession and its Satis Est," *Lutheran Quarterly* 12 (1998): 249-270.

[367] *WA* 30.2:237, 268-356.

possible, even though their former advocate [Luther] now steps forward as a preacher of repentance, ruthlessly exposing the chief evils of the church and relentlessly making the bishops responsible for them — celibacy included. It is a stern love that sketches the portrait of a proper Christian bishop here, not "pussyfooting" like Melanchthon at the end of Article 28 out of respect for episcopal dignity, and begging for tolerance. Luther thunders against a clergy that is heading for ruin: "Your blood be upon your own head! We are and want to be innocent of your blood and damnation."[368]

Excoriating them, while simultaneously injecting himself into the diet's deliberations from the Coburg, Luther lays out four conditions for peace, beginning with a warning, "Therefore, we are offering you a choice" (*Dar umb bieten wir euch an die wahl*).

1) Since you will not perform the episcopal office and work . . . let us exercise your office for which you are responsible. Give us the right to teach the gospel freely . . . serve the poor people . . . Do not persecute and resist . . . what others want to do for you.

2) We do not wish to covet or take anything from you . . . we expect to work, so that you will thus be spared both labor and pay, care and cost.

3) We wish to let you remain what you are . . . you should be allowed to be princes and lords, for the sake of peace, and your properties should be left alone . . . Only keep the peace and do not persecute us! . . . You could help us and we could help you to peace. If you do not do so, then we retain the honor, and you lose

---

[368] Maurer 70. Maurer maintains that there is no theological difference between the *Exhortation* and CA 28, only a difference in tone. He writes, "In this situation, Melanchthon's intention to moderate the basic presuppositions of the planned compromise must have been extremely irritating to Luther, even though his friend reminded him of the agreements made earlier." He adds with regard to CA 28, "Here also Luther, because of the theological incompetence of the bishops, thinks only of separating their jurisdictional and magisterial functions from the preaching office (*WA* 30.2:240.20ff.)," 72, n. 127.

both peace and honor.

4) You could restore episcopal jurisdiction (*zwanck*) [secular and administrative rule] provided you leave us free to preach the gospel.[369] For my part I will readily give help and counsel so that you may have something of the episcopal office after all.[370] Thus you would have two parts of the episcopal office: one, that we and the preachers teach the gospel in your stead; the other, that you assist such with episcopal jurisdiction (*zwangk*). Your person, life, and princely demeanor we leave to your conscience and God's judgment. Up to now we have never taken such jurisdiction (*zwangk*) from you.[371]

That these conditions represent an unsavory juridical accommodation,[372] rather than a desirable reconciliation, is immediately clear from Luther's response to his anticipated evangelical critics:

But someone might at this point think it laughable to hear that the endowment bishops (*stifft bisschove*) should govern the churches,

---

[369] That *zwanck* (a word meaning "coercion") refers to the secular rule of bishops as "sovereigns" of the realm (*episcopus ut princeps*) is clear from Luther's famous letter to Melanchthon, dated July 21, 1530 in *WBr* 5.1656.42-43: "I speak of the church as a church which already has been separated from the political commonwealth." Subjects are required to obey these bishops, says Luther, but "they obey not as members of the church, but as citizens."

[370] *WA* 30 II.342: "*Da will ich fur mein teil auch getrost zu helffen und ra ten, auff das yhr doch ettwas bisschoffliches ampts auch haben mügt.*" This offer to "help" also appears in Ap 14. Cf. *BSLK*, 296-297: ". . . *daß wir zum höchsten geneigt sind, alte Kirchenordnung und der Bischofe Regiment, das man nennet* canonicam politiam, *helfen zu erhalten.*"

[371] *Ibid,* 340-343. In the next paragraph, Luther summarized the four conditions: "We will perform the duties of your office; we will support ourselves without cost to you; we will help you remain as you are; and we will counsel that you have authority and are to see to it that things go right," adding, "What more can we do?"

[372] Including an implicit threat: "If you do not do so . . . you lose both peace and honor."

since it is well known that they cannot and will not learn how . . .
I know well, sad to say, that it is true. But in order that the wicked
people may see that we seek peace and that nothing is lacking in
us, I can put up with their providing parishes and pulpits with
clergymen and thus help to administer the gospel. I would sooner
have the fault be theirs than ours, and God has before now
governed and done good by means of wicked rogues [e.g., King
Herod and the Romans].

In other words, with nose held closed and for the sake of
peace, the endowment bishops could be tolerated if the gospel
can be spread. "If, however, they want to suppress the gospel
or remain so completely unrepentant, they may do so at their
own risk. We shall still preach what we want to . . . The
Lutherans remain masters because Christ is with them and
they remain with him, even though hell, the world, devil,
princes, and all should go mad."[373]

The *Exhortation*, Lewis W. Spitz concludes in *Luther's
Works*, "might be considered Luther's own Augsburg
Confession."[374] When the first five hundred copies of it
arrived in Augsburg on June 7, 1530, they quickly sold out.
An elated Justus Jonas quickly wrote to Luther, "Your truly
prophetic book is read by all the pious . . ."[375]   Just   two
weeks after its publication, in the midst of the uproar it caused,
Cardinal Campeggio ordered his secretary, Daniel Mauch, to
prepare a Latin translation. In a letter dated in Augsburg, June
21, 1530, Mauch wrote to his friend, Wolfgang Richard, a
physician in Ulm, "It is a summary of all Lutheranism. If you
wish to see the whole of Luther, you ought to buy it."[376]

---

373 *Ibid*, 345. *"Die Lutherisschen bleiben wol Meister weil Christus
bey yhn und sie bey yhm bleiben, Wenn gleich helle, wellt, teufel,
fursten und alles solt unsinnig werd."*
374 *LW* 34.7.
375 *WA* 30 II, 238: *Liber tuus vere propheticus legitur ab omnibus
piis, diis et hominibus applaudentibus, stomachante et dentibus
infrendente Satana.*
376 *Ibid*: *Lutherus scripsit nescio quam adhortationem ad Principes
Ecclesiasticos in lingua Germanica; illam Cardinalis me latinam*

What CA 28 clearly is not is Root's *quid pro quo* which "offers the reconciliation proposal . . . If evangelical church practices and the proclamation of the gospel are allowed, a reformed jurisdiction by the Catholic bishops will be recognized."[377] Instead, Luther's offer to allow the bishops to formally retain some of their spiritual duties, but have them carried out by evangelical preachers, is viewed by many scholars as little more than a negotiating ruse, a political tactical ploy.[378] The terms the evangelicals offered, while genuine, were also known by them to be virtually impossible to accept. Says Maurer:

> The bishops, thinks Luther, would never stand for this limitation of their power; if one were to give in to them here, as Melanchthon had suggested in his proposals on July 14, one would become a participant in all their sins. But it would be a sacrilege to want to concede spiritual authority over the church to the bishop insofar as he is a *secular ruler.* In this capacity, of course, he can require obedience of his subjects, even in external matters of church discipline like fasting, but the church as church never owes him obedience. If he demands it, even though it be by force and in the emperor's name, we must resist to the death. All theologically based attempts at accommodation merely disguise the fact that the bishops want to be temporal rulers and to hold congregations in their power by secular law. Luther's polemic is thus directed not

---

facere iussit. Est autem summa totius Lutheranismi. Si totum Lutherum videre vis, emere poteris. It is not known if a Latin translation was ever executed.
Cf. James M. Kittelson, *Enough Is Enough!* "Confusion Over the Augsburg Confession and its *Satis Est,"* http://www.ccmverax.org/kittel.html[377]
[378] Cf. Armin Kohnle, "Luther und das Reich," *Luther Handbuch,* (Tübingen: Herausgeber Albrecht Beutel, Mohr Siebeck, 2005), 199-200: "War Luthers Angebot im Zusammenhang des Augsburger Reichstag von 1530, die Bischöfe sollten ihr geistliches Amt formel beibehalten, aber durch evangelische Prediger ausüben als taktisches Zugeständnis gemeint, rückte er später von der Vorstellung einer Säkularisation der Hochstifte ab, um das Kirchengut weiterhin für eine geistliche Verwendung zu erhalten."

only against Melanchthon's arguments but more broadly against the original plan of compromise for which CA 28 was to form the theological foundation.[379]

Wengert offers a weak counter to Maurer with personal conjecture rather than facts. He writes in *Priesthood, Pastors, Bishops,*

> In his influential article "The Historic Episcopate and the Lutheran Confessions," Robert Goeser tries to summarize the position of early Lutherans leading up to the Augsburg Confession. He mistakenly imagines that Luther only hesitatingly supported the Saxon compromise (obedience to Roman bishops in exchange for married priests, communion in both kinds, and an end to private, sacrificial masses), a premise based on the questionable work of Wilhelm Maurer.

But like Root and Lazareth before him he fails to show how Maurer's work is "questionable," focusing instead on Goeser, (who dissented against historical episcopacy in LED III), and repeating a myth popular among today's crypto-Catholics, saying, "[Goeser] does not understand that the omission in the Visitation Articles of references to ordination by superintendents arose out of political impossibility."

This oft repeated fable, from Piepkorn to present day ecumenists, ignores the fact that the Thuringian Lutherans had at least three superintendents at their disposal at the time who were able and available to ordain: Spalatin, Superintendent of Altenburg; Anton Musa Superintendent of Jena; and Justus Menius, Superintendent of Eisenach. [380] Wengert adds, "Finally, Goeser asserts that Article 14 of the Augsburg

---

379 Maurer 76.

380 Cf. Andreas Baudler, "Die 'Theodore Baudler Collection' in den USA — Odyssee und Auswertung einiger Spalatinhandschriften aus dem ehemaligen Gnandsteiner Burgarchiv," *Die Familie von Einsiedel, Stand, Aufgaben und Perspektiven der Adelsforschung in Sachsen,* (Freistaat Sachsen: Staatsarchiv, 2007), 108.

Confession could not mean ordination by bishops,"[381] —
which, of course, it couldn't given the Latin and the German
texts' clear use of *vocatio* over *ordinatio, berufen* over
ordinieren, and *iure humano* over *iure divino,* which spelled
the end of canonical ordination.

That Luther wasn't on board with the Saxon compromise,
and Lutheran offers were simply a smoke screen in the days
following Augsburg, is beyond dispute. In a letter dated
October 28, 1530, Luther sought to calm an agitated
Landgrave Philip von Hesse, who demanded to know why
they were continuing to offer concessions. Any offers still
being floated from the evangelical side, Luther assured him,
are fakes, decoys meant to make the Catholics look bad. They
are "concessions" the evangelicals knew the papists could
never accept, but they made for good Lutheran propaganda.
And even if they were to accept them, they would be totally
inconsequential.

> I ask your Sovereign Grace not to be shocked that we have once
> more offered a few bits and pieces[382] in some matters, as for
> instance, fasting, feast days, [differentiations in matters of
> certain] foods, and hymns, for we know, of course, that they
> cannot accept [them] to this extent (*denn wir wissen doch, das sie
> es mit solcher masse nicht annemen konnen*). Our purpose in
> doing this is to increase our respectability all the more, so that I
> can emphasize their infamy all the more powerfully in my
> booklet. Even if all [these concessions] should be accepted this
> would not be dangerous for us.[383]

The bottom line is, Luther was never predisposed to
negotiating the *Augsburg Confession,* (well meaning
statements by Gerhard Forde[384] and others aside, maintaining

---

381 Wengert 56-57.

382 *etlichen Stucken*

383 *WA* Br 5.660.

384 Cf. Gerharde O. Forde's otherwise excellent *Justification by Faith
— A Matter of Death and Life,* (Philadelphia: Fortress Press, 1982), 6
ff.

the CA was principally an ecumenical document).[385] He concludes the same missive by offering the landgrave a tantalizing hint of "the resistance" plans he's already involved in, but which he cannot possibly discuss.

Thus, while the CA was a Saxon political document submitted for the forging of a united military and religious front against the ever advancing Turks, ecumenism and unity were not the primary goals for Luther — speaking truth to power was, and that truth was the gospel! Nothing could be clearer on this score for him, nothing more powerful than the presentation of the Confession itself. The task of the evangelical team in Augsburg, in his view, was to simply deliver the goods and come home. "You have given to Caesar the things that are Caesar's," he wrote to the Lutheran team of Jonas, Spalatin, Melanchthon, and Agricola on July 15, 1530, "and to God the things that are God's: perfect obedience to Caesar by appearing [at the diet] at such great expense, hardship, and trouble; and to God the precious sacrifice of the Confession . . . Therefore, in the name of the Lord, I free you from this diet. Home, and again, home!" And once more at the end of the letter, "Home, home!,"[386] switching both times to the German. Their case had been made. Nothing "better or more advantageous" than the CA could possibly be accomplished.

The sum and total of Melanchthon's point in CA 28 is simply this: Bishops, being pastors (*episcopi seu pastores*), have no other authority than the means of grace. They do not have authority to teach, preach, or introduce traditions or

---

[385] Carl Braaten credits Robert W. Jenson with the expression "dogmatic proposal" for the *Augsburg Confession.* Cf. Eric W. Gritsch and Robert W. Jenson, *Lutheranism: The Theological Movement and Its Confessional Writings* (Philadelphia: Fortress Press, 1976). The "proposals" that were for negotiation, however, were not dogmatic, but political in nature, bargaining chips for the sake of peace. Luther believed the diet should confine itself to practical questions and reason. Cf. Maurer 70 f.

[386] *WA* Br 5.479-481: *Immer wieder heim, immer heim!" "Heim, heim!"*

practices contrary to the gospel that can "ensnare consciences" by suggesting these too are a means of grace. When they do, they abrogate their authority. As the article states, "It is patently contrary to God's command and word to make laws out of opinions or to require that they be observed in order to make satisfaction for sins and obtain grace, for the glory of Christ's merit is blasphemed when we presume to earn grace by such ordinances."[387]

---

[387] *CA* 28.35-36.

Chapter 6

The Myth of Anglican Succession

While CA 5 is concerned solely with the means of grace, historical episcopacy's focus is the nomistic organ it deems necessary for the transmittal of that grace: successively ordained bishops traceable to the apostles.[388] Episcopalians go to great lengths to demonstrate they sit on the same successive branch as the Catholic Church, a branch that Rome and history show, the Anglicans themselves have sawn off. In his masterful study of *The Historic Episcopate*, written in the same year in which Pope Leo XIII nullified Anglican ordinations and partially reproduced here, Methodist Episcopal Bishop and church historian R. J. Cooke explains why Anglican pretensions to historical episcopal succession are totally unsustainable.

England had remained religiously and legally Catholic through the reign of Queen Mary until the ascendancy of Princess Elizabeth in 1558, the daughter of Henry VIII and Ann Boleyn. What followed, however, was a confused and even comical series of actions that first canceled, and then commandeered Rome's episcopal succession by the most dubious of means. Cooke writes:

> The [1535] Act of Supremacy also provided that all persons holding office under the crown, civil, military, or ecclesiastical, should take an oath acknowledging the royal supremacy. By this

---

388 Cf. Ernst Käsemann, "Verkirchlichte Freiheit," *Der Ruf der Freiheit*, 5th Edition, (Tübingen: J.C.B. Mohr [Paul Siebeck], 1972), 181-182: "The apostolic succession of the episcopal office is quite simply — naturally I can only speak in the name of historical criticism — one of many Christian fictions. There is only one apostolic succession that allows itself undoubtedly to be proven historically, namely the discipleship of Christ."

requirement every bond between the Roman Church and the Reformed Church was broken. The hierarchy, which Anglicans affirm had undoubted succession, was destroyed. In the whole kingdom there were twenty four episcopal and two archiepiscopal sees. The sees of nine bishops and of one archbishop were vacant. In July, 1559, the remaining bishops and archbishops were summoned by the lords of council and ordered to take the oath; but, with the exception of Kitchin, Bishop of Llandaff, they all refused, and by the end of September they were all deprived of their sees by High Court of Commission. In this manner the Roman sees were emptied of their bishops — a mode quite as legal as that by which the bishops of Edward VI had been deprived in the preceding reign—and there remained now in all England no bishop, except Kitchin, who might lawfully exercise the functions of his office or who could with any assurance transmit the succession.

The archiepiscopal see of Canterbury, the highest in England, being vacant by the death of Cardinal Pole [the papal legate sent to England to restore episcopal succession],[389] it was of prime importance that it should be filled as soon as possible by one in harmony with the new order of things in Church and State. For this purpose Queen Elizabeth, according to her royal prerogative, issued a mandate, September 9, 1559, to four of the Roman Catholic bishops, Tonstal of Durham, Bourne of Bath and Wells, Poole of Peterborough, Kitchin of Llandaff, and to Doctors in Divinity Barlow and Scory, who had been ejected from their sees in Mary's reign, commanding them to consecrate Matthew Parker, who was a professor of sacred theology, Archbishop of Canterbury. The Roman bishops refused to obey the mandate. They recognized neither the spiritual authority of the queen nor the episcopal character of Barlow and Scory.

The attempt to link by royal authority the new hierarchy on to the old proved an embarrassing failure. But the failure to establish with becoming dignity some sort of a hierarchy was not the worst

---

[389] In *Saepius Officio,* the 1897 official response of the Anglican archbishops to Leo XIII's *On the Nullity of Anglican Orders* of 1896, there is the stunning admission that neither Rome nor Canterbury is quite certain what actions Pole actually took to continue episcopal succession in England: "VI. As regards the practice of the Roman Court and Legate in the XVIth century, although the Pope writes at some length, we believe that he is really as uncertain as ourselves."

evil, if evil it was, that shadowed the doubtful birth of that episcopal system which, forgetting its plebeian origin, began in the next reign to assert for itself a divine parentage. By separating from the ancient Church — the treasury of mystical grace — apostolical succession, if there was ever such a thing in the universe, was now made impossible to the new born Church established by act of Parliament. For, although the newly constituted Church might have consecrated ministers and bishops, yet these servants of the crown could not, on modern Anglican principals, be in possession of the succession, since they had severed themselves in matters of faith and practice from that Church which had given them authority and in which they acknowledged the grace and fact of apostolical succession alone to reside. Otherwise, the Arian, Donatist, and Eutychian bishops, validly ordained, but all rejected as heretical, would also be in the succession — an absurd doctrine, rejected alike by Romanist and Anglican.

The failure of this commission resulted in the issuance of another mandate, dated December 6, 1559: *Elizabeth, by the grace of God, of England, France, and Ireland queen, defender of the faith, etc., to the Reverend Fathers in Christ, Anthony, Bishop of Llandaff, William Barlow, sometime Bishop of Bath, now elect of Chichester, John Scory, sometime Bishop of Chichester, now elect of Hereford, Miles Coverdale, sometime Bishop of Exeter, John, Suffragan of Bedford, John, Suffragan of Thetford, John Bale, Bishop of Ossory,* [commanding them to consecrate Matthew Parker Archbishop of Canterbury] *according to the form of the statutes in this behalf set forth and provided; supplying, nevertheless, by our supreme royal authority, of our mere motion and certain knowledge, whatever (either in the things to be done by you, your condition, state, or power for the performance of the premises) may or shall be wanting of those things which, either by the statutes of this realm or by the ecclesiastical laws, are required or are necessary on this behalf, the state of the times and the exigency of affairs rendering it necessary.*

Matthew Parker Archbishop of Canterbury

In obedience to this mandate Matthew Parker, it is said, was consecrated Archbishop of Canterbury in the chapel at Lambeth House, December 17, 1559, by the persons named, except Kitchin, Bishop of Llandaff, Bale, and the Suffragan of Thetford.

Such were the events leading up to, and such were the means by which, the Anglican hierarchy was established. It originated as we see in the civil power, and on that power was and is dependent for its continuance. "It drew its life from Elizabeth's throne," says the historian Froude,[390] "and had Elizabeth fallen it would have crumbled into sand . . . The image in its outward aspect could be made to correspond with the parent tree; and to sustain the illusion that it was necessary to provide bishops who could appear to have inherited their powers by the approved method as successors of the apostles."

Cooke includes an amusing footnote in which Cecil, the queen's own secretary, points with frustration to the impossibility of this situation:

Before this mandate was issued there was no little embarrassment how to proceed. Among the state papers of the time is a letter from Parker to Cecil, Elizabeth's secretary, on the margin of which Cecil made some notes. One refers to Edward's Ordinal; and Cecil writes, "This is not established by Parliament." The other relates to the consecration. Cecil notes, "There is no

---

[390] James Anthony Froude, 1818-1894, English historian, biographer, and founder of the Oxford Movement.

archbishop nor III bishops now to be had; wherefore *quarendum* [by what means]?"[391]

By what means, indeed? Anglicanism's fealty to historic episcopal succession has been historically thrice interrupted and/or discontinued. The first instance was Henry VIII's break with the Roman bailiwick, which as Cooke shows, already ended it then and there. In the second instance, Elizabeth reversed Mary's reinstitution of papal jurisdiction, and in the third, the Church of England completely suppressed historical episcopacy during the Commonwealth period (1649-1660), before reintroducing it after the Interregnum.[392]

In parallel, Sweden's claim to legitimate historical episcopal succession, (hailed by ecumenists today as the "evangelical model"), ended even before England's did, when Gustavus Vasa (King Gustav I) nationalized the Catholic church at the 1527 Diet of Westerås, placing all bishops' appointments under the jurisdiction of the crown,[393] not the pope, the example Henry VIII later followed. Todd Nichol, the sole dissenting author of CCM, notes the precise consecrative episcopal break in the Swedish succession:

> When Gustavus Vasa assumed the Swedish throne in 1523, five sees stood vacant. He sought to fill these in approved canonical fashion and succeeded in the case of Petrus Magni, who was consecrated with papal approval in Rome in 1524. In 1528 Petrus Magni consecrated three bishops, and in 1531 Laurentius Petri was consecrated archbishop (possibly by Petrus Magni). Petri

---

391 R. J. Cooke, *The Historic Episcopate: A Study of Anglican Claims and Methodist Orders,* (New York: Eaton & Mains; Cincinnati: Curts & Jennings, 1896), 29-33.

392 Cf. *Toward Full Communion and Concordat of Agreement,* Lutheran-Episcopal Dialogue, Series III, ed. William A. Norgren and William G. Rusch (Minneapolis: Augsburg Fortress, 1991), 59-62. Hereafter: *LED III.*

393 Cf. Karl Heussi, *Kompendium der Kirchengeschichte,* (Tübingen: Verlag von J.C.B. Mohr (Paul Siebeck), §84, *q.*

performed a final consecration in 1536. Continuity of the inherited order was breached when the king called on two Germans, Conrad von Pyhy and George Norman, to reorganize the Swedish church on the continental model. After their arrival, superintendents were appointed by the king and installed by other ecclesiastics. During this transitional period it seems that the consecrations of Michael Agricola and Paulus Juusten for sees in Finland by Botvid Sunesson of Strängnäs were regarded as valid episcopal consecrations. Some continuity was restored in Sweden with the appointment of Laurentius Petri Gotha as archbishop in 1575. Among the participants in the consecration was Juusten. Scholarly opinion is divided over whether an episcopal *successio personalis* survived in the Swedish church during this period. But it is certain that the prevailing Lutheran pattern eventually established itself in Sweden. For the most part the term "bishop" was discarded, superintendents were charged with duties of oversight, and pastors as well as bishops conducted ordinations. That these things are not reflected in the present episcopal regime in the Church of Sweden is the result of developments in the nineteenth century.[394]

Ten years after Sweden nationalized the Catholic church, Bugenhagen, at the invitation of King Christian III, ended the historic succession of Denmark, Norway, and Iceland, possessions of the Danish crown, by installing seven new bishops on September 2, 1537, (a move hardly in keeping with the reformers' supposed "deep desire to maintain the church polity and various ranks of the ecclesiastical hierarchy" just seven years after Augsburg).[395]

---

[394] Todd Nichol, *Episcopacy, Lutheran-United Methodist Dialogue II,* Edited by Jack M. Tuell and Roger W. Fjeld, (Minneapolis: Augsburg, 1991), 49-50.

[395] Cf. LED III, §35. The reformers included the nobility.

The Myth of CCM

Everyone is entitled to his own opinion, but not to his own facts.

Daniel Patrick Moynihan

In 1999 the Evangelical Lutheran Church in America and the Episcopal Church USA signed the concordat, *Called to Common Mission,* by which the ELCA "adopted" Anglicanism's faux "historical episcopacy," that is, church governance by bishops. For many American Lutherans who had desired a fuller communion with the Episcopal Church at the beginning of the new millennium, but had confessional reservations about adopting "episcopal succession," there was the comforting reassurance offered them in CCM's §11: "In the Lutheran Confessions, Article 14 of the *Apology* refers to this episcopal pattern by the phrase, 'the ecclesiastical and canonical polity' which it is 'our deep desire to maintain.'"

Whatever one might have thought of CCM, few tended to doubt its threefold assumption that the *Apology* itself seems to endorse a return to historical episcopacy, that this was the "deep desire" of the reformers, and that they were only prevented from doing so by the cruelty of the bishops. Therefore, proponents of CCM reasoned, it is time for Lutherans to fulfill the original wishes of Luther, Melanchthon, Jonas, et al. Indeed, grave warnings were issued from high places just prior to the vote of the church-wide assembly against questioning the confessional interpretations of the ELCA already embodied in the *Concordat of Agreement,* CCM's predecessor document.

Writing for *The Lutheran Forum* in the Spring of 1999, Dr. Harding Meyer, of the Institute for Ecumenical Research of the Lutheran World Federation, stated:

> The new CCM as well as the original *Concordat* make it perfectly clear that a Lutheran decision in favor of CCM would correspond to the convictions of the Lutheran Reformation and not betray them. The concern that

hierarchical structures are being elevated over the Gospel is unfounded . . . Article XIV of the *Apology* so strongly affirms . . . the "deep desire" of the Lutheran Reformation to maintain the ancient canonical order of the Church,[396] whoever justifies his or her rejection of the *Concordat* or CCM with the argument that it is in conflict with the Lutheran Confessions is himself or herself in conflict with them.

Meyer's assertion is a repeat of Piepkorn's thirty years earlier, to wit: "Although the hierarchical structuring of the church is of human right only, the symbolical books affirm their preference for episcopal polity (Ap 14, 1.5)." [397]

Similar pre and post CCM commentaries follow, beginning with its chief architect, Michael J. Root:[398] "Some opponents of CCM are insisting that the ELCA will violate its commitment to the Lutheran Confessions if it adopts CCM. For at least some of us who support it, the issue is precisely the reverse. On the issue of ministry, the Confessions call us to embrace the opportunity CCM offers."[399]

Carl E. Braaten, director of the Center for Catholic and Evangelical Theology: "The folks linked to the Word Alone

---

[396] Luther publicly burned the canon law in Wittenberg on December 10, 1520, two articles of which, 14 & 19, are about the canonical order of the Church. Cf. *WA* 7.171-172.

[397] Piepkorn, 110.

[398] Root left the E.L.C.A. in 2010 to become a Roman Catholic.

[399] *dialog: A Journal of Theology,* 38, no. 2 [Spring 1999], 86-87. Root's false claims with regard to *CCM* and the Confessions are well documented by Kittelson and Menacher, the latter noting, "In his article 'Bishops, the Concordat, and the Augsburg Confession' in *Inhabiting Unity* (Grand Rapids: Eerdmans, 1995) p.50, Root writes, 'Episcopal succession in general was not a theme at Augsburg. The issue was more narrowly the status and authority of the Catholic bishops.' That being the case, how did Root manage to help write in *CCM* paragraph 11 that Apology 14 has the Reformers at Augsburg talking of 'episcopal succession' when it was not a theme?" ("Root and Concordat," ccmverax@topica.com, 10 Feb. 2002).

Network[400] claim that the adoption of the episcopal office in apostolic succession would contradict the Lutheran Confessions. If this were the case, why did the primary authors of the confessions — Luther and Melanchthon — express their 'deep desire' to retain the episcopal office? Why did they call it 'good and useful?' The fact is that they saw no contradiction, nor do the majority of Lutheran theologians around the world and most of the seminary faculties of the ELCA."[401]

Robert Jenson, a co-founder of the Center swooned ordination is an "efficacious sign," a "sacrament," which imparts an "indelible character." He called the historic episcopate an "irreversible development," insisting "the divine right of the episcopate cannot be challenged by any principle of the Reformation."[402]

A 1999 ELCA informational brochure entitled *Called to Common Mission: Questions & Answers* asked: "Do the Lutheran Confessions reject the historic episcopate for Lutherans? Nowhere do the Lutheran Confessions reject the historic episcopate. In fact, the *Augsburg Confession* (Article 28) expresses the desire to maintain the traditional ecclesiastical and canonical polity (see paragraph 11 of *Called to Common Mission*)."

David S. Yeago, Lutheran Theological Southern Seminary: "We must say no to polemics, which claim to represent true Lutheranism, but obscure the clear endorsement in our Confessions of that body of practice now called the historic episcopate as a bond of communion between the Churches"[403]

---

400 WordAlone, an early opposition group to CCM within the ELCA, was ill equipped to address the theological and historical issues related to CCM. Ostensibly opposed for confessional reasons, the group quickly became mired in issues of law (gay ordination, church governance, "culture wars," etc.) and faded away.

401 *dialog:* 39, no. 3 [Fall 2000], 218.

402 Robert Jenson, *Unbaptized God,* [Minneapolis: Fortress, 1992], 50, 61,70-71.

403 David S. Yeago, *Lutheran Forum,* "Gospel and Church: Twelve Articles of Theological Principal Amid the Present Conflict in the

Bruce D. Marshal, SMU/Perkins School of Theology: "Yet the Confessions bind Lutherans in perpetuity to a 'supreme desire' for bishops of the traditional kind, historic succession and all."[404]

The 10th Round of U.S. Lutheran-Roman Catholic Dialogue declared: "Regarding 'the order of the church and the various ranks in the church' including bishops, the Apology of the Augsburg Confession testifies that the 'greatest desire' of the Reformers was to retain this ministerial structure. This desire in the Lutheran Confessions still is normative for present day Lutheranism."[405]

The editors of *Lutheran Forum* magazine: "So why are we editors, past and present, willing to endorse *Called to Common Mission*? Because the revised *Concordat* is not contrary to the scriptures, or Creeds, or our Lutheran Confessions."[406]

All such hierarchical histrionics aside, none of the above authors cite any primary sources to back up their claims. Indeed, as we have already seen, much of what is passed off as "confessional research" in American Lutheranism is based on little more than a reliance on secondary translations of original documents, some of which are notoriously unreliable. Yet entire ecumenical agreements are consummated by the ELCA using such questionable sources. CCM and the *Concordat of Agreement* are two such inept compacts. Both rely on the English of Theodore Tappert's *Book of Concord,* (which is a partial translation of the original texts found in the BSLK), and the findings of the *Lutheran-Episcopal Dialogue Series*

ELCA," 34, no. 1 [Spring 2000], 21-22. Yeago now teaches at the Institute of Lutheran Theology (ILT) in Brookings, South Dakota.

[404] Bruce D. Marshal, *Lutheran Forum,* "Can Lutherans Have Episcopal Bishops? Reflections on a Refusal of Communion," [Easter 1998], 36. Marshal left the E.L.C.A. in 2010 to become a Roman Catholic.

[405] *The Church as Koinonia of Salvation: Its Structures and Ministries* — Common Statement of the Tenth Round of the U.S. Lutheran-Roman Catholic Dialogue [2004], 111.

[406] *Lutheran Forum,* [Spring 1999], 8., signed by Ronald Bagnall, Leonard Klein, Paul Hinckly, and Glenn Stone.

(LED) of 1988 and 1991, which are equally devoid of original sources.

LED III, for instance, relies on H. George Anderson's English translation of Maurer's, *Historical Commentary on the Augsburg Confession,* "the most thorough and exhaustive discussion of the historical circumstances surrounding the *Augsburg Confession,* including the attitudes and intentions of Martin Luther and Philip Melanchthon." LED concludes that, "On the basis of the historical perspective provided by Wilhelm Maurer it is evident that the Lutheran confessional documents of the 16th century, normative for the Evangelical Lutheran Church in America, endorse the historic episcopate in principal." All further queries on the subject are then referred back not to Maurer's two volumes, but to Piepkorn's little tract from the 1960s: "It is not necessary here to present a full doctrine on ministry in the Lutheran Confessions. For such a full doctrine see Arthur Carl Piepkorn, 'The Sacred Ministry and Holy Ordination in the Symbolical Books of the Lutheran Church,' in *Eucharist and Ministry,* Lutherans and Catholics in Dialogue IV (1970), pp. 101-119."[407]

But as is the case in Root's lead up to CCM, LED merely uses Maurer out of context to reinforce its predetermined conclusions and ignores him where he disagrees. To create the illusion of Luther as a big supporter and reinforcer of historical episcopacy, for example, it quotes Maurer's reference to churches having the right to ordain, but tempers it with:

> However, says Maurer, "the emergency situation in Bohemia should not lead one to deduce a general rejection of the historic episcopate." Although there were strong tendencies toward secularization of bishoprics on the part of all parties in Germany, "Luther did not simply condemn the late medieval episcopacy."[408]

---

[407] LED III, 45.
[408] *Ibid,* 43.

LED's conclusion? Because Luther didn't condemn it, he endorsed it — another *argumentum ad ignorantiam* for a tea pot on the moon. He didn't condemn it outright for the most obvious of reasons — it was the government. To do so would have been a blatant declaration of war. But he thoroughly condemned it on theological grounds in his *Exhortation to All Clergy Assembled at Augsburg*.[409] Completely disregarded are Maurer's counterweights: "If [Luther's *Sermon on Keeping Children in School,* issued at the height of the Augsburg negotiations] is to be seen as a response to CA 28, it proves how far Luther had distanced himself from the historic episcopacy and how little he counted on the practical implementations of a compromise;"[410] or "Melanchthon himself stated that he did not want to burden the church with episcopal control again in CA 28 even if he granted them a right by human law (*ius humanum*);"[411] or "Luther's indifference to the historic office of bishop is revealed at the end of [*On the Keys*]."[412]

Instead, both LED and Piepkorn rely on a few English texts, thoroughly mixing the two kingdoms under an all-inclusive ubiquitous heading of "historic episcopate" while ignoring Maurer's conclusion: "More clearly than before, Luther, influenced by Augsburg and post-Augsburg 1530, placed the doctrine of the two authorities in the perspective of suffering obedience."

In other words, the Lutherans were willing to suffer under the historic episcopate of "wolves and our enemies," and "wicked rogues," strictly for the sake of the avoidance of war, "because they still possess the office and sit in the place of the apostles."[413] That's hardly a "deep desire" for or ringing endorsement of historical episcopacy, so much as it is the acknowledgment of an occupation force of worldly

---

[409] Cf. *WA* 30.
[410] Maurer, 74.
[411] *Ibid,* 77.
[412] *Ibid,* 79.
[413] *Ibid,* 80.

161

ecclesiasts, or as Luther put it, "a wicked tyrant is more tolerable than a wicked war" (*Ja, ein böser Tyrann ist leydlicher denn ein böser krieg*).[414]

But not to worry. Where Luther doesn't agree with LED, he too is simply dismissed: "Studies of Martin Luther's understanding of ministry abound, sometimes with emphasis on and interpretations of his antipathy to bishops at certain times in his life. But his views have official standing in the Evangelical Lutheran Church in America only in those writings of his which were taken up into the *Book of Concord*."[415] Yet the same *BoC* states in the *Formula of Concord's* affirmation:

> Since Dr. Luther is rightly to be regarded as the most eminent teacher of the churches which adhere to the Augsburg Confession and as the person whose entire doctrine in sum and content was comprehended in the articles of the aforementioned Augsburg Confession and delivered to the Emperor Charles V, therefore the true meaning and intention of the Augsburg Confession cannot be derived more correctly or better from any other sources than from Dr. Luther's doctrinal and polemical writings.[416]

In the end, LED's cherry picking of Luther and Maurer leads it to some very confused and contradictory conclusions, sometimes occuring in the same paragraph:

> It is clear from these extensive citations [TPPP 12-13, 60-66], that during the "confessional phase" (1528-1537) of the reforming movement, before they were separated evangelical churches no longer under the jurisdiction of Rome, there are *consistent statements of commitment* to the church's traditional polity, which *includes both the historic episcopate* and "ranks" in the hierarchy . . . It must be stressed that for the Lutheran confessional tradition, *historical succession* of laying-on-of-hands in the ministerial office *was not theologically primary*.[417]

---

414 *WA* 19.637.
415 LED III, 50.
416 *BSLK* 984-985; *Tappert*, 576.
417 LED III, 53.

But which is it? How can one have both a "consistent commitment" and non-commitment to the tradition of theological primacy (*esse*) historical episcopacy claims for itself? Here we see the early formulation of CCM's schizoid reasoning that the historic episcopate is not necessary though it is necessary, a full decade before its promotion and passage in the ELCA.

The German Text

In Tappert, the *Augsburg Confession* is translated from the Latin and the German — but strangely the *Apology*, translated by Jaroslav Pelikan,[418] is only from the Latin. It's the same thing in the *Triglotta* and the Kolb/Wengert *BC 2000*, the latter misleadingly stating that, "Because Jonas's translation in large measure follows the [Latin] octavo edition, readers will now have a text of the Apology that for the most part corresponds to the text used in the 1580 German Book of Concord."[419] (Instead of Jonas's German translation, however, the reader is given an English translation of the Latin, even though the German contains some major differences, most importantly as we will see in Ap 14).

In his 1959 introduction, Pelikan offered a rather bizarre rationale for not including the German text by claiming it is "a very free translation which has been called a 'pious paraphrase,'"[420] a statement which is itself a pious paraphrase of the BSLK's critical apparatus: *Sie ist aber auch sonst mehr eine freie Bearbeitung* ("But it is otherwise a freer revision [of the Latin])."[421] Pelikan appears to have misunderstood the

---

[418] Pelikan, a Lutheran pastor, whose father and grandfather were Lutheran pastors, left the E.L.C.A. in 1998 to become a member of the Orthodox Church in America.

[419] *BC 2000*, 109.

[420] Tappert 98.

[421] *BSLK* XXIII.

note by assuming it meant the German is thus somehow of lesser value than the Latin. The BSLK goes on to explain, however, that the German is "freer" insofar as it eliminates a number of quotations from the ancients, (which Jonas and Melanchthon obviously felt were unnecessary). This hardly makes it "a pious paraphrase," a very shortsighted assumption that is contrary to history and the authoritative status the BSLK gives the German. Tappert's accolades for the German CA as "critically superior," "typographically incomparable," and "more official" than the Latin, are equally applicable to the Ap, and perhaps even more so, given Melanchthon's high praise of Jonas's translation, which he himself participated in. Indeed, the 1533 *Apology* was in parts strongly reworded and "sharpened" (*verschärft*), and is the version on which all subsequent versions depend.[422]

Whether as a result of Pelikan's statement, or an assumption on the part of the CCM drafters that the Latin is somehow more authoritative than the German, Pelikan's English translation appears to have simply been accepted at face value. The result is an astonishing lack of scholarship on the part of the authors of an ecumenical document that has such far reaching and widespread ecclesiastical ramifications. No mention is ever made of the German text, for instance, in either the *Concordat* or CCM, nor is it ever referenced in any of the statements issued by the various ELCA seminary faculties prior to the deciding vote of the 1999 church-wide assembly.[423] At a minimum, by virtue of the fact that the German and Latin appear side by side in the BSLK (and *Triglotta*), both texts are equally authoritative. Yet there is no evidence that either of the originals was consulted, much less that the German text was paid any heed at all, an English

---

422 Tappert 24. Cf. *BSLK, 2 Übersetzung und Drucke.* XXIII.

423 Luther Seminary, Lutheran Theological Seminary at Gettysburg, Lutheran Theological Southern Seminary, Trinity Lutheran Seminary, and Wartburg Seminary all issued official statements. Of these five, four mentioned the Lutheran Confessions only in passing, and LTSS didn't mention them at all.

translation of the Latin being the only one that was ever looked at. How is one to take such a document seriously when, as Tappert declares in his foreword, "Serious students of the Lutheran Confessions will continue to consult the original Latin and German texts on which the present translations are based"? Perhaps the prevailing assumption of the drafters and faculties was the same as Wengert's: "The German version offers only a modicum of assistance."[424]

Tappert was correct to characterize the German text of the *Augsburg Confession* as "more official." Both the Latin and German texts were made available in Augsburg in 1530, but for reasons of clarity, as well as power politics, it was the German confession (*das deutsche Bekenntnis*) that was read aloud and handed to Emperor Charles V, (though he wished for the Latin to be read). The Elector of Saxony insisted on it, noting they were now assembled on German, not Roman soil. Two months later, the Chancellor of Electoral Saxony, Gregor Brück, again chose to address the emperor and his brother in German before handing them a copy of the *Apology*. These actions placed the emphasis on the German text from day one, bold moves indeed, given that the reformers knew the Spanish emperor spoke nary a word of German.[425]

But why would the evangelicals risk an imperial slight over the language? Because at the Diet of Augsburg, the reformers' appeal, like Luther's a decade earlier, was to the Christian nobility of the German nation, and not to the Holy Roman Empire per se.[426] Luther had used a similar tactic in 1520 to

---

[424] Wengert 41.

[425] It is a modern myth that Charles V fell asleep during the reading of the *Augsburg Confession.* Eyewitness accounts attest to his attentiveness. Cf. Robert Stupperich, *Die Reformation in Deutschland,* DTV, 1972, 94.

[426] The term "Heiliges Römisches Reich Deutscher Nation" was not in use until the 15th century and at the time of the Reformation referred exclusively to the German part of the Imperium. Cf. Karl Heussi, *Kompendium der Kirchengeschichte,* Tübingen, Mohr, 1971, 180. One of the earliest editions of *An den christlichen Adel*

signal severance from Rome when he wrote *The Freedom of a Christian*, *(Tractatus de libertate christiana)*.[427] He addressed it, along with an open letter *(ein offener Brief)*, to Pope Leo X, publishing it not only in Latin, but also for a much wider audience in German, a language he knew Leo didn't know, (while Elector Frederick the Wise knew very little Latin).[428] In Augsburg it was not a general confession the reformers were handing the emperor, but a location-specific one, a "Saxon credo" *(Sächsiche Confession)*, one that Melanchthon allowed only at the last minute to be signed by a broader representation of evangelicals.[429]

But politics wasn't the only factor at play here. So was the importance of clarity. Luther had set the trend the summer before when he wrote to the pope in German, at the Leipzig Debate against Johannes Eck in 1519. Then his appeal, as it would be in Augsburg, was to the German princes (Luther being one of the original authors, or *Verfasser*, of the *Augsburg Confession*, along with Melanchthon, Spalatin, Jonas, and Agricola). Heiko Oberman writes in his book, *Luther, Man Between God and the Devil*:

> On the afternoon of July 5 Luther could no longer contain himself. Violating all the rules of disputation, he interrupted Eck

---

deutscher Nation von des christlichen Standes Besserung, 1520, inserted the words *Teutscher Adel* (German Nobility) before the title. Cf. *WA* 6. 399.

[427] *WA* 7.20-38.

[428] Cf. Walch 15.783; 19.986ff. Cf. Michael Mullet, *Martin Luther*, (London, New York: Routledge, 2004), 115.

[429] Cf. *BSLK* XVII. It was still regarded as a Saxon credo on February 24, 1537, when the *Augsburg Confession*, the *Apology*, and Melanchthon's *Treatise on the Power and Primacy of the Pope* were signed in Schmalkalden: *"Also haben etliche suscribiertt, etliche nitt, doch den gestellten artickell vom gewalt des Bapsts sampt der Sachsischen Confession, vnd apologi habben alle predicanten ainhellig vnderschriben."* Hanz Voltz, ed., *Urkunden und Aktenstücke zur Geschichte von Martin Luthers Schmalkaldischen Artikeln (1536-1574)*, (Berlin, Gruzter, 1957), 173-174.

twice. The next morning at seven, he could bear no more of Eck's barbs [that Luther was a "Bohemian heretic"] and spontaneously changed over to the German language to demonstrate to non-theologians that his rights had been infringed. In subsequent years laymen would preside over Reformation disputations from the start: the search for truth was too important to leave to academic theologians.[430]

Eck vs. Luther at the 1519 Leipzig Debate

In the same way, the *Augsburg Confession* was about rights and about truth, and its appeal was to the laity, to German princes, not academic theologians.

Two years after Luther's old foe, Duke George, died in 1539, all evangelical pastors in Saxony were required to purchase, learn, and teach from the German *Apology* as a matter of "top priority" (*vornemlichen keuffenn sollen*). The requirement wasn't simply a matter of German books for German people, (as a reviewer for *Lutheran Quarterly* once

---

[430] Heiko Oberman, *Luther, Man Between God and the Devil*, (New York: Image Books, Doubleday, 1992), 299-300.

167

wrote to me), but constituted an illegal act in defiance of the Imperial Edict's demand for a return to the *status quo ante,* including a return to the Latin liturgy. Even the local choir boys were required to sing in Latin only. Yet on October 18, 1542, Johann Pfeffinger, the Superintendent of Leipzig, who was a student of Melanchthon's, as well as a friend of Luther and Bugenhagen, and who taught in the Schönburg region of Germany, issued a catalogue "of spiritual books for the churches which must be purchased" (*was man an geistlichen Büchern für die Kirchen anschaffen und müsse*). While the Bible could be either in Latin or German, the *Augsburg Confession,* the *Apology,* and Melanchthon's *Locos communes,* must be (*müsse*) in German, and to quote Hüttel, "the Reformation began on that very day in the Schönburg region."[431] The order of Pfeffinger's cover page follows:

In the Cities

Bible: Latin & *Teütsch*   *Locos communes: Teütsch*
                    CA & Ap: *Teütsch*

In the Castles

Bible: Latin & *Teütsch*   Two Books of Psalms: *Teütsch*
                    CA & Ap: *Teütsch*

---

431 Walter Hüttel, "Zur Geschichte der Reformation im Schönburgischen in Herbergen der Christenheit," *Jahrbuch für deutschen Kirchengeschichte* 1987-88, ed. Karlhein Blaschke, (Berlin: Ev. Verlangsanstalt), 67.

Cf. Andreas Baudler, "Die 'Theodore Baudler Collection' in den USA," 111: "Aus dieser Ansammlung von Visitationsakten ragt besonders die so genannte *Gnandsteiner Gottesdienstordnung* vom 25. April 1540 hervor, in der u.a. geregelt war, dass die Pfarrer verpflichtet seien, wichtige evangelische Bücher sebst zu kauffen und zu lesen. An der Spitze der Visitationskommission befand sich erneut Spalatin, aber auch Heinrich und Abraham von Einsiedel waren als Kommissare d.h. Finanzinspektoren eingebunden."

Bible: *alles Teütsch*   *Locos communes: Teütsch*
                    CA & Ap: *Teütsch*

It was "the German original" — not the Latin *Augsburg Confession* — that Dr. Eck requested for study in preparation for the 1540 debate in Worms, and again for the Council of Trent, a clear indicator of the *gravitas* given it by the Roman Church. [432] When the *Book of Concord* was officially published in Leipzig in 1580 it was in German only — the Latin version only following after another four years.[433] Even though an unofficial Latin *BoC* did appear the same year, it was, as the publisher assured the reader, a translation "from the German." After Melanchthon's death in 1560, the first collection of his teachings, known as the *Corpus Philippicum,* containing both the CA and Ap, appeared first in German — and a year later in Latin. And where there were questions regarding the accuracy of the Latin text, the Latin itself referred readers back to the German original, e.g., in Ap 2, as Tappert renders it, "But to show all good men that our teaching on this point is not absurd, we ask them first to look at the German text of the Confession (*deutsche Confession ansehen/inspiciatur germanica confessio*)." [434] Additionally, the English translation of the *Augsburg Confession* and *Apology* at the court of Henry VIII, published in London in 1536 by R. Taverner, bore the title *The Confessyon of the Fayth of the Germanyes,* indicating the documents were

---

[432] *BSLK* XVIII.

[433] *Ibid,* XVII (*Corpus Reformatorum* 2, 105): *"so ist der im Latein noch garnicht gemacht."* The German was published by Hans Steinmann of Leipzig and bore the Latin title *Concordia, Pia et unanimi consensu repetita Confessio Fidei et doctrinae . . .* Cf. *Bekenntnis und Kirchenheit, 400 Jahre Konkordienformel,* (Nürnberg: Landeskirchliches Archiv, 1977), 58.

[434] *BSLK* 146; Tappert, 100.

regarded first and foremost as German products.[435]

Luther, who was not entirely satisfied with Melanchthon's April/May 1531 Latin text, pressed for the quick distribution of *eine deutsche Apologie,* and even considered writing it himself.[436] While the evangelical camp greeted this prospect enthusiastically, in the end the task was given to Justus Jonas.

Justus Jonas

To the latter's undoubted exasperation, Melanchthon, who regarded the *Apology* as his *Privatarbeit,* (private work), constantly fiddled with the text, making several revisions in the Latin from April to September 1531, with a few insignificant changes occurring as late as 1533. Even Luther, at one point, acknowledged that Melanchthon "would never

---

435 The title "Defender of the Faith," accorded British monarchs, was first awarded to Henry VIII by Pope Leo X, in June 1521, for his attack on Luther in *Assertio Septem Sacramentorum.* In it he referred to Luther as "a wolf of hell . . . limb of Satan . . . How rotten is his mind!" Cf. Mullet,143-145. Cf. Erwin L. Lueker, ed., *Lutheran Cyclopedia,* (St. Louis, Concordia, 1975), 500.

436 Cf. Theodor Kolde, "Augsburger Bekenntnis," *Realencyklopedie für protestantische Theologie und Kirche,* (Leipzig: Hinrichs, 1897), 248, 58-60.

have published his *Apology* if he hadn't been forced to."[437]

Far from being a mere translator, as many American Lutherans have apparently come to assume, Justus Jonas was one of the most brilliant minds of the Reformation, a star pupil of Erasmus, president of the University of Erfurt, and one of the original authors of the *Augsburg Confession*. It is even significant that the German *Apology* doesn't refer to itself as having been "translated" (*übersetzt*) from the Latin, but "put into German," (*aus dem Latein verdeudschet*), a subtle (and untranslatable) distinction, meaning one that is *non verbatim*.

In close cooperation with Luther, Melanchthon, and other Wittenberg theologians, Jonas worked synoptically with the *Editio princeps* and *Octavo* edition of the Latin text to produce the German, which was printed in the Autumn of 1531. The result was a German text of the *Apology* that was so superb, it was given official status along with the German CA already at the Diet of Schweinfurt in 1532, a full five years before Schmalkalden. There the decision was made to position it right next to the CA as its "defense and erudition," (*als eine Schutzrede und Erklärung der Konfession*). That occurred, as Theodor Kolde points out, because the laity of the *Gemeinden* — and not the princes — insisted on it. In fact, subscription to the German *Apology* quickly became the condition for joining the Smalcaldic League.[438] Fifty years later the Lutheran church would call for a return "to the edition of 1531 . . . as having full and primary authority . . . the true *Augsburg Confession*, as it was presented to Emperor Charles in 1530. It is the version that should always be cited. All our churches subscribed to this edition in 1537."[439] Unfortunately English

---

[437] The quote is from Konrad Cordatus, who lived in Luther's house from July 1531 to 1532. He wrote, *"Philippus hätte nie die Apologie geschrieben wenn er nicht gezwungen worden wäre, er hätts immer besser machen wollen."* Walch, *Tischreden*, 636.11.

[438] Kolde, 249, 1-12.

[439] *De Controversiis quibusdam, quae superiori tempore circa quosdam Augustanae Confessionis articulos motae et agitatae Iudicium d. Martini Chemnitii, ed.* Polycarp Leser, Wittenberg, 1594, *Sources and Contexts of the Book of Concord*, Robert Kolb and

speaking audiences have been without a reliable translation of the German *Apology* to the present day.

Besides exhibiting an irrational preference for the Latin, Pelikan (like Kolb/Wengert) apparently failed to take into account the fast moving geo-political events on the ground between the Spring and Fall of 1531 that resulted in the profound changes in the German text. He completely ignores the fact that Melanchthon himself edited Jonas's German just prior to its publication, and that he was so pleased with the final copy that he pronounced it to be "in need of no improvement" (*nicht der Verbesserung bedürftig*).[440] What Pelikan dismissed as "variants in the German version" are not simply variants; they are the original text of the *Editio princeps* of 1531, written by an original author of the CA, personally edited and highly acclaimed by both Melanchthon and Luther, officially adopted in Schweinfurt in 1532, signed by the confessors in Schmalkalden in 1537, incorporated into the Lutheran Confessions of the *Book of Concord* of 1580, and returned to after Melanchthon's *Confessio Augustana Variata* had wandered too far from the original confession.[441]

James A. Nestingen, eds., (Minneapolis: Fortress Press, 2001), 202-203. What the theologians at Schmalkalden actually signed was Jonas's October 1531 *"verbesserte Apologie"* (improved Apology), which is also the one in the 1580 Book of Concord, (and not an earlier October 1530 German Apology). The somewhat misleading language comes from Luther's student, Johann Aurifaber, who in 1565 reported that the theologians had signed "the Augsburg Confession and Apology as handed over to Emperor Charles at the Diet of Augsburg in 1530," (*die Augsburgische Confession vnd Apologia so Keiser Carol Anno zu Augsburg auff dem Reichstag vberantwortet.*) Cf. *BSLK*, p. XXIII.
[440] *CR II*, 542.
[441] Cf. Christian Peters, *Apologia Confessionis Augustanae*, "Untersuchungen zur Textgeschichte einer lutherischen Bekenntnisschrift (1530-1584)," (Calver Verlag Stuttgart, 1997), 194: ["Die deutsche *Oktavausgabe* von 1533] ist es auch, die anläßlich des Tages von Schmalkalden (Februar 1537) zum

verbindlichen Paralleltext der lateinischen *Oktavausgabe* vom September 1531 erhoben wird." Peters's source is *CR* 26, 699f. The signatures of the thirty three evangelical theologians at Schmalkalden in February 1537 appear not on the texts themselves, but on separate sheets (Cf. *Unterschriften in Weimar* LKA Reg H 124, Blatt 40a-41a).

Chapter 7

The Myth of Apology 14

It is therefore quite impossible to enter into any kind of intelligent discussion on the meaning of Article 14, much less incorporate it into an ecumenical document, without consulting the Latin, and most especially the German texts, something the authors of the *Concordat of Agreement* and CCM clearly appear not to have done. Instead, they cut and pasted bits of Tappert together to create CCM's embarrassing §11, which offers a preposterous fictionalized Reformation scenario that never existed. It says:

> "Historic succession" refers to a tradition which goes back to the ancient church in which bishops already in the succession install newly elected bishops with prayer and the laying on of hands . . . In the Lutheran Confessions, Article 14 of the *Apology* refers to this episcopal pattern by the phrase, "the ecclesiastical and canonical polity" which it is "our deep desire to maintain."

By adding the phrase "historic succession" into the mix, (in quotes no less), Martin Marty and his drafting team misled people into believing Ap 14 is discussing episcopal succession.[442] Both proponents and opponents of CCM today

---

[442] The ELCA authors of *CCM* are Martin E. Marty, Michael J. Root, and Todd W. Nichol. The principal ECUSA author is J. Robert Wright. Root, former Dean of Academic Studies at Lutheran Theological Southern Seminary 2000-2009, converted to Roman Catholicism in 2010, offering this departing statement to his faculty: "Over the last year or so, it has become clear to me, not without struggle, that I have become a Catholic in my mind and heart in ways that no longer permit me to present myself as a Lutheran theologian with honesty and integrity." Critics note that he was a theological Catholic long before CCM.

agree that the concept was never on the table in Augsburg, as the *Confutatio,* the Catholic rebuttal to the *Augsburg Confession,* shows. Nor could it have been. The term didn't even exist in 1530, and is not found in any Catholic or evangelical documents until at least a decade later, when it was first used by the Catholic theologian Johannes Groper (1503-1559) somewhere between 1540-42 as a papal invention to counter "irregular" Lutheran calls and ordinations. These were, after all, not only illegal, but also perceived recipes for chaos in the Church, since improperly ordained priests did not possess the "indelible character" (*character indelebilis*) bestowed by a bishop in historical succession, and could therefore not function as proper conduits for the transmittal of sacramental grace, the same argument Rome used against the Bohemians. Ap 14 instead rejects the *Confutatio's* insistence that the phrase "rightly called" (*rite vocatus/recht gebürlich berufen*) be understood as ordination in accordance with canon law (*Corpus iuris canonici*).[443] It is, in fact, an extension of CA 5 (*De ministerio ecclesiastico*), in Tappert "The Office of Ministry," or the "office of preaching" (*das Predigtamt*), which Luther did not regard as "clerical," since the Holy Spirit calls whomever, whenever, and wherever he wishes (*wo und wenn er will*), as the highest calling in Christendom. Service in this office requires a proper call from the congregation (*die Gemeinde*), the *ecclesia particularis,* which is fully church in any given time and place in the unity of the *successio fidelium.*[444]

Ap 14's rejection of canonical ordination is especially remarkable, given that what the evangelical side even meant by "ordination" while in Augsburg, and for much of the Reformation, was a "muddled concept" (*verworrene Begrifflichkeit*)[445] carried into the fourteenth article. And by all

---

443 " . . . it should be understood that 'those rightly called' refers to those called according to the laws and ecclesiastical ordinances that have been observed throughout Christendom." *Confutatio,* Article XIV, Kolb/Nestingen, p. 115.
444 Cf. *WA* 31 I.211.
445 *RGG* IV, 1675.

accounts, Luther appears not to have been in any great hurry to clarify it. Meeting at a theological conference in Wittenberg in 1537, Melanchthon and Spalatin urgently desired to discuss the importance and particulars of the subject, arguing that "it is most important to define how ordinations are to be performed. For all reasonable Christians know that no one should publicly teach without a call. For that reason so much depends on the nature of such a calling. Besides, people need to have respect for those who have been commissioned to teach."[446] But we read in footnote 8 on page 73 of the official minutes *Urkunden und Aktenstücke*, "Luther dealt with neither one of these points in his notes," (*Beide Punkte hatte Luther in seiner Niederschrift nicht behandelt*), while the actual record of the proceedings is even more explicit, listing ordination as one of *The Three Additional Articles Luther Rejected at the Wittenberg Theologians Conference.*[447] Obviously the subject wasn't high on his priority list even seven years after the Diet of Augsburg! As Kittelson once wrote to me, "It was not until 1535 that the Elector John Frederick set out a definite order for the examination, calling, and ordination of candidates, . . . yet the Elector's actual order [*Stadtarchiv Wittenberg* 17 (Bc5), fol. 3], as published in early 1536 or sometime after the decree itself, says not a single word about 'ordination' as such."[448]

When Luther finally did get around to composing a rite — nine years after Augsburg! — "The Ordination of Ministers of

---

[446] *"das aufs hochst von neten sey, wie die Ordination zubestellen sey. Dann alle verstendige Christen wissen, das nyemand on Vocation offentlich leren soll. Derhalben an solcher Vocation mercklich vnd vil gelegen. Dazu mussen die person ein schew haben, das sie in der lere auf andere, so beuelh haben, sehen sollen, etc."* Urkunden und Aktenstücke von Martin Luthers Schmalkaldischen Artikeln (1536-1574), ed. Dr. Hans Volz, (Berlin: Verlag Walter De Gruyter & Co.,1957), 71-73.

[447] *Ibid*, 71: *"7. Die drei von Luther auf der Wittenberger Theologenkonferenz abgelehnten zusätzlichen Artikel - Drey artickel, die anhengig bliben, 1537."*

[448] For more on Luther's lack of concern for a formal ordination rite, see *LW* 53.122-126.

the Word" (*Ordinatio ministrorum verbi*), in which he addresses the candidate as "bishop," his concept remained essentially the same as his suggestion (*Vorschlag*) to the Senate in Prague back in 1523: The *Gemeinde* (church/community) should gather in prayer, choose one or more suitable persons as needed (*auswählen*), confirm their calling through prayer and laying on of hands (*confirmare*), and introduce the ordinand (*commendare*) to the congregation, community, or university, as the case may be.[449] Yet for all of his fervor in seeing to it that his important writings were published in a timely manner, Luther never published this or any other ordination rite.[450]

As Wilhelm Brunotte has shown, for Luther *ordinatio* as a *ritus ecclesiasticus* was the same thing as an *Introduktion*, which was simply the culmination of the longer process of *ordinieren*, which included being called, examined, commissioned, and affirmed (*Erwählen, Prüfen, Beauftragen, Approbation*). What it clearly was not, however, was a consecration. "*Ordinare non est consecrare*," Luther famously declared in his *Winkelmesse*.[451]

He also injected the 1539 Wittenberg rite with bits of irreverent humor. "The ordinator addresses the ordinands in these or similar words: Herein [I Timothy 3] you hear that we bishops — i.e., presbyters and pastors — are called not to watch over geese or cows, but over the congregation God purchased with his own blood . . ."[452] (He also credited himself with having removed "geese, cows, Mohammed, and the wretched atrocities of the Pope," all of which were, of course, edited out of the official books used for ordination.)

A *Bischoff* is "bei Schaff," Luther mused, "by the sheep" with his flock, and the call remains the key. "For to be a pastor one must be not only be a Christian and a priest, but must have

---

[449] This is the same formula described by Tyndale in the Church of England in 1528.

[450] The 1539 rite was nevertheless copied, distributed, and incorporated into numerous church orders.

[451] *WA* 15.721. Cf. BSLK 491 ff. Cf. Brunotte, 182-191.

[452] *WA* 38.427.

an office and a field of work committed to him. This call and command make pastors and preachers. A burgher or layman may be a learned man, but this does not make him a lecturer and entitle him to teach publicly in the schools or to assume the teaching office, unless he is called to it."[453] "I ask the dear tyrants: If bishops are made by the election and call of their own congregation, and if the pope is pope without confirmation by any other authority and by election alone, why should not a Christian congregation, too, make a preacher by its call alone?"[454] And again, "to offer one's service [in the church] is to say, 'I'll be glad to accept it if you can use me in this place.' If he is wanted, it is a true call."[455] To Dorothea Jörger Luther wrote most simply on September 12, 1535, "Whoever is called, is ordained, and should preach to those who have called him; that is our Lord God's ordination and chrism."[456]

That ordination during the Reformation did not have the importance alleged today, is obvious from the histories of such important Lutheran territories as Württemberg. The Church of Württemberg, the second oldest in all of Germany, was quick to embrace the Reformation in 1534 under Duke Ulrich and the Lutheran reformer Erhard Schnepf. It is home to the prestigious Karl-Eberhard Universität in Tübingen, where directly across from the Stiftskirche, Melanchthon lived as a student and lecturer before joining Luther in Wittenberg. (It was also in Tübingen where he was denounced in 1536 by Cordatus, Luther's friend and pastor of Niemeck, for saying works are necessary for salvation). Yet for all of its rich history and prominence in the Reformation, Württemberg never bothered to

---

[453] *Ibid* 31 1.211.

[454] *Ibid* 11.415. Compare Piepkorn's erroneous assertion, "in the mind of the early Lutheran community the mere possession of a call . . . did not authorize the recipient to preside over the eucharistic assembly and pronounce the formula of consecration," 105.

[455] *WATR*, Nr. 483.

[456] *WA Br* 7.271. *Wem gerufen ist, der ist geweihet, und soll predigen denen, die ihn berufen; das ist unseres Herrn Gottes Weihe und rechter Chresem.*

ordain its pastors until 1854 — more than three hundred years after the Diet of Augsburg and Ap 14![457] Yet all of its pastors were obviously regarded as *gebührlich berufen, rite vocatus,* even as the entire Lutheran system in neighboring Saxony was being hierarchically restructured after Luther's death by his nemesis, Elector Moritz. The reformer deeply despised the man, calling him "an evil worm" (*der böse Wurm*), a "Judas" to the Reformation.

A Diminishing Desire

Called to Common Mission makes much ado about the evangelicals' supposed "deep desire to maintain the church polity and various ranks of the ecclesiastical hierarchy," which it simplistically portrays as a desire for episcopalism, a "historic succession" of bishops. How utterly misguided this assumption is, is revealed in a closer examination of Ap 14. The English phrases "ecclesiastical hierarchy," "canonical government," "ecclesiastical and canonical polity," are all rather imprecise. These expressions can easily be misunderstood to be mere matters of "church polity," as if they were applicable and amenable to today's Lutheran congregations, a confusion that emanates from a reliance on English translations rather than the Latin and German texts. The result is the common erroneous conclusion that the phrases "evangelical episcopate" and "canonical polity" are reciprocative, rather than a confusion of kingdoms the reformers knew them to be. Echoing most American Lutheran ecumenists, William H. Lazareth, for example wrote, "The confessors freely declare their preference for a truly evangelical episcopate: 'We want to declare our willingness to keep the

---

[457] Cf. Gustav Bossert, *Die Eigenart der evangelischen Landeskirche Württembergs im Wandel der Zeit,* "Für Volk und Kirche:" Zum 70. Geburtstag von Landesbischof D. Th. Wurm, hg. Ev. Pfarrverein in Württemberg (Stuttgart: Steinkopf, 1938).

179

ecclesiastical and canonical polity, provided that the bishops stop raging against the church' (CA, Ap 14.5)."[458]

Referencing the same passage, Joseph A. Burgess and Jeffrey Gros also concluded, "The emphasis has been added to point to the fact that the churches which accept the doctrinal authority of the *Book of Concord,* as the Evangelical Lutheran Church in America does, are committed in principle to a preference for 'the ecclesiastical and canonical polity' with its 'various ranks of the ecclesiastical hierarchy.'"[459]

George A. Lindbeck went so far as to declare, "The statement of the *Apology* regarding 'our deep desire to maintain the church polity' should be interpreted as an expression of theological principal rather than as a historically outworn response to sixteenth century circumstances."[460]

Jonas and Melanchthon avoided this confusion of tongues by inserting the Latin *terminus technicus, "canonicam politiam"* into the German text in both Ap 14 and 28. *Politia* is derived from the ancient Greek word *polis* ("a walled city"); in Plato's day the "body politic," and appears in Latin most often in conjunction with *res publica,* meaning "the state" or "the republic."[461] *Canonicus* means "one living under rule," in Greek: *kanonikos,* "rod," in this case "ecclesiastical law" (*nach kirchlichem Recht*).[462] From this it is clear that Melanchthon and the reformers are identifying a very specific and well known term in their day, "which one refers to as the *canonicam politiam,*" (*das man nennet canonicam politiam*): namely the princely episcopal body politic, the ecclesiastical republic — a

---

458 William H. Lazareth, *Two Forms of Ordained Ministry,* 29.

459 Joseph H. Burgess, Jeffrey Gros, *Growing Consensus: Church Dialogues in the United States, 1962-1991,* (NewYork: Paulist Press, 1995), 287.

460 George A. Lindbeck, "Episcopacy," in *Promoting Unity, op. cit.,* pp. 52-53.

461 Also the name of one of Plato's works, and meaning "the administration of the commonwealth." Cf. Charlton T. Lewis and Charles Short, *A Latin Dictionary,* (Oxford: Clarendon, 1975), 1391.

462 *Mittellateinisches Glossar,* 2 Auflage, E. Habel, (Schöningh: Paderborn, 1925), 46.

distinct medieval form of government that is hardly adaptable or desirable for the church today. This is the worldly power, the *weltliche Gewalt* that is further addressed in Ap 28. As a direct object, it refers specifically to the *Kirchenordnung,* (for which there is no satisfactory English translation), "ecclesiastical regime" perhaps being the nearest approximation, not to be confused with today's *Kirchenleitung* which is the office of the shepherd of the flock.[463] This regime included the *Bischofe Regiment* which completely mixed the spiritual and secular kingdoms, including military (*potestas gladii*), police, and judicial powers (*potestas jurisdictionis*), as well as real estate and all other worldly possessions and pursuits befitting prince-bishops. They even issued their own arrest warrants of the citizenry. One can argue that since *polis* is the root word for "police," the reformers were in fact dealing with an ecclesiastical police state, the German title for CA 16 actually being, *Von der Polizei und weltlichem Regiment,* "Concerning the Police and Worldly Government."

Pelikan's translations in Tappert for *canonicam politiam* in Ap 14, as well as Kolb/Wengert's "canonical order," fall far short of conveying the secularization of the spiritual estate the reformers were rejecting.[464] The bishops possessed the civil powers of the state, including the power to wage military campaigns. To attack them too harshly in Augsburg would have amounted to nothing less than a declaration of war. It is little wonder then, that Melanchthon and the evangelicals told the bishops that for the sake of peace, they could keep their political estates and property rights, so long as the gospel could be preached in their territories.

---

463 Ernst Kinder u. Klaus Haendler, *Lutherisches Bekenntnis,* (Berlin/Hamburg: Lutherisches Verlagshaus,1962), 144: "Der deutsche Originaltext sagt: 'Kirchenregiment' (lateinisch: *ordo ecclesiasticus*). Damit ist jedoch nicht 'Kirchenleitung' im heutigen Sinne gemeint, sondern das 'Hirtenamt' des 'Weidens,' der geistlichen Leitung der örtlichen Gemeinde." Cf. *LW* 13.147, n. 4; 193 f.

464 Pelikan translates the term first as "canonical government," then as "canonical polity."

It is patently absurd, however, to argue as CCM and others do, that this amounts to the reformers eagerly desiring this hierarchical system, or *Stand*, in their day. Luther summarily dismissed it from the Coburg on Wednesday, August 24, 1530, even as the negotiations in Augsburg were underway. "This [*Stand*] has long since fallen, and there is nothing spiritual to it" (*denn derselbe ist längst gefallen und hat auch nichts Geistliches an sich*)."[465] Nor does he at any time defend the huge "ecclesiastical state" to which the Saxon dioceses of Naumburg, Merseburg, and Brandenburg belonged. Indeed, he was willing to hold out against it until Judgment Day, saying in a table talk (in which he addresses the Archbishop and Cardinal Albrecht von Mainz as "Bishop," rather than "Archbishop," proof he did not think hierarchically), "What Christ will have to say to the pope, Bishop of Mainz, and me on the Day of Judgment, will either help me or hurt me, and I'll leave it at that."[466] Indeed, Luther rejected the canonical polity in a letter to Georg Spalatin already on July 31, 1521, writing, "It would be best if the whole Canon Law were completely removed and that the sovereigns for once showed courage and completely abolished the ecclesiastical jurisdictions and punishments in their territories."[467]

Nor did Melanchthon ever push for a canonical state though he had ample opportunity to do so. One such important occasion presented itself in the *laudatio* he prepared for the funeral of Georg von Anhalt, who died on October 17, 1553. In his eulogy he speaks of "churches" and "states" in the plural, keeping them separate from one another, showing he was no advocate for a *canonicam politiam*. He praises Georg saying, "He was exceptional in piety, learning, and all virtue, and in the churches and states (*deque ecclesiis et politiis*) of this land most

---

[465] *WA* II 10.416-459.
[466] *WATR* 6.296 (6962).
[467] *WA* Br 2.368-369.

well received."[468] In his use of the ablative plural we see Luther's doctrine of the Two Kingdoms, where church and state are held in separate tension, even though Georg was both a worldly prince and a Lutheran bishop. Melanchthon, instead, pits "church(es)" against "state(s)" and makes no plug for the *canonicam politiam* at all, in spite of a huge opportunity to do so in the person of von Anhalt, whom Luther himself had ordained in 1545 in Melanchthon's presence, and who would have been a most excellent "proof" for a desire and fulfillment of a Lutheran "canonical polity" — had the Lutherans at all desired such a thing.

In his first draft of the *Apology* in 1530, Melanchthon had actually expressed a "maximum desire" to preserve the political ecclesiastical state (*maxime cupiamus ecclesiasticam politiam conservare*), not for any reasons of Catholic dogma, but because he considered it "to be useful (*nützlich*) for the tranquility of the church," (*eamque ad tranquillitatem ecclesia podesse iudicamus*). At issue was the growing threat of war. He penned it after the failure of the secret negotiations, but prior to the issuing of the final verdict (*Reichstagsabschied*) of the Diet at Augsburg on November 19, 1530. The verdict, or Imperial Edict, was a virtual sword of Damocles, which specifically forbad among other things, the preaching and teaching of *sola fide* (CA 4), and demanded a return to the *status quo ante* under penalty of death. The reformers' fight wasn't with the emperor, as far as they were concerned, but with the bishops acting as secular lords.[469]

"Apostolic succession," (quite the myth in its own right), via

---

468 Johann Erhard Kapp, *Kleine Nachlese einiger, größten Theils noch ungedruckter, und sonderlich zur Erläuterung der Reformations-Geschichte nützlicher Urkunden*, Bd. 1.1, (Leipzig, 1727).

469 Walch 16.1596-1616, Nr. 115 *Das kaiserliche Edikt, oder Abschied des Reichstages zu Augsburg, so viel die Religion betrifft*, November 19, 1530: *"Etliche haben gelehrt, dass der bloße Glaube allein ohne Liebe und gute Werke selig mache, und die guten Werke gar verworfen,"* e.g., Nicolas v. Amsdorf.

a *successio episcoporum* was never a topic in Augsburg, nor was it ever broached by either party. Luther never spoke of "apostolic succession" (*succession apostolica*), but of the "succession of faith" (*successio fidelium*)[470] The reformers' "maximum desire" at the time was for the preservation of the state through the avoidance of war for the tranquility of the church, with a *canonicam politiam* being useful and desirable only for the purpose of keeping the peace.

Article 14 of the Catholic Confutation (*Confutatione Pontificia*) agrees that the issue was ecclesiastical law and civil order. The CA and *Apology* were, after all, political documents, submitted by political princes to an imperial diet.

Emperor Charles V at Augsburg in 1530

An initial "maximum desire" is also perfectly understandable given the dire situation the reformers found

---

470 Cf. Gerhard Müller, *Causa Reformationis* (Gütersloher Gütersloh 1989), 482, Nr. 62: "Vgl. auch W4.138, 20 wo die *fideles* als *Episcopi Christi* bezeichnet werden, oder W4.224, 21f., wo es heißt: *omnes fideles per Christum sacerdaotem sunt sacerdotes et regnes.* Luther spricht nicht von der *successio apostolica,* sondern von der *successio fidelium,* vgl. darüber jetzt Höhne a a.O.S. 15." Cf. Heinrich Bornkamm, *Luthers geistige Welt,* Carl Bertelsmann Verlag, Gütersloh, 1959.

themselves in at the time. They were, after all, prisoners in Augsburg, a fact one rarely finds mentioned. Soldiers were posted at all of the city gates to prevent their possible escape in the wake of Philipp von Hesse's refusal to negotiate with the Romanists, and his subsequent hasty departure in the night of Saturday, August 6.[471] The emperor had entered the city with an enormous show of military might, bringing two thousand troops and horse drawn artillery with him to ensure civil order. Additionally, Charles and the pope had already agreed to suppress the Reformation by force one year earlier, at the Treaty of Barcelona, June 29, 1529. Eck now insisted the emperor carry out that treaty by beheading the reformers.[472] Added to his voice were the constant bloodthirsty threats from the papal legate, Cardinal Lorenzo Campeggio, in charge of the twenty Catholic theologians assembled in Augsburg. He urged Charles, even during the summer negotiations, to kill the reformers whom he referred to as a "sect," as "noxious and venomous weeds . . . We want to see to it that Germany is swimming in blood (*So wollen wir machen daß Deutschland soll im Blut schwimmen*)."[473] In a letter dated July 8, 1530,

---

[471] Walch 16.1366, Nr. 1037: "*Antwort der protestierenden Stände auf Kaisers Anfrage wegen des Landgrafen Abreise, und über die deshalb vom Kaiser angeordnete Thorwache.*"

[472] Things had gotten off to a bad start in Augsburg when the evangelicals refused to kneel for the opening procession of the Blessed Sacrament.

[473] *WATR* 27.Nr. 56. Cf. Kidd, *Documents of the Continental Reformation,* (Oxford: At Clarendon Press, MCMXI, No.s 112 & 117. In a letter dated January 1530, Campeggio instructed Charles to join him in a twofold strike against the evangelicals. "And I, if there be a need, will pursue them with ecclesiastical censures and penalties, omitting nothing that it may be needful to do. I will deprive the beneficed heretics of their benefices, and will separate them by excommunications from the Catholic flock. Your Highness also, with your just and awful Imperial Ban, will subject them to such and so horrible an extermination that either they shall be constrained to return to the holy Catholic faith, or shall be utterly ruined and despoiled both of goods and life. And if any there should be, which God forbid, who shall obstinately persevere in that diabolical course . . . Your Majesty

Melanchthon wrote to Luther at the Coburg Castle, "the emperor commands that we restore all things to the original state until a council is convened."[474] The reinstatement of the Edict of Worms and the *status quo ante*, required the evangelicals to submit to Roman obedience no later than April 15, 1531, and to restore all lands, churches, offices, estates and practices to the Catholic fold. Failure to comply would result in swift and bloody military action. Melanchthon and the evangelicals were being ordered to make concessions under extreme duress. They had a gun to their head, both figuratively and literally, in both canon and cannon.

But a year later, by September 1531, with the immediate crisis of being held prisoners in Augsburg having passed, Melanchthon's "maximum desire" in Ap 14 is lessened to a "deep desire" as he recalls it (*nos summa voluntate cupere*), and now refers to a past event, "to maintain the church polity and various ranks of the ecclesiastical hierarchy, although they were created by human authority (*iure humano*)." This statement, not found in the first draft, *erste Entwurf,* is nothing short of a complete rejection of the *Corpus iuris canonici,* the canonical polity which insists the bishops' rule and authority are *iure divino*,[475] an extremely daring stance, given the evangelicals' continuing post-Augsburg peril. Jonas then further reduced the "deep desire to keep," to a matter of merely being "highly inclined (*geneigt*) to help maintain" the political estate, the *canonicam politiam* of the prince bishops.[476] However, the inclination to help was now strictly conditional, and was predicated on the bishops' acceptance of the equal status of evangelical pastors and their Lutheran teaching. Melanchthon, after all, had not come to Augsburg just to negotiate. "When a

---

will then take fire and sword in hand, and will radically extirpate these noxious and venomous weeds."

[474] *Melanchthons Briefwechsel MBW*, *WA* Br. 5.446, Nr. 1629.

[475] The Augsburg Interim of 1548 reaffirmed bishops *iure divino* in Article XIII, and the "perpetual succession" of the bishops to their orders through the laying on of hands in Article XX.

[476] *BSLK* 296.

fellow at the Reichstag in Augsburg asked Philip Melanchthon, 'Philip, what is it you're trying to do here?' he immediately replied, 'WIN!'"[477] When the bishops did not accept, however, the inclination was withdrawn.

That it was even still on the table at the end of August 1530 was a point of sharp contention among the Lutherans. Back in June, Jonas and Melanchthon had fought bitterly over the merits of ecclesiastical jurisdiction. Jonas appealed to Luther in a confidential memo dated June 30, "But in this matter you should counsel us, so that the matter may not be harmful for future generations and afterwards sear our consciences."[478] Over the course of the next ten days, Melanchthon negotiated secretly with the papal nunzio Campeggio.[479] In a letter to him dated July 7, he agreed to drop the evangelical insistence on communion in both kinds, as well as priestly marriage, provided Rome was willing to tolerate both practices until a general council of the church could be convened to decide the issues. He also saw the question of the mass as resolvable, and even promised to restore the *potestas iurisdictionis* of the bishops in all of the evangelical lands.[480]

In his famous letter of July 14, 1530, Melanchthon urgently asked Luther to answer once and for all the vexing question of the authority of bishops "for we see that the bishops indeed rule by man-made law." The question was whether they are to be

---

[477] Walch 22.1812f. *"Als jemand auf dem Reichstage zu Augsburg zu Phil. Melanchthon gesagt hatte: Philippe, was wollt Ihr anfangen? antwortete er sogleich: Siegen!"* The source of the statement appears to be Luther himself, recorded by D. Conrad Cordatus in Latin of what appears to have been a German conversation. The sentence is No. 52 and corresponds with the Latin passage of the same number. The original is found in Cordatus's handwritten Latin journal *Tagebuch über D. Martin Luther, 1537.*

[478] *WA* Br 5.428

[479] *MBW,* 1380.Nr. 1043, Vol. 1, Regesten 1-1109 (1514ß1530). Spalatin reported that after five days of negotiations, Eck sarcastically suggested the Lutherans "send [their] *solas* to the cobbler for awhile." *Mann soll die Solen eine Weile zum Schuster schicken.*

[480] *CR* 2.172f.

obeyed in keeping with Paul's dictum in Romans 13:1, ("Let every person be subject to the governing authorities"). If bishops enact statutes that are "not contrary to the faith," that "deal with works which are permitted," Melanchthon reasoned, the bishops must be obeyed for the simple reason that they are the governing authorities (*Recht der Obrigkeit*). This, however, he points out, creates a gordian knot, because "if obedience is required, then there is no freedom, for freedom and obedience contradict one another. This knot," he urged Luther, "has to be untied; for that freedom seems to dissolve obedience, [and this] should not be."

Recognizing that Melanchthon had once again tied himself up in the law, ("here you do have problems"), Luther responded on July 21, by rejecting both the bishops' *potestas iurisdictionis* and Melanchthon's argument of necessary obedience, even where faith is not imperiled, "even if it is permissible and godly, since one ought not to do evil so that good may result" [Romans 13:1]. The problem is not the bishops' statutes per se, but what causes them: canon law, (including the claim bishops have authority *de iure divino*). He warned Melanchthon not to yield (*nicht zugeben*) on the question of bishops mixing the two realms. The roles of prince and bishop are forever to be separated (*unvermengt*), with their governments never overlapping, even if exercised by the same individual.

Not even an evangelical bishop may institute churchly practices in a congregation without its consent, and a sovereign bishop may never do it at all.[481] "Thus we grant neither according to spiritual nor worldly rights power to the bishops to impose anything on the church."[482] "Since the bishops are openly guilty of this mixture [of the two governments], of this tyranny and oppression of the church, we cannot yield to them unless they have first, through public repentance, rescinded and

---

[481] *WA* Br 5.491-495. Cf. Heinz Scheible, *Melanchthon, Eine Biographie*, München, Verlag S. H. Beck, 1977.
[482] Walch 16.1015, 18-23: *"Daher können wir weder nach geistlichem noch nach weltlichen Rechte den Bischöfen die Gewalt beilegen etwas über die Kirche zu verordnen."*

condemned the former laws and all the things they did on the basis of the mixed tyranny." He adds, "And if the bishops should threaten violence and seek to bring this about, we must not obey them or compromise with them, but rather die for the cause of the distinction between these two governments."[483]

The question, therefore, is not one of disobeying bishops "if — only if — bishops teach evil things," as Wengert insists,[484] but of bishops being the evil itself through the imposition of statutes (including godly ones) on churches without their consent, "even so that good may result" (for the *bene esse* of the church). "The bishops are, after all," Luther writes in the same letter, "merely servants and stewards,[485] and not the lords of the church."

Informed by Melanchthon that Campeggio was nevertheless prepared to offer dispensations, Luther replied with a line he attributed to Amsdorf, "I shit on the legate and his overlord's [pope's] dispensations; we'll find our own dispensations."[486] When Melanchthon, nevertheless, offered further compromises that included the return of the evangelicals to episcopal jurisdiction (*Wiederherstellung der bischoflichen Gewalt*) and recognition of the authority of the pope ("We honor the authority of the apostolic see."),[487] Hessen, Lüneberg, Nürnberg, Schirrmacher, Schnepf and Luther all vehemently opposed it, and the signers of the *Augsburg Confession* ordered Melanchthon to make no further concessions.[488] Consequently, the negotiations of the Committee of Six, which had begun on

---

[483] Walch 16.1016, 4-15 of Nr. 1009.

[484] Wengert 84.

[485] I Cor. 4:1, (Οὕτως ἡμᾶς λογιζέσθω ἄνθρωπος ὡς ὑπηρέτας Χριστοῦ καὶ οἰκονόμους μυστηρίων θεοῦ) literally means subordinate servants who use their hands to dispense (*ausreichen*), in this case word and sacrament.

[486] *"Ich schisse dem Legaten und seinem Herrn in seine Disputation, wir wollen Disputationes genug finden."* Walch 21a. 1517-1519, Brief Nr. 1627, Feste Coburg, 15 Juli, 1530.

[487] Karl Brandi, *Deutsche Reformation und Gegenreformation*, I (Leipzig, n.d. [1927]), 236.

[488] *BSLK* 296, n. 3. Cf. *LW* 49.406, n. 19.

August 23, lasted barely a week before collapsing on August 31. Further halfhearted talks sputtered and died between September 8 and 14, Campeggio finally ending it, with neither side showing any interest in further talks.[489] Contrary to popular belief, Ap 14 was never agreed to, but was "admonished" by the *Confutatio,* tabled, (and ultimately rejected), the two sides finding only partial agreement in theory, but not in practice.

On September 22 the emperor offered the evangelicals a general armistice until April 15, 1531, by which time the *status quo ante* and a return to the Catholic faith must be accomplished as set forth in the Confutation. If not, his military might (*Reichskammergericht*) would swing into action. The following day the evangelicals were summoned one last time to Charles V's personal quarters to be informed that the pro-papal estates had already formed a military alliance, and the emperor had joined it. When a final offer to defend their position was met with the demand to submit to the resolution, the evangelicals committed their cause to God, shook hands with the emperor and departed. They had not come to Augsburg seeking papal concessions or even "justice," as Pelikan mistakenly has it in Ap 14, but "equality" (*nihil aequi impetrare potuisse*). They had come, as Melanchthon said earlier, to "WIN!" If they could not achieve that, there was nothing more to discuss. They would go on to form their own defensive league in Schmalkalden over the Christmas holidays.

The fact that the "deep desire" was now a past event, post Augsburg, whose time had clearly come and gone, is clear in both the Latin and German texts, but it is completely lost in the English. Pelikan committed a critical error in his translation of the Latin Ap 14.2, allowing for a seismic shift in ecumenical dialogues which would go on to serve as the basis for CCM's false claims, and is repeated in Kolb/Wengert's *2000BC*, as well as official documents of the ELCA. In Tappert it reads, "Thus the cruelty of the bishops is the reason for the abolition of canonical government in some places, *despite our earnest*

---

[489] *Ibid, Excursus* 423.

desire to keep it (quam nos magnopere cupiebamus conserver)." Pelikan rendered *cupiebamus* in the present tense, indicating a continuous desire, when in fact it is the first-person plural imperfect active indicative, connoting *past* desire, and must therefore be translated "we earnestly desired" to keep it.[490] The critical question then becomes: When? When were the reformers still willing to keep the ecclesiastical polity of government by bishops? Their answer is clear: The year before — at the time of the Diet of Augsburg, well *before* the penning of the German *Apology*! But things had now radically changed. For Luther, Melanchthon, Jonas, and the Lutheran reformers, Ap 14.1's "deep desire to maintain the church polity and various ranks of the ecclesiastical hierarchy" was a thing of the past — but 14.2's "the abolition of canonical government" is in the present.

Pelikan and Kolb/Wengert also translated *in hoc conventu* generically, "in the assembly," a term too vague in the English to be of much use. Which assembly exactly? After all, an assembly could be a gathering anywhere at any time, a local congregation, or Melanchthon and his friends now comfortably enjoying a beer back home in Wittenberg. Hence the need for what the BSLK calls Jonas's *verschärfung,* or "sharpening" of the text with *Reichstage* for *conventu,* removing any ambiguity. The *Reichstag,* or Diet, was a specific event within a given time frame. It had an opening bell and a closing bell. It was strictly limited to nine sessions from June 20 - September 22, 1530, and concluded its business more than a year before the German *Apology*. When it ended, so did any ongoing "deep desire to maintain church polity and various ranks of the ecclesiastical hierarchy."

Pelikan's and Marty's CCM team's error aside, to now suggest a present willingness to keep the episcopal polity creates obvious irreconcilables. If the evangelicals so deeply desired the polity and hierarchy of bishops, why didn't they just go ahead and keep it, starting in the autumn of 1531? If they abolished it in their lands, surely they had the power and

---

490 *Triglotta:* "which we greatly desired to maintain."

wherewithal to reintroduce it, and it would have gone a long way to satisfy the demands of the *status quo ante,* greatly reducing the chances for war. [491] But in fact they hadn't undertaken anything at all to fulfill that "desire" in the intervening thirteen months. Instead, the desire had gone from "maximum," to "deep," to "inclined;" from present to past — from *cupiamus,* to *cupere,* to *cupiebamus.*

The *Smalcald Articles* confirm the same, noting that any desire for canonical bishops' ordinations is a past event: "If the bishops *had wanted* to be true bishops and *had taken* on themselves the church and the gospel, they *might have* been permitted (for the sake of love and unity, but not of necessity) to *have* ordained and confirmed us and our preachers . . ."[492] Tappert and Kolb/Wengert have also incorrectly translated this passage in the present tense. The reformers were prepared to consider such matters, but only during the negotiations in Augsburg, as is clear from such phrases as "offered *until now*" (*bisher auch angeboten*), "*from now on* they won't have it so good" (*soll's ihnen hinfurt nicht mehr so gut werden*), "they should keep their outrages and anointing" (*sie sollen ihren Greuel und Chresem behalten*), etc.[493]

---

[491] Present day suggestions that the evangelicals were prevented from doing so for political reasons are largely fanciful. The very demand of the *status quo ante* presumes their ability to reinstate it. Though the popular vote at the time in Germany was largely against it, (e.g., 87% of the citizenry of Ulm), some city governments chose to keep their options open in order to retain their imperial connections. Cf. Steven E. Ozment, *The Reformation in the Cities:* "The Appeal of Protestantism to Sixteenth-Century Germany and Switzerland," (Yale University Press, New Haven & London, 1975), 128 ff.

[492] *BSLK* 457: "Wenn die Bischofe *wollten* rechte Bischofe sein und der Kirchen und des Evangeliums sie annehmen, so *mochte[n]* man das umb der Liebe und Einigkeit willen, doch nicht aus Not [das] lassen *gegeben sein,* daß sie uns und unsere Prediger *ordinierten* und *konfirmierten...*"

[493] *Ibid* n.3

The Crisis of 1531

How, then, does one account for Jonas's radical surgery of the Latin text in the German, which Melanchthon now hailed as beyond improvement? The answer is that the *Apology* was a work in flux, its position being adjusted in response to the rapidly changing events on the ground but declaring with finality in Ap 14 that, although the Lutherans had once been willing to help maintain the *canonicam politiam,* (strictly for the sake of peace), they no longer were. It was a position they would not waver from. An explosive war of words had quickly escalated in the first half of 1531. Luther, who had fired the occasional warning shot across Melanchthon's bow from the Castle Coburg when he appeared overly eager to make concessions in Augsburg, now answered the *Confutation*'s threats with a broadside of his own, issuing two powerful tracts that appeared almost simultaneously. The first was, *Dr. Martin Luther's Warning to His Dear German People,* written the previous October before the final verdict of the Diet, and published in April 1531. Still careful to portray Charles V as a benevolent Christian potentate who was not to blame for the present crisis but rather his advisors, Luther nevertheless countenanced for the first time defensive military action through passive, and in the worst case, active resistance. He understood it as a regrettable but necessary evil, thereby dramatically upping the ante of his stance on the authority question (*Obrigkeitsfrage*) eight years earlier in *On Temporal Authority, the Extent to which It should Be Obeyed.* He now wrote, "If war breaks out — which God forbid — I will not reprove those who defend themselves against the murderers and bloodthirsty papists, nor let anyone else rebuke them as being seditious, but I will accept their action and let it pass as self defense."[494] And should he himself be murdered, he is prepared to "take a throng of bishops, priests, and monks with me," they

---

[494] *WA* 30 III.282.

all going to hell, and he to heaven.[495]

"The Papal Belvedere"[496]

Appearing at the same time was his *Commentary on the Alleged Imperial Edict,* in which he laid the blame for the day's precipitous events squarely on Pope Clement VII and Campeggio. The Elector John and Landgrave Philip especially regarded the polemics as a healthy warning to the emperor as to the seriousness of their cause. Duke Georg of Albertine Saxony, who had despised Luther since the Leipzig Debate, was only too eager to join the fray against the Lutherans, sharply attacking their position in *Against Luther's Warning,* claiming it was a blueprint for insurrection against the emperor.

---

[495] *Ibid.*

[496] *Lucas Cranach the Elder, from Luther's publication Wider des Papsttum (1545). The caption reads: "No Pope, don't frighten us with your ban, and don't be so furious, so furious a man. Otherwise we will counter where, we will show you our derrieres." (Nicht Bapst: nicht schrecken uns mit deim ban, Und sey nicht so zorniger so zorniger man. Wir thun sonst ein gegen wehre, Und zeigen dirs Belvedere).*

Cochläeus, the third of Melanchthon's chief antagonists in Augsburg after Eck and Campeggio, quickly capitalized on the anonymously published work as further evidence that the Lutherans were a seditious, rebellious lot, who were seeking nothing less than a complete German rebellion against the empire. All of these exchanges took place in April.

Things got worse in May. Luther quickly responded with *Against the Assassin at Dresden,* accusing Georg and the Catholics of seeking a pretext for war through the Imperial Edict. He argued that by going against God's word, they should indeed "be tortured by anxiety and fear that rebellion would occur," and offered his earlier stance in the Peasant's War as clear proof that revolution itself was not his cause.

But with this last exchange, in which both emperor and pope now bore full responsibility for the impending conflagration, Luther had entered new territory. As Kittelson put it, "Luther's decision that his Catholic opponents were beyond redemption had far reaching consequences. Earlier he had declared that he and his supporters could no longer pray for them. Now he added that true prayer carried with it curses on the papacy."[497]

Indeed, those consequences played themselves out in June, in events in Saxony that would have a direct bearing on the German changes to Ap 14. The Imperial Edict had banned the preaching of Article IV of the *Augsburg Confession,* the article on justification, the very heart and soul of the Reformation. Anyone found guilty of doing so would be proclaimed a heretic, and stood to lose both property and life, arranged through Clement VII's licensure to Campeggio on April 28, 1531.[498] Duke Georg's answer to Luther was not to issue another tract, but to take forceful action instead. Eager to implement the Imperial Edict as quickly as possible, and unwilling to wait for the convening of a general council, he issued his own edict on May 11, demanding strict compliance under the severest of penalties. Among other things, it

---

[497] James M. Kittelson, *Luther the Reformer,* (Minneapolis: Augsburg Publishing House, 1986), 259.
[498] Cf. Kidd, No. 112.

prohibited rebaptism, use of both kinds in the sacrament, disobedience, blasphemy against the Virgin Mary, and blasphemy against the saints. His ruling was to be strictly enforced by the Saxon nobility.

Literally caught in the middle of this verbal crossfire was the fortress, Burg Gnandstein, the ancestral home of the aristocratic family von Einsiedel, and its sister castle, Kohren.[499] The Einsiedels were very close friends of and collaborators with Luther, Melanchthon, Jonas, and Spalatin.[500] Their bond with Luther dated back to their attendance at the Leipzig Debate in 1519, and is an extraordinary Reformation history in its own right ranging from Heinrich Abraham von Einsiedel standing front and center, third from Luther at the Diet of Worms, to Haubold von Einsiedel being responsible for the publication of the *Book of Concord.*

These castles, which guarded the main commerce routes midway between Berlin and Prague, found themselves on opposite sides of the dividing line between Albertine (ducal) and Ernestine (electoral) Saxony.[501] Kohren was situated in evangelical territory, Gnandstein in Catholic. Heinrich Hildebrand von Einsiedel, the lord of Gnandstein, and his brother Heinrich Abraham, had committed themselves to the cause of the Reformation even before Leipzig, employing pastors who were evangelical in preaching and teaching.

---

[499] Kittelson highlights the dilemmas of the nobility in October 1532, and the town council of Leipzig in 1533. But the crisis in Gnandstein occurred earlier and preoccupied Luther, Melanchthon, and Jonas in the spring and summer of 1531, the precise time of the writing of the German *Apology.*

[500] Cf. Andreas Baudler, "Die 'Theodore Baudler Collection' in den USA, 101-125. Cf. Andreas Baudler, "Luther, der 'Fürstenknecht,'" *Frankfurter Allgemeine Zeitung,* 30. Januar, 2013, Geisteswissenschaften, Seite N4, Nr. 25.

[501] Cf. *Die wettinischen Länder 1485-1554,* map prepared by K. Blaschke in H. Eberhardt *et al.* (eds.), *Die Reformation in Documenten* (Weimar, 1967), Appendix.

On January 10, 1528 they had been ordered by Duke Georg to fire a pastor from each castle for administering Holy Communion in both kinds and seek legal absolution for their crime from the Bishop of Merseburg. Should they refuse to do so, Georg would seize their properties by whatever means necessary. In a document entitled, *Discussions Related to the Question: Is It Permissible for Evangelicals to Wage War Against the Emperor? (Verhandlungen über die Frage: Ist ein Kampf der Evangelischen gegen den Kaiser erlaubt?)*, they appealed to Luther and the Wittenberg theologians for help via Georg Spalatin. To what degree, they asked, was it permissible for the evangelical nobility to resist the duke, including refusing to even publish the Imperial Edict in their domains? The brothers refused to seek absolution, in part, because Luther had written to them saying, "Master Philip and I would not like to see that," (*Magister Philippus und ich würden es ungern sehen*), and the case remained open into the summer of 1531 when all three of the reformers responded vigorously *de negotio Einsiedeliorum* in the latter half of June. On the 26th, in a letter signed by each, Luther, Melanchthon, and Jonas counseled the Einsiedels to stand fast in the face of Duke Georg's tyranny, whom Luther referred to as "the masked emperor," (someone who liked to play emperor without actually being one). Johannes Brenz even joined the fray from Swabia, denouncing the persecution of the Einsiedels by "the tyrant of Dresden!

Luther conferring with Heinrich Hildebrand von Einsiedel[502]

Melanchthon suggested the nobles do the same thing as the city of Ulm, which in the days immediately following the Edict of Worms in 1521, had agreed to publish the ban, but refused to either protect or punish citizens who chose to side with the evangelical cause. They advised the brothers Einsiedel to do the following: 1) The nobility should not resort to defensive actions on behalf of their subjects. 2) Every citizen must decide for himself and at his own peril to exercise and confess his faith. 3) The nobles are right to publish the edict in compliance with the holy estate of temporal authority (*Recht der Obrigkeit*), even though they regard it as grossly unjust. 4) But since Duke Georg is clearly guilty of mixing the two realms, the Einsiedels should take it a step further and include the following *Protestatio* as formal notice, framing it in the words of the *Augsburg Confession*:

In opposition to the Imperial Edict they regard as fully correct the teaching that the forgiveness of sins is already theirs *condonari nobis peccata* (CA 4); that they have a merciful God (CA 5); that they have eternal life (CA 4); that these things are theirs by grace through faith in Christ *in propter Christum* (CA

---

[502] It is unknown whether Luther ever visited Gnandstein, though his communications with the Einsiedels were extensive.

4), not through merits or works; and that any teaching contrary to this doctrine is a violation of the gospel. Further, they will refuse to punish anyone in their domains for violating the ban on celebrating the sacrament according to the gospel. Luther urged them to trust in God, commit their cause to him, and cling to the *Augsburg Confession*. In short, the reformers' counsel is not armed resistance, but resistance in, with, and through the gospel, through noncompliance with the Imperial Edict's ban on justification by faith alone and the sacrament in both kinds. Jonas and Melanchthon wrote, "It is imperative that you and all Christians know, confess, and uphold this article, and that you prosecute the knowledge and honor of Christ, for thus it is written, 'Whosoever confesses me, so also will I confess him.'"[503] They were to stand firm in their faith, trust God above all, and if suffering should occur God would reckon it to them and be their present help. Finally, they also reserved the right to take their case against the Imperial Edict to the Imperial Court in Speyer; in other words: to sue the emperor.

---

[503] *"Dieser Artickel ist euch und allen Christen not zu wissen, zu bekennen, und helfen zu erhalten, und belanget die erkentniß Christi und ehr, darumb der spruch dahin gehört, Wer mich bekennet, will ich widder bekennen, etc."*

Chapter 8

The Jonas Text

Burg Gnandstein

The *causa Einsiedelorum* lay particularly close to Luther's heart. So impressed was he with this family that he would later write to Spalatin in 1541, "The Einsiedels are a rare and one of a kind light in the darkness of the most confused nobility of the century."[504] All of these threatening events were occurring just as the Latin *Apology* was going to press in April, 1531, and Jonas was beginning his work on the German text. At the height of this clash over the essence of the gospel, with Luther's obvious oversight and approval, and with Melanchthon's editing, Jonas now proceeded to "delete" what amounts to fully one third of the Latin text of Ap 14, including

---

[504] *"Die Einsiedels sind ein seltenes und einzigartiges Licht im Dunkel jenes verworrensten Adels dieses Jahrhunderts."* Burg Gnandstein, Falk Schulze, (Horb am Neckar: Geiger Verlag GmbH,1996), 32.

the parts of 14.1 and all of 14.5 which serve as the basis for CCM's claims. What had been a rejection of obedience to a canonical government of bishops "in some places" in April/May 1531, is now a total abandonment by October 1531, given these and other new developments on the ground. The Latin passages missing in the German *Apology* have been struck through in Tappert below, with corrections to Pelikan's English translation italicized and footnoted:

Article XIV from the Latin: Of Ecclesiastical Order

1   With the proviso that we employ canonical ordination, they accept Article XIV, where we say that no one should be allowed to administer the word and sacraments in the church unless he is duly called. On this matter we have given frequent testimony in the *assembly*[505] to our deep *desire*[506] to keep the church polity and various ranks of the ecclesiastical hierarchy although they were created by human authority.[507] ~~We know that the Fathers had good and useful reasons for instituting ecclesiastical discipline in the manner described by the ancient canons.~~

2   But the bishops either force our priests to forsake and condemn the sort of doctrine we have confessed, or else, in their unheard of cruelty, they kill[508] the

---

[505] "Assembly" is somewhat imprecise. Jonas translates *conventus* as *Reichstag,* ("Diet"). Cf. *Mittellateinisches Glossar,* Habel-Gröbel, (Paderhorn), 186.

[506] *nos summa voluntate cupere conservare*

[507] By making church polity and ecclesiastical hierarchy *iure humano,* Melanchthon has in fact rejected it, since it claimed to be *iure divino.* CA/Ap XIV was subsequently rejected by Article XIII of the Augsburg Interim on May 15, 1548, which reaffirmed the rule of bishops *iure divino.* Cf. *Das Augsburger Interim von 1548,* "Texte zur Geschichte der evangelischen Theologie 3," Joachim Mehlhausen, ed., (Neukirchen-Vluyn: Neukirchener Verlag, 1970).

[508] *occident* = past tense: "they killed," a possible reference to Jan Hus, etc.

unfortunate and innocent men. Thus the cruelty of the bishops is the reason for the abolition of canonical government in some places, *which we earnestly desired to preserve.*[509] Let them see to it how they will answer to God for disrupting the church.

3   In this issue our consciences are clear and we dare not approve the cruelty of those who persecute this teaching, for we know that our confession is true, godly, and catholic.

4   We know that the church is present among those who rightly teach the word of God and rightly administer the sacraments. It is not present among those who seek to destroy the word of God with their edicts,[510] who even butcher anyone who teaches what is right and true, though the canons themselves are gentler with those who violate them.

5   ~~Furthermore, we want at this point to declare our willingness to keep the ecclesiastical and canonical polity, provided that the bishops stop raging against our churches. This willingness will be our defense, both before God and among all nations, present and future, against the charge that we have undermined the authority of the bishops. Thus men may read that, despite our protest against the unjust cruelty of the bishops, we could not obtain *equality*.~~[511]

Article XIV from the German

1   In the fourteenth article, where we say that we permit no one to preach or distribute the   sacraments in the

---

[509] *nos magnopere cupiebamus conservare* = first-person plural imperfect active indicative ("which we earnestly desired to preserve"), not the Tappert/Kolb-Wengert present tense ("despite our earnest desire to keep/retain it").

[510] E.g., Duke George's edict of May 12, 1531.

[511] *aequi* = "equality," not Tappert/Kolb-Wengert's "justice."

churches,[512] "except those who are duly called," they accept it if we understand the call of the priests as those ordained or consecrated in accordance with the Canon. On this matter we've let ourselves be heard from several times in this Diet, that we are inclined in the highest to help maintain[513] the old ecclesiastical regime and Bishops' Regiment,

2 known as the *canonicam politiam,* provided that the bishops allow our teaching and accept our priests.[514] But up to now the bishops have persecuted our own[515] and murdered them contrary to their own laws. And so we are not yet able to achieve that they cease their tyranny. For this reason the blame lies with our opponents that *our obedience to the bishops is withdrawn,* and we are excused before God and all people of faith. Because the bishops will not except ours,

4 they depart from this teaching, which we have proclaimed and which we are obligated before God to confess and keep, *we must abandon the bishops* and be more obedient to God, and know that the

4 Christian church is there where God's word is properly taught. Let the bishops see to it how they will answer for the tyranny by which they tear the churches apart and lay them waste.[516] [Italics added.]

---

512 *"Kirchen"*

513 Jonas has downgraded *summa voluntate* ("deep desire"), to *geneigt/libenter* ("inclined").

514 I.e., CA 4 and pastors as equals.

515 I.e., the laity, especially the nobility.

516 Art. XIV *Vom Kirchenregiment:* "Im vierzenten Artikel, da wir sagen, daß man niemands gestate zu predigen oder die Sakrament zu reichen in der Kirchen, 'denn allein denjenigen, so recht gebührlich berufen sein,' das nehmen sie an, wenn wir den Beruf also verstehen von Priestern, welche nach Inhalt der Canonum geordiniert oder geweihet sein. Von der Sache haben wir uns etlichemal auf diesem Reichstag hören lassen, daß wir zum höchsten geneigt sind, alte Kirchenordnung und der Bischofe Regiment, das man nennet

In their introductions to the *Apology*, Pelikan and Kolb/Wengert suggest that the differences between the Latin and German texts are either minor or insignificant.[517] While that is true for some articles, it is certainly not the case for Article 14, which Wengert rightly calls "one of the most hotly contested articles among American Lutherans."[518] Yet, for all of the modifications made to the various articles during the Reformation, (for example: 4, 5, 6, 12, 15 and 20), only one has remained forever unaltered from the moment it was penned: The German text of Ap 14.

Events and attitudes had changed dramatically over the course of a year, making the article especially significant for what it was no longer saying in the German. Gone is any acknowledgment "that the Fathers had good and useful reasons for instituting ecclesiastical discipline" described in the ancient canons. Gone is the "willingness to keep the ecclesiastical and canonical polity," though the estates may remain. Gone is any need to offer a defense before God and the nations that the authority of the bishops was being undermined — that defense having already been made on June 25, 1530. The Latin's subservient tone is replaced by a bold German declaration of independence. Where canonical government was abandoned "in

---

canonicam politiam, helfen zu erhalten, so die Bischofe unsere Lehre dulden und unsere Priester annehmen wollten. Nu haben die Bischofe bis anher die Unsern verfolgt und wider ihre eigene Recht ermordet. So können wir auch noch nicht erlangen, daß sie von solcher Tyrannei ablassen. Derhalben ist die Schuld unsers Gegenteils, daß den Bischöfen der Gehorsam entzogen wird, und sind wir für Gott und allen frommen Leuten entschuldigt. Denn dieweil die Bischofe die Unsern nicht dulden wollen, sie verlassen denn diese Lehre, so wir bekannt haben und wir doch für Gott schuldig sind, diese Lehre zu bekennen und zu erhalten, müssen wir die Bischöfe fahren lassen und Gott mehr gehorsam sein und wissen, daß die christliche Kirche da ist da Gottes Wort recht gelehret wird. Die Bischöfe mögen zusehen, wie sie es verantworten wöllen, daß sie durch solche Tyrannei die Kirchen zerreißen und wüst machen." *BSLK 296-297.*

[517] Tappert 98; Kolb/Wengert 109.
[518] Wengert 41.

some places" in the Latin, it is now (twice) abandoned in the German.

The reformers' offer in Augsburg was already strictly conditional from Day 1: They were inclined to help the bishops keep their political estates, with all of their legislative and judicial accoutrements (including police, military powers, etc.), provided Lutheran pastors are accepted as "equals" (*aqua*) and their teaching on justification is accepted — something that is not the case even today, (as any Lutheran who has recently attempted to receive the sacrament in a Roman Catholic Church knows).

As George Carlin might say, much of this was about "stuff." Melanchthon's quick note to Luther from Augsburg saying the *status quo ante* was being imposed, was another way of saying, "They want their stuff back." And it was a lot of stuff, including ecclesiastical offices, jobs, monasteries, churches, and real estate including whole towns, cities, castles, and territories. The bishops not accepting "ours" (*Unsern*) in Ap 14, refers to the Christian nobility (*christlicher Adel*), as distinguished from the preceding "our priests" (*unsere Priester*). The nobility, as we saw, had been ordered to abandon the CA, or face confiscation and incarceration. Jonas's response in Ap 14.2 is that rather than abandon the *Augsburg Confession*, the evangelicals will instead abandon the bishops and their entire canonical system.

In fact, he notes, they already have. Whereas in the Latin text canonical government has been abolished "in some places" — in the German it is abandoned altogether. The term "abandon" is the German idiomatic expression *fahren lassen,* which can also be understood as "to heck [or hell] with" the bishops. Luther had employed the same words two years earlier in the fourth stanza of "A Mighty Fortress" (*Ein Feste Burg*): "If they take our body, goods, land, child, and wife, to heck [hell] with it! They have no win, the kingdom remains ours," (*Nehmen sie den Leib, Gut, Her, Kind, und Weib, laß fahren dahin! Sie haven's kein Gewinn; das Reich muß uns doch bleiben*).

The gates of hell and who belonged there were never far

from the evangelicals' minds, including Melanchthon's. There is an amusing incident in which the normally contemplative reformer, who was not known for outbursts, loses his cool in Augsburg. During a break in the negotiations, a wealthy *Bürger* invited the two sides including Master Philip, Brenz, Jonas, Cochläeus, Wimpina, and others to dinner. When the food arrived, Melanchthon began to offer the table grace. Upon hearing him pray, Wimpina (one of the top Catholic negotiators) turned to Cochläeus and expressed surprise that the Lutherans even knew how to pray. Outraged, Master Philip told the Catholics they were clueless when it came to prayer and needed to learn it from the Lutherans, who alone pray correctly, and not the papists! A huge argument ensued, at the conclusion of which Cochläeus announced that the reformers could say whatever they wished, he would stay faithful to his mother, the holy Christian Church. Melanchthon retorted, "So what? We will remain with the Father, and we'll see who goes to the devil first!" (*wer eher zu Teufel fahren wird!*).[519] Finally, it is worth noting that the last answer to the emperor in Augsburg had come from Duke John, who stated that the Lutheran cause was firmly rooted in the word of God, and the gates of hell would never prevail against it.

Immediately upon Duke Georg's death in 1539, the Saxons produced the German *Apology* of 1540 in his territory. If one turns to Ap 14 of an original copy, one finds that the wording is *exactly* the same as that of 1531 — wording that has remained unaltered to the present day.

---

[519] *WATR* 4.42. Melanchthon's retort is a stinging rejoinder to the old Catholic dictum, "You cannot have God for your father unless you have the church for your mother" — the same rationale employed by today's crypto-Catholic movement, e.g., Carl E. Braaten in *Mother Church* "Ecclesiology and Ecumenism," [Minneapolis: Augsburg Fortress, 1998]. Where the reformers saw the church as the priesthood of all believers (*communio sanctorum*) recognizable by faith alone, Braaten and many ecumenists see it as an Alveldian Roman hierarchical construct.

Rite Vocatus

CCM postulates the fantastic notion that the reformers possessed a desire, even a "deep desire," to be part of a hierarchical clerical structure (later) known as "historical episcopacy." How completely erroneous this is, is easily demonstrated in Luther's Saxony. In the aftermath of the Diet of Worms of 1521, the emperor, who needed Lutheran cooperation to defend against the growing Turkish threat, had been stymied in his efforts to enforce the Diet's Edict. When the Diet of Speyer subsequently met in 1526, it unanimously resolved that, "Each one is to rule and act for himself as he hopes and trusts to answer to God and the Imperial Majesty." Lohse observes that as a result of this new princely participation in the reorganizing of the church, "Luther himself understood the resolution of Speyer as the end of episcopal jurisdiction."[520] He points to Luther's letter to the elector, dated November 22, 1526, in which he writes, "Papal and clerical coercion and regulation are now abolished in the Electorate of Your Electoral Grace. All of the cloisters and religious foundations are falling into the hands of your Electoral Grace as the supreme head; with these institutions also come the duties and burdens associated with their management. Yet there is no one else who can or should assume them."[521]

The decline of episcopal jurisdiction post-Augsburg, and the hastening of it by the Lutherans, played itself out in rather dramatic fashion in many places, but nowhere more so than in Luther's own Saxony, two prominent examples of which follow.

The diocese of Merseburg was one of three governed by the powerful Wettin princes. Centered in Leipzig and founded in 955, it dissolved in 1561 after having a history of 43 bishops. Throughout the centuries until 1544, there are endless lists of

---

[520] Lohse 63.
[521] *WA Br* 4.1052, II. 21-25.

the Catholic ordained under the "grades" of "Tonsured, Acolytes, Subdeacons, and Presbyters." None are listed in terms of a call (*Berufung*), but rather as "ordained clergy," *ordinaciones clericorum.* But in 1544 the bishop's seat went to a Lutheran, Superattendent Anton Musa, in office from 1545-1548. During this period one finds that under the Lutherans the title *ordinaciones clericorum* was immediately dropped — and replaced with *vocatus ad* — "called to," e.g., *vocatus ad Parochiam, vocatus ad Diaconatum,* etc..

With his archenemy Duke Georg now dead, Luther preached in Merseburg Cathedral on August 2, 1545, and performed several ordinations. Had "ecclesiastical discipline in the manner described in the ancient canons," or "canonical polity" so as not to "undermine the authority of the bishops" been the deep desire of the Lutherans after Augsburg, Musa, not Luther, would have done the ordinations. Nor would Luther have done any other ordinations for that matter. Yet it is clear that until the end of his life, Luther did not regard ordination, or the exclusive exercise of it by bishops, to be a big deal or even necessary.

After the defeat of the Protestants in 1547, the Catholic Michael Helding, who would be the last Bishop of Merseburg, immediately reversed the Lutheran practice, and returned the diocese to the Catholic sacrament of *ordinaciones clericorum.*

The lack of desire for anything even resembling a so-called "historical episcopacy" is best seen at ground zero of the Reformation itself. If one consults the registry of the *Wittenberger Ordiniertenbuch* between 1537 — the year of the Smalkald adoption of the CA and *Apology* as confessional writings — and Luther's death in 1546, one finds that an astonishing total of 738 persons were "ordained." Every last one of them, however, is registered as *vocatus ad.* Not a single one is *ordinaciones clericorum.*[522] And not a single one was

---

[522] Piepkorn used the *BSLK* (501, n.1) in referencing the Ordination Register, but obviously either completely missed or ignored the *ordinaciones clericorum* vs. *vocatus ad* distinction.

ordained by a bishop! Given these facts, Wengert's enthusiastic claim that "far from overturning apostolic, historic succession among bishops, Luther sought to uphold it and revive it in the face of papal abuse,"[523] appears all the more absurd. If that were even remotely true, why didn't Luther simply implement it in his own backyard all those years? Why didn't he counsel the Bohemians to seek a rapprochement with Rome to establish a canonical system of bishops and archbishops, or send the fellow from Breslaw back home, or to Rome, or at least to a bishop sympathetic to the Reformation? In fact the Lutherans did the exact opposite, placing the entire emphasis not on ordination by a bishop, but on one's call from the priesthood of all believers, the *Gemeinde,* the *communio sanctorum, rite vocatus.*

These practices in Merseburg and Wittenberg, indeed throughout Saxony, were in keeping with the express wishes of the reformers themselves, specifically Elector John the Steadfast. As the ruler of Saxony at the time of the presentation of the *Augsburg Confession,* he had also signed it, along with his son and successor, John Frederick the Magnanimous. In a signed document in the *Urkundenbuch der Universität Wittenberg* dated May 5, 1536, John Frederick, along with his brother, in fulfillment of their father's last will and testament, decreed an end to episcopalism with its attendant hierarchy — what Pelikan/Tappert and Kolb/Wengert respectively refer to as "the various ranks of the church," the "ecclesiastical hierarchy." Holdovers from that system with its ecclesiastical "dignitaries," would be allowed to live out their remaining days, after which time the entire Catholic hierarchy, with all of its titles and names, was to be "completely wiped out and extinguished!"[524]

---

[523] Wengert 24.

[524] *"So wollen wir auch himit die titel und namen der digniteten, auch canonien, vicarien, caplanen nach beurter personen abgang genzlichen ausgelescht und extinguirt haben!"* Walter Friedensburg, *Urkundenbuch der Universität Wittenberg,* Teil I: 1502-1611, (Magdeburg: Selbstverlag HKPSA, 1926), 180. Cf. M. Bierbaum,

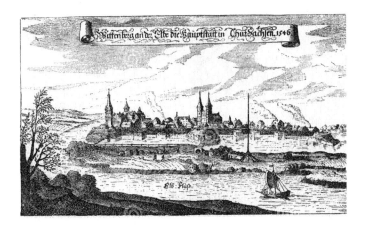

Luther's "Little Wittenberg" 1546

The importance of this document cannot be overemphasized against the false claims of CCM that the reformers "deeply desired" a return to Catholic church polity and ecclesiastical hierarchy, if only they had been able to do so. As the list of ranking officials at the Diet (*Sitzordnung des Heiligen Römischen Reiches Deutscher Nation, Worms 1507-08*) clearly shows, the Saxon electors represented fully two thirds of the electorate (*Weltliche Kurfürsten*), controlling three bishoprics belonging to the Holy Roman Empire of the German Nation, more than any other territorial princes. And they fully intended to reform them, beginning already in Augsburg. When at the presentation of the *Augsburg Confession* not a single bishop agreed to sign it, the Elector and his son signed it for them.

Luther, himself, had declared after reading the Imperial Edict of September 22, 1530, "As far as the spiritual jurisdiction is concerned, the thing certainly appears to have an inequality to it, so that the *Kirchenregiment* still compels our priests in many burdensome things, much of it opposed to one's

---

"Domkapitel," *Lexicon für Theologie und Kirche,* (Freiburg, Herder, 1959): "Besetzung. Die Dignitäten verleiht der Hl. Stuhl, die Kanonikate u. Vikarien der Bischof (vorbehaltl. c. 1435) Mitwirkungsrechte."

conscience and the gospel. For this reason their jurisdiction and *Kirchenregiment* [Tappert's "ecclesiastical order," Kolb/Wengert's "church order"] can in no way ever again be reestablished or reintroduced."[525] In 1533 he announced in *The Private Mass and the Consecration of Priests* [526] that "henceforth it will not go well" for the bishops; they can keep their "atrocities and their anointing, we will see to getting our pastors and preachers through baptism and God's word, without their anointing, ordained and certified through our choosing and calling."[527]

The "atrocities" (*Greuel*) or "outrages" of which Luther speaks are not simply physical cruelties, as is often portrayed today, which once halted, would cause the reformers to embrace episcopalism,[528] but spiritual violence against the gospel, which included the Edict's ban on the preaching of justification in CA 4.

He made perhaps his most famous anti-episcopal succession statement in his *Chronikon* on the tenth anniversary of the printing of the Latin and German *Editio princeps* of the *Augsburg Confession*:

> In the church, the succession of bishops does not make a bishop, but the Lord alone is our bishop. He awakens bishops where, which, and when he wishes, as we have seen in Hieronymous, Augustinus, Ambrosius, Hus, and also in us, *getting rid of the succession* (*Beiseitesetzung*), which the papists praise so highly.[529]

And yet the persistent myth floated pre and post-CCM,

---

[525] Walch 16.1541, Nr. 19, 1-9.

[526] *Von der Winckelmesse und Pfaffen Weyhe, WA* 38.195-256.

[527] *WA* 38.236, 23f.

[528] A common misconception of *CCM* advocates.

[529] Walch 14.600: *So macht in der Kirche nicht die Succession der Bischöfe einen Bischof, sondern der Herr allein ist unser Bischof. Der erweckt Bischöfe, wo, welche, und wann er will, wie wir sehen an Hieronymus, Augustinus, Ambrosius, Hus, und an uns selbst, mit Beiseitesetzung der Succession, welche die Papisten rühmen.* Also *WA* 53.74.

quoting Wengert's book, is that "far from overturning apostolic, historic succession among bishops, Luther sought to uphold it and revive it in the face of papal abuse,"[530] a fallacious claim and concept never discussed in Augsburg. How great a fable Luther's supposed desire to uphold and revive it is, can also be seen in the high profile "blessed examples" that occurred in his and Melanchthon's lifetimes, with Luther often being the prime instigator.[531]

At the death of Duke Georg in Albertine Saxony, for example, Luther quickly advised his brother and successor, Duke Henry (1539-1541) to introduce the Reformation into his lands through visitations.[532] Henry's two bishops, Johann von Maltitz, of Meissen (1534-1549), and Sigismund von Lindenau, of Merseburg (1535-1544) vigorously objected, with Maltitz protesting that the duke's visitations did not have their consent and was strictly the purview of the office of the bishops (*quod absque suo consensu visitationem Dux instituerit quae pertineat ad officium episcopi*). But it was to no avail. and the Visitation was rapidly undertaken by visitors from Wittenberg.[533]

When Henry's son, Maurice (1541-1553), succeeded him, instead of supporting the bishops, he replaced them with consistories and superintendents.[534] By 1573 ordinations were being done by the *Generalsuperintendent + Assessoren des Konsistoriums* (*Oberkirchenrat*), "and a number of pastors and private citizens," *und einige Pfarrer und Privatpersonen* (*Lehnherren*),[535] and were taking place in Wittenberg, Berlin, Stendahl, Werben, Wittstock, and Neustadt-Brandenburg. The *Privatpersonen* (laymen!) who took part in ordinations were the

---

530 Wengert 24.

531 Contrary to Bergendoff's assertion in *LW* 40, x.

532 Veit Ludwig von Seckendorf, *Historia Lutheranismi,* 217. The focus of the Visitations was education, not episcopal station.

533 Emil Sehling, *Die evangelischen Kirchenordnungen des 16 Jahrhunderts,* Institut für Evangelisches Kirchenrecht, I. i. 257 sqq.

534 *Ibid,* 95.

535 *Gnandsteiner Kirchenordnung, Mark Brandenburg,* Sonderdruck aus dem Wichman Jahrbuch XIX u. XX, 1965/1966, Beate Fröhner, s. 8.

schössene Lehnherren, (*schoß* from Mittelhochdeutsch: *schoz,* meaning "tax," *Zoll, Steuer*). Not the farmer or the baker were the "selected laymen" to participate in the ordinations, but the tax-paying feudal lords of Saxony — as they already could in 1530. And in Luther's day there were 440 such feudal tax-paying families to choose from.

Very similar circumstances unfolded with Luther's guidance in Electoral Brandenburg under Elector Joachim II (1535-1571).[536] While this prince was favorable toward the Lutheran Reformation, he nevertheless sought to create a conservative program of his own, and in 1539 established a commission for reform that included Melanchthon and the Erasmian Georg Witzel. On March 1, 1540 after consulting with Luther,[537] the towns and nobles of the Diet "but not the spiritualty [bishops], [538] accepted the 1540 *Brandenburger Kirchenordnung* (church regulation), and swiftly followed it up with a Visitation. Pastoral candidates were to be examined by the superintendent, (in this case Jakob Stratner), or by a similar colleague, before assuming the office of *Pfarrstelle.* The old forms of worship were kept, though the retention of the episcopacy remained an open question. Ordination could only be performed by a bishop who was committed to the Reformation. But of the three bishops in Brandenburg at the time, Busso von Alvensleben, Bishop of Havelsberg; Georg von Blumenthal, Bishop of Lebus; and Matthias von Jagow, Bishop of Brandenburg; only Jagow (1526-1544) had joined the evangelical cause. He had embraced the Lutheran Reformation with gusto, offering communion in both kinds in 1539, and taking a wife in 1541. But Alvensleben and Blumenthal filed formal protests against the new church regulation, and even Jagow, (who some might today refer to as an "evangelical bishop"), felt compelled to write to the Elector requesting that his "episcopal rights and jurisdiction might not

---

536 Cf. Kidd, 304-307.
537 W.M.L. de Wette, *Dr. Martin Luthers Briefe, Sendschreiben, und Bedenken,* Vol.V. 232.
538 Sehling, iii., 28 sqq.

be abridged." [539] Whether evangelical or not, however, "episcopal authority soon proved incompatible with the new regime, and it was denounced as 'tyranny' by the preachers."[540]

When Jagow died in 1544, he was succeeded by the evangelical bishop, Joachim von Münsterberg-Oels. But in 1550, with Münsterberg-Oels still in office, the Brandenburg legislature (*Landtagsrezeß*) replaced the bishops with consistories and superintendents, turning the examination and ordination duties of the bishop back over to the superintendent, (the equivalent of today's "dean" or *Dekan* in Germany), referring to him as "our spiritual bishop" (*unserem geistlichen bischofe*).[541]

Now it must be said, if there was ever a huge opportunity for 16th century Lutherans to institute and showcase Lutheran bishops in "apostolic succession," and in premier locations — (Berlin among them), this was it! But instead of embracing historic episcopalism, they showed their true evangelical colors by returning to the Visitations and dispensed with the old Catholic system in favor of deans. The *Landesherr,* or territorial prince, in the mean time, was dubbed the *summus episcopus* and did the bureaucratic chores of the *Landeskirchen,* of which there were more than two dozen in Germany. The Lutheran churches in the land of Luther would not only go on to survive without historic episcopal succession — they would thrive without bishops for the next four hundred years![542]

In short, the German *Apology* to which the reformers, electors, nobility, and the German nation all subscribed, edits

---

[539] A.F. Riedel, *Codex Diplomaticus Brandenburgensis,* III. iii. 480.

[540] *Ibid* I. ix. 462.

[541] LThK, *Lexikon für Theologie und Kirche,* Bnd. 2, "Brandenburg," B. Stasiewski, 645-646.

[542] Historical episcopacy was first introduced into German Protestantism by Adolf Hitler as part of the 1933 *Führerprinzip.* Bishoprics were created in the Reichskirche under Reichsbischof Müller in the states of Hannover, Bavaria, and Württemberg. In 1945, two of these nationalistic bishops, Wurm and Meiser, were retained for their leadership qualities, but have come under closer scrutiny in recent years for their suspect stances on the Jews. Cf. *RGG,* I, 1307.

out any desire for a *canonicam politiam,* the "usefulness" of which, other than for ecclesiastical tyranny, had long since come and gone. CCM presents a false scenario by equating the reformers' desire for peace through maintenance of the bishops' political estates, with a longing for episcopal governance. The negotiations in Augsburg were first and foremost about the avoidance of war, and the evidence strongly suggests the only reason the reformers put the "desire to help maintain" the estates on the table in the first place was as a tactical bargaining chip (*als taktisches Zugeständnis*) in anticipation of the Diet's demand for the restoration of the *status quo ante*.

Thus there can be no surprise that the "desire" of Ap 14 in the German is rendered in the past tense and no longer on the table. As Martin Lehman points out, after Melanchthon and Jonas had communicated to Luther that Albrecht von Hohenzollern, the Archbishop of Mainz, desired to come to terms with the evangelicals in Augsburg, Luther wrote to him "on July 6, 1530, in which he asked this powerful prince in the Church of Rome to use his influence in seeking to bring about a peaceful settlement of the religious controversy.[543] Albrecht had in fact demonstrated an irenic spirit in the negotiations that took place at the diet. However, when in 1531 he proceeded to take stern repressive measures against members of the city council at Halle who refused to participate in the Easter mass under one kind, Luther became indignant at the archbishop's conduct."[544] His response is *The Private Mass*, in which he pulled the plug on the offer to accept canonical ordination for the sake of peace. "Such humility we have also tendered *until now* (*bisher auch angeboten*) to our present day Antiochuses and Demetriuses, namely, that they should have the power to confirm our pastors in their calling, even though they may be our enemies, in order that they might not be able to complain that we were proud and would do or permit nothing for the sake

---

[543] *WA* 30 II.397-412.
[544] *Ibid,* 38.141-142.

215

of peace and unity."[545] The evidence clearly shows, however, that latest by 1531 Luther and the Wittenberg reformers had no intention of returning to an episcopal hierarchical system — assuming they ever did.[546] It also thoroughly debunks the myth of CCM, perpetuated by the ELCA seminaries, that "far from overturning apostolic, historic succession among bishops, Luther sought to uphold it and revive it in the face of papal abuse." Nothing could be further from the truth.

In summary:

   • The term "historical episcopacy/historic succession" did not exist at the time of the presentation of the *Augsburg Confession* and *Apology.*

   • Episcopal/apostolic/historic succession was never discussed in Augsburg.

   • Ap 14 refers to the political princely bishops' estates, not to any ecclesiastical "succession."

   • Both the Latin and German texts of Ap 14 make clear any "desire" to maintain the bishops' estates for the sake of peace, is a past event.

---

[545] *Ibid* 236.

[546] Cf. Kurt Schmidt-Clausen, *Episcopacy in the Lutheran Church?* "The Development of Offices of Leadership in the German Lutheran Churches: 1918-Present," (Philadelphia: Fortress Press, 1970), 72-73: "The office of bishop in German Lutheranism is a relatively recent institution. It came into existence when the end of the monarchy in Germany in 1918 brought with it the discontinuation of the so-called 'Government of the Church by secular authorities' (i.e., princes) . . . First of all of great importance is the fact that with a few exceptions not worth noting there have been no bishops as chief officers of the Church throughout the four-hundred-year history of German Lutheranism."

- The German Ap 14 omits any willingness to keep the "ecclesiastical and canonical polity."

- The only "succession" of interest to the reformers is the *successio fidelium.*

- CCM subverts CA 4 & 7 that faith alone (and not a *successio episcoporum*) creates true Christian unity.

- Ap 14's focus is "call" (*vocatio*), not "ordination" (*ordinatio*).

Coepiscopos

The origin, structure, and phrasing of Melanchthon's Ap 14 statement of "desire" is especially interesting. Articulated as a gambit, his original offer "to help maintain the church polity and various ranks of the ecclesiastical hierarchy, (although they were created by human authority),"[547] is withdrawn in the very same paragraph, the bishops' raging against the gospel being "the reason for the abolition of canonical government in some places, though we were earnestly desiring to keep it." This rather facetious wording is uncannily similar to Luther's preface (*Vorrede*) to Melanchthon's *Instructions to the Visitors* of 1528, penned three years before the *Apology*: "We would gladly have reestablished the 'proper' (*recht*) office of bishop and visitation, as the highest of necessities, but [instead] we've decided to stay with the office of love, common to and commanded of all Christians, thus S.K.F.G. [the Elector] ordained/ordered (*ordenen*) several capable persons to this office, namely Knight Hans von der Plantiz, Dr. Hieronymus Schurf, Asmus von Haubitz, and Philip Melanchthon."[548]

---

[547] Melanchthon's use of *humana auctoritate* violates Canon Law's premise that ecclesiastical hierarchy is divinely established.

[548] *"Wir hetten gerne widder (das) recht Bischoflich und besucheampt, als auffs höhest von nöten angericht gesehen, Aber da haben wir zur*

217

This preface is very important for a number of reasons: 1) Luther's words, "We would gladly have reestablished the 'proper' office of bishop and visitation, as the highest of necessities," were written, of all places, on the cover page of Melanchthon's famous *Instructions* booklet for oversight by superintendents. Melanchthon paraphrased it three years later in Ap 14 with the phrase: "we have given frequent testimony... to our deep desire to maintain the church polity and various ranks of the ecclesiastical hierarchy." 2) Luther's words are rife with sarcasm, pretending the reformers would just love to reestablish the "*proper* office of bishop" of the ecclesiastical hierarchy, (which they've just finished demolishing), but alas, they'll stick with the office of Christian love instead, (it being the only true office there is). 3) None of the ordained mentioned here are clergy, making it clear Luther did not understand ordination "clerically/clericalistically." Melanchthon is the only theologian in the bunch, yet all are *recht gebührlich berufen* (rightly and duly called) in accordance with Ap 14, laymen ordained (*geordenet*) by a layman (the elector) to the bishop's office of visitation. Far from "eliminating the laity as a separate category of Christian existence" (Wengert), Luther emphasized their premier role in the confessional life of the church by pointing to the greatest of all church councils, called and convened not by any clergy, as he noted in his *Appeal to the Ruling Class of the German Nation (*1520), but by a layman: the emperor. "Further, the bishop of Rome neither called nor sanctioned the Council of Nicaea, the most celebrated of all, but the emperor, Constantine. After him, many other emperors did the same, and these councils were the most Christian of all. Moreover, when I examine decisions of those councils which the pope himself called, I find they did nothing of special importance."[549]

Von Haubitz and von Plantiz, as members of the priesthood

---

liebe ampt ordenen, nemblich: Ritter Hans von der Plantiz, Dr. Hieronymus Schurf, Asmus von Haubitz, und Philip Melanchthon." WA 26.197, 17f.
[549] *WA* 6.413.

of all believers of the Christian nobility of the German nation, already had a special responsibility of oversight (*bischoflich*) of their people. Hieronymus Schurf, on the other hand, was Luther's lawyer (*Jurist*) who defended him before the emperor in Worms, and whom he may have had in mind, along with other jurists such as Fabian von Freilitzsch, when he penned his vision of a priesthood of all believers in *A Sermon on Keeping Children in School.*[550] He considered them properly called and "ordained" (*geordenet*), "rare birds," "the new generation of clergy," "true bishops before God," and "preachers."

Hieronymus Schurff

Attempting to strictly limit such examples to the "metaphorical," (though all of the aforementioned calls were real), Wengert quips that after all, "no one talks about the bishopric or papacy of all believers."[551] But Luther did precisely that, not least in his famous pronouncement that all who have crawled out of the baptismal font are all equally priests, bishops, and popes. He bestowed bishop's titles left and right to friends and colleagues — certainly reckless behavior, one would think, for one desiring so deeply to "revive and

---

[550] Cf. *LW* 46.239, n. 47.
[551] Wengert 12.

uphold. . . apostolic, historic succession among bishops."[552] In a letter to Spalatin in Altenburg on August 15, 1539, (in which he thanks the von Einsiedel family for various things), Luther not only accords him the title of bishop, but of "archbishop," a title he had also given to Jonas, addressing him in the vocative: *"Georgia Spalatino, Archiepiscopo Misnen"* (*Erzbischofe der Kirchen zu Meißen*).[553] Spalatin had no diocese, though he was active in the temporarily vacant Diocese of Meissen following the death of Bishop Johannes von Schleinitz (1518-1537). In the same letter Luther asks Spalatin to greet his "fellow bishops," *"Saluta D. Ionam et alio coepiscopos!"* These included at least three laymen, Melchior von Creutzen, Caspar von Schönberg, and Rudolf von Rechenberg, with Justus Jonas being the only theologian in the bunch!

Bugenhagen did the same. Ludwig Binder points to a 1544 letter Bugenhagen sent to Johannes Honterus in Ungern (today's Romania). He addressed it to "The Bishop of the Diocese of Kronstadt" (*Superintendenten der Kronstädter Diözese*) at a time when Honterus was not even ordained, much less a pastor in Kronstadt, underscoring the fact that Bugenhagen, "like Luther, was quite unconcerned about assigning [ecclesiastical] titles,"[554] titles the ELCA and others

---

[552] *Ibid* 24. Cf. Walch 21a.12, 30f.: In a very early alert to the corrupting influence of hierarchical episcopacy, Luther, in a letter dated June 8, 1516, urged his friend Staupitz to decline the Elector's offer to make him the Bishop of Chiemsee. Staupitz, he insisted, was simply much too good to be a bishop.

[553] Walch 21.2572. Luther addressed Justus Jonas as the "Archbishop of Saxony" a decade earlier in a letter dated April 19, 1529, *WA* Br 5.1410: *Reuerendiss[imo] in Christo Patri ac Domino D. Iusto Ione, Archiepiscopo Saxonie . . .*

[554] Ludwig Binder, "Die Entstehung der lutherischen Superintendentur in der Siebenbürgisch- sächsischen Kirche," *Beihefte der Kirchlichen Blätter,* Monatsschrift der Ev. Kirche A.B. in der Sozialistichen Republik Rumänien, Heft 2, BKB 2, 1980, Seite 75. "Im Jahre 1544 schreibt Bugenhagen aus Wittenberg an Johannes Honterus einen Brief, in welchem er ihn als Superintenten [Bischof] der siebenbürgischen Kirchen, so doch als einen solchen über einen

are now trying so hard to press into frames. But as we've seen, titles and ordination were no big deal for the Wittenberg reformers; publicly proclaiming justification by grace through faith in one's baptism, on the other hand, was everything.

Melanchthon had issued an early warning to those who get hung up on church polity in his 1528 *Instructions for the Visitors of Parish Pastors in Electoral Saxony* — "On the Human Order of the Church," (*Von menschlichen kirchen ordenung*): "It is obvious that much confusion has resulted from an unrestrained preaching about church order (*Kirchenordenung*). Therefore the pastors have been admonished to give greater attention to important subjects, such as Christian repentance, as treated above, faith, good works, the fear of God, prayer, the honoring of God, etc. . . . these subjects are of greater importance," and "the people are to be taught to speak with restraint about such matters as church order," since "the only reason for keeping [it] is to learn the word of God."[555]

---

größeren Kirchenkreis bezeichnet. Honterus wird als Superintendent betitelt, noch bevor er überhaupt als Pfarrer von Kronstadt Geistlicher war . . . Bugenhagen war wohl über die genauen Verhältnisse in Kronstadt bei Abfassung seines Briefes nicht unterrichtet, und war wie Luther etwas sorglos in der Zuteilung von Ehrenbezeichnungen."
[555] *WA* 26. 222-223.

Chapter 9

_____

*"I've been thinking a lot lately about the power of doctrines —
how support for a false dogma can become politically
mandatory, and how overwhelming contrary evidence only
makes such dogmas stronger and more extreme.*"[556]

Paul Krugman

A Pious Plethora

Called to Common Mission is, without a doubt, the most
egregious theological and historical fraud ever foisted on
American Lutheranism. Just as Bohemia's sixteenth century
subterfuge sought to create a semblance of successive
episcopal governance through Italian ordinations, (condemned
by Luther in *De instituendis ministris*), CCM seeks to create
the same semblance through twenty-first century imitation
Anglican ordinations. Its genius was to sell itself as an
adiaphoron, a matter of theological indifference and simple
church polity, rather than the confessional train wreck that it
is. By introducing the confusion of CCM into the clarity of
CA 7's *satis est* for true unity, the means to an end were
achieved. Viewed by most ELCA sheep as little more than an
in-house policy squabble among clerics, interest quickly
waned in what appeared to be nothing more than a
disagreement over ecclesiastical administration. Once this
elephant in the room had been successfully passed off as a
mouse (gospel as law), a more protracted fight over a mouse
many perceived to be an elephant (homosexuality) could begin
(law as gospel). CCM was piously celebrated as a *fait
accompli* and the total confusion of law and gospel it ushered

_____

[556] *The New York Times,* May 16, 2014, A27. Krugman is a Nobel
prize winning economist.

in persists to the present day.

In 2004, the fifth anniversary of its adoption, the ELCA quietly reversed itself in a stunning admission that the very premise of CCM is complete fiction.[557] But by then people no longer cared. In §80 of *The Church as Koinonia of Salvation: Its Structures and Ministries* — "Common Statement of the 10th Round of the U.S. Lutheran-Roman Catholic Dialogue," the ELCA admits:

> Prior to the late 1530s the theme of succession played little role in the Reformation debates on the role and authority of the bishops. The authority and ministry of the bishops, not any particular concept of succession, were the subject of the debate. The Lutheran Confessions explicitly regret the loss of the "order of the church" (Apol. 14.1) that resulted from the presbyterial ordinations the Lutherans judged to be necessary for the life of their churches, but neither Article 28 of the Augsburg Confession on the power of bishops nor the response by the imperial Catholic theologians to it in the Confutation refers explicitly to succession.[558]

This constitutes an astounding disavowal of the very heart of CCM's "Agreement in Ministry §11:

> "Historic succession" refers to a tradition which goes back to the ancient church, in which bishops already in the succession install newly elected bishops with prayer and the laying-on-of-hands. At present the Episcopal Church has bishops in this historic succession, as do all the churches of the Anglican Communion, and the Evangelical Lutheran Church in America at present does not, although some member churches of the Lutheran World Federation do. The Chicago-Lambeth Quadrilateral of 1886/1888, the ecumenical policy of The

---

[557] Cf. Mark D. Menacher in *Logia: A Journal of Lutheran Theology, Called to Common Mission: A* Lutheran Proposal? (Epiphany 2002), 11: 1, 21-28.

[558] As with *CCM,* the Dialogue teams did not rely on the original Latin and German texts, but on the inferior English translation of Kolb/Wengert's 2000 version of the *BoC.*

Episcopal Church, refers to this tradition as "the historic episcopate." *In the Lutheran Confessions, Article 14 of the Apology refers to this episcopal pattern by the phrase, "the ecclesiastical and canonical polity," which it is "our deep desire to maintain."*

This 2004 rejection of CCM's *raison d'être* raises huge questions for both American Lutherans and their ecumenical partners. If episcopal succession wasn't discussed in Augsburg after all, was the ELCA rank and file intentionally duped into accepting an agreement based on false and misleading information? Is CCM based on a lie, or on historical and confessional incompetence, or both? Is it morally justifiable to adopt a confessional statement with one ecumenical partner, while agreeing to its complete opposite with another for the sake of "mission and unity?"[559]

The statement also adds further fiction to the mix. As has already been shown, Ap 14 and 28 express no "regret" whatsoever for "the loss of the 'order of the church'" (misleadingly put in quotes and attributed to Ap 14.1), but explicitly reject canonical ordination, stating emphatically, "In

---

[559] ELCA Bishop Michael Rogness (St. Paul Area Synod) acknowledged the deception in his 2008 review of Wengert's book *Priesthood, Pastors, Bishops:* "Far from the reformers' desire that pastors and bishop are both part of the same office, the ELCA has adopted the rituals which have elevated the office of bishop above that of a pastor. Anyone who compares the ordination of a pastor with the installation of a bishop cannot escape that conclusion. Supposedly the ELCA does not embrace the belief of 'episcopal succession,' that is, that 'apostolic succession' is symbolized and conveyed through the office of bishop, a position which Wengert also disavows. But with *Called to Common Mission* (CCM) we have adopted the rituals of those who do believe that, and we have accordingly agreed that pastors cannot officiate at ordinations. Apparently to demonstrate that we really do not concur theologically with what we have adopted liturgically, we allow 'exceptional' ordinations by pastors, and then make the process so formidable that only a few venture to request it. All this we have done with scant theological discussion."

this issue our consciences are clear." Nor is it true, as the ELCA asserts, that the cause of the "loss of the 'order of the church'" was Lutheran presbyterial ordinations (the Romanists' claim), but was the result of Rome's infidelity to the gospel. And contrary to both statements' claims regarding 16th century ecclesiastical polity, neither the Latin nor the German Ap 14 texts advocate a return to it, nor do they support anything even remotely resembling "historical episcopacy." The absurd conclusion of the U.S. Lutheran-Roman Catholic Dialogue, "that the 'greatest desire' of the Reformers was to retain this ministerial structure" which "still is normative for present-day Lutheranism," amounts to the ELCA agreeing with Eck, Campeggio, and the Augsburg papists that the reformers were the cause of "the loss of church order," though Ap 14 clearly states "the blame lies with our opponents . . . they tear the churches apart." According to this skewed logic, a return to the medieval "episcopal pattern" ought to be normative for the church today.[560]

It is thus with no great shortage of irony that Wengert dismisses detractors of episcopalism as democratic "fanatics," power grabbing "pietists," and the priesthood of all believers as a "pious" seventeenth or nineteenth century myth (depending on which chapter you're in), all the while ignoring the fact that historical episcopal succession is itself an 18th century pious myth imported from Germany — literally.

This ecclesiastical Trojan horse arrived on American shores courtesy of the Moravian pietists of Herrnhut

---

[560] The ELCA expressed its deep desire for Canon Law and the *canonicam politiam* (political bishops) much earlier in *Toward Full Communion and Concordat of Agreement,* Lutheran-Episcopal Dialogue, Series III, William A. Norgren and William G. Rusch, eds., (Minneapolis: Augsburg, 1991), 50. The editors highlighted Ap 14.5 in Tappert (omitted by Jonas) and stated, "The emphasis has been added to point to the fact that churches which accept the doctrinal authority of the *Book of Concord,* as the Evangelical Lutheran Church in America does, are committed in principal to a preference for 'the ecclesiastical and canonical polity' with its 'various ranks of the ecclesiastical hierarchy.'"

(Berthelsdorf)) by Dresden, a town belonging to the Austrian count, Nikolaus Ludwig Graf von Zinzendorf. Von Zinzendorf was a follower of Philipp J. Spener (1635-1705), a pastor in Frankfurt-am-Main, foe of Lutheran orthodoxy, and the author of *Pious Desires* (*Pia Desideria*), also known as the "Pietist Manifesto," who sought to change Lutheranism from being a "religion of the head," to a "religion of the heart." After being banished from Saxony, Zinzendorf became the Moravian bishop in Berlin in 1737, and travelled throughout Europe and the U. S., establishing Moravian communities, (e.g., in Bethlehem, Pa.). In his *Introduction to Lutheranism,* Eric Gritsch makes the following observation:

> In 1727, Zinzendorf granted a group of Czech Protestants permission to settle in Herrnhut. These refugees were Moravian Brethren, disciples of the Prague reformer Jan Hus who had been burned at the stake in 1415. Moravians had since become pacifists and were committed to an intensive, pious community life and to a Christian unity made visible by the ancient tradition of having bishops in apostolic succession. Zinzendorf, who was deeply involved in the Herrnhut community, was seen as something of a father figure there. He was consecrated bishop of the Moravian Brethren in 1737 in Berlin by the Reformed Court Preacher Daniel E. Jablonski,[561] who claimed to be in apostolic succession with all other Christian bishops. Through his consecration, Zinzendorf established a link between Lutheranism and a historical Protestant episcopate.[562]

Zinzendorf, he notes, is regarded by some as "the patriarch of American Lutheranism." So in the end, the old Bohemian fixation with the pious myth of successive episcopal ordination that was rejected by Luther, managed to leapfrog his Saxony, only to find a new home on American shores. ("Houston, the episcopate has landed.")

---

561 Cf. *RGG,* 507.
562 Eric W. Gritsch, *Introduction to Lutheranism,* (Minneapolis: Fortress), 1994, 34.

Yet such ecclesial zealotry (*Schwärmerei*) came not only from Germany, but from England as well. The question today is: Why should we as Lutherans say "Yes and Amen" to a theological theory that was first approved by the Church of England more than a hundred years after Luther's death, and to a church that is neither theologically nor historically a Reformation church?

In the 17th century rumors began to circulate in England that Luther had acknowledged a number of theological errors, among them, his less than flattering ideas on ordination, (e.g., "Ordination is no big deal!"), especially those recorded in his table talks. The first English copy of *Table Talk* appeared in a book entitled, *Captain Henrie Bell's Narrative or Relation of the miraculous preserving of D. Martin Luther's Book, entituled Colloquia Mensalia.*[563] It was printed in London "by William Du Gard, dwelling in Suffolk-lane, near London-stone." In an early 1652 edition of Captain Bell's book, housed at the British Library, one finds a commentary on the inside cover written by its first owner, a priest, with the initials "S.T.C." Addressing the controversial topic of the day, the attempt to justify "apostolic succession" in light of Luther's words, he writes, "One argument strikes me in favor of the tenet of apostolic succession in Ordination of Bishops and Presbyters as taught by the Church of Rome, and by the larger part of the earlier Protestant Church of England, which I have not seen in any of the books on the subject." What follows is a rather subtle, even comical attempt to show that "apostolic succession" must be understood in "miraculous terms." Using a series of outlandish pictures, he writes, "Jack's Crepitus" (presumably meaning "thunder," from the Latin *crepitus:* "rustle, noise, rattle") was followed by a "Flash of Lightening that struck and precipitated the Ball on St. Paul's Cathedral." S.T.C. concludes, "The initiative alone is supernatural . . . the beginning necessarily miraculous . . . the miracle becomes perpetual, still beginning, never ending," etc.

---

[563] *A Copy of the Order from the House of Commons,* 24th February, 1646.

This contemporary commentary is of interest insofar as it shows how desperate the Church of England still was in the 17th century to find a convincing theological theory to justify the historical episcopate ten years before it became legally binding through the intolerant 1662 *Act of Uniformity*.[564] But before then, as Bell's book shows, (and Cooke's study of *The Historic Episcopate* reveals), the Anglican Church struggled mightily in its attempt to validate its decision to copy the "tenet of apostolic succession in the Ordination of Bishops and Presbyters as taught by the Church of Rome."[565] In the end, however, Rome quashed the Anglican pretensions to its historical episcopacy on September 15, 1896 with Pope Leo XIII's issuance of *On the Nullity of Anglican Orders Apostolicae Curae*. The title speaks for itself. Issued as a papal bull, it can never be undone and Anglican "historical episcopacy" can never be recognized by the Vatican.

Therewith ends Anglicanism's ecumenical selling point of being the *via media* (middle way) between Catholicism and Reformation theology, the supposed "bridge" to Rome, though it is neither a Catholic nor Reformation church. By hitching its wagon to the Anglican episcopal succession of CCM, the ELCA has unwittingly driven its ecclesiastical horse and buggy across a bridge to nowhere.[566]

---

564 See herein Ch. 6

565 The *Act of Uniformity* was directed against the Lutherans (and other Protestants), and is now bizarrely embraced by the ELCA. Cf. Mark D. Menacher, *Called to Common Mission:* Visible Unity Through Grand Deception," http://www.ccmverax.org/GrandDeception.htm: "Unbeknownst to many, the unity prescribed by *Called to Common Mission* is grounded not in the Lutheran Confessions but rather is derived from the English Parliament's 1662 *Act of Uniformity* (cf. *CCM* paragraph 16). By adopting *CCM,* the ELCA has pledged to conform its ordination structure and practice to the dictates of seventeenth century English episcopalian intolerance."

566 Cf. Mark D. Menacher, *Called to Common Mission*: "A Lutheran Proposal?" Logia: A Journal of Lutheran Theology, (Epiphany 2002), 11: 1, 21-28: " . . . by putting the legal principles of episcopalian

"That a Christian Congregation"

The Catholic doctrine of historical episcopal succession rests on the claim that Jesus ordained his apostles at the time of the Last Supper, "the first graduating class," as New York's Cardinal Timothy Dolan referred to them in a recent homily to newly ordained priests. This "first ordination" was meant to perpetuate the priesthood of Christ in the "unbloody" sacrifice of the Eucharist.[567]

Luther responded forcefully to this myth of apostolic succession in the year in which he formulated the heart and soul of his theology, 1520, in the *Babylonian Captivity of the Church*:

> The Romanists adduce their strongest argument, in that, at the Last Supper, Christ said, "This do ye in remembrance of me." "Look," they say at this point, "Christ ordained his disciples as priests" . . . They assert what they like on the basis of Christ's word no matter what the occasion . . . Why do they not argue that He ordained as priests those on whom He laid the office of the word and of baptism when He said, "Go ye into all the world, baptizing them in the name," etc.? . . . Not one of the ancient Fathers asserts that priests were ordained when those words [Lk.22:19] were used.
>
> What then is the origin of this new piece of intelligence? Perhaps they sought by this means to establish a seed bed of unappeasable discord, through which clergy and laity were to be more widely separated than heaven and earth; yet this has proved to be unbelievably hurtful to baptismal grace, and to

---

religious intolerance before the promises of the gospel and by putting the sinister statutes of the seventeenth-century English kingdom before the rightful domain of the kingdom of Christ, the ELCA has created for itself a series of crises with respect to academic credibility, historical reality, intellectual integrity, and ethical accountability."

[567] As taught by Thomas Aquinas (*Summa theologica* III, qu. 79 a. 7; ad 3; qu. 81 a. 4), and dogmatized at the Council of Trent (Sess. XXII, cap. 2).

the confusion of fellowship based on the gospel. Here is the root of the terrible domination of the clergy over the laity.[568]

"The perpetuity of the office," he declared to the Bohemians who desired historical episcopal succession, "is shown to be fictitious."[569] He rejected Augustine's claims, (which are the same as CCM's), that bishops represent a visible and tangible sign of the unity and presence of the church. The latter is recognized only through the signs of word and sacrament. Where these occur, one can reasonably expect to find the church. Bornkamm writes:

> Luther clearly perceives the contradiction. Only for a few years did he endure the vagueness and the half measures of Augustine. The church is not a visible organization; it extends over all the world. But it is a real communion, which rallies about Christ, its common Head. It no longer finds its unity in the Catholic episcopal succession (*successio episcoporum*) but in the hidden yet uninterrupted continuity of believers (*successio fidelium*). Only for a short time after this [1517] do we still find an unrelated external acknowledgement of the hierarchical church in Luther.[570]

Just as it was demanded of the Lutherans at the Diet of Augsburg, Christian unity in CCM is predicated on ceremonial uniformity *iure humano* (contrary to CA 7), not on *sola fide iure divino* (contrary to CA 4), the article by which the church stands or falls.[571] As such it requires adherence to "apostolic succession" for the sake of unity in a "visible church," neither of which exists, since the constitutive element of Christ's

---

568 *WA* 6.563.

569 *WA* 12.190; (40.35).

570 Bornkamm, *Luther's World of Thought,* 143.

571 There is no record of Luther actually using the phrase *iustificatio articulus stantis vel cadentis ecclesiae*. It may be based on his words in *WA* 40 III.352: *quia isto articulo stante stat Ecclesia, ruente ruit Ecclesia* ("Because if this article [of justification] stands, the church stands; if this article collapses, the church collapses.")

church is the word alone, received by faith alone, known to God alone. For this reason all the creeds begin with "I believe," as all things therein are discerned only by the eye of faith, from the existence of the church to the resurrection of the dead. This is Luther's *Deus absconditus* in his *theologia crucis*, a God who is hidden in his revelation through the cross. Alister McGrath writes,

> In a remarkable sermon, he delivered on 30 November 1516, Luther points to the crucifixion as a paradigm for the relation between faith and sense-perception: just as Christ was raised from the ground upon the cross, so that his feet did not rest upon the earth, so the faith of the Christian is denied any foothold in experience.[572]

In contrast to an empirical church that is based on experience and sensory perception, rather than faith, the *communio sanctorum* remains hidden under the cross until the last day. "The cross alone is our theology."[573]

For decades "congregationalism" was taught as the Lutheran ecclesiastical model in such American Lutheran educational materials as Jerry L. Schmalenberger's booklet, *Lutheran Christians and Their Beliefs,*[574] in contrast to presbyterianism, episcopalianism, and the European Lutheran state churches. Referencing Luther's priesthood of all believers, it offered a "bottom up" versus "top down" constitutional form of church governance. With the rise of ecumenism's focus on "visible unity" through historical episcopal succession, however, the congregational model was replaced in the ELCA with something called "wider church," that focused on "leadership" in "three expressions": congregations, synods, and a "church-wide assembly." The

---

[572] Alister E. McGrath, *Luther's Theology of the Cross,* (Oxford: Basil Blackwell, 1985), 168.
[573] *WA* 5.176.32-33: *CRUX sola est nostra theologia.*
[574] *Lutheran Christians and Their Beliefs,* Jerry L. Schmalenberger (Lima, Ohio; Fairway Press, 1984).

latter acts as the ELCA's "highest legislative authority," consisting not of delegates, but of "voting members" who represent only themselves, not their congregations. Direct representation, such as it is, ends at the synodical level, allowing for a massive church-wide representational disconnect in which approximately .02% of the membership make all the decisions for the other 99.8% of its 3.7 million members.

It is perhaps not by accident then, that Luther's famous congregational "civil rights" declaration of 1523 appears only as a footnote in Wengert's *Priesthood, Pastors, Bishops*, and not at all in ELCA generated materials. With its long, in-your-face title, *That a Christian Assembly or Congregation Has the Right and Power to Judge All Teaching and to Call, Appoint, and Dismiss All Teachers, Established and Proven by Scripture*,[575] the tract was written as a succinct defense for the people of the small town of Leisnig in Saxony. They had joined the Reformation, but their *episcopos*, the Abbot Antoninus of Buch of the nearby Cistercian monastery, remained hostile to it. Oversight by the abbot's office had been granted the monastery back in 1191 by Emperor Henry VI, and formally recognized by Pope Martin V in 1419. Antoninus appointed one of his monks, Heinrich Kind, to be the Leisnig parish priest, but when Kind embraced the Reformation, the abbot quickly recalled him. He sent the congregation a new priest, but they refused to accept him, and sent an appeal to Luther instead, asking him to provide them with a written biblical defense for them to call their own pastor and preacher. After he visited them on September 25, 1522, they elected Kind to be their priest, (and Johann Gruner their preacher). A round of negotiations with the abbot followed that included offering him a bribe in the form of an annual "stipend," (which pleased him greatly, but which his monks refused), and the situation remained unresolved until the elector officially recognized the parish's evangelical status

---

[575] *WA* 11.408-416.

in the Visitation of 1529.[576]

Leisnig on the Mulde River in Saxony

Luther begins his treatise to the Leisnig congregation by making it clear that it is the local congregation (*Gemeyne*) he is speaking of, "which does not engage in human affairs," identified as that assembly wherever the gospel is preached, "no matter how few and how sinful and weak they may be," (language he would also use a few months later with the Bohemians in *Concerning the Ministry*).[577] Where it is being preached, no appeals to ecclesiastical hierarchy, old church customs, or traditions are valid. Christ alone is our bishop, he gives oversight (*episcope*) to all Christians.

> In this matter of judging teachings and appointing or dismissing teachers or pastors, one should not at all care about human statutes, law, old precedent, usage, custom, etc., even if they were instituted by pope or emperor, prince or bishop, if one half or the whole world accepted them, or if they lasted one year or a thousand years. For the soul of man is something eternal, and

---

[576] Cf. *LW* 45.161-168.

[577] Cf. Walch 10.1599.88: *so schon nur zehn oder sechs wären* ("even if there are only ten or six").

more important than every temporal thing. That is why it must be ruled and seized only by the eternal word; for it is very disgraceful to rule consciences before God with human law and old custom.[578]

God's word inevitably clashes with human law and custom when these try to rule the soul.

One hears almost nothing from them but such boasting that they have the power and right to judge what is Christian or what is heretical. The ordinary Christian is supposed to await their judgment and obey it. Do you see how shamelessly and foolishly this boasting, with which they intimidated the whole world and which is their highest stronghold and defense, rages against God's law and word? Christ institutes the very opposite. He takes both the right and the power to judge teaching from the bishops, scholars, and councils and gives them to everyone and to all Christians equally when he says, John 10 [:4], "My sheep know my voice." [579]

While bishops, popes, scholars, "and everyone else" have the right to teach, only the sheep have the power to judge whether what is being taught is the word of God.

My dear, what can these water bubbles say against it, with their foot stomping, "Councils, councils! One must listen to the scholars, the bishops, the crowd; one must look at the old usage and custom"? Do you think the word of God should yield to your old usage, customs, and bishops? Never! That is why we let bishops and councils decide and institute whatever they please; when God's word is on our side we — and not they — shall judge what is right or wrong and they will have to yield to us and obey our word[580] . . . wherever there is a Christian congregation in possession of the gospel, it has not only the right and power, but the duty — on pain of losing the salvation of its souls and in accordance with the promise made to Christ in baptism — to

---

[578] *WA* 11.408-409.

[579] *Ibid.*

[580] Cf. Luther's October 26, 1522 Sermon in Weimar, *WA* 10 III. 397-398.

avoid, to flee, to depose, and to withdraw from the authority that our bishops, abbots, monasteries, religious foundations, and the like are now exercising, whose teaching is clearly contrary to the word of God.

Pointing to the priesthood of all believers he states, "For no one can deny that every Christian possesses the word of God and is taught and anointed by God to be a priest, as Christ says, John 6 [:45], 'They shall all be taught by God,' and Psalm 45 [:7], 'God has anointed you with the oil of gladness on account of your fellows.' These fellows are the Christians, Christ's brethren, who with him are consecrated priests, as Peter says too, I Peter 2 [:9], 'You are a royal priesthood so that you may declare the virtue of him who called you into his marvelous light.'"[581]

Already anticipating the question regarding a proper call that would be addressed in CA 14, he asks rhetorically, "If you say, 'How can this be? If he is not called to do so he may indeed not preach, as you yourself have frequently taught.'" His answer is twofold: First, if a Christian is in a place where there are no Christians, he or she is called by God to proclaim the gospel. Second, if they find themselves in a place with other Christians, they should await a call from their fellows to preach and teach. If there is a lack of teachers in that place, they may teach without a call from men, "provided [they do] it in a decent and becoming manner."

"Any congregation" *igliche Kirch* [582] (even one in Montana), may elect and call one or some of its members to preach and teach whenever there is a need, wherever the divine word is absent, (the proverbial "emergency"), "for need is need and has no limits — just as everyone should hurry to the scene of a fire in town and not wait until asked to come." Indeed, "a simple layman, armed with scripture, is to be

---

581 *Ibid,* 309.
582 Cf. *TPPP* 67.

believed above a pope or a council without it."[583] Further, "no bishop should institute anyone without the election, will, and call of the congregation. Rather, he should confirm the one whom the congregation chose and called; if he does not do it, he [the elected one] is confirmed anyway by virtue of the congregation's call." He concludes by saying that if there is no bishop to provide evangelical pastors, the example of Titus and Timothy is invalid, and the congregation must call one of its own, who may exercise all of the duties of the pastoral office — or decide only to preach, leaving baptism "and other lower offices to others — as Christ and all the apostles did, Acts 4."

The Unity Myth

After burying the priesthood of all believers as "a pious myth," then resurrecting it metaphorically in the form of Emser's *zwei Stände Lehre,* Wengert offers his "Concluding Thoughts":

> First and foremost, the priesthood of all believers is not a scheme for giving power to the laity, nor is it an excuse for dividing up Christ's church or diminishing its public offices. When Luther says that we are all priests, bishops, and popes, it is one of his most poignant pleas for unity in the church, that is, for unity among the members of the body of Christ. To say "we are priests because we share Christ's priesthood in baptism" is the same as saying "through baptism we are the body of Christ." There are no loose cannons on the ship of the church.[584]

Nor, apparently, ever a need for "a wild boar in the Lord's

---

583 Luther's retort to Eck at the 1519 Leipzig Debate. Cf. Roland H. Bainton, *Here I Stand — A Life of Martin Luther,* [New York - Nashville, Abingdon - Cokebury Press, 1950], 116-117.
584 Wengert 103.

vineyard."[585] One of the distinct features of the ELCA's selling of CCM and related myths, is the lack of any genuine debate in matters of confessional history and theology. Seen as a threat to the unity and security of the institution, debate is piously touted as being contrary to the gospel and the common good. Wherever dissent does not meet with the institution's official teaching magisterium, debate is stifled at every turn, suppressed at every carefully choreographed gathering of its "threefold expressions" and in all of its publications: censorship for the sake of "unity." As Kittelson once wryly observed, "The constant banging of the drum for unity is yet another tool in Satan's nefarious bag of tricks."

Yet nothing could be more Lutheran, indeed more Melanchthonian, than the art of evangelical disputation, nothing more vital for the proclamation of the gospel, for the sharpening of confessional minds, and the prevention of the onset of a *mirabilis stupor* (amazing trance) of the church into pseudo-theological banalities. That disputation was and is the norm, and not the exception to meaningful theological discourse among Lutherans, is already established in the Ninety-Five Theses and seen in its title, *"Amore et studio elucidande veritatis. Hec subscripta disputabuntur Wittenburge Presidente R.P. Martino Luther."*[586]

Spalatin hailed the rebirth of the gospel through disputation as having its start in 1517 in the indulgence controversy,[587] and brought to full force in the Leipzig Debate. When after sixty years the University of Wittenberg allowed courses in the art of disputation to fall into disuse in 1577, (because

---

[585] Pope Leo X's description of Luther in the papal bull *Exsurge Domine*, June 15, 1520 threatening him with excommunication.

[586] The German title for the 95 Theses is *Die unterstehenden Sätze, die aus Dran und im Streben nach Erforschung der Wahrheit aufgestellt sind, sollen erörtert werden zu Wittenberg unter vorsitz des ehrwürdigen Vaters Martin Luther.*

[587] In his *Ephemerides Spalatini,* which covers the years 1480-1544, he notes concerning 1517: *"MDXVII. Hoc anno...renatum est Evangelium gratiae Dei Witebergae... tum Augustiniano Monacho, cum disputare coepisset..."*

Luther and Melanchthon were no longer around to oversee them!), the *Visitationskommission,* under the leadership of Chancellor Haubold von Einsiedel, Jakob Andreae (Chancellor of Tübingen), and Erbmarschall Hans Löser, demanded they be reinstated. [588] Luther had repeatedly defended the vital importance of vigorous confessional jousting (*Anfechtung*). In his July 7, 1542 preface to *The disputation of Master Heinrich of Lüneburg for his diploma, Dr. Martin Luther presiding,* he wrote:

> Our doctrine and especially that article concerning justification is always assailed, not only from without, but even from within and in our hearts, which happens for our own great benefit. We ought to thank God, therefore, because we do not teach and live so listlessly. If we were not attacked, we could easily become languid and decadent. On account of the adversaries it is necessary for us to be energetic and lively so that we may defend the wisdom of God against them to his glory and for the salvation of mankind, since the wisdom of God is more powerful than all. Hence this custom has arisen that we often debate and battle among our own selves, the one eluding the other, as it were. These propositions have been written so that we may offend. It is proper to entice the devil in order that the wisdom of God may become clear and begin to shine, as Paul says, in our folly, yes, in our warfare [Cor. 1:21]. [589]

Thus, to abrogate the protest is to cease to be Protestant. Giving offense in the gospel is for the spiritual good of the hearer [Rom. 10:19], and so even heretics are highly useful Luther insisted.

Anfechtung for the sake of the gospel, however, appears to

---

[588] Ulrike Ludwig, *Zwischen Philippismus und orthodoxem Luthertum: Der kursächsische Reformprozess und das Melanchthonbild in Kursachsen in den Jahren 1576 bis 1580.* Leucorea-Studien zur Geschichte der Reformation und der Lutherischen Orthodoxie (LStRLO), Bd. 13, hg. Irene Dingel und Armin Kohnle (Leipzig: Evangelische Verlagsanstalt, 2011), S. 106.
[589] *WA* 39 II.191.

have little place in ecumenism's present striving for unity *über alles*. The pursuit of institutional "visible church" predicated on and safeguarded by bishops in succession, has its roots, not in Reformation theology, but in the social ideal of scholasticism's inability to clearly distinguish between the secular and spiritual realms. It is evidenced in ecumenical discussion groups where preeminence is given to ecclesial fraternity over confessional fidelity to the gospel, a prime example of which is found in the writings of Michael J. Root, principal CCM author and former ELCA ecumenical negotiator. In an essay for *Episcopacy, Lutheran-United Methodist Dialogue II*, entitled "Bishops as Points of Unity and Continuity,"[590] Root, now a Roman Catholic, expressed his vision for visible church unity through something he calls clerical "collegiality," that is, (Catholicism's claim) of unity in the hierarchy. In language that prefigured CCM he wrote: "As ordained ministers are one in their proclamation of the gospel in word and sacrament, the church is one," — suggesting the oneness of the church is dependant on the unity of the clergy rather than their "conformity with a pure understanding of the gospel."[591] Root espouses the *Unité, Égalité, Fraternité* of the clergy as a sign and preserver of visible church. "The unity of the ordained ministry is thus a sign and means of the needed unity of the church," — though ordination constituted neither for the Lutheran reformers, nor does the church "need" unity beyond what the Holy Spirit already creates through faith alone.

Quoting not Luther, but Marquette Catholic theologian Bernard Cooke, who maintained that the ordained are the "'link' position who unify the communities into 'the great church,'" (though the Holy Spirit alone does this), Root posits the "collegial character" of the clergy as a constituting and maintaining element of the church, and expresses a deep

---

[590] Michael J. Root, *Episcopacy, Lutheran-United Methodist Dialogue II*, Edited by Jack M. Tuell and Roger W. Fjeld, (Minneapolis: Augsburg, 1991), 118-125.
[591] CA7

desire for a return to the pre-Reformation clerical order. "Such an understanding of the collegial nature of ordained ministry has a strong foundation in the pre-Reformation tradition and may seem obvious to Methodists." But when it comes to returning to this tradition, "Lutheran uneasiness at any hint of the creation of a separate clerical caste may be a problem here." Nevertheless, "As this collegial character is realized, and the ordained ministry is one in its witness to the gospel, the oneness of the church is realized."[592]

Or said differently, the church is a lady in waiting for the clerical caste to get its unifying act together. "The unity of the bishops," he continues, "becomes a special means and sign of the unity of the church," (though the church's only means and sign of unity are word and sacrament, CA5). He fixates on the office-holder, of whom CA 5 says nothing, rather than the office of means, and concludes in a section called, "Episcopacy and the Continuity of the Church:"

> If certain complications are ignored, what has been said about episcopacy and the unity of the church can easily be transformed to apply to episcopacy and the continuity of the church. Continuity is simply unity across time. As bishops oversee the integrity and identity of the church's mission, they

---

[592] A present example of a neo-monastic clerical fraternity can be found, for instance, in the Society of the Holy Trinity (STS), founded in 1997 by disaffected Lutheran clergy who emphasize the "otherness" of the ordained. Its "Senior Pastor" Frank Senne, maintained in a 2005 interview "that the Society does not exist to reflect the church as it is but to model the church as it can become by God's grace. You can't be that without taking some risks. It has been the nature of religious communities and orders to be in a liminal or marginal relationship to the Church [sic]." http://www.societyholytrinity.org/ Luther rejected sodalities for devotional purposes. He castigated their spiritual pride in e.g. *A Treatise Concerning the Blessed Sacrament* (1519), and regarded the communion of saints as the only legitimate Christian fraternity. Judging from their governing statements, STS members apparently have no plans to "sin boldly," (Luther's advice to a troubled Melanchthon on August 1, 1521. Cf. Walch 15.2589).

also oversee its continuity . . . If the church's unity in this gospel is preserved, then the church's continuity is also preserved. The bishop's distinctive ministry of oversight is thus a ministry at the service of the church's continuity. When BEM[593] describes the bishop as a minister of oversight, unity, and continuity, it is ascribing one ministry to the bishop, not three . . . The unbroken continuity of ordination is a sign of the continuity of the church in the one message.

Having thus made the church's unity and continuity dependent on an ecclesiastical rite *iure humano* via the *successio episcoporum*[594] — rather than guaranteed in the cross — Root casts a longing eye to "the creation of a separate clerical caste." "The ecumenical goal should be the restoration of collegiality in ministry and episcope," (though the reformers' goal was simply the faithful proclamation of the gospel).

---

[593] *Baptism, Eucharist and Ministry,* Faith and Order Paper No. 111, World Council of Churches, Geneva, 1982. BEM declared that historical episcopacy is "a sign, but not a guarantee," of unity, (repeated in CCM). The official Roman Catholic response, though, rejected BEM by reasserting episcopacy as both a sign and a guarantee (*Churches Respond to BEM,* "Faith and Order" Paper 144; ed. M. Thurian; Geneva: WCC, 1988, 5:26, 33). Therewith, as Burgess notes, "the eschatological proviso involved in faith in the promise has been eliminated." *Lutheran Forum,* Vol. 26, No. 4, 35 n.38.

[594] Cf. Burgess, 33: "In the course of church history bishops have been as great a source of disunity as of unity. Major tensions and disagreements among early bishops cannot be overlooked; it was not all sweetness and light . . . It appears that at one moment in the 4th century there were no fewer than six bishops in Antioch, each claiming to be the sole representative of the authoritative and valid succession from the days of the apostles. On balance bishops go with the flow, that is, serve the establishment, as can be seen in the fact that in a crisis, which is when teaching authority is really needed, they have tended to line up with the establishment: for example, at the time of the Arian heresy, on the side of the Arians and the Arian emperor . . . at the time of the Reformation, on the side of the pope and the emperor."

Nine years later he'd weave this old Roman episcopal theory of ecclesiastical unity through clerical "collegiality" into CCM.[595] There he employed the term in paragraphs 2, 4, 5, 7, 12, 13, 14, 17, 19, and 24, reinforcing in a clerical compact what Luther rejected as "Emserian *priesterey*," Wengert's "special and external" clergy,[596] and Piepkorn's divine "sacrament of orders,"[597] a continuity of unity through clerical fraternity which Luther dismissed as utterly "fictitious," and a "laughing stock."

Visible unity was strictly a secular matter for Luther, as he wrote to Elector John during the Augsburg negotiations, "ordained by the secular government as a secular ordinance,"[598] useful, for instance, for showing pope and emperor a united political and military front, but never a matter of the gospel. *Christus non curat politiam aut oeconomiam* ("Christ does not concern Himself with the state or with political economy"),[599] including the "ecclesiastical jurisdiction" of bishops (*potestas iurisdictionis*).[600] While the church has externals indicating its presence (preaching, sacraments, call, praise, etc.), Luther was simply not a believer in "visible church,"[601] nor was such unity ever his goal —

---

595 Cf. Root's references to clerical collegiality in CCM, e.g.: "We believe that a ministry of pastoral oversight (*episkope*), exercised in personal, *collegial*, and communal ways, *is necessary* to witness to and *safeguard the unity* and apostolicity *of the church*." (A.5)

596 Wengert, 22.

597 Piepkorn, 116.

598 *WA* Br 5.574.

599 *WATR* 1.932. Christ is most certainly not invested in today's free will "culture wars" that preoccupy so many Americans through the mixing of the kingdoms.

600 Cf. *Urkundenbuch zu der Geschichte des Reichstages zu Augsburg im Jahre 1530,* ed. K.E. Förstemann (Halle, 1833-1835; reprint: Hildesheim, 1966), 2, 250 Section One.

601 E.g., *Answer to the HyperChristian Book, WA* 7.687: "I trust that the holy Christian church cannot be demonstrated physically but can only be believed. Contrary to Murner and all the papists, it will have to remain a spiritual place standing in the Spirit, invisibly built on the

truth and peace were, his negotiation with Zwingli over the Lord's Supper being a case in point, instigated under strong political pressure for the sake of visible unity, but foundering on the issue of truth. The latter is strictly the work of the Holy Spirit who through means (CA 5) of the proclamation of justification alone creates "spiritual unity," as Luther called it, in hearts known only to God. The unity of the church isn't predicated on church government, but on faith in God's word. When Eck insisted at the Leipzig Debate that Christ's words to Peter, "feed my sheep" (John 21) refer to church government, Luther countered with I Corinthians 12:28 to show that church government is only a minor grace, the unity of the body of Christ is preserved by faith without a visible head.[602] "Do not hope for unity or concession," he wrote to the Lutheran negotiators in Augsburg on July 15, 1530, "For this I have never pleaded at God's [throne], since I know that it is an impossibility."[603]

What made it impossible, and was the reason canonical order was abandoned, was not the cruelty of the bishops, as is simplistically touted today in Lutheran-Roman Catholic dialogues, but the complete irreconcilability of the opposing dogmatic positions: free will vs. bondage of the will, law vs. gospel — diametric opposites that cannot possibly coexist in the same human heart. Any attempts to reconcile them, Luther repeatedly stated in the summer of 1530, would be as futile as

---

rock of Christ." *Against Hans Wurst*, *WA* 51.469-572: "The church is a high, deep, hidden thing which one may neither perceive nor see, but must grasp only by faith, through baptism, sacrament and word." *How Christians Should Regard Moses*, *WA* 16.363-393, text "U": "this kingdom we cannot see, because it consists only in faith and will continue until the Last Day;" Ap VII.18 in the German: "Even if [the church] is not yet revealed for the world, but is hidden under the cross" (*ob es wohl fuer der Welt noch nicht offenbart, sondern unterm Kreuz verborgen ist*).

[602] Cf. W.H.T. Dau, *The Leipzig Debate in 1519*, [St. Louis: Concordia Publishing House, 1919], 170.

[603] *WA* Br 5. 479-480.

"to have Belial reconciled with Christ."[604] What was rendered to God in the *Augsburg Confession* was simply not negotiable; only what was rendered to Caesar. Hence, the *only* thing remaining to be discussed and hoped for was a political solution leading to peace in the empire, he adding in the same letter, "I wish and almost hope that the dissension in matters of statements of faith may be set aside and a political unity be brought about."[605]

In a particularly sharp jab at the negotiators, he wrote to Spalatin on August 29, 1530, "I hear that you people, like it or not, have begun a strange project, that is, to bring about unity between the pope and Luther. But the pope will not want it, and Luther sees no possibility of it. Watch out that you don't use all this effort for absolutely nothing," adding sarcastically, "If you people can accomplish [this unity], even though it is contrary to the will of both parties, then I shall soon follow the example you set, and reconcile Christ and Belial."

But he saved some of his most pointed pokes for Melanchthon, a dabbler in astrology, whom he now saw as seeking dogmatic unity out of a superstitious fear of ghosts, telling Jonas, "I know that you were not pushed into this pointless work by your own will, but by chance — or rather by the masked ghosts of Speyer."[606] Believing rumors that a mysterious group of ghostly monks had cruelly beaten some ferrymen into taking them across the Rhine River near Speyer, and were now headed to Augsburg to cast an evil spell on the Diet, Melanchthon had fearfully written to Luther, "The ghost of the monks at Speyer . . . definitely signifies a terrible tumult."[607] One of the Nürenberg delegates would later report that only Erhard Schnepf kept his cool and held fast in the confidence of his faith during the negotiations. "Schnepf is the only one who still has a beak to sing [is still credible in the

---

604 Belial = Satan. II Cor. 6:15.
605 *WA* Br 5.458.
606 Cf. *LW* 49.413 n. 11.
607 *WA* Br 5.542.

Lutheran faith]."[608]

Fidelity to the word was what mattered to Luther. A few months later he took to the pulpit to declare:

> No, my dear man, do not recommend to me peace and unity when thereby God's word is lost, for then eternal life and everything else would be lost. In this matter there can be no yielding nor giving way, no, not for love of you or any other person, but everything must yield to the word, whether it be friend or foe. The word was given to us for eternal life and not to further outward peace and unity. The word and doctrine will create Christian unity or fellowship. Where they reign all else will follow. Where they are not no concord will ever abide. Therefore do not talk to me about love and friendship, if that means breaking with the word, or the faith, for the gospel does not say love brings eternal life, God's grace, and all heavenly treasures, but the word . . . [609]

Eight years later, in 1539, in a conversation recorded by Anton Lauterbach, he reflected on the negotiations in Augsburg saying, "I had to attack [the *Confutatio*] more sharply because Philip was too modest. As a result of his modesty, at all events, the papists were puffed up. Out of love Philip wants to be of service to everybody. If the papists came to me this way, I'd send them packing." Pondering what had nevertheless been accomplished, in spite of their different temperaments, he added, "In the Acts of the Apostles you have a description of us. James is our Philip, who in his modesty wanted to retain the law voluntarily [Acts 15:13-21]. Peter signifies me, who smashed it: 'Why do you put a yoke on the neck of the disciples' [Acts 15:10]? Philip lets himself be devoured. I devour everything and spare no one. So God accomplishes the same thing in two different persons.'"[610]

Yet, that same year Melanchthon would write one of the

---

[608] *C.R.* 3.364.
[609] *WA* 34.11, 387.
[610] *WATR* 4.4577.

boldest statements of the Reformation against the mythology of historical episcopal succession:

> This testimony is cited by one, so that it will be thought firstly what the church might be, and the spirit is separated from the carnal opinions, which imagine the church to be a state of bishops and bind it to the orderly succession of bishops, as the empires consist of the orderly succession of princes. But the church maintains itself differently. Actually, it is a union not bound to the orderly succession but to the word of God. The church is reborn where God restores the doctrine, and gives his Holy Spirit. Paul testifies in Eph. 4 [:11] that the church is ruled and preserved in this manner, not by orderly succession: "He gave gifts to men, apostles, prophets . . ." He teaches that the true church is where Christ is at work and where he bestows true teachers. . . . Let us not permit ourselves to be scared away from the word of God by the false protection of the name church.[611]

He reiterated the same to Emperor Charles V at the 1541 Regensburg Conference. In the end, Luther saw the quest for dogmatic unity in Augsburg as little more than the devil's work, an exercise in law elicited by fear and superstition. His creedal belief in the priesthood of all believers was not a "poignant plea for unity in the church," but an immutable truth in the gospel that was simply not negotiable. The Confession at Augsburg, he declared in 1533, "is truly the last trump before the Day of Judgment . . . [It] is therefore deserving of all praise. Nobody should regret what it cost because the word of God was spread abroad contrary to the intention of all people, of the emperor, of the pope, etc. They wanted to extinguish it, but the blaze grew and spread."[612]

---

[611] *Melanchthons Werke in Auswahl,* ed. Robert Stupperich, [Gütersloh: Gerd Mohn, 1951], 1:330, 16-23. Cf. Philip Melanchthon, *Commentary on Romans,* Translated by Fred Kramer, (St. Louis: Concordia Publishing, 2010), 239-284.
[612] *WATR* Nr. 297 4b.

The Cathedral in Speyer

"An Imagined Priestly Dignity"

"In a word, a priest was a man who could say mass, even though he could not preach a word and was an unlearned ass. Such in fact is the spiritual estate even to the present day."[613]

Luther

While the ELCA's teaching magisterium pays much lip service to bishops, pastors, and parishioners being "servants" of the word, the structure, organization, websites, mailings, and educational materials it produces all hail a ministry of primacy, of "leadership" instead. Central to its focus on ministerial careerism, this culture of leaders is raised up and promoted throughout the institution's "three expressions" (congregation, synod, and church-wide assembly). An endless stream of letters and promotional materials is sent to "pastoral leaders," "youth leaders," "stewardship leaders," and "congregational leaders."[614] In assemblies "synodical leaders"

---

[613] *WA* 30 II.529b, 32f.

[614] Its newest glossy addition is *L Magazine*—"Empowering ELCA Leaders for Vital Ministry," from Logos Productions. It also

247

are "lifted up," and "voting members" are all encouraged to see themselves in "leadership roles."[615] In such a pervasive atmosphere of oversight which thoroughly embraces an ecclesiastical *Sehnsucht nach dem Recht der Obrigkeit* (deep desire for authority), there appears to be very little emphasis on, or room for, true servanthood. It seems the pious continuously seek to separate the sheep from the goats, as they look from faith to reason and from hiddenness to visibility.

This deep desire for a Lutheran "episcopal dignity" in a CCM world has led in recent years to the conferring of some very ridiculous orders indeed, ones that would undoubtedly have spilled Luther's beer. In April 2003, for example, Metropolitan New York Synod pastors were presented with three documents from the bishop's office addressing the question of lay persons possibly presiding at Holy Communion, and the use of so-called "reserved elements."[616] The first, *An Order for Public Worship with Communion by Extension,* included a farcically choreographed liturgy in which the laity were told to "stand back . . . in a visible location not near the elements." Lay persons were forbidden from ever stepping into the pulpit, even if they were reading a sermon written by the pastor. "In the absence of the Presider, it is appropriate for the one sharing the meditation to speak from a place other than the pulpit." This curious *modus tollens*

---

promotes a three year curriculum for pastoral and congregational leaders called "Leading Well: Equipping for Leadership in God's World," in which participants "explore their gifts and their implications for how they lead" and "practice what it means to live and lead well."

615 All ELCA seminaries tout a mission of producing "leaders." E.g., "Luther [Seminary's] mission is equipping leaders for the world today, in communities so diverse that we will need all the innovation we can muster." (President Rick Foss, quoted in *The Lutheran,* May 2013, 44.) The ELCA's scholarship fund is called the "Fund for Leaders."

616 Luther rejected the practice of a "reserved host," deeming the sacrament efficacious only as a single act of the words of institution, the distribution, and the reception of the elements.

implies that in their pulpit and altar roles, ordained clergy serve as nomistic organs of grace over and against the centrality of the word, prompting one bemused German theologian to label it *Tabernakelfrömmigkeit* (tabernacle piety).

One idea presently being discussed in many synod offices for preventing laypersons trespassing on holy ground, is to retain their ordinations in the bishop's office. Wengert proposes, "The question of 'laypersons' (synodically approved ministers) presiding regularly at Holy Communion . . . might be resolved if the ordination and call of such persons were held not by the individual ordained as if they were rights[617] but by the synod council and bishop" — (apparently to be kept under glass and broken only "In Case of Emergency.") Luther called such schemes "tomfoolery," and those who hold them members of an "Emserian *priesterey*," "licentiates of canon law" (*Licenciat facrorum Canonum*), who have "a license to babble" whatever they please, but "a prohibition against proving anything."[618]

The second document, *That They May Be Fed,* by then New York Bishop Steven P. Bouman, contains sweeping and undocumented claims, to wit: "An historical overview of the role and person of the presider makes clear that the ordained have presided over the eucharist from antiquity; . . . a review of biblical and other sources makes this thesis clear." The only two biblical sources he cites, however, are Hebrews 9:11-12, which is, in fact, the consummate affirmation that Christ alone is our Presider and High Priest, and 1 Peter 2:9-10, Peter's declaration that we are all "a chosen race, a royal priesthood, a holy nation, God's own people." Bouman bafflingly concludes from these, (in language virtually identical to Wengert's), "Importantly, Peter does not say that all are 'priests,' but that all are true members of the one priesthood." With total

---

[617] Luther called it "the general right common to all Christians," (*De instituendis, WA* 12.191-192.)
[618] *WA* 7.632.

disregard for the proper translation of *ierateuma* ("the office of priest"), Bouman misses the glaring irony of Luther's specific reference to 1 Peter 2:9 in *De instituendis,* in which he debunks any elevated notion of ordination relative to the ministry of word and sacrament. Luther wrote:

> Apollos who came to Ephesus without call or ordination. . . By what right, I ask, did he exercise the ministry of the word except by the general right common to all Christians, as described in 1 Cor. 14:30 . . . This man was afterward even made an apostle without the formality of ordination, and not only functioned in the ministry of the word, but also proved himself useful in many ways to those who had already come to faith.[619]

Bouman, (once again channeling Piepkorn and Wengert), writes, "Current thinking in the ELCA, reflected in the *Study of Ministry,*[620] tends to move in the sacramental direction, holding that ordination is a divine office given to the candidate by God, thus the point of origin is not the congregation." This was also the papists' argument against the Lutherans in Augsburg, insisting ordination is *iure divino,*[621] but rejected by Ap 14. What is divine is not ordination, which is merely an affirmation *iure humano* of an existing call — but the office of preaching — the call to which (*vocatio ad*) is from God (*iure divino*) through the congregation (*vocatio mediata*). Yet, pointing to Clement of Carthage in support of priestly dignity, Bouman adds, "He [Clement] holds that the bishop is the 'High Priest' in that he presides over the eucharistic sacrifice of the people of God of the new covenant," but concludes almost reluctantly that Clement "does use the term 'hiereis' (priests) for the laity (laos) following the royal priesthood metaphor of 1 Peter 2.9." Neither statement is confessional, (the sacrifice not being ours, nor 1 Peter 2:9 being a metaphor), but embraces ELCA's sentimentalism for Roman

---

[619] *WA* 12.191-192.

[620] ELCA documents overwhelmingly quote each other, rarely if ever scripture or the Confessions.

[621] Touted by Piepkorn and present-day crypto-Catholics.

hierarchical sacramentalism. Melanchthon in the Lutheran Confessions dismissed the writings of Clement as "spurious," as "fictitious" as those of Dionysius.[622]

The third document, *When An Ordained Pastor Cannot Preside,* by Paul R. Nelson, the ELCA Director for Worship, exhibits utter confusion with regard to ordination. It contains such bizarre statements as, "When the Lutheran Confessions say: 'It is taught among us that nobody should publicly teach or preach or administer the sacraments in the church without a regular call' (CA XIV), I believe it is referring to the practice of ordination as the confessors had known it. The fact that the Roman Confutation of the Augsburg Confession does not dispute this definition also tends to support this reading."

He errs in his reading of both documents. *Confutatio Pontificia* XIV strictly qualifies *rite vocatus* in canonical terms "in accordance with the form of law and the ecclesiastical ordinances and decrees hitherto observed everywhere in the Christian world, and not according to a Jeroboitic call (1 Kings 12:20),"[623] (that is, by election of the people — but not by God). Melanchthon rejected the qualifier when he substituted *iure humano* for *iure divino* in Ap 14, marking the Lutherans' complete break with the Roman

---

622 *BSLK* 492.71.

623 *Ibid* 296, n.2: *qui secundum formam iuris iuxta ecclesiasticas sanctiones ac decreta ubique in orbe christiano hactenus observata vocatur, non secundum Ierobiticam vocationem.* Jeroboam ruled Israel from 931-910 BC. His call to be king was illegitimate because he was not "rightly" called by God, but by the tribes. But the Lutherans were "rightly called" because post-Pentecost, God calls his ministers through the *communio sanctorum.* Cf. *WA* 40 I.59, *Luther's Lectures on Galatians:* "God calls in two ways, either by means or without means. Today he calls all of us into the ministry of the word by a mediated call (*vocatione mediate*), that is, one that comes through means, namely, through man. But the apostles were called immediately (*immediate vocati*) by Christ himself, as the prophets of the Old Testament had been called by God himself." Luther makes the same in *Concerning the Ministry.*

understanding and system of canonical ordination.[624]

Arguing that pastors should "pre-consecrate" elements for lay distribution, Nelson offers four nonsensical reasons: "1) It preserves the relationship of the ordained to the sacrament. 2) It relies on a sacramental theology of the Eucharist which is extremely 'realistic' in nature. 3) It is convenient and manageable — concerns which ought never to be despised. 4) It is not forbidden by the confessions."[625] At one point he ponders, "The ancient practice of the 'fermentum' (the sending of a piece of consecrated bread from the bishop of Rome's celebration to other churches across the city on the same day) is also worth exploring. Could not the bishop of an ELCA synod simply preside at a celebration of Holy Communion and 'send' the consecrated elements to parishes without pastors?" (The choice of delivery system aside — whether by UPS, FedEx, or carrier pigeon — this laughable scenario prompted one Metro NY Synod pastor to suggest the local bishop simply rotate 360° with outstretched arms while saying the Words of Institution from atop the Empire State Building.)[626]

---

624 Cf. *BSLK*, 69 n. 1. Melanchthon understood "regular call" (*ordentlichen Beruf*) as *rite vocatus* in opposition to Eck's Article 267 f. *ordinatione canonica*, and in keeping with Luther's *"Die vocatio tut dem Teufel sehr wehe,"* (the call hurts the devil very much), *WATR* I 90. Compare *LED III's* blatantly false claim that "Melanchthon accepted the interpretation of the phrase 'regular call' as *ordinatione canonica* (canonical ordination) on which the opponents had insisted," 46.

625 The practice is rejected in among other places *FoC*, SD VII.83-87, "if, for instance, the blessed bread is not distributed, received, and eaten but is locked up, offered up, or carried about," the "entire action" being necessary, i.e., "the consecration or words of institution, the distribution and reception, or the oral eating of the blessed bread and wine . . . inviolately . . . before our eyes . . . Apart from this use it is not to be deemed a sacrament."

626 At a 1985 Long Island, NY interns' meeting a candidate for ministry related to me how his pastoral supervisor, who was in a hurry to leave for vacation, paused before a locked cabinet, quickly said the Words of Institution and made the sign of the cross, thereby

In an equally bizarre article in which he asserts the word alone (*verba nuda*) is not enough, New York Bishop Robert Rimbo wrote in the October 2006 issue of *The Lutheran,* the ELCA's official magazine, "In assemblies where the consecration is reduced to the words of institution, we risk losing the connection with Jesus' own act of institution — blessing God."[627] The reformers, of course, could never have conceived of such a "risk," as Luther Reed properly noted in *The Lutheran Liturgy:*

> Luther, under the prevailing scholastic and Roman view that consecration was effected solely by the recitation of the Verba, and possessed by his dynamic conception of the supremacy of the word (whether this meant the whole gospel, the Holy Scriptures, or the second person of the Trinity), cut out everything except the Dominical Words.[628]

"It is faith that receives this blood," Steven Paulson notes,

---

"blessing" a year's supply of reserved elements for distribution by the deacons.

Luther condemned bishops' staffs and miters (*Bisschoffhut*) as pompous displays that "only lead away from [the church] into hell — still less are they signs of the church," *Wider Hans Worst, WA* 51.507-508. In *De instituendis ministris* he strongly advised the Bohemians against their use, saying, "For in Paul's view he is certainly a bishop who takes the lead in the preaching of the word. Such is your Gallus though he is not resplendent in bishop's miter and staff and other pride and pomp, which are only meant to amaze the stupid crowd (*irritabula stulti vulgi tantum*)." *WA* 12.194. ELCA Bishop William H. Lazareth issued a directive for the burial of pastors of the Metro NY Synod. It included dressing them in their alb, ordination stole and cross, and in the case of a bishop, with miter and staff.

[627] p. 46.

[628] Luther D. Reed, *The Lutheran Liturgy, A Study of the Common Liturgy of the Lutheran Church in America,* (Philadelphia: Muhlenberg Press,1947), 362. Unlike Rome's, Luther's concept was of Christ's perpetual, not re-instituted, consecration through the Words of Institution.

"(not the Father in heaven, or the law, or the devil), thus reversing and bringing to a halt all sacrifice that proceeds from sinners to God."[629] "Therefore," Luther wrote in *The Private Mass*, "we cannot make anything else out of [the Lord's Supper], but must act according to his command and hold to it. However, if we alter it or improve on it, then it is invalid and Christ is no longer present, nor is his ordinance."[630]

The myth of priestly consecration and Luther's dismissal of anything other than the Words of Institution and Lord's Prayer aside, Rimbo's solipsistic claim ignores CA 8's dictum that the efficaciousness of the sacrament does not depend on the administrator, his or her prayers, words, ordination or the lack thereof, but solely on "the *institution* ['he took . . . he broke ... he gave . . . he said'] and *command* of Christ ['eat this . . . drink this . . . do this'], even if they are administered by evil men" (*Et sacramenta et Verbum propter ordinationem et mandatum Christi sunt efficacia, etiamsi per malos exhibeantur*),[631] the *verba nuda*. To ensnare and unsettle consciences with the diabolical proposition that Christians "risk losing the connection with Jesus" unless they embellish the word, is to preach a blatant free will theology, (as if one could "fall out of one's baptism," as Luther put it.) To argue the *verba nuda* is not enough, is to heretically say the emperor (Christ) has no clothes.

Luther called such smells and bells and chancel prancings that include eucharistic prayers, blessings, fastings, consecrations, special vestments, gospel processions, and preparations for the sacrament so much "plucking of feathers,"[632] modern ecclesiastical enthusiasms resulting from

---

629 Steven D. Paulson, *Lutheran Theology*, (New York, T & T Clark International, 2011), 93.

630 *WA* 38.240.

631 *BSLK* 64.

632 In one of its more pretentious rituals, the bishop of the Metropolitan New York Synod of the ELCA gathers the clergy together for an annual "Chrism Mass." All clergy are asked to bring cruets enough for a year's supply of oil, which the bishop "blesses"

the Dunning-Kruger effect (being too theologically incompetent to recognize one's incompetence). Lutherans today would do well to remember the lament of the late beloved Cardinal Carlo Maria Martini, the former Archbishop of Milan and once possible successor to Pope John Paul II. In a shockingly candid interview he gave to the popular Italian daily *Corriere della Sera,* published only hours after his death on September 1, 2012, he indicted a church he called "200 years out of date," saying, "Our culture has aged, our churches are big and empty and the church bureaucracy rises up; our rituals and our cassocks are pompous . . . The church must admit its mistakes and begin a radical change, starting from the pope and the bishops."[633] Whether Lutheran or Catholic, in the end all ecclesiastical *Schwärmerei* (pseudo-pious pap) meant to dress up the word amounts to one and the same thing: a rejection of the bondage of the will.

---

in large quantity in a solemn "mass of the blessing of the oil," after which all the clergy "renew" their ordination vows.

[633] Pope Francis I appears to have heeded Martini's call to make the Church of Rome more appealing to the common man, but to date there have been no doctrinal changes.

Chapter 10

Beware the Ghost of Speyer

"I told them that I'd come to do some theology, but they just laughed at me."

Pastor Dick Smith attending his first Lutheran pastors' conference, Bismarck, N.D., 1963.

The Lutheran theologian Friedrich Bente, (1850-1930), like St. Paul before him, prophetically foresaw "the time is coming when people will not endure sound teaching, but having itching ears they will accumulate for themselves teachers to suit their own likings, and will turn away from listening to the truth and wander into myths" (2 Timothy 4:3-4). Predicting the marginalizing of the *Augsburg Confession* as 16th century doctrine in need of some 21st century "progress," he wrote in his 1921 preface to the *Concordia Triglotta* words that eerily anticipate the rise of mythology for the promotion of administrative episcopal group-think, words that no doubt make many a latter day ecumenist cringe:

> The Lutheran Church differs from all other churches in being essentially the church of the pure word and unadulterated sacraments. Not the great number of her adherents, not her organizations, not her charitable and other institutions, not her beautiful customs and liturgical forms, etc., but the precious truths confessed by her symbols in agreement with the Holy Scriptures constitute the true beauty and rich treasures of our church, as well as the never-failing source of her vitality and power. Wherever the Lutheran Church ignored her symbols or rejected all or some of them, there she always fell an easy prey to her enemies. But wherever she held fast to her God-given crown, esteemed and studied her confessions, and actually made them a norm and standard of her entire life and practice, there the

Lutheran Church flourished and confounded all her enemies. Accordingly, if Lutherans truly love their church, and desire and seek her welfare, they must be faithful to her confessions and constantly be on their guard lest anyone rob her of her treasure.[634]

Tappert expressed the same concerns thirty years later as American Lutheranism began its long drift into episcopalianism, asking,

> Is there the beginning of a tendency today to adopt the theology and the practice of a neo-Romantic remythologization which is currently flowering in our environment? This is not an idle question, for it is always a sign of weakness rather than strength when the church drifts on what some fondly call "the wave of the future." What such "waves" have done to the Lutheran Church in the past, both in Europe and in America, history amply testifies. This appears to be a time for earnest self-examination.[635]

He, like Bente, Bornkamm, Oberman and others (to borrow a Reformation phrase), "smelled the roast" (*hat den Braten gerochen*) that was beginning to burn in the ontological oven. Historical episcopacy is at its core not simply an appeal to ecclesiastical tradition, a mere matter of adopting quaint Anglo-Catholic rites and rituals, but a distinct doctrine that stands in sharp contrast to the confessional Pauline theology of "the priesthood of all believers" wherein all the baptized are equally priests, bishops, and popes. One's rejection of episcopal myth, as well as the institutions and ecumenical concordats that tout it, is a matter of Christian conscience, not one of democracy, congregational rights, or pious fanaticism. *Called to Common Mission* declares justification by faith in the *verba nuda* to be insufficient for ecumenical unity by imposing law over gospel through the requirement of same ceremonies, and in so doing contradicts scripture, the

---

[634] F. Bente, *Concordia Triglotta,* (St. Louis: Concordia Publishing House, 1921), iv.

[635] Theodore G. Tappert, "Directions in Lutheran Losses to Other Communions," *Lutheran Quarterly,* Vol. 8 (1956): 362-4.

Confessions, Reformation history, and common sense.

The huge irony here, of course, is that the only true ecumenists left standing in the room are those who have declared CCM to be completely unnecessary for full Lutheran-Anglican communion, who see human requirements beyond agreement in the gospel as the trouncing of grace by law, and who have departed the captivity of a free will system.

Ecclesiastical institutions that bind themselves to a *successio episcoporum* in pursuit of visible unity, Bornkamm concluded, are little more than ancient Judaism revisited, possessing the pious passions of temple service, a sacerdotal caste, and a slavish tradition that embraces such second century absurdities as the claim, "Whoever breaks with the bishop parts company with the church!"[636]

At it's 2011 annual Church-wide Assembly in Orlando, Florida, the ELCA adopted a document for incorporation into its constitution called, "Living Into the Future Together (LIFT)." In §8 it directs that, "The responsibility for this church's theological discernment be located in the Office of the Presiding Bishop, which will assist this church in better understanding its identity, recognizing the theological, relational and educational gifts God has given this church and the power of these gifts to provide Christian leadership and partnership in today's rapidly changing world." And there we have it. With this statement and the push of voting members' buttons, the ELCA has with a hail and hearty "Aufwiedersehen," successfully ushered Luther's treatise *That a Congregation Has the Right and the Power to Judge All Teaching* safely into heaven, creating for all rights and purposes a papistic "Lutheran" magesterium in which there is no more imaginary priesthood of all believers, no congregational autonomy, or lay authority, or congregational rights and powers — in short, "no loose cannons in the church." No theological debate will be countenanced to challenge such recent official statements as, "Ecumenical rapprochement requires . . . that Lutherans not condemn

---

636 The rule of the See of Peter.

Catholic teaching about the practice of indulgences as inherently contrary to the Gospel."[637]

At the close of *Priesthood, Pastors, Bishops,* Wengert issues a stern warning to anyone who is contemplating leaving an ecclesiastical institution such as his, or of not participating in its present ecumenism, listing three necessary criteria he says he gleaned from Melanchthon's TPPP. "Rule in the church, ungodly doctrine, and claims of divine right to rule must all converge before one can remain outside such a gathering . . . This sets the bar for rejection of ecumenism or walking out of a church extremely high. If, and only if, the one who controls the meeting is Antichrist does an evangelical Christian have reason not to attend or not to remain in communion with another person or group." [638] (His dire warning is perfectly understandable given the ELCA's staggering losses since its founding in1988 of more than 1.7 million members or 31% and over 1000 congregations,[639] making it the fastest declining denomination in America).

But in reality, Melanchthon and the Lutherans set the bar very low already in Augsburg — in CA 7, which says simply that the church is there where the gospel is preached in its

---

[637] *The Hope of Eternal Lif* — "Common Statement of the 11th Round of the U.S. Lutheran-Roman Catholic Dialogue, (Lutheran University Press, 2011), 70.

[638] Wengert 92. The reference is to *TPPP* 60-61. Notice his repeated hierarchical mistranslation of *furstehen/praesunt* as "rule" (`a la Piepkorn), instead of "watch over, shepherd, preside."

[639] As reported on the ELCA's 2016 website. Cf. *The Lutheran,* "The Shrinking Church," January 2013, p. 23: "Nearly 30 percent of ELCA churches reported an average worship attendance of fewer than 50 people in 2010. From 2003 to 2011, average weekly worship attendance dropped 26 percent. And from 2009 to 2010, ELCA membership decreased 5.9 percent, the sharpest rate of decline among mainline denominations, according to the National Council of Churches." From 2000 to 20013 the ELCA lost 24.6% of its membership as reported by the same magazine, August 2015, p. 20.

purity and the sacraments are administered according to it. Where they are not, there is no church to walk out of. Its "purity" is CA 4, the doctrine of justification by grace through faith alone in Christ alone. That word is the *esse,* the very essence and being of the church, and it is enough (*satis est*) "for the true unity of the Christian church" (CA 7.2). It is not a matter of indifference or *adiaphoron,* (a non-essential church rite neither commanded nor forbidden in God's word), nor is it simply for the well-being (*bene esse*) of the church, (which *adiaphora* can also supply), but is the constituting element of the body of Christ, faith in whom alone unites the *communio sanctorum,* God's holy people, his royal priesthood. Thus, "It is not necessary for the true unity of the Christian church that ceremonies, instituted by men, should be observed uniformly in all places" (CA 7.3). Indeed, to make it so would be to make of the gospel a new law.

But *Called to Common Mission* makes it so. It announces there can be no unity in pulpit and altar fellowship ("full communion") between Lutheran and Episcopalian Christians unless both groups uniformly observe the man made ceremony of Anglican historical episcopal ordination, (a position not dissimilar from Catholicism's requirement that all must first be part of the See of Peter). CCM at its core declares CA 4 to be *non satis est* for true unity, and affirms the false claim of the 1989 Anglican-Lutheran *Niagara Report* that the bishops are "necessary to . . . safeguard the unity and apostolicity of the church," a claim Luther flatly rejected already in 1521 at the Diet of Worms. That historical episcopal succession must be observed by all Christians in all places is the stated Anglican "common mission," (hence CCM's title) without which there can be no hope of rapprochement with Rome. These requirements are not surprising, given that Canterbury and Rome have never signed on to the *Augsburg Confession* — which the ELCA, with its embrace of episcopalianism, apparently no longer does either.

At the height of the CCM sales pitch its theological significance was downplayed by proponents as a mere *adiaphoron* for the *bene esse* of the church, a simple matter of church governance. "We have no problem with it," a Metro N.Y. bishop's assistant told me, "since we consider it a matter of the kingdom of the left" (the civil realm). Even opponents of CCM unwittingly referred to historical episcopacy as an *adiaphoron*, clumsily adopting the term without understanding that by compromising the second half of CA7's rejection of the need for same rites, the first half (the sufficiency of same faith) is negated — a substitution of law for gospel. It's as if one were to adopt the Anabaptists' rejection of infant baptism in the second half of CA 9 as a matter of indifference, while agreeing to its efficacy in the first half; or accepting the Novatian rejection of absolution in the second half of CA 12, while adopting absolution in the first half, and so on. Did Martin Marty's CCM drafting team really not understand that the *Augsburg Confession* (and CA 7 in particular), is a presentation of doctrinal opposites: This is what we believe versus this is what we do not? Sufficiency of the gospel versus the insufficiency of ceremonies was never a "yes . . . and" for the Lutheran reformers, but an "either . . . or."[640] Either being baptized into Christ's death by grace alone, through faith alone, in Christ alone is sufficient for the true unity of the Christian church, or it isn't. CCM declares that it isn't — more is needed. God needs our help.

Enter canonical ordination conferred through historical episcopal succession. Many echoed Wengert's mitigating assertion that the reformers were indifferent in the matter, making it perfectly harmless for Lutherans to drink the canonical Kool-Aid: "[In Ap 28] Melanchthon simply refused

---

[640] In 2002 the WordAlone movement fatally sought to harmonize the theological irreconcilables of Ap 14 — of canonical and evangelical ordination — by drafting an "Admonition." Written in part by Dorothea Wendebourg and other theologians, it sought a compromise with the ELCA over CCM if that institution would accept evangelical ordination "in equal standing" with historical episcopal ordinations. This political *faux pas* led to the departure of a number of confessional theologians from the movement and its credible end.

to discuss questions of canon law. That law, which required that bishops be in communion with Rome and thereby to be under Rome's claim to apostolic succession, was a simple adiaphoron, not worth arguing about."[641]

But Melanchthon did not regard it as a matter of indifference, nor do the Roman Catholic and Anglican communions.[642] The reason it wasn't worth arguing about in Ap 28 is because he had already addressed and debunked the myth in Ap 14. The papists' claim to a *successio episcoporum iure divino* wasn't allowed to stand for the very reason that it isn't an *adiaphoron,* but a false teaching "for the false protection of the name of church," as he put it in his *Commentary on Romans.* Yet the claim continues to be made today by those who speak of a need to "rescue" or "save the church," (as if the church were not already the rescued and saved, the united and safeguarded). Indeed, it is in this very article (Ap 28.15-16) that the Lutheran reformers established the adiaphoral litmus test, Melanchthon writing:

> In the Confession we nevertheless added the extent to which it is legitimate for the them to create traditions, namely, that they must not be necessary services (*Gottesdienst/necessarios cultus*) but a means for preserving order in the church, for the sake of peace. These must not ensnare consciences as though they were commanding necessary services. This is what Paul teaches when he says (Gal. 5:1), "Stand fast in the freedom with which Christ has set you free, and do not submit again to a yoke of slavery." Therefore the use of such ordinances ought to be left free, only that offenses should be avoided and that they be not regarded as necessary services. Thus even the apostles ordained many things that were changed by time, and they did not set them down as though they could not be changed. For they did not contradict

---

641 Wengert 81.

642 Each of the church bodies officially embraces ontological ordination. "Both traditions affirm . . . the sacramental nature of ordination, as to which there is no significant difference between them." *The Final Report of the Anglican-Roman Catholic International Commission* (Cincinnati: Forward Movement Press, 1982; Elucidation 3).

their own writings, in which they worked hard to free the church from the idea that human rites are necessary services.[643]

For Melanchthon, "not necessary" meant, "It is patently contrary to God's command and word to make laws out of opinions . . ."[644] According to CA 28, not only may human traditions not be necessary for justification — they may also not be made necessary for necessity's sake (*Meinung Gesetze*), both of which can unsettle consciences:

> Inasmuch as ordinances which have been instituted as necessary *or* instituted with the intention of meriting justification are in conflict with the Gospel, it follows that it is not lawful for bishops to institute such services *or require them to be necessary.*[645]

He offers the contradictory example of the observance of the sabbath, saying, "Some argue that the observance of the Lord's Day *is not* indeed of divine obligation but *is* as it were of divine obligation . . ."[646] The same Emserian illogic pervades CCM's mitigating attempt to introduce historical episcopacy into American Lutheranism. One reads in paragraph A.5:

> We believe that a ministry of pastoral oversight (*episkope*), exercised in personal, collegial, and communal ways, *is necessary* to witness to and safeguard the unity and apostolicity of the church.

But in paragraph C.18:

> By thus freely accepting the historic *episcopate,* the Evangelical Lutheran Church in America does *not thereby affirm that it is*

---

[643] *BSLK* 400-401.
[644] *Ibid,* 126.35.
[645] *Ibid,* 128.50.
[646] *Ibid,* 130.63.

necessary for the unity of the church.[647]

Addressing such double talk, Melanchthon asks incredulously:

> What are discussions of this kind but snares of conscience? Although they try to mitigate the traditions, moderation can never be achieved as long as the opinion remains that their observance is necessary. And this opinion must remain where there is no understanding of the righteousness of faith and Christian liberty.[648]

Indeed, he asks, "Where did the bishops get the right to impose such traditions on the churches and thus ensnare consciences when Peter forbids putting a yoke on the disciples and Paul says that authority was given for building up and not tearing down?"[649] "The bishops," he concludes, "might easily retain the lawful obedience of men if they did not insist on the observance of traditions which cannot be kept with a good conscience."[650]

Thus, the only question remaining is: Does historical episcopal succession require "necessary services" that can "ensnares consciences?" Proponents answer, "No," its adoption simply doesn't rise to that level. As proof, they offer CCM itself, which as we have seen, contradicts itself. Opponents, of course, point to the obvious oxymoron and ask the quintessential Melanchthonian question: If historical episcopal succession is not necessary for unity — why is it necessary?[651]

---

647 Cf. Joseph A. Burgess, *Lutheran Forum,* Vol. 26, No. 4, 32. On the question of the historic episcopate, a key to the adiaphoristic principle is "that an *adiaphoron* is only an *adiaphoron* when it is an *adiaphoron* for both sides involved."

648 *BSLK* 131.4-14.

649 *Ibid,* 127.42.

650 *Ibid,* 131.69.

651 Cf. *WA* Br 5.491-495: Melanchthon wrote to Luther during the negotiations regarding the supposed necessity of unnecessary episcopal dictates on July 14, 1530, "If obedience is required, then

The Catholic/Anglican answer is that it is and always has been necessary, because it is a sacrament in which the distinction or "order" of priests and bishops has been divinely instituted, and is thus a holy, divine thing and sign.[652] Central to this understanding is the notion of sacrifice, both through the consecratory actions of the priest, and offerings of thanksgiving and praise from the communed, the focus thereby being on *our* actions and reactions rather than Christ's action alone "in the night in which he was betrayed."

Henry VIII's Archbishop Thomas Cranmer declared, "Scripture openly teaches that the order of priests and bishops was not instituted by human authority, but divinely . . . who must consecrate the body and blood of Christ in the sacrament of the altar . . . and the power, function, and ministration of these ministers is necessary to the church as long as we fight on this earth against the flesh, the world, and Satan, and on no occasion must it be abolished" (*De ordine et ministerio sacerdotum et episcoporum*).

Cranmer's dictate is expressed in successive Anglican ordinals from 1550 to the present. Quoting the 1550 Ordinal in the lead up to the vote on CCM, the Ecumenical Officer for the Episcopal Diocese of Chicago, William D. Roberts, asked the ELCA in his keynote address to the 1999 annual gathering of the Metro Chicago Synod:

> Why are Lutherans so committed to an ordering of ministry which defies what is "evident unto all men, diligently reading

---

there is no freedom, for freedom and obedience contradict one another." Luther concurred, saying it is a mixing of the two kingdoms, "Thus we grant neither according to spiritual nor worldly rights power to the bishops to impose anything on the church," even if it is for the *bene esse* of the church. See Ch. 7 above, "A Diminishing Desire."

652 Cf. Melanchthon in *BSLK,* 125.30: "Besides, it is disputed whether bishops or pastors have the right to introduce ceremonies in the church and make laws concerning foods, holy days, *grades or orders of ministers,* etc." (*gradibus ministrorum seu ordinibus; von unterschiedlichen Orden der Kirchendiener*).

Holy Scripture and Ancient authors" and undoes what "for a thousand five hundred years and upward . . . [has] continued under the sacred regiment of bishops?" This statement from the Ordinal, with its references to "ancient Authors" — such as Clement of Carthage! — and the "Offices . . . evermore had in such revered estimation" adds the weight of church tradition to that of Scriptural authority for continuing the historic episcopate.[653]

Roberts conveniently failed to mention that between Edward VI's Ordinal of 1552, and Queen Elizabeth's Act of Uniformity in 1662 reinstating episcopal succession as necessary for valid ministry, a full century had elapsed during which the Anglican hierarchy had become extinct. Hence, Pope Leo XIII's perfectly reasonable 1896 postmortem issuance of a death certificate for what was already a fact, the *Nullity of Anglican Orders.* Like Monty Python's dead parrot, Anglican succession had "ceased to be," "was no more," had "expired" was "bereft of life," and if the English crown "hadn't nailed it to the perch, it'd be pushing up the daisies! Its metabolic processes are now history!"

Said history, however, appears to have completely escaped the Lutherans at the assembly. There is no official record indicating the ELCA responded to Roberts by directing him to Article 14 of the *Apology* which states that the "various ranks of the ecclesiastical hierarchy . . . were created by human authority." Or to Melanchthon's *Commentary on Romans* stating "the church maintains itself differently" from those "who bind it to the orderly succession of bishops." Or to his *Treatise on the Power and Primacy of the Pope,* "Since the distinction between bishop and pastor is *not by divine right,* it

---

653 From *Let's Talk,* Living Theology in the Metropolitan Chicago Synod, Evangelical Lutheran Church in America, Vol. 4, No. 2, Pentecost 1999, *Called to Common Mission.* "I think they [ELCA leaders] see us as possibly helping them recover the ancient catholic tradition which they had prior to the Reformation." J. Robert Wright, *Living Church,* 2001, p. 15. Wright is the principal Episcopalian author of *Called to Common Mission.*

is manifest that ordination administered by a pastor in his own church is valid by divine right." Or to the same's insistence that the "the writings of Clement are spurious," because the power of the keys, and electing and ordaining of ministers "is given to the church and not merely to certain individuals," citing I Peter 2:9 "You are a royal priesthood," and Matthew 18:20 "Where two or three are gathered . . . ," all of which predate the English ordinals. "What happened to the Confessions?," Kittelson asked, "Did they just get misplaced somewhere?" Have they "become mere historical 'documents' of antiquarian interest only?"[654]

There is, however, record of enthusiastic applause from the assembly to Roberts's demands — who it must be said was completely honest and candid with his audience in citing James Addison: "The Reformation in England was . . . not doctrinal but constitutional. The Church of England had reformed in one respect only. It had denied the supremacy of the Pope and had broken relations with Rome. In doctrine and liturgy and orders . . . it remained a Catholic Church."[655] It seems not to have occurred to anyone present to ask why then a Lutheran church would want to adopt the spurious claims and rites of what is, by its own admission, not a Reformation, but a Catholic church.[656]

To the present day, there is not agreement within the Anglican communion itself on a theology of historical episcopacy.[657] The history remains splintered, offering three different positions since the latter half of the 17th century.

---

[654] James Kittelson, *Enough is Enough!*

[655] James Thayer Addison, *The Episcopal Church in the United States 1789-1932.* Archon Books, 1969, 6.

[656] Cf. J. Robert Wright, *Called to Common Mission:* Our Best Opportunity, *Word & World from LutherSeminary,* Vol. 19, No. 2, 1999, 183: " . . . I am convinced, especially with these changes, the *CCM* is the best opportunity anywhere for the church that is the 'highest' of the Protestant tradition, the ELCA, to embrace fully that church which is the 'lowest' of the Catholic tradition, the Episcopal Church."

[657] *LED III,* 62-64.

Latitudinarians see episcopacy as a "secondary matter . . . a convenient and traditional manner of ordering ministry." Followers of John Henry Newman (1801-1890), on the other hand, see episcopacy as "primary," bishops being the *esse* of the church. The third, and perhaps most widely held view today is that of F. D. Maurice (1805-1872), who taught that historical episcopacy is "one of the appointed and indispensable signs of a spiritual and universal society,"[658] bishops having a direct commission from Christ as assuredly as the first apostles. The ecumenical irony here, though, cannot easily be missed: Anglicanism's insistence on denominational unity through historic episcopacy — which it doesn't itself possess — is surely proof it is neither a sign nor a safeguard of Christian unity.[659]

Returning to the adiaphoral litmus test of Ap 28, the question remains: Is historical episcopal successive ordination "a necessary act of worship?" That it is "necessary" is integral to its mythology, certainly at least since the Quadrilateral of 1886 when it became *conditio sine qua non* (something absolutely indispensable or essential) for valid ministry, being of the *esse* of the church, (along with the Old and New Testament, and the sacraments of baptism and the Lord's

---

[658] Frederick Denison Maurice, *The Kingdom of Christ*, (1838; reprinted London: S.C.M. Press, 1958, ed. A. R. Vidler), Vol. II, 106.

[659] In an article in *The Huffington Post*, Religion News Service, 11/25/2013, "Church of England Faces Extinction, Says Former Archbishop of Canterbury Lord George Carey," Trevor Grundy reports in 2013 that Carey issued a dire warning to three hundred worshippers gathered in Shropshire, West England. "He said that every one of the church's 43 dioceses (territorial units governed by bishops) could disappear within 25 years if an urgent campaign to attract the young was delayed. 'There is a prevalent view that people don't want to hear what we have to say anymore.' There are 25 million baptized Anglicans in England and Wales but fewer than one million of them attend services on Sundays, church statistics show."

Supper).[660] Though episcopalian ordination is described by some as *plene esse* (for "the fullness of the church"), the dictum "No bishop, no church" remains in keeping with the Roman ontological bestowal of an indelible character, meaning once a priest, always a priest.[661] London Archbishop Wand wrote in 1961:

> Theologians argue over the respective merits of *esse, bene esse,* and *plene esse.* But since the Oxford Movement, popular opinion has hardened in favour of the strict view that apostolic succession of the ministry through episcopacy is necessary to the proper constitution of a church. That is always made a *sine qua non* in Anglican negotiations for reunion with other Christian bodies, and forms indeed, together with Bible, Creed, and Sacraments, a part of the famous "quadrilateral" or four-fold basis for ecclesiastical reunion.[662]

---

[660] Cf. *An Episcopal Dictionary of the Church: A User-Friendly Reference for Episcopalians,* Don S. Armentrout and Robert Boak Slocum, Editors, (New York: Church Publishing Inc., 2000), 189.

[661] Luther found the idea of an indelible character ludicrous, calling it "a fiction" and a "laughingstock" (*WA* 6.567). Cf. *LW* 36.111, n. 201: "The so-called *character indelebilis,* peculiar gift of ordination, meant that 'once a priest, always a priest.' This 'indelible mark' received authoritative statement in the bull *Exultate Deo* (1439). Eugene IV, summing up the decrees of the Council of Florence, says: 'Among these sacraments there are three — baptism, confirmation, and orders — which indelibly impress upon the soul a character, i.e., a certain spiritual mark which distinguishes them from the rest.' The Council of Trent (1563) further defined the correct Roman teachings as follows: 'The Holy Synod justly condemns the opinion of those [e.g., Luther] who assert that the priests of the New Testament have only temporary power, and that those once rightly ordained can again be made laymen, if they do not exercise the ministry of the word of God.' *PE* 2, 68 n. 5."

[662] Wand 54. The Chicago-Lambeth Quadrilateral requires a four-fold adoption for church reunion: 1) the Bible 2) Apostles' and Nicene Creed 3) Baptism and Holy Communion 4) the Historic Episcopate.

But is it an "act of worship?" The Lima text of the World Council of Churches' *Baptism, Eucharist, and Ministry,* to which the ELCA and ECUSA subscribe, states:

> 41. A long and early Christian tradition places ordination in the context of worship and especially of the eucharist. The act of ordination by the laying on of hands of those appointed to do so is at one and the same time invocation of the Holy Spirit (*epiklesis*); *sacramental sign;* acknowledgment of gifts and commitment.

> 43. Ordination is a sign of the granting of this prayer by the Lord who gives the gift of the ordained ministry. Although the outcome of the Church's *epiklesis* depends on the freedom of God, the Church ordains in confidence that God, being faithful to his promise in Christ, *enters sacramentally* into contingent, historical forms of human relationship and uses them for his purpose.[663]

The operative word here is "*epiklesis.*" What would normally be any bidding prayer for the gift of the Holy Spirit, is in the Anglo-Catholic tradition a prayer for special grace or power (*charisma*) conferred exclusively on the ordinand with respect to the sacrament, through the laying on of hands via the historic episcopate.[664] Lima makes no effort to explain what that special grace or power might be or what it means "especially for the eucharist," though it is well understood in

---

[663] *Baptism, Eucharist, and Ministry,* "Ministry," (Faith and Order Paper, No. 111, WCC, Geneva, 1982).

[664] Cf. *Catechism of the Catholic Church,* (Liguori, Missouri; Liguori Publications, 1994), 1566: "The Ordination of Priests: 'It is in the Eucharistic cult or in the *Eucharistic assembly* of the faithful (*synaxis*) that they exercise in a supreme degree their sacred office; there, acting in the person of Christ and proclaiming his mystery, they unite the votive offerings of the faithful to the sacrifice of Christ their head, and in the sacrifice of the Mass they make present again and apply, until the coming of the Lord, the unique sacrifice of the New Testament, that namely of Christ offering himself once for all a spotless victim to the Father.' From this unique sacrifice their whole priestly ministry draws its strength."

Catholicism to be the specific power given to clergy to confect (transubstantiate) through epicletic prayer the elements of Christ's "unbloody sacrifice."[665]

Signers to Lima define ordination as a "sacramental sign," though Luther and the Confessions rejected any notion of it containing either a promise or sign of special grace. Lima's intentionally ambiguous language in flirtation with the Roman Sacrament of Ordination is meant, it is said, to entice non-episcopally successive churches into alignment with Anglo-Catholic practices — the encroaching episcopalism Oberman, Tappert, Bente and others have repeatedly warned against.

When it came to Holy Communion, Luther Reed correctly noted, "Luther rejected the entire Canon [including all of the Offertory prayers] and retained only the scriptural narrative of the institution and the Lord's Prayer. The Verba thus received a new and significant emphasis as proclaiming the heart of the gospel."[666] In fact, Luther could think of no need for, nor more fitting an *epiklesis* than the Lord's Prayer, which he placed right after the Words of Institution in the *Deutsche Messe*. If one wants to praise and give God thanks during the sacrament, he reasoned, what better praise and thanksgiving could there possibly be than the Lord's Prayer?

But instead of celebrating Luther's rediscovery of freedom in the *verba nuda* from the pious liturgical clutter of the past, Reed strangely deemed it insufficient on the grounds that the

---

[665] Carl E. Braaten believes the third round of Lutheran-Roman Catholic Dialogues sufficiently addressed any possible confessional objections in "The Eucharist as Sacrifice." He writes in *Essential Lutheranism*, p. 99: "Lutherans have feared that Catholics teach that the sacrifice of Christ is repeated in the Eucharist. This is not what Catholics intend to say. Catholics clarified that what they mean is not a repetition but re-presentation, not doing the sacrifice over again but making the once-for-all event of salvation present again and again." The end result, however, is the same: a focus on our "doing," our "presenting," our "making Christ present" versus Christ's doing, presenting, and omnipresence in the *verba nuda* "given and shed for you."

[666] Reed 335.

reformer couldn't possibly have had access to all of the earlier scholarly conversations on liturgy available to us today. Hence, his focus was more on purifying the existing Roman rite of false doctrine than on creating new sacramental formulae. While his was a start, he concludes, it falls short of the Anglican "improvements" of Archbishop Cranmer who emphasized "the 'offering of ourselves, our souls and bodies,' in union with the holy sacrifice, which had been so strongly emphasized by Augustine," adding, "[Cranmer] stressed the note of thanksgiving, which Luther and his followers failed to do."[667]

In light of this perceived "failure," he praises succeeding prayer books that reintroduced the invocation of the *epiklesis* which "served as a model for the later Anglican 'prayers of consecration' in the Prayer Books of the American Episcopal church . . ."[668] which they have now "gifted" the Lutherans with.[669] In other words Reed, like Rimbo, the ELCA, and CCM, finds *sola fide* in the *verba nuda . . . non satis est.*[670]

---

[667] Luther rejected anything that took the focus off of Christ's supreme sacrifice, including "eucharistic prayers" and "epiklesis," which redirect attention from what Christ has done for us, to what we can do for Christ.   Instead of the word "eucharist," meaning "thanksgiving," he used the terms *das heilige Abendmahl* ("the Holy Evening Meal"), or *Das Sakrament des Altars* (*sacramentum altaris*). In his *Treatise on the New Testament, that is, the Holy Mass* he wrote, "For a testament is *nit beneficium acceptum, sed datum* ("not a benefit received but a benefit conferred") . . . in the mass we give nothing to Christ, but only receive from him, unless they are willing to call this a good work: that a person sits still and permits himself to be benefited, given food and drink, clothed and healed, helped and redeemed. Just as in baptism, in which there is also a divine testament and sacrament, no one gives God anything or does him a service, but instead takes something, so it is in all other sacraments and in the sermon as well." *WA* 6, 364.

[668] Reed 362.

[669] Both CCM and Wengert speak of historical episcopal "gifting."

[670] American Lutheran liturgy increasingly emphasizes in the *Lutheran Book of Worship,* and its successor volume, what we can do for God, offering Him "ourselves, our time, and our possessions," to

The Anglican Church (being a constitutional Catholic church according to Wand, Roberts, and Wright) teaches that for the sacrament to be "valid," it must be consecrated[671] by a priest properly ordained into holy orders by a bishop in historic succession.[672] The consecration can occur through two kinds of clergy: the ordinary and the extraordinary, without whom there can be no preternatural effect. A sacrament administered by anyone else is both illicit and invalid — a claim which essentially renders the efficacy of the Words of Institution a moot point given that the priest, and not Christ, now becomes a nomistic organ of grace — indispensable for the dispensing. (Luther insisted if the devil himself said the words, the sacrament would be valid.) The requirement of this supplementary faith leads to unsettled consciences and disquieted hearts, where Christ the Mediator is in need of a mediator. It is, when all is said and done, nothing more than a return to Emser's "two kinds of priesthood, a lay priesthood and a priestly one."[673]

---

whom "we dedicate our lives" (absolution, offertory, offertory prayer, fraction, epiklesis, eucharistic prayers), rather than what God has done for us. See Oliver K. Olson's critique "Luther's Catholic Minimum," *Response XI*, (1970), 17-31.

[671] Holy Communion, for Luther, is the distribution (*ausreichen*) of what Christ already consecrated at the Last Supper. The status of the distributor is completely immaterial.

[672] *Book of Common Prayer*, (1979), 510.

[673] Cf. *BSLK*, 127.43-46: "Yet there are clear testimonies which prohibit the making of traditions for the purpose of appeasing God or as if they were necessary for salvation. In Col. 2 Paul says, 'Let no one pass judgment on you in questions of food and drink or with regard to a festival or new moon or a sabbath.' Again, 'If with Christ you died to the elemental spirits of the universe, why do you live as if you still belonged to the world? Why do you submit to regulations, 'Do not handle, Do not taste, Do not touch' (referring to things which all perish as they are used), according to human precepts and doctrines? These have an appearance of wisdom.' In Tit. 1 Paul also says, 'Not giving heed to Jewish myths or to commands of men who reject the truth.' In Matt. 15 Christ says concerning those who require traditions, 'Let them alone; they are blind and leaders of the blind.'"

To be sure, many Episcopalians tend to be rather ambivalent on the issue of transubstantiation, with some parts of the Anglican communion fully subscribing to it, other parts not. Either way, however, a theology of sacramental ordination runs counter to the Lutheran teaching on the Sacrament of the Altar, since Christ, having died "once for all" (Rom. 6:10), cannot be re-sacrificed (even in "an unbloody manner"), nor "re-presented" (being omnipresent), but is remembered in the one and only continuous Supper, in the sufficiency of the *verba nuda* "in the night in which he was betrayed," in the words "given for you, shed for you, etc.," and not in re-presented, reconstituted, transubstantiated suppers.[674] Wengert, nevertheless, cautions that during the Reformation:

> Only when ordinances led to the servitude under the law or to the crushing of consciences did a God-given reason to resist the church's proper pastoral or episcopal authorities arise . . . This means that in the Lutheran churches, one must first demonstrate that a bishop or an episcopal form of governance or an ecumenical agreement contradicts the gospel itself before one can counsel people to oppose it or their bishops. Arguments from tradition — whether from the ancient church or from the more recent past — hold no water. If a practice maintains good order in the church and does not contradict the gospel's freedom by making the practice necessary for salvation (!), then well-meaning Christians cannot object to its institution."[675]

Yet in its appeal to precisely such an errant tradition, and not scripture,[676] CCM makes a number of assertions that

---

[674] The ELCA employs a number of "eucharistic prayers" in its communion liturgy, which place an increased emphasis on the sacrament as the "high point" of worship, even though, as Luther repeatedly made clear, "We hold that the sacrament is less important than preaching." *WATR* 1. Nr. 512.

[675] Wengert 75-76.

[676] This is characteristic of the Emserian *priestery*. *LW* 39.157 n.30: "Luther ridiculed Emser's bad logic [in his *Answer to the HyperChristian Book*]: Emser proved the priestly estate (*prius*)

contradict the gospel's freedom:

1) Luther stated unequivocally at the 1521 Diet of Worms: bishops, councils, and popes can err, and thus cannot be "a sign . . . of the unity and apostolic continuity" of the church today, any more than they weren't in the 16th century (contra CCM §12).

2) Bishops cannot "safeguard the unity and apostolicity of the church" — only the Holy Spirit can — who also safeguards the church from erring bishops who think they can (3rd Article of the Creed vs. CCM §5).

3) The call (*vocatio*) and the means of grace (word & sacrament) are divinely instituted. Ordination, which contains neither grace nor promise, is not (Ap 14 vs. CCM §5).

4) CCM's embrace of historical episcopal succession ensnares Christian consciences in the false belief that bishops are "necessary to witness to and safeguard the unity and apostolicity of the church," thereby imperiling salvation through the false teaching that a sacrament not administered by episcopally ordained sequential sacerdotes is illicit and invalid for the forgiveness of sins. This was the false argument of the papists in Augsburg which the Lutherans rejected in CA 14, not as *adiaphora*, but as out and out "false teaching" (CA 7 vs. CCM §5).

James Kittelson arrived at the following conclusion in his rebuttal to Michael Root, in *Enough is Enough!*

---

through its long historical tradition (*posterius*) or usage, thus begging the question of its cause, or foundation (*principium*)." Cf. *WA* 7.632: "Human traditions and human laws," Luther wrote to Emser, "have at all times damaged and obscured divine laws, as Christ teaches in Matthew 15 [:3-9] and as Paul teaches everywhere."

At least in passing, it is certainly not too much to observe in addition that today's bishops or ecclesiastical overseers (episcope') by any other name have far more at their disposal than the sword of the spirit. It is no longer "political power" in the strict sense, but (to put it as generously as possible) "administrative authority" from which the offices of teaching and providing spiritual leadership all too often have been shorn. In terms of what they actually do from day to day, bishops are the officials of both the ELCA and the Episcopal Church USA. They therefore participate far more in the realm of temporal affairs than Root and many others are willing to admit. Seen from the vantage point of pastors and parishioners, conditions and even the nature of the episcopacy are not all that different from those that prevailed in the Late Middle Ages.[677]

And it seems the ELCA, in its perpetual search for "signs," agrees. The *Lutheran-Episcopal Dialogue, Series III* declares, "There are signs that the office of bishop continues to evolve in the Evangelical Lutheran Church in America." There being no biblical basis for this, we are prompted to ask: Into what exactly is it evolving? Quoting Maurer in a chapter *LED III* calls "The Lutheran Confessional Heritage," the ELCA unwittingly equates its bishops with those of the Late Middle Ages:

> From the perspective of suffering obedience, Luther was willing to accept the jurisdiction of bishops, even if they "were wolves and our enemies" — "because they still possess the office and sit in the place of the apostles" — as long as pure doctrine would be guaranteed.[678]

From this they giddily conclude, "On the basis of the historical perspective provided by Wilhelm Maurer it is evident that the Lutheran confessional documents of the 16th

---

[677] James M. Kittelson, *Enough Is Enough!* "Confusion Over the Augsburg Confession and its *Satis Est.*" http://www.ccmverax.org/kittel.html
[678] Maurer 80.

century, normative for the Evangelical Lutheran Church in America, endorse the historic episcopate in principle."[679] Seemingly oblivious of the fact that Maurer and Luther here are speaking of the despised *stifft bisschove* (prince/endowment bishops), the ELCA foolishly compares its own bishops to "wolves" and "enemies" of the gospel, who "possess the office and sit [illegitimately] in the place of the apostles." Their confusion stems, in part, from their inability to properly distinguish "biblical" episcopacy from "traditional" or "monarchial" episcopacy, a distinction that Luther, the Confessions, and even Piepkorn all make. In "A Lutheran View of the Validity of Lutheran Orders,"[680] his "sequel" to "The Sacred Ministry and Holy Ordination in the Symbolical Books of the Lutheran Church," Piepkorn admitted that there is no biblical evidence whatsoever to support the idea that bishops were sole ordinators, or that there even was an ordination rite prior to its later liturgical development in the tradition of the monarchial episcopate. He writes:

> Turning to the question of the minister of the sacrament of order, a Lutheran cannot find in the sacred scriptures evidence that bishops (in any sense that this term came to acquire in the patristic church) were the only ordinators in the apostolic period. Certainly, he feels, this cannot be proved by the passages conventionally alleged — Acts 6:6; 14:22; I Timothy 5:22; II Timothy 1:6; Titus 1:5. He observes further that the liturgical evidence of a later period is not decisive for establishing the principle that only bishops can ordain. We do not have any descriptions of or extensive allusions to the rite of ordination prior to the period in which the monarchial episcopate triumphed.

Indeed, as Luther stressed in *The Babylonian Captivity*, none of the apostles were ordained nor is ordination ever mentioned in the New Testament.[681] The "monarchial" or

---

[679] *LED III* 45.

[680] *Lutherans and Catholics in Dialogue IV*, 209-226.

[681] *WA* 6.560.

277

"traditional" episcopate, on the other hand, first appeared in Syria c. 115 A.D., and not in Rome before 140-154 A.D. [682] When Piepkorn thus writes in his sequel that, "The Lutherans stand committed to the desirability of the *traditional* episcopal polity by their symbolical books (Apology 14, 1.5),"[683] he is speaking of the later development — as are the Confessions whenever they speak of the *stifft bisschove*. The only difference is that Piepkorn is for it, the Confessions are against it. Luther and the reformers are for a return to the pre-traditional or biblical precedent and example instead, the period prior to the monarchial episcopate when the church had "an earlier kind of health . . . in the old manner . . . in the form and manners of the early church,"[684] a simpler time of elders or presbyters, in which ordination isn't even mentioned, much less hierarchically structured.

Yet the ELCA awkwardly seeks to straddle both worlds, embracing Piepkorn even as it conflates the two periods, the biblical with the traditional, into something it calls an "evangelical episcopate" within an "historical episcopacy." The resulting incongruity is obvious: Whenever the ELCA is asked to define an "evangelical episcopate," they answer it is "bishops according to the gospel." But bishops according to the gospel,[685] as Piepkorn pointed out and Luther and the

---

682 Cf. Heussi, 36, §10c.

683 Piepkorn, 213.

684 *WA*, Br 2, 388: *ut fieret consuetudo libertatis introducende & in prisce Ecclesie faciem & mores restituende;* ". . . *sodaß (oder damit) daraus die Gewohnheit enstünde, die Freiheit (nach dem Vorhergehenden und Folgenden: in bezug auf die Laienprediger und das allgemeine Priestertum) einzuführen und wiederherzustellen, sodaß das Antlitz und die Sitten der alten Kirche wiederkehrten.*"

685 I.e., elders/presbyters, e.g., 1 Timothy 3:6. Cf. *WA* 41, 208, Luther's sermon on Psalm 110: "In the scriptures they are called servants, bishops, that is: overseers, or as the apostles call them, presbyters, seniors (*Seniores*), that is: the eldest, since the word presbyter doesn't mean anything other than 'an old man.' Thus were chosen the best persons to the office, those who had attained such

Confessions have shown, were not hierarchical, monarchial, in historic episcopal succession, or even traditional, but just elders as pastors. But none of this matters, apparently, to an institution devoted to the *Führerprinzip*, or "leadership principle" over the simple proclamation of the gospel as it struggles to "live into" its 1999 CCM sales pitch: "You don't have to believe it; you just have to do it."[686]

Ecumenical Enthusiasms

"It is obvious in all three [predecessor churches that formed the ELCA] that a development occurred in the office [of bishop] and in the expectations of it as a direct result of the change in title. There was a greater regard for the pastoral character of the office and for its function as a symbol of unity . . . the synod bishops were given a somewhat

---

age, who were tried, learned, practiced, and experienced, as befits all administrations, scripture commanding us to choose such persons."

[686] Subsequent official statements exemplify the breadth and depth of the ELCA's confusion and use of fiction in its lead-up to the vote on the *Concordat* and *CCM*. E.g., "In terms of the historic Lutheran confessional formulations, the Lutheran churches agree, as stated in Article 14 of the Apology of the Augsburg Confession that they share a 'deep desire to maintain the church polity and various ranks of the ecclesiastical hierarchy' as they have existed throughout catholic history [sic]. Article 14 expresses our 'willingness to keep the ecclesiastical and canonical polity,' a proposal which is still in place. Already in 1537 our churches understood that such threefold ordering of ministries was the past and therefore the future polity of the Church, and thus recognized the ecumenical implications of their ordering of Lutheran ordained ministries. This statement in Apology 14 remains the basis of any Lutheran 'agreement' in the future, and the Concordat only reaffirms this abiding proposal of Apology 14 as the future pattern of ordained ministries in the Church [sic]" (*Concordat:* Concerns Addressed, March 1997), 20.

enhanced pastoral role . . . There are signs that the office of bishop continues to evolve in the Evangelical Lutheran Church in America."

Lutheran-Episcopal Dialogue, Series III, 42.

"Somehow it seemed as though the farm had grown richer without making the animals themselves any richer except, of course, for the pigs and the dogs. Four legs good, two legs better. ALL ANIMALS ARE EQUAL BUT SOME ANIMALS ARE MORE EQUAL THAN OTHERS. The creatures outside looked from pig to man, and from man to pig, and from pig to man again; but already it was impossible to say which was which."

George Orwell, *Animal Farm*

Church governance (*administratio*) is not the only reason ELCA theologians give for the adoption of CCM. They also offer episcopal succession as a sign and safeguard against a perceived pietistic *Übertragungslehre,* a doctrine which says that the congregation, as the priesthood of all believers, "transfers" power and authority to the pastor by its call. One can debate the meaning of "tranfers" until the cows come home, but some arguments against the *Übertragungslehre* are even more misguided than the *Lehre* itself.

Lazareth, for example, in his promotional book for an "evangelical episcopate," *Two Forms of Ordained Ministry,* wrote:

> Confessionally, the locus classicus for this view of the "power bishops" as delegated from below for the sake of "good order" (rather than as conferred from above for the sake of the "means of grace") is supposedly to be found in Ap 15.20. It is immediately apparent, however, that the explicit reference there is to adiaphoral "rites and seasons . . . traditions profitable to good order," and not to the regularly called ordained ministry "to the gospel" (CA 14). It is also important to note that 1 Peter 2:9 ("You are a chosen race, a royal priesthood, a holy nation, God's own people . . ."), the scriptural proof-text most frequently

280

misused for this view within later Lutheran popular tradition, is cited only once in the entire *Book of Concord*.[687]

The *locus classicus*, however, has never been Ap 15, but the very *BoC* Melanchthon quote he points to: 1 Peter 2:9 in TPPP.[688] Nor does its single citation diminish its importance — it also appears only once in scripture.[689] Luther quotes it another 44 times for example in *Luther's Works*, and its authority is fully affirmed in the *Formula of Concord*.

Wengert sees the *locus classicus* in CA 5, but then claims the article must be understood "clerically" as the clergy's domain alone (except in extreme emergencies). He bases this on the title given it (later), and castigates the Lutheran half of the EKD (Evangelische Kirche in Deutschland), VELKD (Vereinigte Evangelisch-Lutherische Kirche Deutschlands), for translating *Predigtamt* as the "office of proclamation." Mistranslating VELKD as "the People's Evangelical Lutheran Church in Germany," (as if it were a remnant of the former communist East Germany), though it is the "United Evangelical-Lutheran Church of Germany," he writes, "Thus, they invariably paraphrase (and thereby distort) CA 5's *Predigtamt* by using a word that is completely foreign to sixteenth-century German: *Verkündigungsamt,*"[690] that is, the office of "proclamation."

Setting aside for a moment that preaching and proclamation are obviously the same thing, his distinction is utterly

---

[687] Lazareth 32. His statement again appears lifted from Piepkorn, who wrote: "The classical prooftext for this teaching, I. Peter 2:9, is cited only once in the symbolical books." Piepkorn, 107-108.

[688] Cf. *WA* 8.252 ff. for Luther's explanation of this key passage.

[689] The verse is an expansion of Exodus 19:6.

[690] Wengert 39-40, 124 n.24. That Luther thought of the preaching office as the office of the proclamation of the gospel, is obvious from his Bible of 1545, e.g. 1 Johannes 1:5: *"Und das ist die Verkündigung, die wir von ihm gehört haben und euch verkündigen, daß Gott Licht ist und in ihm ist keine Finsternis."* Also, the kerygma of God (*kerykeuo = verkündigen, bekanntmachen*) is "to proclaim, make known."

frivolous given his own translation of *Predigtamt* as "proclamation" in his Kolb/Wengert *2000 BC*. In Ap 24.34, for example, the Latin term for the office appears twice as *praedicationem evangelii*, which he renders first as "the preaching of the gospel," then as "the proclamation of the gospel," though the German word in both cases is *Predig(t)amt*.

To make historical episcopacy, on the other hand, an *Übertragungsersatz* for Christ's church is to offer it a red herring. Nothing says "power transfer" more pietistically and more enthusiastically than the myth of historical episcopal succession as a "safeguard" for the gospel as CCM's "Agreement in the Doctrine of the Faith" does.[691] Both ELCA and ECUSA accept:

> the ordinations/installations of their own bishops as a sign, though not a guarantee, of the unity and apostolic continuity of the whole church. With the laying-on-of-hands by other bishops, such ordinations/installations will involve prayer for the gifts of the Holy Spirit. Both churches value and maintain a ministry of *episkope* as one of the ways in which the apostolic succession of the church is visibly expressed and personally symbolized in fidelity to the gospel through the ages.[692]

This unguaranteed and thoroughly unreliable "sign" of "apostolic succession" in historical episcopacy is the sacrament of ordination through the laying on of hands with

---

691 *Baptism, Eucharist, Ministry*, "Ministry," 26.

692 *CCM*, A.5, 12. With this statement the ELCA essentially endorses the Romanist rebuttal of the Lutheran Confessions in Articles XIII and XX of the 1548 Augsburg Interim, which reaffirmed bishops *iure divino* and their "perpetual succession" through the laying on of hands. For a brief synopsis of the failed history of the *episkopoi* as a visible sign of the unity of the church, see Joseph A. Burgess, "Evangelical Episcopate, Yes — Sacramental Requirement, No," *Lutheran Forum*, Vol. 26, No. 4, November 1992.

epicletic prayer.[693] Through it "gifts" are said to be received (especially with regard to the sacrament) so that grace may be conferred.

Anticipating resistance from confessional Lutherans, (whom he called "such sticklers for dogmatic precision"), Anglican Archbishop Wand wrote in 1961 what could pass for an update of "Jack's Crepitus"[694] in Henry Bell.

> It may well be asked why it should be thought necessary to lay so much stress on the outward form; would it not be enough to preserve the inward life? The answer is that the outward form is itself the best guarantee of the preservation of the inward life. It is the shell that preserves the kernel from harm.[695] This is in conformity with the general sacramental principle by which the existence of the church is governed. The physical continuity is the outward and visible sign of the inward and spiritual grace. Just as in the sacrament of the Eucharist and of Baptism we are always careful of the outward elements,[696] so in the continuous life of the Church one would naturally be anxious to preserve intact the outward succession by which the inward life is symbolized and conveyed.[697]

---

[693] Cf. *Anglican Ordination Rites,* The Berkeley Statement: 'To Equip the Saints,' Findings of the Sixth International Anglican Liturgical Consultation, Berkeley, California, 2B, Appendix E.

[694] A supposed miraculous outward sign for historical apostolic succession. Cf. Chapter 9.

[695] At the very least, the sexual abuse scandal of the Catholic episcopate in recent decades dispels this notion. Sensitive to historical Eastern Orthodox and Lutheran claims that the Anglican shell contains no theological kernel, Wand agreed with G. F. S. Gray, *The Anglican Communion* (SPCK, 1958, 11) that the Anglican Church is nevertheless "the most elastic Church in Christendom," Wand 229.

[696] Luther advised baptizing with beer if water wasn't to be had. *WATR* 394, December 1532.

[697] Wand, 52. He agrees with Gray "that there is no special Anglican system of theology in the sense that, for example, there is a Calvinist system; nor is any one doctrine given such overwhelming importance

The Lutheran objection is that scripture teaches precisely the opposite, namely that the word begets the church, never the church the word, or if you will, the kernel protects the shell, not the other way around. As the 3rd Article to the Creed makes clear, the Holy Spirit, not the church, guarantees, sanctifies and preserves the church through the word which alone is its life. Lutherans have thus traditionally rejected the Anglican notion expressed by Wand that:

> What may seem, at first sight, to be merely mechanical continuity will wear a different aspect when it is seen as part of the outward sign by which the grace of ordination is conveyed to the candidate for the ministry. In this, as in other sacraments, one will naturally exercise care and reverence in regard to the outward sign, not thinking it all-important in itself but honoring it for the treasure it conveys.[698]

Seeing this "care and reverence in regard to the outward sign" in a new light, (what Luther referred to as "a carnival mask"), became the magical breakthrough to "solving" the seemingly irreconcilable barrier between Anglicanism's "ontological" and Lutheranism's "functional" understanding of ordination in the walkup to CCM. Its "discovery" was championed by LWF ecumenist George Lindbeck:

> What the Reformers objected to was the idea that succession constitutes a guarantee or criterion of apostolic faithfulness, but once one thinks in terms of the sign value of continuity in office, this difficulty vanishes. Signs or symbols express and strengthen the reality they signify, but the sign can be present without the reality, and the reality without the sign (as for example, is illustrated by the relation of the flag and patriotism). Thus it is apostolicity in faith and life that makes the episcopal sign fruitful, not the other way around, but this ought not be turned into an

---

as Lutherans give to the doctrine of justification by faith alone . . . two extreme doctrinal positions," 229, 21.
[698] Wand, 54.

excuse for neglecting the sign.[699]

What the reformers rejected was not only the notion that succession constituted "a guarantee or criterion of apostolic faithfulness," but the very idea of a "sign value of continuity in office" beyond word and sacrament itself, something Luther had already rejected at the Leipzig Debate (against all appeals to tradition, councils, bishops and popes). A sign is only ever as good as its guarantee. What good is a sign for gas if there is no guarantee of a gas station? What good are the signs of water, bread, and wine if they are not guaranteed in, with, and under the word they contain? The "sign value of the continuity in office," indeed, its very guarantee, is not successive ordinations, but baptism — "the sign of Jonah" (Matthew 16:4), given to the priesthood of all believers. "Apostolicity in faith and life" is not what makes a sign "fruitful," but the word alone which creates faith and life, guaranteed through the cross and heard in the command and promise of Christ ("baptize," "eat," "drink"). While Zwingli, for example, possessed an outward sign in the controversy over the Lord's Supper, it came without the guarantee of the word, "This IS (*est*) my body/blood." Without it, the sign was merely an *alleosis,* [700] an empty symbol. And so it is for "the ordinations/installations of [the ELCA's and ECUSA's] own bishops as a sign, though not a guarantee, of the unity and apostolic continuity of the whole church."[701]

Without a guarantee (found only in word and sacrament), historical episcopal ordination is a trope, a metaphorical expression in the ELCA's pantheon of "expressions" that contain neither grace nor promise. (What, indeed, is faith, if not the absence of the need for symbols and signs in the first

---

[699] George A. Lindbeck, "Episcopacy and the Unification of the Churches: Two Approaches," in *Promoting Unity,* edited by H. George Anderson and James R. Crumley Jr. (Minneapolis: Augsburg, 1989), 53-54.

[700] *BSLK,* 1024.

[701] *CCM* A.5, 12.

place, "the assurance of things hoped for, the conviction of things not seen"?) [702] By contrast, the priesthood of all believers, which is said by many in that institution to be metaphorical, is in fact the real deal, containing the guarantee, the grace, and the promise of Christ in Galatians 2:20.[703] As Lutherans, Joseph A. Burgess notes, "We are irrevocably committed to the view that the authenticity of the gospel is the only guarantee for the legitimacy of the structures of the church — rather than the converse, that the legitimacy of the structures of the church guarantee the authenticity of the gospel." [704] But hailing Lindbeck's supposed breakthrough, LED III declares:

> If the sign/substance way of understanding the impasse has been resolved by a deeper perception of the category of "sign" such as Lima developed, then this really constitutes (in Lindbeck's words) "a shift in the perception of the diachronic dimension, that is, in the way in which succession and apostolicity are perceived." [705]

Translation: If the perception of the sign of historical episcopal succession has changed over time, it could and should be acceptable to Lutheranism. But how has the perception changed according to LED III? Have Episcopalians now agreed that successive episcopal ordinations are not a sacramental sign from God after all, possessing neither grace nor promise? Do they believe with Luther and the Confessions that there is in fact nothing ontological about ordination, which Lutherans from Mathesius to Maurer have said is simply the selection of a pastor?

---

[702] Hebrews 11:1

[703] "I have been crucified with Christ; it is no longer I who live, but Christ who lives in me; and the life I now live in the flesh I live by the faith of the Son of God, who loved me and gave himself for me." (RSV)

[704] Joseph A. Burgess, *Lutheran Forum*, Vol. 26, No. 4, 31.

[705] *LED III*, 22.

LED III:

> The historic episcopal succession has traditionally been seen by "high church" Anglicans as being ontological, even an essential element of the gospel given for all time, whereas "low church" Lutherans have traditionally emphasized that the ordained ministry is strictly functional in character, having no ontological dimension whatsoever, especially insofar as ordination might then be seen as establishing a superior or higher class of Christians within the church. But now, increasingly within both churches, ordination — and even the office of bishop — is being seen by historians, theologians, and others as being functional in origin, and ontological upon reflection. Once the historically functional origin is agreed, there can then also be agreement, as is obvious, that the reflection upon ordained ministry — even by the laity of both churches — does indeed posit a certain "ontological" dimension to it, provided always that it is not accorded a status higher than those whom it serves. Thus Lutheran clergy after ordination, just like clergy of the Episcopal Church, are commonly accorded the title "The Reverend" in front of their names, indicating some change, but not elevation, of status.[706]

In other words, Lindbeck's "shift in the perception of the diachronic dimension," is simply the decision — "upon reflection" — by some Lutheran ecclesiasts to accept the Anglo-Catholic myth of ontological ordination. It's a return to Emser's *Allotria* (monkey business) and twofold *priesterey*, to Wengert's "clericalistic" CA 5. Reflecting on their reverential reflections, Lindbeck and LED apparently concluded that Lutheran "functional" ordination (the call to proclamation and distribution) is itself *non satis est* when it comes to episcopal dignity, and in need of a bit of clerical cachet, of priestly panache.[707] They thus posited it with "a certain dimension" of ontological aura, giving it a status supposedly not higher "than those whom it serves" — (even though the title "The

---

706 *Ibid,* 23.
707 *Scheinheiligkeit* ("holy aura")

287

Reverend," means "worthy to be revered,"[708] and connotes an elevated status, to say nothing of the addition of miters and staffs). And therewith, in the words of Froude, "The image in its outward aspect could be made to correspond with the parent tree; and to sustain the illusion that it was necessary to provide bishops who could appear to have inherited their powers by the approved method as successors of the apostles."

When it came to such supercilious claims of an "ontological dimension" to ordination, Luther pulled no punches, declaring in *Concerning the Ministry:*

> There is something ridiculous (*ridicule*) about this conferring of orders. For the episcopal dignity is not a sacrament nor has it a "character." Yet it gives a priestly dignity and power supposedly above all others. Though the episcopal authority ranks as the highest since it grants the ordination and "character" of a priest, it is at the same time inferior since it is not itself an order or in possession of a peculiar "character." So the lesser bestows what is greater. And since it proved necessary to dress up this absurdity they created this fictitious distinction between dignity and power. What else was possible once the imprudent lie got started, but to continue to vacillate? Wherefore Christ predicted how all things in the papal realm would be guided by no consistent reason but overleap the bounds of common sense. So it is not surprising that they concede the priestly sacrament of baptism to all, yet lay claim to the exclusive possession of the priesthood.[709]

Yet, five centuries after the Reformation rejected such pious posturing, affirming instead with Luther that "one cannot recognize a church by its outward customs; it is recognizable through the word of God alone," the 21st century American Lutherans finally blinked.

Ordination (*"if it is anything at all"*) is not a sacrament, but simply the choosing of a preacher, a rite containing no grace,

---

708 *Webster's Third New International Dictionary of the English Language,* (Chicago: Encyclopedia Britannica, Inc., 1986), Vol. II, 1943. Some ELCA pastors now prefer the title "The Very Reverend."
709 *WA* 12.182.

promise, or "ontological dimension," all present ELCA efforts to sacramentalize the rite as a sign aside. While bishops (pastors) are "watchmen" (*Wächter*), servants, and shepherds, they are not the guardians or preservers of the church. Luther quashed such episcopal ecstasies in *Against the Antinomians*:

> A thousand years ago you and I were nothing, and yet the church was preserved at that time without us. He who is called "who was" and "yesterday" had to accomplish this. Even during our lifetime we are not the church's guardians. It is not preserved by us, for we are unable to drive off the devil in the persons of the pope, the sects, and evil men. If it were up to us, the church would perish before our very eyes, and we together with it as we experience daily. For it is another Man who obviously preserves both the church and us . . . It is a tragic thing that there are so many examples before us of those who thought they had to preserve the church, as though it were built on them.[710]

While one can "Protestantize" such episcopalian ecstasies in order to make them ecumenically friendly by neutering the language of the indelible character to one of "epiklesis" — in the end the herring is still a herring, whether viewed from above or seen from below. Whether a lay or episcopal *Übertragungslehre*, both are pietistic schemes, both are concerned with ontological status and hierarchical structure — the one from the bottom up, the other from the top down. According to the Wittenberg reformers, though, the church subscribes to neither. Luther's paradigm is flat, it is horizontal within *das einzige gemeinsame Priesterthum* of the single Christian *Stand* with many *Stände,* exercised through the law of love.[711]

Which brings us back to Lohse who correctly stated, "Luther did not design a *fixed* program for the execution of the Reformation or for the construction of the new form of the

---

[710] *WA* 50.477. An expanded version of this paragraph is found in Luther's preface to Volume II of the Wittenberg edition of his German works, published in 1548. Cf. *WA* 54.470, 8-26.
[711] Cf. *BSLK* 430 (SA II.IV.9).

evangelical church." Such a bold claim spreads panic among ecclesiastical hierarchists whose mission is "good order" for the sake of "unity" in a "visible" church for the purpose of "saving" and "rescuing" the body of Christ to "increase justice in social, economic, and political terms."[712] They point with trepidation to possible chaos in the church from "rampant congregationalism," "democracy," "congregational rights," "loose cannons," and out of control parishioners in Montana. While some may concede that Luther believed congregations are indeed free to organize and associate in ways that best befit the proclamation of the gospel (CA 7), they also point to the supposed eschatological exceptionalism of Luther's day, to the "emergency" that gripped his time. Luther, they argue, believed the church and the world to be in the throes of the last days, with all signs pointing to the immanent return of Christ.[713] So understandably, in the same way that marriage and property were of little interest to St. Paul, the creation of a fixed program for a future evangelical *Kirchenleitung* was not a preoccupation of Luther's — but it must be in our day! Yet as an astute member of one of my congregations recently asked, "How, exactly, has the nature of the church or the eschatological clock changed since Luther's day?"

Indeed, while the reformer clearly battled the unlearned *Schwärmer* of his time from both the top down and the bottom up, insisting on a thorough liberal arts and confessional

---

[712] Carl E. Braaten, *Principles of Lutheran Theology,* (Philadelphia: Fortress Press, 2007), 68.

[713] That Luther expected Christ to return in his lifetime is also largely a modern myth, perpetuated by Root and others. In CA 17 the Lutheran reformers rejected the eschatological teachings of Hans Hut and a number of Jews from Worms, who insisted the Millennium would be ushered in during Easter, 1530. One of their leaders, Augustin Bader, was executed in Stuttgart on March 30, 1530. Cf. *BSLK* 72 n. 3. Cf. Scott H. Hendrix, *Luther and the Papacy,* Stages in a Reformation Conflict, (Philadelphia, Fortress Press, 1981), 194 n.22: "Apocalyptic concerns never dominated Luther's theology as they did Hoffman's. See K. Deppermann, *Melchior Hoffman,* (Göttingen, 1979), 67-68."

education for all those called to public ministry, he also had a deep abiding faith in the power of the word alone to bring order out of chaos, of the Holy Spirit to "call . . . enlighten . . . sanctify the whole Christian church on earth and preserve it in union with Jesus Christ in the one true faith" (SC, III). This royal priesthood, the priesthood of all believers, is therefore what it is: the *communio sanctorum simul iustus et peccator,* God's holy people of saints and sinners gathered around word and sacrament.

Bornkamm summarized the problem of hierarchization most aptly in his answer to the question, "What is the Church?"

> The words spoken by Luther of the individual Christian also apply to the church: It is not in the stages of having become but of becoming (*Sie steht nicht im Gewordensein, sondern im Werden*). But this did not go far enough for people who were anxiously concerned about the reality of the church. They thought it was a disparagement of the church. This was already apparent in Melanchthon. He fretted over the Catholic sneer that the Protestant Church was only a *civitas Platonica,* a cloudland. It can be observed how little by little a second idea insinuated itself, at the side of Luther's, into Melanchthon's consciousness. The church is also an outward sociological institution as, e.g., the state, cities, guilds, etc., are. At first this second concept occupies a very secondary position, but gradually it thrust forward, and finally a second, equally justifiable concept of the church was adopted by the Lutheran orthodoxy determined by Melanchthon: the visible church at the side of the invisible. This division into two parts is never found in Luther. It stands to reason that the visible church is of far greater interest to theologians, church politicians, and particularly to the jurists. Finally the Lutherans followed in the train of Calvin: The invisible church is disposed of with the elaboration of a few principles, and with a reverential bow it is ushered into heaven. Then exclusive attention is directed to the tangible problems of the so-called visible church. In this way a new legal form of the church developed. It is an institution of public life and may be defined as such according to form, purpose, personal relationships, etc., as other sociological entities

are. Thereby Luther's profound and unified concept of the church was destroyed.[714]

Five hundred years after the Reformation, sociological legalism is *de rigueur* for much of what passes for Lutheranism in the U.S. and around the world. The pursuit of a shining church on a hill through an imagined earlier visible unity is at best a fundamental misunderstanding, and at worst a complete ignoring of Luther's theology of death and new life, a theology that, as Forde put it, undermines "all ordinary ideas of progress according to moral and legal schemes." He adds:

> Catholic suspicion and the constant fire of moralists have gradually taken their toll on the confessional position. All too often Protestants have not had the courage of their convictions. They have gone on the defensive, made concessions, and ended by adopting one form or another of the patronizing rhetoric of their adversaries, usually for the sake of so-called "practical" exigencies. It just isn't "practical" to preach or teach an "unconditional" promise.[715]

---

[714] Heinrich Bornkamm, *Luther's World of Thought,* 149-150.
[715] Gerhard O. Forde, *Justification by Faith - A Matter of Death and Life, (Philadelphia:* Fortress Press, 1982), 43-44.

Chapter 11

There's no place like Rome!

"Then close your eyes, and tap your heels together three times and think to yourself, 'There's no place like home.'"

The Good Witch Glinda to Dorothy in the Land of Oz

Many apologetic Lutheran ecumenists, (not in defense of, but apologizing for Lutheranism) would have us believe as Carl E. Braaten[716] does that Lutherans are homeless wandering Arameans, "exiles" hoping to return to Rome, who though they "sometimes become smug and self-sufficient and convert their interim status into a permanent establishment . . . the fate of Protestantism," nevertheless "dream of reunion with their fellow countrymen." [717] Former conservative Lutheran theologian Richard John Neuhaus concluded before converting to Roman Catholicism and being re-ordained a Catholic priest, that the Lutherans are "a people driven into exile who did so well and found themselves so comfortable that they forgot about returning to their home country"[718] — though "home" for Luther was never Rome, but God's word

---

[716] Braaten is a co-founder of the "Center for Catholic and Evangelical Theology," along with Robert Jenson and their wives.

[717] Braaten, *Principles of Lutheran Theology,* 56.

[718] *The New York Times,* September 9, 1990, Peter Steinfels. Neuhaus believed that Vatican II sufficiently addressed the concerns of 16th century Lutheranism, and later pointed to what he saw as significant progress in the Roman Catholic-Lutheran *Joint Declaration on the Doctrine of Justification (JDDJ).* But while conceding in *JDDJ* that salvation is by grace through faith — though not "alone" — the Roman Catholic Church continues to be predicated on Aquinas's synergistic system of the cooperative nature of man for justification.

293

alone.[719] According to this "ecumaniacal"[720] longing it is imperative they pursue a "path that leads to the recovery of unity," as Braaten put it, without which "the goal of more faithfully embodying the attributes of the true church of Jesus Christ is then made more distant."[721]

Braaten, who was raised a mid-western Norwegian Pietist, is clearly a man on a mission, (a word he employs often and with no small amount of frustration). In *Essential Lutheranism,* his sequel to *Principles of Lutheran Theology* and dedicated to his clerical fraternity "The Society of the Holy Trinity," he appears to despair of the Holy Spirit ever getting the job of Christian unity done, pointing to the sorry state of American Lutheranism today in three models.

"The first type aims to be gnesio-Lutheran, that is, to be authentically Lutheran by appealing to the *Book of Concord* and the period of seventeenth century scholastic orthodoxy."[722] The result, he believes, is an inward focus on Lutheran exclusivity and anti-ecumenism exemplified by the Missouri (LCMS) and Wisconsin Synod (WELS) Lutherans.

"The second type of Lutheranism is motivated by various social agendas," bereft of any theological acumen. Such is the Evangelical Lutheran Church in America (ELCA).

"A third type of Lutheranism includes chiefly the office

---

[719] Rumors were in circulation that the Lutherans were already "crawling back" to Rome at the time of the 1528 *Instructions*, based in part on Luther's advice that the people make confession to a pastor prior to Holy Communion. Erasmus, and others, fed the rumor. Cf. *WA* 26.183: ". . . besonders die Forderung, die Sünde nicht bloß vor Gott, sondern auch dem Priester zu beichten, hatte die Meinung aufkommen lassen, daß die Evangelischen 'zurückkröchen.'" Luther replied in the preface, "Already [the devil] has used our enemies to criticize and condemn us so that some boast that we have regretted our teaching and are retreating and recanting" *WA* 26.200.

[720] I thank Mark Menacher for this inventive term.

[721] Braaten, *Principles of Lutheran Theology,* 57 ff.

[722] Carl E. Braaten, *Essential Lutheranism,* "Theological Perspectives on Christian Faith and Doctrine," [Dehli, NY: ALPB Books, 2012], 12.

managers who have a nose for where the money and levers of power happen to be. They have technical expertise that could be useful in any business enterprise, and it doesn't particularly matter which one. The ELCA is currently run by these bureaucrats who excel in loyalty to the party apparatus that pays their salaries, but are not motivated by theological convictions. They are not opposed to Lutheran orthodoxy; they just don't know what it is. If they happen to know a little theology and speak glibly on church matters, they might even become bishops. Understanding the doctrines of the Christian faith is not a prerequisite."[723]

The solution, he believes, is a fourth type of Lutheranism: "Evangelical Catholics" (ECs), who believe "that the evangelical catholic understanding of the biblical Christian faith is the most faithful interpretation of the Lutheran theological heritage in an ecumenical age." Their motto, whether large "C" Catholic or small, (it doesn't seem to matter to Braaten, who constantly mixes them up), is "dogma is more important than denomination."

That is, until it isn't, all of the above being essentially the same — steeped in law — ECs included. But as the supposed true Lutheranism that offers a way forward, Braaten's "fourth group" bears some closer scrutiny.

Though he often describes the doctrine of justification by faith in glowing terms, "the one big thing for Lutherans" which arose out of Luther's experience, he wonders, "Now what if later Lutherans did not share the same sort of negative experiences or at least not to the same degree? Would the doctrine of justification through faith alone apart from the works of the law enjoy the same premier status?"[724] He concludes that it needn't do so as it is proving to be an inconvenient truth for accomplishing visible church unity.

When it comes to this dogma, some Lutheran theologians have

---

[723] *Ibid*, 13.
[724] *Ibid*, 22.

attempted to organize the whole of theology around the doctrine of justification by faith alone. I think that is an abuse of the doctrine, even though I am fully committed to its use as an indispensable criterion for constructing the doctrine of salvation — soteriology. I am also greatly in favor of its hermeneutical function in biblical interpretation and its homiletical value in sermon preparation. I became convinced of this mostly by reading Luther's commentaries and sermons. However, I believe that it would be wrong to try to derive the whole of Christian doctrine from this article.[725]

Among the Lutheran theologians who have organized "the whole of theology around the doctrine of justification by faith alone" are Luther and Melanchthon, the former insisting "the article of justification . . . is the centerpiece (*das Häuptstücke*), cause, and source of all other promises; where it remains pure and perseveres, there the church also remains pure."[726] "Because if this article stands, the church stands; if this article collapses, the church collapses."[727] Melanchthon pronounced it to be "the highest and chief article of all Christian teaching,"[728] in the opening of Ap 4. But with nary a reference to justification's central role in the *Bondage of the Will*, Braaten credits Martin Kähler's and Gerhard Ebeling's "attempts" at a

> reduction of Christian doctrine by making the category of faith serve as the hub around which all the other articles of faith revolve. Nevertheless, such an approach is impossible today in light of our knowledge of the origins of the Christian faith, the history of dogma, and the ecumenical dialogues with Roman

---

[725] *Ibid*, 14.

[726] *WATR* 3.444: *"Der Artikel von der Rechtfertigung . . . der das Häuptstücke, Ursache, und Quelle ist aller anderen Verheisungen; wo der reine bleibt und bestehet, so bleibt auch die Kirche rein."*

[727] *WA* 40 III.352: *quia isto articulo stante stat Ecclesia, ruente ruit Ecclesia.*

[728] *BSLK* 159: *"dem höchsten fürnehmsten Artikel der ganzen christlichen Lehre"*

Catholics and the Eastern Orthodox theologians. In light of these factors we know that systematic theology that claims to be evangelical, catholic, and orthodox is based on the twin towers of Trinity and Christology. The article of justification by faith functions as a critical soteriological principle within this dogmatic framework and cannot by itself constitute it. That may sound like an unLutheran concession, but to require this one doctrine to be generative of all others is based on a misinterpretation of the Lutheran Confessions, the *Book of Concord.*[729]

Although he offers in the opening chapters of *Principals of Lutheran Theology* and *Essential Lutheranism* to explain himself, he never does, leaving his only point to be that if Lutherans don't begin to back off of the article of justification (CA 4), their ecumenical colleagues will no longer speak to them. "A Lutheran theology," he insists, "that would restrict itself to Luther's theology or the Lutheran Confessions would be an abrogation of their intention to serve as a reforming movement within western Christianity."[730]

As James Kittelson wrote to me in 2002, "These people are therefore not Lutherans by their confession. Why, then, do they arrogate to themselves responsibility for the future of Lutheran churches in North America?" Why indeed? While the ecumenists claiming to represent them are conducting a confessional yard sale, Lutherans are increasingly joining Alice in Wonderland in asking,

"Who in the world am I? Ah, that's the great puzzle."

When it comes to downplaying the confessional Lutheran identity, a tool popularly employed by ecumenists for nudging the Lutheran diaspora back to Rome is the word "catholic" in reference to the "catholicity of the church."

Braaten, who appears infatuated with the word over and against Luther's substitution of "Christian," writes, "By 'catholicity of the church,' we have in mind the universal

---

[729] Braaten, *Essential Lutheranism,* 14-15.
[730] *Ibid,* 15.

297

scope of the apostolic mission. The mission is universal because of its eschatological character. Therefore, a church can be apostolic only if it is also catholic, working in line with the universal scope of the apostolic commission."[731]

Even if read repeatedly the statement makes little sense, a non sequitur of the kind Kittelson liked to call "an effort to introduce confusion where clarity abounds." Catholicity (or the universality of the church), results from the proclamation of the gospel. The word alone creates the where and when of the church, never the church the word. Hence, the church neither creates nor becomes catholic — it simply is — wherever the Spirit creates faith through preaching. "Evangelical Catholics" could save themselves and others a good deal of confusion if they'd simply use the phrase the 1580 BoC uses: "one holy, Christian, and apostolic church."[732]

But Braaten won't have it: "In many Protestant circles the word 'catholic' in the Nicene Creed was dropped in favor of the word 'Christian.' This was a weak move because the word 'Christian' is more suitably an equivalent for the word 'apostolic,' concentrating on the identity principle of the church."

If this were actually true, one would need to count Luther, Melanchthon, Jonas, Bugenhagen, and the Wittenberg reformers among the "weak," since they too, translated *catholicam* as "Christian" (*Christliche*), and not "catholic" (*katholische*), something the German churches had already begun to do well before Luther's time. It is also the official German translation in *The Three Chief Symbols* (Apostles', Nicene, Athanasian Creeds) in the 1580 *Book of Concord*. In his 1538 exposition on the Trinitarian formula of the *Smalcald Articles* entitled, *The Three Symbols or Creeds of the Christian Faith*, Luther contrasts the two terms, writing in the

---

[731] Braaten, *Principles of Lutheran Theology*, 64.
[732] Cf. Kolb/Wengert, *2000BC*, 22, n.12: "*catholica*: this word, lacking in many texts of the Old Roman Creed, is translated 'Christian' in both the German (already before the Reformation) and the traditional English version."

margin of the third petition of the Nicene Creed, "*Catholica* can have no better translation than 'Christian,' as has been the case up to now. That is, although Christians are to be found in all the world, the pope rages against that, and wants to call his court alone the Christian Church, but he lies, just like his idol the devil."[733]

And when it came to the Latin phrasing "*sanctam ecclesiam catholicam*," Luther's emphasis lay less on the catholicity of the church (a word which simply describes its eschatological location: "everywhere"), and more on its holiness as the *sanctam ecclesiam,* from the original Greek αγιαν εκκλεσιαν, the *Gemeine der Heiligen,* a phrase already in use in Germany at the time of Charlemagne.[734]

"The word 'catholic,'" Braaten says, "now has been restored to the creed for common liturgical use; this gives rise to the salutary quest for authentic catholicity so conspicuous by its absence in many churches."[735] This idea, though, is patently absurd and a quixotic contradiction of the 3rd Article of the Creed, as one can hardly go on a quest for the "everywhereness" of the church which is hidden in the cross which alone determines its authenticity. But even viewed practically, the word is nothing if not problematic today with its undue emphasis on the Latin, as any Lutheran pastor can

---

[733] "*Catholica kan man nicht wol besser deudschen denn 'Christlich,' wie bis her geschehen, Das ist wo Christen sind in aller Welt, da wider tobet der Papst und wil seinen hoff allein die Christliche Kirche geheissen haben, Leugt aber, wie der Teuffel sein Abgott.*" *WA* 50.283. Melanchthon defended the word "catholic" strictly in terms of universal correct teaching in *de appellation ecclesiae catholicae* in *Corpus Reformatorum* (Melanchthon), Vol. 24, cols. 397-399. The papal position aligning catholic with Roman was reaffirmed in the declaration, *Dominus Iesus,* "On the Unicity and Salvific Universality of Jesus Christ and the Church," issued on August 6, 2000, by the Congregation for the Doctrine of the Faith, headed by the Prefect Joseph Cardinal Ratzinger, (elected as Pope Benedict XVI, April 19, 2005).

[734] *BSLK* 24.

[735] Braaten, *Principles of Lutheran Theology,* 65.

attest to who has had to explain to parishioners *ad nauseam ad infinitum,* "No, the word doesn't mean 'Catholic,' it means 'universal.'"

Nor is it sacrosanct. Like ecumenism's other *Lieblingswörter* (beloved phrases) "apostolic succession" and "mission,"[736] it is not found anywhere in the Old or New Testament. "The word 'catholic' is in the ancient creed," Braaten insists, "the word 'Roman' is not,"[737] — though neither word is found in the most ancient of creeds, the *Roman Creed,*[738] the predecessor to the *Apostles' Creed* and in widespread use throughout the West by the 3rd century. It speaks only of the "Holy Church," with *catholicam* not making its creedal debut before the 4th century and not appearing in its present form before the 6th - 8th centuries.[739]

When the word "catholic" is spoken hearers cannot distinguish an upper from lower case "C," and when it is read

---

[736] The ELCA and her offshoots perpetually speak of the church's "mission," a word that scripture, Luther, and the Confessions never use. Christ declared "mission accomplished" from the cross: John 19:30 τετέλεσται = perfect passive indicative: "It has been accomplished." (Luther's Bible 1545: *"Es ist vollbracht!"*) Luther also never spoke of a *successio apostolica,* only of a *successio fidelium.* "Apostolicity," or the apostolic office for Luther was nothing more than "to preach the gospel, whereby God is made known and glorified" *WA* 45.651. In contrast the *Niagara Report* states: "The apostolicity of the Church is the mission of self-offering (not self-preservation) for the life of the world." I.23; and LED III: "For apostolicity means that the Church is sent by Jesus to *be* for the world, to participate in his mission and therefore in the mission of the One who sent Jesus, to participate in the mission of the Father and the Son through the dynamic of the Holy Spirit." 32.

[737] Braaten, *Essential Lutheranism,* 74.

[738] "I believe in God the Father Almighty and in Christ Jesus, His Son, our Lord, and in Holy Spirit, Holy Church, and resurrection of the flesh."

[739] Cf. *The Oxford Dictionary of the Christian Church,* Edited by F.L. Cross and E. A. Livingstone, (Oxford: Oxford University Press, 1997), 1181. Cf. *Lutheran Cyclopedia,* Edited by Erwin Lueker, [St. Louis: Concordia, 1954], 324.

few Catholics and Protestants know the difference, especially where they are used interchangeably. If "Evangelical Catholics" wish to be truly consistent, why not insist that the English version of the creed not only "restore" *catholica,* but also *unam sanctam* and *apostolicam ecclesiam*? Surely these "sacred" Latin words merit equal billing. In fact, why not insist the entire creed be spoken in Latin? Is the insistence that we say "catholic" on Sunday mornings simply because some of us enjoy saying "catholic," in the same way Jerry Seinfeld said "some people just like to say the word 'salsa'"? Clearly for the sake of clarity, it can be said the word "catholic" has outlived its usefulness in the 21st century in much the same way "bishop" has, both terms having already begun to wane among the reformers in the 16th century.

But "Evangelical Catholics" beg to differ, contending that it is really the word "Lutheran" that has outlived its usefulness, a name they find unhelpful for ecclesiastical homogeny. "In 2017," Braaten predicts, "Lutherans and Catholics from around the world will celebrate the 500th anniversary of Luther's nailing of his 95 theses to the Castle Church in Wittenberg, Germany, the event that triggered the Reformation."[740] While it remains to be seen how hardy the Catholics will party, the bigger question is, will any Lutherans celebrate the event? Reformation Day — once the biggest confessional day of the year for Lutherans around the world, when congregations sang loudly "A Mighty Fortress is our God," pastors preached rousing sermons on justification by grace through faith alone, and Sunday Schools reenacted Luther's nailing of the 95 theses to the Castle Church door — has now all but disappeared from the liturgical calendar. Gone are most mentions of the Reformation except as a regrettable schism. Luther the confessor has been replaced by Luther the cantankerous German of ill tone and ill health who needs to be apologized for and explained away. Ecclesiastical publishing houses fastidiously avoid the mention of Luther or "Lutheran"

---

[740] Braaten, *Essential Lutheranism,* 18.

301

in their congregational materials,[741] while new congregations avoid adding the name "Lutheran" over their door and old ones remove it altogether.[742] In this ecumenically correct and interfaith age of "Why can't we all just get along?," it's just too embarrassing to be a Lutheran,[743] a term that now connotes church jellos and Garrison Keillor more than biblical confessional theology. In lieu of confessional competence, it is vogue today for many self-described "Lutheran" academics and clerics to apologize for Luther to the world, for the schism his Reformation has wrought, and to seek to "repair the breech" through episcopal unity and "concrete visible structures," — "God's work, our hands."

Attempting to give credence to the modern myth that even Luther didn't wish to be thought of as a Lutheran, ecumenists trot out as one of their standard talking points a single quote

---

[741] E.g., on Reformation Sunday 2013 Fortress Publishing put a picture of a Luther statue on its bulletin cover for the first time in years but made no mention of the man anywhere in the text. In tiny print at the bottom of the back panel was written, "Cover: Statue of Martin Luther, Stuttgart, Baden-Württemberg, Germany. The following year neither Luther nor the Reformation was mentioned at all.

[742] E.g., the Metropolitan New York Synod ELCA St. Peter's Church, housed in the iconic CitiCorp Center in Manhattan, was St. Peter's Lutheran Church before it dropped the name "Lutheran." Newly formed LCMC congregations Transformation Christ Church in Lake Orion, Michigan and Grace Community Church in Belleville, Michigan do not include the name "Lutheran."

[743] ELCA Metro New York Bishop Robert Rimbo, Oct 24, 2013, Sermon for the Reformation/Reconciliation Mass at The General Theological Seminary, New York City: "Frankly, I don't like Reformation Day. I much prefer re-focusing on Reconciliation. The danger Lutherans face in marking Reformation without Reconciliation is we so often pat ourselves on the back that we come dangerously close to dislocating our shoulders. Since it was decided to mark Reformation/Reconciliation today, I've thought back over listening to Reformation Day sermons for over 60 years and preaching nearly 40 years of them. I find them, often — including when I've preached them — to be exercises in self-aggrandizement."

from the early Luther in his 1522 *Sincere Admonition to all Christians to Guard Against Insurrection and Rebellion*. He wrote it a year after being declared an outlaw and two years before the outbreak of the Peasant's War to show his teaching was in keeping with the *Urkirche*:

In the first place, I ask that men make no reference to my name; let them call themselves Christians, not Lutherans. What is Luther? After all, the teaching is not mine [John 7:16]. Neither was I crucified for anyone [I Cor. 1:13]. St. Paul, in I Corinthians 3, would not allow the Christians to call themselves Pauline or Petrine, but Christian. How then should I — poor stinking sack of maggots that I am — come to have men call the children of Christ by my wretched name? Not so, my dear friends; let us abolish all party names and call ourselves Christians, after him whose teaching we have.[744]

But as Albrecht Beutel has shown in *Wir Lutherischen*, the passage has been accorded undue and disproportionate importance over Luther's evolving use and full embrace of the name "Lutheran" post-1522. Showing that Eck was the first to apply the slur four days into the Leipzig Debate (*plurimi . . . Lutterani*), Beutel traces Luther's self-identification with the term from an initial slander to a salutary declaration in which he transitions from simply identifying evangelicals as "the"

---

[744] *WA* 8.685. Cf. Albrecht Beutel, "Wir Lutherischen," *Zeitschrift für Theologie und Kirche*, [Mohr Siebeck, 110 Jahrgang Heft 2 Juni 2013]: "'man wolt meynes namen geschweygen und sich nit lutherisch, sondern Christen heyssen,' zählt zu den meistzitierten Selbstaussagen des Reformators." Luther's thought obviously didn't cease to evolve in 1522 any more than it did in 1510 when a thoroughly medieval Luther still thought that faith alone cannot justify, or in 1517 when he still believed in purgatory and indulgences in the *Ninety Five Theses* (69, 71). Cf. Alister E. McGrath, *Luther's Theology of the Cross*, [Oxford, Basil Blackwell, 1985], 81 ff. Cf. Heinrich Bornkamm, *Der weltgeschichtliche Sinn von Luthers 95 Thesen*, [Berlin, Heliand Verlag, 1941], 2. Auflage, 3.

Lutherans, to identifying with "his" Lutherans.[745] Kittelson noted a decade before Beutel, that he'd crossed that nomenclatural Rubicon in 1530 when in his *Exhortation to all Clergy Assembled at Augsburg,* he switched from "the poor Lutherans" (*die arme lutherisschen*) to "we poor Lutherans" (*wir arme lutherisschen*),[746] and repeatedly thereafter to "us Lutherans" (*uns Lutherischen*) and "we Lutherans" (*wir Lutherischen*),[747] all the while maintaining the proper tension between "Lutheran" and "Christian" in which the former is simply the proclamation of the latter. Indeed, Luther was perfectly happy to accept the Lutheran *nom de guerre* whenever and wherever it meant the proclamation of the gospel. For him, Beutel insists, the designations *christlich, evangelisch,* and *lutherisch* were forever synonymous. That "Lutheran" meant the confessing church for him is clear from his *Exhortation*: "If, however, they want to suppress the gospel or remain so completely unrepentant, they may do so at their own risk. We shall still preach what we want to . . . The Lutherans remain masters because Christ is with them and they remain with him, even though hell, the world, devil, princes, and all should go mad."[748]

He'd made the same confessional claim three years before Augsburg in his tract against the Sacramentarians' charge that he cared little for their idea of Christian unity, saying, "Well, since they are so completely wicked as to mock the whole world, I shall add a Lutheran warning (*eine Lutherische warnunge*) and say: Cursed be such love and unity . . ."[749] Kittelson points to Luther's equally powerful identification of the name with the gospel in his 1534 *Letter of Dr. Martin*

---

[745] *WA* 38.339.

[746] *WA* 30 II.304, 336; Cf. Beutel, 158-186.

[747] *WA* 38.339.

[748] *WA* 30 II.345. Beutel relates an incident of vandalism in 1527 in the Sacco di Roma, when someone used a nail to scratch the name 'LVTHER' into the Vatican fresco *Disputa del Sacramento* by Raphael, p. 172.

[749] *WA* 23.81. Kittelson mistakenly has the phrase appearing in 1528. It appeared in the Spring of 1527 and was formulated in 1526.

Luther Concerning his Book on the Private Mass, in which the reformer contrasts it with such titles as pope, bishop, cleric, etc.

> Finally, this is what I want you to consider: If the mass carries and gives so little temporal honor, riches, and power as the precious gospel and truth give, how many ardent celebrants of the mass, do you think, one would find today? In truth, for the past six hundred years (I do not want to calculate backward too far) we would have seen neither pope, cardinal, bishop, nor other servants of the mass, but they all would have become evangelical or Lutheran, and we would at the present time truly wonder what these names, pope, cardinal, bishop, mass, clerics, etc., meant, and what kind of creature they would have been, whether elf, dwarf, water nymphs, or malicious demons.[750]

"At the very least," Kittelson insists, "by late April 1530 he himself was using 'Lutheran' nomenclature in just the manner he himself had apparently forbidden only eight years earlier."[751] By the time of the Diet of Augsburg the name referred to very specific confessional teaching, as Kittelson and Beutel highlight, both noting, "This point of reference also received an unlikely endorsement from the first session of the Council of Trent . . ."[752]

But sadly, the name today is little more than a vacant historical footnote for many North American Lutherans. "Specific, normative teachings," Kittleson observed more than a decade ago, "do not lie behind the naked term 'Lutheran,' which has now become virtually void of concrete confessional and easily accessible doctrinal content." With Beutel he asked, "How and for what reasons has this one quotation [of 1522] against the riotous label 'Lutheran' come to reign supreme over Luther's many other positive uses of 'Lutheran' that have definite and easily knowable doctrinal content?" With his eye

---

750 *WA* 38.269.

751 James M. Kittelson, "Luther on Being 'Lutheran,'" *Lutheran Quarterly* 17 (2003): 103.

752 *Ibid,* 107.

on the rise of today's ecumenical enthusiasms, he added:

> Paul Tillich and Jaroslav Pelikan may have preferred to speak of
> "catholic substance and Protestant principle," and some who feel
> ecumenically burdened by the label "Lutheran" may currently
> prefer to call themselves "evangelical catholics," but none of
> them should force these preferences back into Luther's self-
> naming and self-identity. Beyond the one famous early quotation
> within its context of rebellion and riot, Luther frequently and
> consistently accepted and used the label "Lutheran" for the sake
> of its doctrinal content. Whatever else might be said of him,
> Luther knew who he was and so announced himself. So, too, did
> his followers, and so might they still.[753]

Braaten is one who seeks to force his preference back into
Luther's self-naming and self-identity. Quoting the 1522
statement while ignoring its Pauline point and all of the
reformer's subsequent Lutheran affirmations, he declares
against all evidence, "He was a Catholic [sic] until he was
excommunicated, and when he was forced into exile. He
remained a Catholic in exile until the day he died."[754] But as
history clearly shows, neither Luther nor the Catholics who
condemned him — from Leo X's excommunication to the first
session of the Council of Trent [755] — considered him still a
Catholic.

Braaten figures, "It has been said so often it's about time
that Lutherans start believing it: Luther did not set out to start
a new church."[756] Whether he did or didn't, one thing is clear:
He had absolutely no interest whatsoever in preserving
Rome's church. Such trite statements much bandied about by
ecumenists, overlook the fact that Luther's point of reference
for the church was altogether different, his focus being not on
the physical "where" (*catholica*) but on the eschatological
"who" and "what" (*christlich*) of the church: "sheep who hear

---

[753] *Ibid,* 108-109.

[754] Braaten, *Essential Lutheranism,* 20.

[755] December 13, 1545 to December 4, 1563.

[756] Braaten, *Essential Lutheranism,* 19.

the voice of their Shepherd," "hidden under the cross."

Repeating an oft repeated ecumenists' fable, Braaten opines, "His focus was not on substituting his church for the one in which he was baptized, confirmed, and ordained"[757] — a complete denial of history showing Luther's radical dismantling of the Catholic system as the Reformation progressed — from canon law, to church administration, to the clergy caste, to liturgy, sacraments, bishops, education, ordination, and the pope, including recruiting electoral help wherever it was needed to officially introduce and legally secure its replacement. As we've already seen, he was absolutely for substituting the churches of the Augsburg Confession for the Church of Rome at every opportunity, (e.g., *Wider Hans Wurst*), and personally facilitated it throughout Europe, which ignited the Catholic demand for a return to the *status quo ante*. Indeed, as Luther saw it, there wasn't even a church under the papacy to replace. Since meritocracy and works righteousness was being preached instead of Christ, there was no Holy Spirit present he recalls in the 3rd Article of the *Large Catechism*. "Therefore, there was no Christian church,"[758]

Yet Braaten, like Root, waxes nostalgic for a pre-Lutheran, pre-Reformation ecclesiology, for a return to what he calls the "Great Tradition" of Lutheranism's antecedents. He laments that "Lutheran identity takes us back five centuries at the most . . . Christian truth takes us back to the beginnings — *ad fontes* — to the original sources of ecclesial identity in the Holy Scriptures, which cradle the truth of God's definitive revelation,"[759] — a sophomoric abdication of the Confessions and a repeat of the papistic charge in Worms that Lutheran teaching isn't Christian truth, hence the need to appeal to tradition. But not only is confessional Lutheranism the Pauline theology of the *Urkirche* — its very moniker, the "Lutheran Church," pre-dates the "Roman Catholic Church" by half a

---

[757] *Ibid.*

[758] BSLK 665.45 *Darümb ist es auch kein christliche Kirche.*

[759] Braaten, *Essential Lutheranism,* 117.

307

century, the latter not appearing in print before 1580. Lutheranism is therefore neither new, nor Roman, unless the gospel itself be new and Roman.

Nevertheless, Braaten and his "Evangelical Catholics" are determined to press on in pursuit of a visible ecclesiastical unity that exhibits a total confusion in the bondage of the will, the definition of the church, a misunderstanding and misrepresentation of Luther's theology of the cross, of justification, sanctification, the roles of the two kingdoms, and the proper distinction between law and gospel. In a section he antithetically calls, "Lutheran Catholicism," Braaten writes:

> Evangelical catholics share a vision of the church that exists in historical and spiritual continuity with the apostolic church founded by Jesus and the apostles and that continued through ancient medieval times up to the sixteenth century Reformation.[760] Continuity is the important concept. Evangelical catholics believe that modern Protestantism prides itself in breaking away from institutions and sacraments that provide continuity. Especially in an ecumenical age evangelical catholics tend to draw from the traditions they share with the Roman Catholic and Orthodox Churches.[761]

He lists their recidivistic goals as follows: "Evangelical catholics generally call for the restoration of episcopacy in apostolic succession, the celebration of Holy Communion as the central act of Christian worship, the return of private confession, the use of a rich array of liturgical forms, as well as the establishment of religious societies, and in a few cases, even monasteries."[762]

---

[760] The cause of the Lutheran Reformation was that the apostolic faith was no longer being preached. Continuity isn't the key, as Luther wrote to the Senate of Prague, truth is, even if it were a new thing.

[761] Braaten, *Essential Lutheranism,* 35.

[762] *Ibid.* Cf. Luther's *Kirchenpostille, WA* 10 II.74-75: "What does it avail your neighbor if you should build a church out of pure gold? What benefit does he derive from the great display of pomp and

His list leaves no doubt that upper case "C" is the proper designation for "Evangelical Catholics," private confession being the only item of interest to Luther, who didn't believe in episcopal succession, the primacy of the sacrament over preaching, lavish and lengthy liturgics with gospel processions, or pious clerical societies and monasteries.

Still, Braaten's ECs believe it is possible to organize the church as a kind of Christocentric one-world-order, a Christian United Nations made up of Dominicans, Jesuits, Benedictines, Lutherans, Anglicans, Methodists, Baptists, etc. all under one general secretary: the pope. While he acknowledges that Roman Catholic-Lutheran differences over core issues in the gospel remain, these need not hinder empirical unity through a Roman absorption of Lutherans. To that end, the greatest ecumenical achievement "since the Reformation," he believes, is the 1999 Roman Catholic-Lutheran World Federation consensus paper, the *Joint Declaration on the Doctrine of Justification* (JDDJ).[763] He writes, "according to the JDDJ Lutherans and Catholics confess together certain basic truths:

1) that all persons depend completely on the saving grace of God for their salvation;

2) that God forgives sin by grace and at the same time frees human beings from sin's enslaving power and imparts the gift of new life in Christ;

3) that sinners are justified by faith in the saving action of God in Christ;

---

pretense in the churches by means of vestments, reliquaries, statues, and vessels made of silver? What benefit does he derive from the making of lots of noise, murmuring, the singing of vigils and masses? Do you think God will permit himself to be paid off by means of the ringing of bells, the smoke of candles, the display of gold and other nonsense?"

[763] For all of Braaten's claims of Catholic-Lutheran rapprochement, it is worth remembering that the June 15, 1520 papal bull *Exsurge, Domine* (Arise, O Lord), condemning Luther as a heretic, and his subsequent excommunication, still stand.

4) that in baptism the Holy Spirit unites one with Christ, justifies, and truly renews the person5);

5) that persons are justified by faith in the gospel "apart from works prescribed by the law;"

6) that the faithful can rely on the mercy and promise of God;

7) that good works — a Christian life lived in faith, hope, and love — follow justification and are its fruits."[764]

Ignored is that all of these "truths" are in agreement with the Council of Trent's standing declaration of the insufficiency of the Lutheran *sola*'s, maintaining instead that justification is a synergistic process of infused righteousness involving human cooperation with (*co-operare*) and free will assent to (*assentire*) God's grace, rather than a forensic declaration of imputed righteousness from the cross. In order to be declared just in Catholicism, one must first *become* just — contrary to Luther's theology of the cross. Rather than rejecting the Council of Trent's condemnations against the Lutherans, JDDJ simply says they no longer apply — the reason ostensibly being that the Lutheran negotiators of JDDJ have now moved closer to the Catholic position in regard to the cooperative nature of man.

Before it was consummated in Augsburg on October 31, 1999, two hundred fifty one German university professors signed a protest manifesto, including such world renowned theologians as Peter Stuhlmacher, Martin Hengel, and Otto Betz of the University of Tübingen (hardly a bastion of conservative theology), stating "the content of its statements fundamentally calls the Lutheran Doctrine of Justification into question, presupposes an ecumenical notion of purpose which is irreconcilable with Reformation criteria, has not received the consent of the instances responsible for doctrinal

---

764 Braaten, *Essential Lutheranism*, 29-30.

questions, and results in no practical consequences for ecumenical togetherness on the ground."[765]

Braaten, who concedes "they may be right about that," nevertheless writes, "In my view the JDDJ is a miracle of divine grace. There is nothing of its kind in the last 500 years." Frustrated, however, with JDDJ's failure to launch fourteen years hence, he adds, "This does not mean that the Roman Catholic Church is yet prepared to lift the ban of welcoming Lutherans to the same Table of the Lord." Though he finds it unacceptable, he bafflingly concludes,

> Now, if the doctrine of justification is the one big thing for Lutherans, then according to this document a person may become a Roman Catholic, join the Roman Catholic Church, without having to renounce his or her Lutheran beliefs.[766] That is exactly what some Lutherans, for example, Richard John Neuhaus, have said when they entered into the Roman Communion. My rejoinder is that signing the JDDJ is a necessary step but still insufficient, because the big elephant in the room remains standing, and that is the dogma of papal infallibility and the papal claim to universal jurisdiction.[767]

The cognitive dissonance and confessional disconnect here are truly jaw dropping. The elephant that remains standing in the room is not papal infallibility or jurisdiction, but *das Hauptstück,* "the centerpiece," the same elephant that stood in the bishop's palace in Augsburg in 1530 — Justification! The rejection of the justified, (in this case Lutherans at the Lord's Table unless they join the Church of Rome), is a rejection of all of JDDJ's points.

Justification (CA 4) is the article by which ecclesiastical consensus papers either stand or fall, and JDDJ falls with a mighty crash through a CCM-style inverse on Lutheran participation in the sacrament: You don't have to do it; you

---

[765] http://www.wordalone.org/docs/wa-german-professors.shtml
[766] Unless those beliefs include Christ's invitation to non-Catholics to his Supper by justification.
[767] Braaten, *Essential Lutheranism,* 28-31.

just have to believe it. What justified Neuhaus's presence at the Lord's Table in the eyes of Rome was his conversion to Catholicism, not his prior conversion to Christ.

In a pitch for a Calvinist progressive version of the church militant (*ecclesia militans*), Braaten writes in *Principals of Lutheran Theology,* in a chapter called, "The Ecumenical Principle":

> Lutherans have been able to enter into many different relationships with state and society. Calvinists, by contrast, have shown a greater desire to enlist the power of the state to carry out the will of God in political and cultural life. The "social gospel" earlier in this century and today's "Conservative Coalition" both are products of Calvinist activism. Lutherans, by comparison, look like a bunch of "quietists."[768]

But, "many Lutherans are now renewing the effort to restore something lost during the sixteenth-century schism," he continues, although "Christianity will not again become a meaningful social force, checking the excesses of the ruling *isms,* until it overcomes the denominational conflicts of the past and constructs new forms in which its own vision of life can once again become a resource for good."[769]

Its ruling *ism* apparently not being baptism, Braaten envisions cementing the final brick into place for his shining church on a hill, a church of "concrete visible structures."[770] "The reconstructed unity of the church does not mean that the church will aim to restore the authoritarian structures of a medieval Christendom that claimed to exercise the lordship of God over the state and over all believers; it may well be that a reunited church will be no more than a creative minority in a pluralistic culture."[771]

He accuses those who point to the sufficiency of the

---

768 Braaten, *Principles of Lutheran Theology,* 55.
769 *Ibid,* 59.
770 Braaten, *Essential Lutheranism,* 78.
771 Braaten, *Principles of Lutheran Theology,* 59.

existing unity in the cross of engaging in "ecclesiological docetism," of "gnostic heresy" for not seeing visible disunity as a sin.[772] ECs believe true unity still needs to be "lived 'into'" (CCM) and the Confessions still need to be "realized," (though CA 7's "true unity" cannot be made any truer, nor the unnecessary more necessary.)

Though ECs express their devotion to Lutheranism's dogmatic antecedents, they reject as *non satis est* the existing "preserved oneness"[773] of the church testified to in those very same antecedents, in the ancient creeds of the church and Luther's explanation to the 3rd Article in the *Large Catechism*:

> This is the sum and substance of this phrase [*communio sanctorum*], I believe that there is on earth a little holy flock or community of pure saints under one head, Christ . . . It is called together by the Holy Spirit in one faith, mind, and understanding . . . *it is united* (*einträchtig*) in love without sect or schism.[774]

And where does this *Einträchtigkeit* (unity) already exist? Wherever the gospel is preached! But as Braaten is quick to remind us, *"Was Luther sagt* does not necessarily prove something is true."[775]

As if they could know who is a Christian, Braaten and the ECs seek proof — physical proof — through rites, rituals, signs, institutions, bishops, successions, guilds and monasteries. Expressing disappointment in Lutheranism's simple stress on the humiliation of faith over ecclesial triumphalism, he states "ecclesiology has not been the strong suit of Lutheranism. In fact it has been something of an

---

[772] In an "Open Letter to Bishop Mark Hanson," dated July 13, 2005, Braaten bemoaned the ecumenical brain drain of ELCA colleagues departing for other denominations (mostly the Roman Catholic Church).

[773] *erhält eine einzige, conservare unam*

[774] *BSLK* 657-658.

[775] Braaten, *Essential Lutheranism,* 117.

embarrassment."[776] Waxing nostalgic for a visible unity that never existed in the church even from the time of the apostles,[777] ECs appeal to a common misreading of Christ's unity prayer in John 17:21, "that they may all be one; even as thou, Father, art in me, and I in thee, that they may also be in us, so that the world may believe that thou hast sent me." From this they conclude that if only the world could see all Christians "united" (however that might look) under one head as part of one overarching institution, it would believe in Christ and satisfy Pilate's ancient query, "Where is your kingdom?" Braaten admits,

> There is nothing we can do to make the church one. The church is already one in Christ. All we can do with our ecumenical dialogues and concordats is to discover better ways to express our ecclesial unity in Christ. So why is this unity such a big deal? There is only one answer that matters, given in the words of Jesus — "that they may all be one . . . so that the world may believe."[778]

Abridged thusly, the inference is "seeing is believing" — that unity creates faith. If only the world could see the church's oneness, it would somehow believe. "Show us the Father," Philip said similarly to Jesus, "and that will be enough for us" (John 14:8). But the word alone shows us the Father, preaching alone creates unity in faith (CA 7; SC II, 3) which comes not by seeing, but by hearing. Luther explained the proper meaning of John 17:21 in a sermon on October 17, 1528, declaring that preaching creates unity in faith which just creates more preaching: "This is the fruit that should follow through and from this unity, namely that *Christ's word*

---

[776] *Ibid*, 36.

[777] Cf. *BSLK,* 242 n.2. In the Paschal Controversy at the end of the second century Roman Christians excommunicated Christians in Asia Minor. In the Iconoclastic Controversy in the eighth century the Lateran Synod condemned the Synod of Constantinople. In 1054 the pope excommunicated the Eastern Orthodox.

[778] Braaten, *Essential Lutheranism,* 77.

continue to break forth and be received in the world as God's word, in which there is an almighty, godly, unassailable power and eternal treasure of total grace and holiness."[779] In other words: The church's unity results from and is known through the preaching of the word, not "concrete visible structures."

He expounded on it again in his June, 1542 *Lectures on Genesis.* Reflecting on the meaning of Jacob's ladder (Genesis 28:12-14) which refers to "the wonderful union of the divinity with our flesh," he wrote:

> Later there is another union — a union between us and Christ, as John expresses it in a very beautiful manner. "I am in the Father, and the Father is in me," says Christ (John 14:10). This comes first. Later he says: "You in me, and I in you." (John 14:20). This is the allegorical meaning of the ladder. But the allegory should nourish our faith and not teach about our affairs or our works. Therefore we are carried along by faith and become one flesh with him, as Christ says in John 17:21: "That they may all be one; even as thou, Father, art in me, and I in thee, that they may also be in us." In this way we ascend into him and are carried along through the word and the Holy Spirit. And through faith we cling to him, since we become one body with him and he with us. He is the head; we are the members. On the other hand, he descends to us through the word and the sacraments by teaching and by exercising us in the knowledge of him. The first union, then, is that of the Father and the Son in the divinity. The second is that of the divinity and the humanity in Christ. The third is that of the church and Christ.[780]

Braaten too speaks of ladders in a chapter, "On Tearing Down the Ladders to Heaven." He notes, "It is in the nature of religion to construct ladders to heaven. It is in the nature of the gospel to tear them down. There are three stairways to heaven

---

[779] *WA* 28.185: *Das ist die frucht, die durch und aus solcher einigkeit soll folgen, nemlich das Christus wort weiter ausbreche und jnn der welt angenommen werde als Gottes wort, darin eine allmechtige Göttliche, unüberwindliche krafft und ewiger schatz aller gnaden und seligkeit stehe.*
[780] *WA* 43, 582.

that Lutherans love to tear down." These are the ladders of "intellectualism," "moralism," and religious "emotionalism," and he concludes confessionally, "Christ alone is our ladder to heaven, so all the other ladders must come down. We do not need to climb any ladder to heaven, not even Jacob's ladder, whose every rung goes higher and higher. That is what the doctrine of justification by faith alone is all about. It is the one big thing, the one thing needful that Mary learned sitting at Jesus' feet."[781]

The question today is whether Braaten and the ECs have learned it, or is their conviction just another rung on the emotional ladder? If indeed "Christ alone is our ladder . . . the one big thing, the one thing needful . . . what the doctrine of justification by faith alone is all about," how is it also a "reduction of Christian doctrine by making the category of faith serve as the hub around which all the other articles of faith revolve"? Why is "such an approach impossible today in light of our knowledge of the origins of the Christian faith, the history of dogma, and the ecumenical dialogues with Roman Catholics and the Eastern Orthodox theologians"? If "systematic theology that claims to be evangelical, catholic, and orthodox is based on the twin towers of Trinity and Christology," how is it that, "the article of justification by faith functions as a critical soteriological principle within this dogmatic framework and cannot by itself constitute it"? Why can Lutherans not "require this one doctrine to be generative of all others," and how is it "a mis-interpretation of the Lutheran Confessions"?[782]

Braaten provides no answers and is given to frequent theological contradictions. In discussing the need to tear down the ladder of intellectualism, for instance, he says, "Although I work hard to understand and teach the true doctrines of the church, I do not place my trust in the most gnesio-Lutheran confessional theology I know," even though the most gnesio-Lutheran confessional theology there is, is the article on

---

[781] Braaten, *Essential Lutheranism,* 45.
[782] *Ibid,* 15.

justification which presupposes the bondage of the will, which is the gospel itself.

Under moralism's ladder he writes, "The Christian moralist sees Jesus as a second Moses, one who came to give a new law."[783] But in a section called "Theology of Mission and the Mission of Theology," he writes, "Every good teacher knows it makes no sense to take every single word and sentence in the Bible literally. Therefore biblical texts must be interpreted by obeying the hermeneutical principle — interpret the parts in light of the whole,"[784] a principal he seems unwilling to apply, for example, to homosexuals in the church, against whom he moralizes at great length. "The moralist," he writes in a confusion of free will, "stands erect before God and prays, 'God, I thank you that I am not like those people over there.' We should strive to be as good as the Pharisees, knowing full well that it is not good enough."[785]

What indeed are Evangelical Catholic calls "for the restoration of episcopacy in apostolic succession, the use of a rich array of liturgical forms, as well as the establishment of religious societies, and even monasteries," but appeals to the ladder of emotionalism, of *Schwärmerei*? Though he decries such ladders, Braaten substitutes them for sound doctrine throughout *Essential Lutheranism*, some brief examples of which follow:

In "The Princeton Proposal"[786] (for the achievement of visible church unity), he rightly notes, "Perfect church unity will never exist before the eschaton," but then wrongly concludes, "The marks of the church, its oneness, holiness, catholicity, and apostolicity, are not descriptive of what is already the case, but prescriptive of goals to be pursued to the end." The statement is a clear contradiction of the creeds' testimony to the present existence of the "one, holy, Christian,

---

[783] *Ibid*, 43.
[784] *Ibid*, 134.
[785] *Ibid*, 44.
[786] Named after the town in New Jersey, not the university.

apostolic church," and of Luther's 3rd Article which declares the "community of saints" to already be in possession of the signs (*Zeichen*) bestowed in baptism, even as it is being perfected through sanctification by the Holy Spirit, and not by any goals pursued by us. Braaten writes:

> Sanctification is a word that describes the life that follows — the life-long pursuit of holiness. The "Princeton Proposal" does not mince words. It calls the separation of the churches a sin. Our churches have been divided so long, that division has come to appear as normal, as something we should simply accept as fixed forever. It is easy for Americans to accept it: competition is thought to be a good thing. It keeps everyone on their toes. But alas, that contradicts the picture of the church we find in the New Testament. The competition between Peter and Paul and James on law and gospel and on faith and works in the Jerusalem church was perceived as a threat to their apostolic mission, as an obstacle that had to be overcome for the sake of the gospel and its mission to Jews and Gentiles.[787]

His Norwegian Pietism is much in evidence in his equating of sanctification with personal pursuits of holiness vs. the work of the Holy Spirit alone through preaching. Instead of Luther's call to *Anfechtung* (theological jousting in the gospel for the avoidance of a *rigor mortis theologica*), Braaten is for visible peace and unity because he thinks it is Christian.

But it wasn't the competition between Peter, Paul and James that posed a threat to the proclamation of the gospel — it was the preaching of a false gospel, of "goals to be pursued" in the law, of the required "concrete visible structures" of circumcision, dietary laws, etc.. which were the "obstacle that had to be overcome." Indeed, it was the competition, Paul's take-no-prisoners preaching against Jewish legal recidivism, that saved the early church: the word alone vs. the pursuit of empirical goals. Competition wasn't "a threat" to the mission

---

[787] Braaten, *Essential Lutheranism*, 118.

— it *was* the mission.[788] *Anfechtung* in the word was the saving grace in Christ's warning that he has come "not to bring peace, but a sword"[789] through a gospel that pits father against son, mother against daughter, etc.

Papal jurisdiction and infallibility are the last remaining obstacles for ecclesial homogeny for Braaten's ECs, provided the elephant of justification can be made a bit smaller. To that end he writes:

> Article VII of the Lutheran *Augsburg Confession* defines the church as "the congregation of saints in which the gospel is rightly taught and the sacraments are rightly administered." This is a partial definition. What it says is important, even essential, but what it omits reveals a deficiency from which present-day Lutheranism still suffers. There is no mention in this classic definition of the church's orientation to the kingdom of God and the world. The omission of explicit references to the eschatological and missionary dimensions of the church's existence accounts for a serious blunder in the history of Lutheranism: the rejection of world missions in the period of seventeenth century scholasticism.[790]

Add to this his strange claim, "The reason that no article concerning the church appears in the Lutheran Confessions is that the authors took the reality of the church of which they were members for granted,"[791] — even though CA 7,[792] CA 8,[793] Ap 7 & 8,[794] SA XII,[795] SC II,3[796] LC II,3[797] are all

---

[788] "The reason is that the devil must sow his seed among the good seed (Matt. 13:25); and wherever God builds a church, he builds his chapel or tabernacle next to it." *WA* 32.474.

[789] Mt. 10:34.

[790] Braaten, *Essential Lutheranism*, 51.

[791] *Ibid*, 36.

[792] *BSLK* 61. *Von der Kirche, De ecclesia.*

[793] *Ibid*, 62. *Was die Kirche sei?, Quid sit ecclesia?*

[794] *Ibid*, 233-246. *Von der Kirchen, De ecclesia.*

[795] *Ibid*, 459-460. *Von der Kirchen, De ecclesia.*

[796] *Ibid*, 511, 5-6. *Der dritte Artikel*

[797] *Ibid*, 653,34-661,69. *Der dritte Artikel*

articles "Concerning the Church." Not only do they take the reality of the church for granted but also its unity through righteousness by faith, Ap 7 stating:

> We are talking about true spiritual unity, without which there can be no faith in the heart nor righteousness in the heart before God. For this unity, we say, a similarity of human rites, whether universal or particular, is not necessary. The righteousness of faith is not a righteousness tied to certain traditions, as the righteousness of the law was tied to the Mosaic ceremonies, because this righteousness of the heart is something that quickens the heart. To this quickening human traditions, whether universal or particular, contribute nothing; nor are they wrought by the Holy Spirit[798]. . . . But as the different lengths of day and night do not harm the unity of the church, so we believe that the true unity of the church is not harmed by differences in rites instituted by men[799] . . . Before the Council of Nicaea some people celebrated Easter at one time and others at another, but this difference did no harm to faith[800] . . . But why discuss it? Our opponents completely misunderstand the meaning of the righteousness of faith and of the kingdom of God if they regard as necessary a uniformity of observances in food, days, clothing, and similar matters without divine command. But see what religious men our opponents are! They require uniform human ceremonies for the unity of the church while they themselves have changed the ordinance of Christ in the use of the Lord's Supper, which certainly was previously a universal ordinance.[801]

Braaten faulting the Confessions for lacking "explicit references to the eschatological and missionary dimensions of the church's existence," (though they're too numerous to list here), spectacularly misses the implicit nature of the gospel purely preached, "Go ye, therefore, and teach all nations, baptizing them in the name of the Father, and of the Son, and of the Holy Spirit, teaching them to observe all things

---

[798] *Ibid,* 241.31.
[799] *Ibid,* 242.33.
[800] *Ibid,* 244.42.
[801] *Ibid,* 245.45-46. E.g. JDDJ.

whatsoever I have commanded you, and, lo, I am with you always, even unto the end of the ages" (Matthew 28:19-20). To borrow from Shakespeare, "The fault is not in our stars, but in ourselves, that we are underlings,"[802] — practitioners of free will and ecclesial works, pursuers of visible goals, concrete structures and missions to "make" disciples of all nations, (a mistranslation of the Greek) — a people who refuse to die. (Not only don't dead men wear plaid; they can't "make" anything, least of all the church on earth.) Our Lord's command is not to go out and *make* anything, ("It is finished!"), but to "preach/teach/ proclaim" (διδάσκοντες)[803] the good news in Jesus Christ. "For Jews demand signs and Greeks seek wisdom, but we preach Christ crucified, a stumbling block to Jews and folly to the Greeks."[804]

There is no blunder or deficiency in CA 7, just a lack of faith on the part of ecumenical empiricists in the Holy Spirit getting the job done. They are, in effect, Nicodemus revisited, asking "How can this be?" to the news the Holy Spirit blows where and when he wills, creating unity by faith in believers scattered hither and thither, one church out of nothing, where all that is needed is a preacher.

Braaten often tries to sell Lutherans on Catholic dogma, [in brackets below], by misinterpreting history, scripture, and the Confessions. He writes of the first three centuries of the church, "We should note that there never was a gathering for worship on the Sabbath that did not include the breaking of bread and sharing the cup to celebrate the presence of Jesus in the church"[805] [eucharistic primacy], though he obviously wasn't there. While Luther suggested the sacrament be made available each Lord's Day, he also wrote to Lazarus Spengler in 1528, "First of all, it is proper and prudent not to compel anyone to come to or abstain from the sacrament, or to appoint

---

802 William Shakespeare, *Julius Caesar* (1.2.135).

803 Mt. 28:20.

804 1 Corinthians 1:22-23.

805 Braaten, *Essential Lutheranism*, 59.

particular times or places for it, thus trapping consciences."[806]

Braaten insists, "I and II Timothy and Titus . . . make clear that by the end of the first century the church had established a threefold ordering of its ministerial leadership"[807] [holy orders]. Yet, there is no record of "ordering" nor sacramental ordination in the pastoral epistles where "bishop," "elder," and "presbyter" connote the same person with the same function, as is clear in the Greek, Luther, and the Confessions.

He asserts, "For Luther faith alone never meant without good works"[808] [justification by faith plus works], though for justification, he meant exactly that.

He frequently conflates confessional Lutheranism with contemporary Protestantism, when for example, he invites Roman Catholics to "struggle with the dogma of papal infallibility" and authority, "in a way not unlike the struggle of Protestants with the doctrine of a verbally inerrant Bible and its infallible authority," (though Lutheran theology struggles with neither, both being forms of idolatry).[809] "To speak of the infallibility of the church is not wrong," he continues, "but we must be aware that it is a roundabout way of referring to the unfailing action of God's grace in keeping Jesus' promise that 'the gates of Hades will not prevail against the church.'"[810]

Claims for the "infallibility of the church," however, are neither biblical nor confessional, the church merely being the fallible forgiven (*simul iustus et peccator*) who have strayed from the gospel throughout history as Luther showed at the Leipzig Debate.[811] It is the confession of Peter, "You are the

---

806 *WA, Br* 4.534.

807 Braaten, *Essential Lutheranism,* 59.

808 *Ibid,* 55.

809 *Ibid,* 79. Worshipful reverence for the letter of the bible over the Christ it reveals, with appeals to textual literalism, inerrancy, and infallibility is known as "bibliolatry." Luther's hermeneutical treatments of the Book of Esther, and the "straw gospel" of James, are just two examples of his clear rejection of this practice.

810 *Ibid.*

811 Cf. *Teaching Authority and Infallibility in the Church,* Lutherans and Catholics in Dialogue 6 [Minneapolis: Augsburg, 1980], 157,

Christ, the Son of the living God" (Matthew 16:16), possessed and confessed by the true church, against which Hades cannot prevail, which preserves the elect through justification.[812] The word is the rock. It alone is infallible, the Reformation slogan being *sola scriptura,* not *sola ecclesia.* The church that proclaims the word in its purity and administers the sacraments according to the gospel is infallible in its proclamation. In, with, and under the church God keeps his true church, his faithful remnant, sheep who hear their shepherd's voice and who, proclaiming the same in its purity, are without error (CA 7).[813]

He falsely maintains that, "According to the apostolic tradition the authority of Christ is bestowed on those called by the Spirit into the service of the church by means of the sacrament of ordination through the imposition of hands and prayer [sacramental ordination]. This is not merely the doing of human beings [divine ordination]. It is not merely a dispensable church ceremony [indelible character]. It is an act of God, or it is not worth doing at all."[814]

As we have seen, Luther and the reformers frequently decided it was not worth doing at all, maintaining that none of the apostles were ordained; that the Holy Spirit is bestowed through baptism, not ordination; that ordination is not a sacrament *iure divino,* but a rite *iure humano* (Ap. 14); and that it is entirely dispensable when the call has ended. Braaten's large "C" Catholicism comes to the fore when he says:

Lutheran Reflections #16: ". . . the language of infallibity continues to seem dangerously misleading to most of us even when applied to the Bible, and to all of us when used in reference to popes, councils, or doctrinal formulations. It can too easily be abused to detract from the primacy of God's justifying act in Jesus Christ."

[812] *BSLK,* 178.85; 211.260; 264.63; 352.12; 477-478.22; 479.25; 560.2; 817.5; 1066.8.

[813] Cf. *WA* 18.649-652, *The True Church, Which Does Not Err, Is Hidden from Men's Sight;* Cf. *WA* 51.507 ff., *Against Hanswurst.*

[814] Braaten, *Essential Lutheranism,* 86.

To emphasize the quality of permanence Catholics have used the term *"character indelebilis"* a term absent from Lutheran vocabulary. However, Lutherans too stress the indelible character of ordination as a divine calling enacted by the church for life-long service. Ordained ministers may betray their calling, stray into heresy, and even commit apostasy, but they can never remove the mark the Spirit has etched upon their souls for service in Christ's church.[815]

This is *Schwärmerei in excelsis,* unsupported by scripture, Luther, and the Confessions, none of which subscribe to the validity of the term, its divine origin, or its permanence.[816] Indeed, Luther completely rejected this fantasy already at the Diet of Worms in 1521. "For that fiction of an 'indelible character' has long since become a laughingstock," he wrote in *The Babylonian Captivity*. "I admit that the pope imparts this 'character,' but Christ knows nothing of it; and a priest who is consecrated with it becomes the life-long servant and captive, not of Christ, but of the pope, as is the case nowadays."[817] Yet amazingly, so-called Lutheran ecumenists recently agreed to sell out the witness of scripture, Luther, and the Confessions in a statement of the 10th Round of the Roman Catholic-Lutheran dialogues, which Braaten hails as an "audacious recommendation": "We recommend that Roman Catholic criteria for assessing authentic ministry include attention to a ministry's faithfulness to the gospel and its service to the communion of the church, and that the term *defectus ordinis* as applied to Lutheran ministries be translated as 'deficiency' rather than 'lack.'"[818] Braaten's own

---

815 *Ibid,* 101.

816 Luther dismissed the notion as ludicrous already in 1520 in his *Address to the German Nobility, WA* 6.408: "It is thus most true that a priest is never a priest when he has been deposed. But now the Romanists have invented the idea of *characters indelebiles,* and prattle on about a deposed priest being different from an ordinary lay person . . ."

817 *WA* 6. 567. Cf. *The Freedom of a Christian.*

818 Braaten, *Essential Lutheranism,* 113.

presumably deficient ordination aside, some of his claims are real hermeneutical head-scratchers:

> What did Jesus have in mind when he talked about the kingdom? As a good Jew Jesus expected that God would overthrow the dominion of Satan and create a new world of lasting righteousness and blessedness. Jesus expected that God would establish the power and glory of his kingdom on earth, as it is in heaven . . . But we know what actually happened. The hopes of Jesus and his disciples were shattered on the cross.[819]

Yet according to scripture, Jesus was never under any illusion as to the purpose and fate of the Son of Man, announcing already at the beginning of his ministry, "Tear down this temple and I will rebuild it in three days" (John 2:19), and "Just as Moses lifted up the serpent in the wilderness, so must the Son of Man be lifted up" (John 3:14). To Pilate he said, "My kingdom is not of this world. If my kingdom were of this world, then my servants would fight, that I should not be delivered to the Jews: but now is my kingdom not from here" (John 18:36).

Braaten offers the same muddled concept of the church he used when arguing for episcopal succession in CCM:

> Here is a heavy phrase one hears from time to time — ecclesiological docetism. Docetism is the ancient heresy, commonly attributed to the Gnostics, that Jesus only seemed to have a physical body, that in reality he was merely a spiritual and invisible essence. Applied to the church, it would be docetic to claim that the true church is invisible (*ecclesia invisibilis*), and that therefore church structures are matters of indifference. That would be a misinterpretation of the concept of the "invisible church." The true church is said to be invisible in contrast to the visible church which contains a mixture of the saved and the lost, a distinction known only to God. This distinction between the invisible and visible church does not mean that the church can exist in history without structures that give expression to the faith, hope, and love that drive Christians to be obedient in their

---

[819] *Ibid*, 64-65.

mission to the world. Since Christianity is an historical social reality, it will always embody itself in concrete visible structures. To talk about the unity of the church, therefore, in strictly spiritualistic terms is the heresy of ecclesiological docetism.[820]

The Lutheran church, however, does not speak of an "invisible church," a phrase that is itself invisible in the Lutheran Confessions. It speaks not of an *ecclesia invisibilis*, but of a *quia nondum revelatum est regnum Christi; dieweil das Reich Christi noch nicht offenbart ist*, a church that "has not yet been revealed," *sive sit tectum cruce; unterm Kreuz verborgen ist*, "hidden under the cross,"[821] yet recognized in the word. As the *Apology* clearly states:

> It is rather, made up of persons scattered throughout the world who agree on the gospel and have the same Christ, the same Holy Spirit, and the same sacraments, whether they have the same human traditions or not . . . If we were to define the church as only an outward organization embracing both the good and the wicked, then people would not understand that the kingdom of Christ is the righteousness of the heart and the gift of the Holy Spirit but would think of it as only the outward observance of certain devotions and rituals. [822]

In search of visible signs and structures for evidence of unity Braaten adds:

> Apostolicity, is a mark of continuity with the apostolic origins of the church. For continuity to succeed, there must be signs of succession . . . The apostolic church, led by the Spirit, developed links to the future of the church in history until the end of time — signs and structures that ensure faithful continuity with the apostolic foundations of the church. To confess the apostolicity of the church without concrete visible signs and instruments of continuity is docetism.[823]

---

820 *Ibid*, 77-78.
821 *BSLK*, 237.
822 *Ibid*, 235-236.
823 Braaten, *Essential Lutheranism*, 86-87.

"If you are troubled and anxious as to whether or not you are truly a church of God," Luther famously told the Bohemians, "I tell you, one cannot recognize a church by its outward customs; it is recognizable through the word of God alone."[824] It is the Holy Spirit, not ecclesial structures, who ensures continuity of faith by means of word and sacrament alone, creating something out of nothing. Docetism is the denial of the reality of God made flesh in Christ. To demand additional visible signs and instruments for proof of continuous faith is itself docetic, "for the Jews require a sign, and the Greeks seek after wisdom" (1 Corinthians 1:22). Missing from Braaten's "concrete visible structures" is the indwelling Christ, who says, "The kingdom of God is not coming with signs to be observed; nor will they say, 'Lo, here it is!' or 'There!' for behold, the kingdom of God is in your midst" (Luke 17:20-21). Indeed, "'A wicked and adulterous generation looks for a sign, but none will be given it except the sign of Jonah.' Jesus then left them and went away" (Matthew 16:4).

"It Shall Become Even Worse"

Ecumenism's present pursuit of the unicorn of visible church embraces a number of pious myths, including the belief that the church once enjoyed empirical unity beyond Peter's confession,[825] that it has both the power and mission to "reconstruct" it, that when reconstructed it will be less sinful than it already is, that the *Augsburg Confession* was an "ecumenical proposal" to achieve this, and that the territorial churches of the *Augsburg Confession* were thus created with an eye to impermanence — ecclesiastical apparitions meant to

---

824 *Walch* 10.1599.88: *Die Kirche kann man an auswendigen Sitten nicht erkennen; man erkennt sie allein aus dem Wort Gottes.*
825 Matthew 16:16.

dissipate with the morning fog once their confessional demands had been met.

Hard pressed to actually identify any time when the church was ever truly united beyond faith, or what they even mean by it, the hands of the ecumenical clock are usually set to a minute before midnight, just before the Reformation, when "Lutheran" had not yet come to mean a separate movement with separate congregations.

In order to put the troublesome Lutheran genie back into the Roman bottle, the myth of Lutheranism as a temporary phenomenon needed to be created. Braaten:

> Lutheranism is not essentially a church but a movement. It is not essentially an independent church in competition with other denominational churches. It is a confessional movement that exists for the sake of reforming the whole church of Christ by the canon of the gospel. The ecclesiastical, organizational structures of Lutheranism are interim measures, ready to go out of business as soon as their provisional aims are realized.[826]

Such is the eschatological case for all churches, Rome included. "The doctrinal controversies of the sixteenth century" says Braaten, "disrupted the unity of the medieval order," caused the "social and political impotence of the churches," gave rise to "secularism in modern culture, the neutralizing of the state in matters of religion, and the tendency to make faith a purely private thing." Therefore the onus is on ecumenists to "reconstruct the unity of the church," because "the church can fulfill its mission in the world only by constructing a form of unity true to its essential nature as the one embodiment of Christ in history." To that end he adds, "One of our traditional slogans has been *ecclesia semper reformans* ('the church always reforming'). In keeping with this, many Lutherans today have renewed the original self-understanding of Lutheranism as a confessing movement for the sake of the church catholic."[827]

---

[826] Braaten, *Principles of Lutheran Theology*, 57.
[827] *Ibid*, 56.

The original phrase is actually *ecclesia reformata semper reformanda secundum verbi dei* ("the reformed church is always being reformed according to the word of God"), and it is not Lutheran in origin or theology[828] — since the reformed are already the forensically justified.

Ecclesia semper reformans is a continuation of the synergistic theories of the scholastics, supposing the church to be in perpetual need of doctrinal "progress" for a legal sociological mission "to increase justice in social, economic, and political terms."[829] The result is a church that is constantly laying down new floors in the mistaken belief that the existing foundation is not solid enough. Short shrift can then be given to the *Preface* to the *Book of Concord's* definition of the *Augsburg Confession* as the "final explanation" of the true Christian faith, fully sufficient "to regulate all religious controversies and their explanations according to it."

It is popularly claimed, especially among ECs, that Luther's and the Wittenberg theologians' intent was to "reform" the Catholic church. Far more accurate is to say they wished to expose it as a false church in their day and see it converted through the proclamation of the gospel in the Augsburg Confession. *Reformatio* (transformation) results from *conversio* (conversion) through the preaching of the gospel. Luther affirms this distinction in *The Bondage of the Will,* saying, "God cares nothing for your reformers (*correctores*) without the Spirit, since they are hypocrites. But the elect and the godly will be reformed by the Holy Spirit,

---

[828] It cannot be shown that any reformer ever said this phrase, its origin being dubious, though some attribute it to the Dutch Reformed theologian Jodocus van Lodenstein (1620-1677), *Beschouwinge van Zion (Contemplation of Zion),* Amsterdam, 1674. In Lutheran theology, however, it is not the church that reforms, but the word that reforms the church.

[829] Braaten, *Principles of Lutheran Theology,* 68. Cf. *WA* 51.238. Luther felt that Christians possessed no special talents for governing and that secular societies can function just as well without God's kingdom.

while the rest perish unreformed."[830]

When Melanchthon first employed the term in a letter to his good friend Hugold von Einsiedel on February 5, 1522, in which he announces (via Einsiedel to the elector), "a reformation now exists" (*es ist eine Reformatio vorhanden*), he declares his inability to contain what the Spirit has unleashed in the word, "I cannot hold the waters back" (*Ich kann aber das Wasser nicht halten*); "May God grant that it be to his glory" (*Gott gebe, daß sie zu seiner Ehre gereiche*),[831] (including Carlstadt's misguided activities).

In "Against Hans Wurst" (*Wider Hans Worst*, 1541), Luther clearly rejects *ecclesia semper reformans*, demanding to know from the hyper-Romanist Heinz von Braunschweig-Wolfenbüttel[832] why a church that is already holy would ever need to be reformed.

> If your church is holy, why is it afraid of a council? Why does it need[833] reforming or a council? If it needs a council, how is it holy? Do you wish to reform her holiness too? We, for our part, have never desired a council to reform our church. God and the Holy Spirit already sanctified our church through his holy word and, indeed, purged away all papal whoredom and idolatry, so that we have everything (God be praised) pure and holy — the word, baptism, the sacrament, the keys, and everything that belongs to the true church — without the addition and filth of human doctrine . . . But we desire a council so that our church may be examined and our doctrine come freely to light — and your whoredom in the papacy be recognized and condemned. Thus everyone who is misled by it may, together with us, be converted to the true holy church and sustained in it.[834]

---

830 *WA* 18.632.

831 *CR* 1, 546 (Nr. 192).

832 A.k.a. "Hans Worst.," a very powerful and early Catholic foe of the Reformation and close personal friend of Emperor Charles V. Cf. Friedrich Koldewey, *Heinz von Wolfenbüttel. Ein Zeitbild aus dem Jahrhundert der Reformation* (Halle:1883).

833 *darf* = *bedarf* from *bedürfen* = "need."

834 *WA* 51.528-529; This tract was originally written in German, Cf. Walch 17.1312, 1350. Luther had expressed similar intent a decade

Put into the vernacular: "We never asked for a council but we'll take it for the publicity. Let them see what a real church looks like!" What it clearly doesn't look like, according to Luther, is one that proclaims with Braaten, "The marks of the church, its oneness, holiness, catholicity, and apostolicity, are not descriptive of what is already the case, but prescriptive of goals to be pursued to the end,"[835] a total contradiction of the Three Chief Symbols and the 3rd Article of the Creed.

But instead of the Confession being "truly the last trump before the day of judgment,"[836] it is dismissed today as a mere "proposal," a poker chip to be placed on the ecumenical bargaining table. The Reformation begun in Luther is viewed as dogmatically incomplete, awaiting its final consummation in a "reconstructed" visible unity "embodying the attributes of the true church of Jesus Christ" on this side of the eschaton.

But not just any construct will do. It is essentially the Roman ecclesiastical and organizational structure the ecumenists seek.[837] Lutherans can fold up their tents and come

---

earlier when the evangelicals offered "concessions" at the Diet of Augsburg, the purpose of which was to expose the false church by proclaiming the treasures of the true church.

[835] Braaten, *Essential Lutheranism,* 51.

[836] *WATR,* Nr. 297 4b.

[837] The so-called "Evangelical Catholic" movement seeks a reintegration of Protestantism with Roman ecclesialism. Luther, on the other hand, challenged the notion of Roman preeminence by pointing to the Council of Nicaea (325 AD) as having expressly granted the primacy and honor of "mother church" to the Church of Jerusalem, a subject he discusses at length in *On the Councils and the Churches:* "The third [offence to the bishop of Rome] is the worst, that they call the church in Jerusalem the mother of all churches because Christ the Lord himself had been bishop there, and in proof of this had sacrificed himself on the cross for the sins of the whole world; there the Holy Spirit had been given from heaven on the day of Pentecost; there all the apostles had afterward ruled the church together (not only Peter, of whom the bishop of Rome boasts). Not one of these events had occurred in Rome. Thus they gently admonished the bishop of Rome to consider that he was far from

331

home to Rome, according to Braaten, when Catholicism's walls of separation have been overcome: the superiority of the pope and clergy over the laity, the exclusive right of the pope to interpret scripture authoritatively and call a council, the doctrine of transubstantiation, and the teaching of the Mass as a good work and sacrifice. "As these walls come tumbling down, the reasons for Lutherans to continue their protest movement against the *Romanization* of the church catholic seems to be greatly diminished."[838] Eliminate the papal claim to infallibility through dialogue, Braaten maintains, and

> the papal office can serve well as a symbol and servant of the universal unity of the communities of faith working for the transformation of the world. The various denominations could well continue as distinct communities in a new order; just as there are Dominicans, Benedictines, and Jesuits within the Roman Catholic Church, there could be Methodists, Presbyterians, Lutherans, and others who bring their best traditions into a richer mix of the one holy, catholic, and apostolic church. The negative aspects of denominationalism may be swallowed up and transcended by its positive aspects within a comprehensive unity of faith administered by a papal presidency and an episcopal magisterium.[839]

As staggeringly naive and confessionally incoherent as this statement may be, it is in keeping with the myth long promoted by "home-to-Romers" that Luther didn't really have a problem with the papal office per se, provided the toxic elements of the *Pontifex Maximus* could be removed, with all

---

being the bishop of Jerusalem, of the mother church, but that his church in Rome was a daughter church which did not have Christ and the apostles and which did not bring Jerusalem to the faith; but rather, he and his church had been brought to the faith through the church in Jerusalem — so had St. Paul humbled the Corinthians, telling them that the gospel did not come from them, but from others to them [II Cor.10:14]." *WA* 50.577.

[838] None of these walls can tumble, of course, as this would spell the end of Roman Catholicism.

[839] Braaten, *Principles of Lutheran Theology,* 71-72.

papal abuses corrected and a right theology acquired. This is the ecumenical pièces de résistance — the Evangelical Catholics' Holy Grail.

Except that Luther had no use for a papal office at all, not even one purged of abuses, a hypothetical he raised at the Leipzig Debate, and addressed in 1536 in the *Smalcald Articles,* the latter written on instructions from the elector to summarize the Lutheran position in preparation for the Council of Mantua, which was unexpectedly called by Pope Paul III.[840] The *Articles,* while not formally adopted at Schmalkalden,[841] nevertheless spell out at a minimum what concessions the Lutherans could and could not make to the Catholics. Adopting a papal office is not one of them. Suppose, Luther muses,

> that the pope could actually renounce his claim to be the head of the church[842] for the sake of unity and to guard against sects and heretics. And suppose further that people could actually elect this pope, and even depose him at will. If, I say, the pope and the see of Rome were to concede and accept this (which is impossible), he would have to suffer the overthrow and destruction of his whole rule and estate, together with all his rights and pretensions. In short, he cannot do it. Even if he could, Christendom would not be helped in any way. There would be even more sects than before because, inasmuch as subjugation to such a head would depend on the good pleasure of men rather than on a divine command, he would very easily and quickly be despised and would ultimately be without any adherents at all. He would not always have to have his residence in Rome or some other fixed place, but it could be anywhere and in whatever church God

---

[840] The Council did not actually meet until 1545, and then in Trent instead.

[841] The *Articles* were not adopted at the time because Luther was too ill to attend and discuss them, and Melanchthon was concerned about the doctrinal disputes it could ignite. It was, however, later incorporated into the Lutheran Confessions of the *Book of Concord.*

[842] Established by Pope Boniface VIII's bull *Unam Sanctam* (1302): "It is altogether necessary to salvation for every human creature to be subject to the Roman pontiff."

would raise up a man fitted for such an office. What a complicated and confused state of affairs that would be![843]

Rejecting a single presidency for the church, he wrote immediately following the Leipzig Debate:

> The first, [argument], is that every community (*gemeyn*) on earth must have one visible head under Christ. This is simply not true. How many principalities, castles, cities, and houses there are where two brothers or lords reign with equal authority! The Roman Empire governed itself for a long time, and very well, without one head, and many other countries in the world did the same. How does the Swiss Confederacy govern itself at present? Likewise in the government of the world there is not one single overlord although we are all one human race descended from one father Adam. The kingdom of France has its own king, Hungary its own, Poland, Denmark, and every other kingdom its own, and yet there are one people, the temporal estate in Christendom, without one common head; and still this does not cause these kingdoms to perish. And if there were no government constituted in just this manner, who could or would prevent a community from choosing not one but many overlords, all clothed with equal power? Therefore it is a very poor procedure to measure the things which are of God's appointing by such vacillating analogies of worldly things when they do not hold even in the appointments of men. But suppose I should grant this dreamer [the Franciscan monk Augustine Alveld] that his dream is true and that no community (*gemeyn*) can exist without one visible head, how does it follow that it must likewise be so in the church (*in der Christenheit*)?[844]

Yet, undeterred in his quest to conjure the church of the Society of the Holy Trinity's Frank Senn, who piously stated "the Society does not exist to reflect the church as it is but to model the church as it can become,"[845] Braaten triumphantly announces, "Lutherans are not Roman Catholics, to be sure, but they are Catholics [*sic*] — Evangelical Catholics of the

---

843 *BSLK*, 429-430.

844 *WA* 6.292.

845 http://www.societyholytrinity.org/

Augsburg Confession."[846]

Their zeal for establishing empirical ecclesial unity through concrete visible structures is at its core a theology of glory and an exercise in the avoidance of death, an ecclesiology bereft of the bondage of the will reflected in the terrified plea of the Wizard of Oz in the midst of the growing storm, "I don't want to die! I haven't accomplished anything yet!"[847]

Truth — not visible unity — was what mattered to the reformers. Lutheranism, for Luther, was nothing more than the proclamation of the gospel. To disavow it, he wrote already in 1522, is to disavow Christ "if you are convinced that Luther's teaching is in accord with the gospel."[848]

Wherever the word is proclaimed, ecclesiastical and organizational structures will of necessity follow until the last day, since pastors need to be called and *Seelsorge* (the care of souls) must be provided, the precise organizational structure of which is nevertheless a matter best left to the agreement of pastor, patron, parishioner, and prince for the sake of the gospel. The Lutheranism of the *Augsburg Confession*, was for Luther, nothing other than the summation of the Christian faith itself. The "ecclesiastical, organizational structures of Lutheranism are ready to go out of business" only when the preaching of the gospel itself goes out of business, when Christ has gathered the wheat into his granary, the nets have all been filled, the wedding guests have all been assembled and the doors have been closed.

The Preface to the CA, to be sure, speaks of a hope for ecclesiastical unity provided agreement can be reached on its articles, but as we've already seen, the evangelicals had long since crossed the theological Rubicon and were far down the road in the dismantling of canonical government by the time they arrived in Augsburg. Only peace was still worth maneuvering for as far as Luther was concerned, under the ruse of concessions if need be, but the truths of the Confession

---

[846] Braaten, *Essential Lutheranism,* 74.

[847] *Oz the Great and Powerful,* Walt Disney Productions, 2013.

[848] *WA* 10 II. 38 f.

were not negotiable. Accordingly, the reformers allowed the demand for the *status quo ante* to run off the clock even as they advocated for, and the evangelical sovereigns established, "the churches of the Augsburg Confession" in accordance with Luther's "blessed examples."

If the truth of the gospel the Wittenberg reformers recovered through the *Augsburg Confession* is not "truly the last trump before the day of judgment," all bets on what Lutheranism is are off. The goal posts can now be moved in the name of "mission," "unity," "visible church," "episcopal succession," and any number of other pious pursuits. The goal's absurdity becomes clear in the questions that must naturally follow: When did the Confessions' "rule and norm" become a mere "proposal"? How is unity defined outside of CA 7, who defines it, and at what point is it truly achieved? How is the God who is hidden revealed in anything other than word and sacrament? What about the *communio sanctorum* who never meet ecumenism's criteria for visible unity,[849] but without whom there can never be true unity? How does a God who reveals himself in opposites in the *deus absconditus* of Luther's theology of the cross (strength out of weakness, life out of death), not also reveal himself in unity out of disunity? Alister McGrath observes Luther's rejection of such a theology of glory:

> The scene of total dereliction, of apparent weakness and folly, at Calvary is the theologian's paradigm for understanding the hidden presence and activity of God in his world and in his church. Where the church recognizes her hopelessness and helplessness, she finds the key to her continued existence as the church *of God* in the

---

849 E.g., *Dominus Iesus,* the 2000 Roman Catholic encyclical, reaffirmed by Pope Benedict XVI in 2007, which says Christ "established here on earth only one church." Non-Roman Catholic churches therefore "cannot be called 'churches' in the proper sense" because they do not possess the apostolic succession, the ability to trace their bishops back to Christ's original apostles. The Orthodox Church, which has bishops in succession, but no allegiance to Rome, is recognized by the Vatican as a "church," albeit a "defective" one.

world. In her very weakness lies her greatest strength. The "crucified and hidden God" is the God whose strength lies hidden behind apparent weakness, and whose wisdom lies behind apparent folly. The theology of the cross is thus a theology of hope for those who despair, then as now, of the seeming weakness and foolishness of the Christian church. How can it survive, let alone prosper? For Luther, the answer was clear . . . "It is not we who can sustain the church, nor was it those who came before us, nor will it be those who come after us. It was, and is, and will be, the one who says: 'I am with you always, even to the end of time.'"[850]

At the Diet of Worms, Luther had refused to recant the apostolic faith unless convinced otherwise by scripture or sound reason. Examining the unreasonableness of church unity through an historic episcopate, Gregory Dix asks a lengthy and perfectly reasonable (if not hitherto obvious) question:

Even that unhappy phrase "the historic episcopate," with which well-meaning ecclesiastical diplomats have sought so earnestly to unite us all by a misunderstanding, proves at this point quite unhelpful to their purpose. What could be meant by the "historic episcopate" apart from one particular "theory" of its nature and origin? How could anyone possibly bring under the heading of a single historical institution embodiments so diverse as the pre-Nicene bishop, with his strong resemblance to the elected city-magistrate of antiquity; the hereditary patriarch of the Assyrian Church; the imperially-nominated Byzantine spiritual bureaucrat; the ordaining bishop of the Celtic Churches, without see or jurisdiction; the prince-bishop of the Middle Ages; the solitary bishop (*abouna*) of the Abyssinian Church, always a foreigner ordained abroad and under oath never to consecrate anyone to the episcopate; the Tudor or Stuart functionary in episcopal orders whose principal raison d'être was to administer certain Acts of Parliament for the Uniformity of Religion — how could one possibly bring all these and other equally variant manifestations of the episcopate under a single heading from the single similarity, that each in its own age and place was regarded as the unique depository or embodiment of the apostolic office and

---

850 McGrath, 181.

power to ordain?[851]

The perfectly reasonable perspective of the Lutheran reformers, on the other hand, was that what the world perceives as Christian disunity, is in fact not — not even the East-West divide,[852] (with Luther frequently giving God thanks for the Eastern Church) — if faith is not imperiled and righteousness is not lost. This is the only bar that anyone may set when pining for empirical unity, and it is the one today's ecumenists refuse to recognize. Lutheran-Catholic consensus papers on apostolic succession and adiaphoristic pursuits amount to so much "plucking of feathers," but have virtually nothing to do with faith. Unity for empiricism's sake, is not unity.[853] Luther addressed the pursuit of such ecclesiastical windmills already in the days immediately following the Leipzig Debate, in his response to the Franciscan monk Augustine Alveld, who attempted to prove from scripture that the *successio apostolica* and See of Peter are divine institutions. He writes in *On the Papacy in Rome Against the Most Celebrated Romanist in Leipzig* (*Von dem Bapstum zu Rome: widder den hochberumpten Romanisten zu Leiptzck*):

> [The church] community or assembly (*gemeyne odder samlung*) consists of all those who live in true faith, hope, and love. So the essence, life, and nature of the church is not a bodily assembly (*sey nit leyplich*) but an assembly of hearts in one faith, as Paul says in Ephesians 4 [:5], "One baptism, one faith, one Lord." Though they be a thousand miles apart in body, yet they are called an assembly in spirit because each one preaches, believes,

---

851 Gregory Dix, *The Ministry in the Early Church,* in K.E. Kirk, *The Apostolic Ministry:* "Essays on the History and Doctrine of Episcoapcy," (London: Hodder & Stoughton, 1957), 296 f.

852 E.g., Ap VII & VIII cites the example of the unimportance of the disunity of the East-West observances in the Paschal Controversy.

853 Today's ecumenical drive for progress in the creation of visible church unity finds its parallels in a shared free will DNA with the "church growth" and "church prosperity" movements, all of which stress ecclesiastical "progress" over suffering and death.

hopes, loves, and lives like the other. So we sing of the Holy Spirit, "Though who through divers tongues gatherest together the nations in the unity of the faith." This really means a spiritual unity (*geistliche einickeit*), and because of it men are called a community of saints (*gemeine der heiligen*). This unity alone is enough (*wilche einickeit alleine gnug ist*) to make a church, and without it no unity, be it of place, of time, of person, of work, or of whatever else, makes a church. On this point we must hear the word of Christ, who, when Pilate asked him concerning his kingdom, answered, "My kingdom is not of this world." [John 18:36]. This is a clear passage which distinguishes the church from all temporal communities (*gemynen*) and asserts that it is nonphysical (*das sie nit leiplich sey*). Yet this blind Romanist makes of it an external community like any other. Christ says even more clearly in Luke 17 [:20 - 21], "The kingdom of God is not coming with signs to be observed; nor will they say, 'Lo, there!' or 'Lo, here!' for behold, the kingdom of God is in the midst of you." I am surprised that these Romanists regard such a clear and strong saying of Christ as nothing but a carnival mask. Everyone can clearly understand from it that the kingdom of God (for this is what he calls his Christendom) is not in Rome, is not bound to Rome, and is neither here nor there. Rather, it is where there is inward faith, whether the man be in Rome, or wherever he may be . . . Inasmuch as the unity of the Christian church is separated by Christ himself from all material and temporal localities and places and transferred to spiritual realms, is it not a terrible error when these preachers of dreams locate it in material communities, which must of necessity be bound to localities and places? How is it possible, or whose reason can grasp it, that spiritual unity and material unity should be one and the same?[854]

Nor did he see visible ecclesial unity as the agent for addressing society's ills, but rather the law of love heard in the gospel, created by faith whenever and wherever it occurs. Reflecting in a sermon on Jesus's parable of Lazarus and the Rich Man, he said, "The believer sets no store by himself but takes comfort solely in divine mercy. This he regards as his riches. And even though he has much, even the treasures of all kings, still his heart is not attached to these, but he always

---

[854] *WA* 6.293-294.

looks down humbly, takes the troubles of all people to heart, and serves all those who are in need. And whatever face he has inwardly before God he shows outwardly." [855] As Bornkamm observed:

> Luther's view of the church helps to overcome the dilemma of denominational divisions. All external church fences fall before his concept. True belief in Christ may exist in all Christian denominations, for God's Spirit blows where it wants to. This opens the portals wide. Who can know where God has his true believers? This makes us modest; we need to engage in competition among ourselves. Every church which styles itself as Christian may be concerned that it really does become the body of Christ, that faith and love dwell richly in its midst.[856]

Right teaching is what matters, as Melanchthon makes clear in his discussion on the unity of the church in Ap 7 & 8. Faith is not harmed by the separation of Christian communities through different ceremonies and rites (CA 7); it is harmed by false doctrine, of which ironically the doctrine of the necessity for empirical unity is one. It is the same false demand that was made in Augsburg by emperor and pope, for imperial and empirical unity — the one to present a united political front to the Turk, the other to present a united visible Church to the world. But for Lutherans the church united already exists within its many churches, (*e pluribus unum,* if you will), one true church sanctified and preserved in perfect union with Jesus Christ in the one true faith of justification by grace through faith alone (SC II, 3; CA 4; CA 7).

The life of this church is not known nor defined by visible unity, concrete structures, dogmatic progress, or successive hierarchies of episcopal leadership — it is known only through death and dying. "[The word of God]," Luther wrote, "is accepted by none but the dying, the despairing, the weak sinners, and those weaned entirely from the flesh."[857] To the

---

855 *WA* 10 III.180.
856 Bornkamm 151.
857 *WA,* 31 II.160.

340

church's signs of word and sacrament, Luther added not social militancy or ecclesial hierarchy, but suffering. "Suffering, suffering, cross, cross is the Christian's prerogative, that and no other." [858] This is the dogma that supersedes denominationalism and all strivings toward ecclesial empiricism. The church shares the same fate as her Lord and only Bishop: to suffer and to die. Where there is suffering, there one finds the church (*ecclesia penitens*), in both the afflicted and the caregiver. For this reason, "The only progress [Luther] expected from the Reformation," Oberman wrote, "was the devil's rage, provoked by the rediscovery of the gospel." Things will not improve. He directs those who eagerly await "a new 'optimistic' interpretation of the visible renewal of the church" to Luther's conclusion in the *Confession of Faith which Robert Barnes . . . Made in England*.[859] "The last words of the foreword show with eminent clarity what progress and success consist of: 'It shall become even worse. Amen.'"[860]

"Home," Luther wrote to the negotiators in Augsburg, "And again I say home!"[861] Home was not the *canonicam politiam* or *successio episcoporum* of Rome, but the confessional preaching of Wittenberg concerning the priesthood of all believers who proclaim unceasingly and uncompromisingly the gospel of justification by grace alone, through faith alone, in the word alone, which alone creates true ecumenism through the gospel paradox of suffering, death, and new life.

It is a message being rapidly lost on a dwindling American Lutheranism. It would appear that when all is said and done, today's deep desire to negotiate dogmatic proposals for the reconstruction of visible church unity through the hierarchy of

---

[858] *Ibid,* 18.310.

[859] Robert Barnes, prior of the Augustinians at Cambridge, friend and house guest of Luther's and the first Lutheran martyr, burned at the stake July 30, 1540.

[860] Oberman 267-271.

[861] Luther rendered this line in German.

a mythical historical episcopal succession, has very little to do with any confidence in the unifying power of the Holy Ghost — and very much to do with a deep seated, superstitious fear of the Ghost of Speyer.

O foolish Galatians! Who has bewitched you, before whose eyes Jesus Christ was publicly portrayed as crucified? Let me ask you only this: Did you receive the Spirit by works of the law, or by hearing with faith? Are you so foolish? Having begun with the Spirit, are you now ending with the flesh? Did you experience so many things in vain? — if it really is in vain. Does he who supplies the Spirit to you and works miracles among you do so by works of the law, or by hearing with faith?

Galatians 3:1-5

"Wir sein pettler. Hoc est verum"[862]

---

[862] *WATR* 5.318. "We are beggars. This is the truth." Luther's last words found scribbled on a piece of paper in his coat pocket.

Index

Act of Supremacy: 95, 150

Agricola, Johannes: 14, 136, 148, 166

Albrecht von Mainz: 100, 182, 215

Aleandro, Girolamo: 18, 20

Alveld, Augustine: 206, 334, 338

Ambrose: 69, 80, 86, 99

Amsdorf, Nicolaus von: 12, 111, 124, 126, 128-129, 132, 136, 183, 189

Anhalt, Georg von: 96, 124, 126, 128-129, 134, 182-183

Anhalt, Joachim von: 103

Apology of the Augsburg Confession: 76, 78, 84, 90, 94-95, 99, 123, 156, 163, 164-172, 184, 191, 193, 196, 200, 204, 206, 208, 216-217, 279, 326

Ap 4: 139, 195

Ap 13: 71-72

Ap 14: 95, 112, 156-157, 159, 174, 180, 183-184, 191, 193, 195, 201, 205, 214, 224, 266, 278-279

Ap 22: 29

Ap 24: 4

Ap 28: 71, 139

Aquinas, Thomas: 14, 229, 293

Augsburg Confession: 25, 27, 29-30, 37, 46, 59, 64, 76-78, 94-95, 98-99, 103, 116-118, 121, 123, 129-130, 137, 140-141, 144-148, 157, 160, 162-163, 165-169, 171-172, 175, 189, 195, 198-199, 205, 282, 209-211, 216, 244, 246, 251, 256, 260-261, 276, 307, 327, 329, 335-336

AC 5: 27, 31

AC 7: 319

AC 28: 139, 158, 223

Augsburg, Diet of: 29, 63, 122-123, 141, 148, 165, 172, 176, 179, 183, 191, 193, 215, 230, 244, 275, 305, 331

Augsburg Interim: 186, 201, 282

Augustine: 65, 80, 99, 124, 230, 272

Barnes, Robert: 99, 341

Barth, Hans Martin: 70, 90, 91

Baudler, Andreas: 146, 168, 196

Baudler, Theodor: 146,168, 196

Bente, Friedrich: 256-257, 271

Bergendoff, Conrad: 39, 128, 212

Beutel, Albrecht: 145, 303-305

Birnstiel, Johannes: 82

Bishops: 2-4, 6-7, 11, 14, 30, 32, 34-35, 38, 42, 44-45, 47, 49-51, 60, 62-64, 67-71, 73-75, 78, 80, 86, 88, 92-95, 97-99, 101, 104-106, 110-112, 115-116, 119-121, 123-129, 132-148, 150-157, 159, 162, 174, 177-181, 183, 186-193, 201-205, 207-209, 211-217, 219-220, 223-228, 230, 232, 234-236, 239-243, 246-247, 253, 255, 257, 259-260, 262-266, 268, 274-280, 282, 285, 288-289, 295, 307, 313, 336

Bohemia: 5, 11-12, 24, 39-50, 57-58, 60, 74-78, 83-84, 86, 102, 105, 112, 126, 134, 160, 167, 175, 209, 222, 226, 230, 233; Diet of: 47, 75

Bondage of the Will: 81, 243, 255, 296, 308, 317, 329, 335

Bora, Katherina von: 102

Bornkamm, Heinrich: 32-33, 39, 69, 113, 184, 230, 257-258, 291-292, 303, 340

Bouman, Stephen P.: 249-250

Braaten, Carl E.: 41, 148, 157, 206, 271, 290, 293-301, 306-329, 331-332, 334-335

Brecht, Martin: 10, 52, 79, 92, 127, 132

Brenz, Johannes: 87, 136, 197, 206

Brunotte, Wilhelm: 8, 108, 131, 177

Bugenhagen, Johannes: 86, 104, 106-107, 126, 136, 155, 168, 220-221, 298

Burgess, Joseph A.: 42, 180, 241, 264, 282, 286

Called to Common Mission (CCM): 26, 41, 95, 103, 115, 119, 139-140, 145, 154, 156, 158-160, 163-164, 174, 179, 182, 190-191, 201, 207, 210-211, 215-217, 222-224, 228, 230, 237, 239, 241-242, 248, 257-258, 260-261, 263-267, 272, 274-276, 279-280, 282, 284-285, 311, 313, 325

Campeggio, Lorenzo: 144, 185, 187, 189-190, 194-195, 225

Character indelebilis: 27, 73, 95, 175, 269, 324

Charles V: 15, 17-18, 29, 104, 123, 162, 165, 171-172, 184-185, 190, 193, 246, 330
Clement of Carthage: 250-251, 266-267
Clement VII: 43, 194-195
Cochläeus, Johannes: 195, 206
Confutation: 175, 184, 190, 193, 223, 245, 251
Cooke, R.J.: 95, 150, 153-154, 228
Council of Constance: 12
Cranach, Lukas: 25, 102-106, 108-109, 111, 194
Cyprian: 80
Democracy: 7, 257, 290
Dulles, Avery: 91
Dürer, Albrecht: 8, 22
Ebner, Hieronymus: 8, 22
Eck, Johannes: 10-12, 14-15, 166-167, 169, 185, 187, 195, 225, 235-236, 243, 252, 303
Ecken, Johannes von der: 15
Ecumenism: 26, 148, 206, 231, 239, 259, 294, 300, 327, 336, 341
Einsiedel: 146,168, 196-198, 200, 220, 238, 330
Einsiedeln: 132
Emser, Hieronymus: 4-7, 10-12, 14-15, 20-23, 25-26, 35-36, 51-54, 58, 63, 89, 100, 138, 236, 242, 249, 263, 273-275, 287
Episcopalism: 26, 179, 209, 211, 214, 225, 271
Episcopal Church: 94, 115, 156, 223, 267, 272, 276, 287
Evangelical Lutheran Church in America (ELCA): 3, 28-29, 94, 156, 160, 162, 180, 223, 225, 263, 266, 276-277, 280, 294
Evangelical Lutheran Church in Germany (VELKD): 281
Forde, Gerhard: 147, 292
Förstemann, Carl Eduard: 17
Frederick the Wise: 5, 8, 23, 69, 166
Frederick, Elector John: 176, 209
Gnandstein: 146, 168, 196, 198, 200, 212
Goeser, Robert: 146
Gritsch, Eric: 32, 148, 226
Hendrix, Scott H: 140, 290
Henry VIII: 94, 97, 100, 126, 150, 154, 169-170, 265

346

Hesse, Philipp von: 147, 185

Hitler, Adolph: 214

Hus, Jan: 11-12, 39, 41, 43, 99, 201, 211, 226

Jenson, Robert: 148, 158, 293

Joint Declaration on the Doctrine of Justification (JDDJ): 293, 309-311, 320

Jonas, Justus: 110, 136, 144, 148, 156, 163-164, 166, 170-172, 180, 186-187, 191, 193, 196-197, 199-201, 203, 205-206, 215, 220, 225, 244, 298

Kattenbusch, Ferdinand: 32-33, 39

Kittelson, James M.: 140-141, 145, 157, 176, 195-196, 237, 267, 275-276, 297-298, 304-305

Kolb/Wengert *BC* 2000: 32, 91, 114, 117, 119, 133, 163, 172, 181, 190-192, 202, 204, 209, 211, 223, 282, 298

Lazareth, William H.: 117-118, 132, 146, 179-180, 253, 280-281

Leipzig Debate: 8, 10-11, 69, 166-167, 194, 196, 236-237, 243, 285, 303, 322, 333-334, 338

Leo X: 12, 15, 22, 166, 170, 237, 306

Leo XIII: 150-151, 228, 236, 266

Link, Wenzel: 8, 22

Lindbeck, George: 91, 180, 284-287

Lohse, Bernhard: 119, 121-122, 132, 138-139, 207, 289

Luther, Johannes (Hänchen): 102, 107

Luther, Martin: 2-12, 14-15, 16-27, 31-93, 95-148, 156-158, 160-162, 165-168, 170-172, 175-179, 182-184, 186-189, 191, 193-200, 204-222, 226-227, 228, 240, 242-244, 246-254, 258, 260, 264-265, 269, 271-278, 281, 283-286, 288-310, 313-314, 318, 320-324, 327, 329-333, 335-338, 340-341, 343

Luther's Writings:

Address to the Christian Nobility: 12, 15, 22, 37, 68, 80, 89, 104, 122, 166, 324

Against the Assassin at Dresden: 195

Against the Heavenly Prophets: 63, 121

An Example of the Way to Consecrate a True Christian Bishop: 124

Answer to the HyperChristian, Hyperspiritual, and Hyperlearned Book of Goat Emser of Leipzig: 5, 20, 242, 274

347

Appeal to the Ruling Class of the German Nation: 40, 218

A Sermon on Keeping Children in School: 63, 85, 91, 161, 219

A Sermon on the Ten Lepers: 22

Babylonian Captivity of the Church: 15, 17-19, 37-38, 56, 72-73, 87, 112, 122, 229, 277, 324

Catechism, Small/Large: 5, 34, 36, 61-63, 87, 95, 133, 307, 313

Commentary on the Alledged Imperial Edict: 194

Concerning the Ministry: 5, 24, 28, 30, 39, 44-45, 47-48, 51, 54, 56, 74, 102, 107, 222, 233, 250-251, 253, 288

Confession Concerning Christ's Supper: 122

Confession of Faith which Robert Barnes . . . Made in England: 341

Dr. Luther's Retraction of the Error Forced Upon Him by the Most Highly Learned Priest of God, Sir Jerome Emser, Vicar in Meissen: 10, 23, 52

Dr. Luther's Warning to his dear German People: 193

Exhortation to All Clergy Assembled at Augsburg: 141-142, 144, 161, 304

German Mass: 119-121

How One Should Choose and Put in Place Church Servants: 46

On the Councils and the Churches: 58, 331

On the Papacy in Rome Against the Most Celebrated Romanist in Leipzig: 338

On Temporal Authority: 193

The disputation of Master Heinrich of Lüneburg for his diploma, Dr. Martin Luther presiding: 238

The Freedom of a Christian: 166, 324

To the Goat (An den Boch): 15

Sermon on Good Works: 33

Sincere Admonition to all Christians to Guard Against Insurrection and Rebellion: 303

Smalcald Articles: 88, 112, 136-137, 139, 192, 298, 333

That a Christian Assembly or Congregation Has the Right and Power to Judge All Teaching and to Call, Appoint, and Dismiss All Teachers, Established and Proven by Scripture: 47, 116, 134, 229, 232

The Private Mass and the Consecration of Priests: 36, 93, 125, 211, 215, 254, 305
The Bondage of the Will: 296, 329
The Misuse of the Mass: 10
The Private Mass and the Consecration of Priests: 36, 93
To the Councilmen of All Cities in Germany That They Establish and Maintain Christian Schools: 65
Treatise on the New Testament, that is, the Holy Mass: 14, 37, 129, 272
Madson, Meg: 116-117
Marty, Martin E.: 174, 191, 261
Mathesius, Johannes: 76-78, 86-87, 100-101, 286
Maurer, Wilhelm: 64, 84-86, 89, 115, 118, 120-122, 132, 135, 140-142, 145-146, 148, 160-162, 276-277, 286
McGrath, Alister E.: 231, 303, 336-337
Melanchthon, Philip: 4-5, 7, 14, 31, 33, 35, 64, 71-72, 76, 85-88, 93-100, 103, 105-107, 109-112, 115-118, 121-124, 127-129, 132-137, 139-143, 145-146, 148, 156, 158, 160-161, 164, 166, 168-173, 176, 178, 180-183, 185-191, 193, 195-201, 205-206, 212-213, 215, 217-218, 221, 237-238, 240, 244-246, 251-252, 259, 261-266, 281, 291, 296, 298-299, 330, 333, 340
Melanchthon's Writings:
Corpus Philippicum: 169, 299
Instructions for the Visitors of Parish Pastors in Electoral Saxony 120-121, 127, 217-218, 221, 294
Locos communes: 168-169
Treatise on the Power and Primacy of the Pope: 5, 79, 85-86, 93, 116, 128, 134-137, 166, 235, 259, 266, 281
Menacher, Mark: 4, 65, 157, 223, 228, 294
Mont, Christopher: 94, 96-97, 99
Mullett, Michael A.: 104, 166, 170
Nelson, Paul R.: 251-252
Nichol, Todd W.: 154-155, 174
Oberman, Heiko: Prologue, 166-167, 257, 271, 341
Ordination: 59, 71-74, 76-86, 88-89, 91-101, 104, 111-113, 115-116, 120-121, 124-127, 129, 134, 146-147, 150, 155, 159-160, 175-178, 192, 201, 208-209, 212-215, 217-218, 221-229, 239, 241, 249-255, 260-262, 267-271, 274-275, 277-278, 282-

288, 307, 322-325

Papal Bull (*Exsurge Domine*): 22, 71, 237, 309

Parker, Matthew: 151-153

Pelikan, Jaroslav: 35, 163-164, 172, 181, 190-191, 201, 204, 209, 306

Petrus Magni: 154

Piepkorn, Arthur C.: 25-26, 30, 37, 59, 72, 79, 81, 83, 106, 110, 118-119, 126, 132, 135, 137-138, 146, 157, 160-161, 178, 208, 242, 250, 259, 277-278, 281

Plato: 180

Prague: 11, 24, 39-40, 44-46, 57, 77, 79, 105, 116, 134, 177, 196, 226, 308; Diet of: 46

Regensburg Conference: 99, 137, 246

Reed, Luther D.: 253, 272

Rietschel, Ernst: 66

Rietschel, Georg: 121

Rimbo, Robert: 253-254, 272, 302

Roberts, William D.: 265-267, 273

Root, Michael J.: 118, 126, 139-140, 145-146, 157, 160, 174, 239, 241-242, 275-276, 290, 307

Schwabach Articles: 122

Schweinfurt, Diet of: 171-172

Spalatin, Georg: 5, 8-10, 16-18, 73, 107, 109-111, 125, 130, 132, 136, 146, 148, 166, 168, 176, 182, 187, 196-197, 200, 220, 237, 244

Spengler, Lazarus: 22-23, 321

Speyer, Diet of: 207

Sutel, Johann: 81-84, 86

Tappert, Theodore: 28, 31-32, 91, 118, 133, 139, 159, 162-165, 169, 174-175, 181, 190, 192, 201-202, 204, 209, 211, 225, 257, 271

Torgau Articles: 122, 129

Tucher, Anton: 22-23

Valerius, Bishop of Hippo: 124-125

Wand, J.W.C.: 96, 269, 273, 283-284

Wartburg: 10, 19, 22-23, 109

Wendebourg, Dorothea: 30-31, 53, 261

Wengert, Timothy J.: 3-4, 6-7, 10-11, 14, 19, 25, 28-36, 43-

48, 50-54, 57-59, 61, 63, 68, 71-72, 74, 78, 86-87, 91, 94, 96, 100, 105-106, 109, 111, 113-119, 121-124, 128-130, 132-134, 138-139, 146-147, 163, 165, 172, 181, 189-192, 202, 204, 209, 211-212, 218-219, 223-225, 232, 236, 242, 249-250, 259, 261-262, 272, 274, 281-282, 287, 298

Westerås, Diet of: 154

Wittenberg: 5, 8, 13-14, 40, 63, 76, 78-79, 86, 92, 96, 102-104, 106-110, 131, 133, 157, 171, 176-178, 191, 197, 208-210, 212, 216, 220-221, 237, 289, 298, 301, 329, 336, 341

Worms, Diet of: 15-16, 18, 20-22, 140-141, 196, 207, 219, 260, 275, 307, 324, 337

Wright, J. Robert: 174, 266-267, 273

Wycliffe, John: 11-12

Zinzendorf, Nikolaus Ludwig von: 226

Made in the USA
Middletown, DE
25 October 2016